NO PARTIALITY
THE IDOLATRY OF RACE & THE NEW HUMANITY

DOUGLAS R. SHARP

InterVarsity Press
Downers Grove, Illinois

InterVarsity Press
P.O. Box 1400, Downers Grove, IL 60515-1426
World Wide Web: www.ivpress.com
E-mail: mail@ivpress.com

InterVarsity Press® is the book-publishing division of InterVarsity Christian Fellowship/USA®, a student movement active on campus at hundreds of universities, colleges and schools of nursing in the United States of America, and a member movement of the International Fellowship of Evangelical Students. For information about local and regional activities, write Public Relations Dept., InterVarsity Christian Fellowship/USA, 6400 Schroeder Rd., P.O. Box 7895, Madison, WI 53707-7895, or visit the IVCF website at <www.ivcf.org>.

Scripture quotations, unless otherwise noted, are from the New Revised Standard Version of the Bible, copyright 1989 by the Division of Christian Education of the National Council of the Churches of Christ in the USA. Used by permission. All rights reserved.

Cover photograph: Melissa Hayden/Photonica

ISBN 0-8308-2669-6

Printed in the United States of America ∞

Library of Congress Cataloging-in-Publication Data

Sharp, Douglas R., 1949-
  No partiality : the idolatry of race and the new humanity / Douglas R. Sharp.
    p. cm.
  Includes bibliographical references.
  ISBN 0-8308-2669-6 (paper : alk. paper)
    1. Race relations—Religious aspects—Christianity. 2. Racism—Religious
  aspects—Christianity. I. Title.
  BT734.2 .S416 2002
  261.8'348—dc21
                                                                                    2001051599

18	17	16	15	14	13	12	11	10	9	8	7	6	5	4	3	2	1
15	14	13	12	11	10	09	08	07	06	05	04	03	02				

For Linda,
my beloved,
who knows . . . and loves still

CONTENTS

Acknowledgments _____ 9

Introduction _____ 11

1 **THE LANGUAGE OF RACE** _____ 19

    The Dis-ease of Conversation: Talking About Race and Racism_____ 20

    The World of Language: Building Common Sense_____ 30

    Building Race: How to Make Things with Words_____ 40

2 **THEORETICAL CONSTRUCTIONS OF RACE AND RACISM**_____ 58

    Rational Dimensions of Race and Racism_____ 61

    Psychological Dimensions of Race and Racism _____ 66

    Sociopolitical Dimensions of Race and Racism _____ 73

    Socioeconomic Dimensions of Race and Racism_____ 85

    The Significance and Limitations of Constructive Theories_____ 95

3 **THE SOCIALITY OF RACE** _____ 99

    A Trip to the Library, a Look at People _____ 100

    Race as a Social Construct: The Objective Reality of Race_____ 103

    Making Sense of Difference: The Science of Race _____ 114

    Typifying Actors and Activities: The Habit of Race_____ 125

    Institutionalizing the Social Order: The Culture of Race _____ 140

    Maintaining the Universe: The Problem of Race _____ 158

4 **THE CONSCIOUSNESS OF RACE** _____ 172

    Race as a Mythical Construct: The Subjective Reality of Race _____ 173

    Embracing Ideology: The False Consciousness of Race_____ 192

    Colorizing People: The Disposition and Conservation of Racial Identity __ 207

    Racial Attitudes: Americans' Opinions on Race _____ 217

5 **FRAMING A THEOLOGY OF RACIAL RECONCILIATION** _____ 235

    Destabilizing Our Universe: The Initiatives of God _____ 240

    The Functions of the Christian Story_____ 244

The Difference Sin Makes: The Response of Humanity _____ 251

Vacating Habits: A New Vision _____ 260

Having Second Thoughts: The Art of Contestation _____ 275

To Have and to Hold: *Embracing* All "Others" _____ 284

Postscript _____ **300**

Bibliography _____ **304**

Index _____ **315**

Acknowledgments

I wish to express my appreciation to several people who provided support and encouragement while this project was unfolding. Special thanks are due to my brother, Tom, and his wife, Sandy, for making their condo in Steamboat Springs available to me for writing several weeks during the past summers. There I met Diane Scott, a true neighbor whose friendship and interest in this project was shown on a daily basis.

I am grateful to my colleague Charlie Cosgrove and my friend Geneace Williams for the extraordinary time they took to read earlier versions of the manuscript and to engage me in rigorous conversation. Others who read and responded to portions of the manuscript are Willie and Minnie Doss, Emma Justes, Bob Price, Kevin Blair, Donna Jorgensen, Georgia Selman, Chris Payne, Jose DeOliveira, Darlene Abernathy, Rupert Simms, Vincent Bacote and Dan Lee. I may be overlooking others, and to them I apologize for my forgetfulness.

It is important to acknowledge my gratitude to InterVarsity Press for their interest in this project, and especially to my editors, Cindy Bunch and Ruth Goring. Their suggestions were always appropriate and contributed to making this a better book. Its flaws, however, are mine alone.

I have only inadequate words to express my love and gratitude to my wife, Linda. She endured several extended periods of my absence from our home in order to make it possible for me to write, and throughout these times she offered great encouragement and support. It is therefore to her that this book is dedicated.

Introduction

Dear Reader,

This book is about how we make sense of race and racism. I'm not using "make sense" to mean "make something understandable, reasonable, lucid or sane," and I'm certainly not using it to mean "justify" or "legitimate." You need only browse white supremacist websites like White Aryan Resistance, or Reconstructing a National Identity for Christian Whites, or World Church of the Creator to see how *race* and *racism* make sense idiomatically. Rather I'm using the phrase in its literal meaning: how we *manufacture* ideas and practices on the basis of the stimulation of our *senses*. Race and racism are not only concepts that have been *made* by human beings, but they are also the principal way we in the United States have made *sense* of ourselves and others.

So my concern in this book is to examine and analyze the phenomena of race and racism with a set of rather elementary questions: How is it that we are led to recognize and believe that there is such a thing as "race," how does it happen that members of one "race" are treated differently from members of another, and why is it this way? This concern is motivated by a set of basic convictions: that both race and racism are deeply embedded in our social and cultural lives, that they have been working for a long time to shape American national history as well as our personal and communal identities, and that on all counts they are *wrong*. And my effort is motivated by an even more fundamental set of theological convictions: race and racism challenge Christian faith and contradict the gospel of Jesus Christ because they are expressions of human sin.

This book is written by a European American, and it is written primarily for reading by other European Americans, though I hope that its reading by members of other people groups will contribute to our intergroup dialogue and our joining in a shared commitment to dismantle both race and racism. I can neither speak nor write for such groups as African Americans, Hispanic Americans, Asian Americans. Each of these people groups is as culturally diverse as the countries from which they or their ancestors came. Arguably, I cannot even speak or write for other European Americans for the same reason.

This book is written by a Christian primarily for reading by other Christians because I hold two other convictions: the gospel of Jesus Christ most emphatically addresses our situation of race and racism, and the churches of Jesus Christ can and must take greater responsibility in dismantling them both. There are many books on racism written by Christians, and I cite some of them in this book. But I want to take a somewhat different approach. The Christian groups that I've been involved with, the Christian literature on racism that I've read, my experience of dialogue with members of various people groups in the United States, and my teaching in multicultural settings have left me with several impressions. Many European-American Christians ignore racism while acknowledging the reality of race(s). Others acknowledge the reality of racism and believe that it is wrong but that there is not much we can do about it. Still others engage racism without questioning the reality of race(s) or taking the initiative to study the social and cultural roots of historic and contemporary expressions of racism.

My approach comes as a result of two considerations. The first has to do with my theological method (which I describe at length in chapter five). Developing theological understanding involves interaction with what I call a constellation of resources. These include (1) the Bible and the Christian traditions that have mediated it to us. By "traditions" I mean not only the formal histories of the church, theology and biblical interpretation but also the local histories of communities of faith that have been shaped by their response to the reading or hearing of the Scriptures. Another resource is (2) the context in which Christians endeavor to live out their faith. Here I have in mind not so much the contemporary era as the geographical and sociocultural settings of Christian communities. "Context" refers not only to sociocultural environments as the combination of external conditions and structures that affect human life but also to the ways these environments and effects are analyzed and described by those who think about them. (3) Personal and communal experiences of participants in Christian communities and sociocultural worlds are further resources. By "experiences" I mean the particular ways persons regard and interpret themselves in relation to others and their environment in order to discern meaning in their lives. Experience involves not only what and how persons think and feel but also the beliefs, attitudes and values that shape and are influenced by their interactions with their world and others. How persons gauge their experience of others and their environment contributes to the development of an internal sense of themselves. In this book, then, I use a theological method that attends to these three types of resources.

The second consideration is that much of the Christian literature on racism has not interacted with the critical literature generated from such contextual disciplines as history, social science, cultural anthropology and culture criticism. The result of this neglect is a weakened analysis and understanding of race and racism. This book seeks to interact with these other disciplines, taking their analyses seriously as ways to understand the personal, social and cultural dimensions of our situation—and to help develop a theological basis for racial reconciliation.

This book asks, How did we build and how do we maintain a culture of race and racism? How then should we regard our culture of race and racism, and respond to it as believers whose primary resource—the Scriptures—offers a radically different vision for humanity? I am not suggesting that the context determines an understanding of the gospel or that the analyses of social-science disciplines take precedence over the gospel. Rather, the gospel is given to us in our situation, so it becomes necessary to develop an understanding of our context in order to address and bear witness to it.

I grew up in a small southern Colorado town where everyone knew everyone and anybody's business was everybody's business. It was one of those almost idyllic communities of the late-nineteenth- to early-twentieth-century American West, a region developed by the grit of settlers who migrated from the East. My little town was a monocultural community, consisting mostly of people whose surnames might also have been found on the public tax rolls of England, Scotland, Ireland, France, Germany, Sweden or Poland. The local economy was dependent on the popularity of potatoes and sugar beets, a modest amount of barley (most of which went north to the Coors brewery), the Rodeo Cowboys of America circuit, Texans' taste for rainbow trout from Colorado mountain streams, and, as the years went by, increasing numbers of winter sports aficionados. It was a wonderful place to grow up. I go back as often as I can to visit.

I don't mean to imply that everyone in my hometown was of European extraction. True, we were a monocultural community, but not everyone in my hometown was culturally "mono." Truth to tell, I, my immediate family, and my closest friends and their families, as well as the local druggists, the people who owned or worked in the stores and the Sears catalog outlet, the folk who ran the grain elevators or fixed Fords and Chevrolets at the local garage, the kind-hearted citizens who handled our money in the bank or starched our shirts at the one cleaner in town—we were all just *Americans*. Our ancestors came over the mountains and settled the land. They forged a living out of the dried prehistoric lakebed called the San Luis Valley, and they brought culture and sensibility and know-how and determination and respect and God and country to that place, and gosh-darn-it, don't ya stand in my way—I'm makin' America here! No, as residents of *Monte Vista* (and *Del Norte*, and *Alamosa*, and *Pagosa*, and *Antonito*, and *Saguache*, and *Blanca*, and *La Garita*, and *Hispaniola*, and *La*

Veta, and *La Jara*—all the towns nestled in the *Valle de San Luis* bounded on the east by the peaks of the *Sangre de Cristo* range of the Rockies' *San Juan* Mountains in the state of *Colorado*), we were an ethnically diverse group of descendants from many European countries, but we all shared a common culture and spoke one language, English.

But before it was a state, even before it was a territory, Colorado had been *Mexico*, as the names of these towns and mountains suggest. Oh, in addition to us European Americans, there was another people group where I grew up. In fact, there were two other people groups, each with its distinctive culture, heritage and language: Mexican Americans and Native Americans. But they lived separately from us; the Mexican Americans lived in neighborhoods on the edges of Monte Vista, and the Native Americans lived mostly on the Ute Indian Reservation in southwest Colorado and came to the valley once a year to work the potato fields during harvest.

For all practical purposes, so far as the European Americans were concerned, these people groups were invisible except when they shopped in the local stores, where they were watched carefully and frequently humiliated by the discriminatory behavior of employees. For the most part the Mexican Americans lived in poverty, earning a living by manual labor or housekeeping in the homes of European Americans, or operating and working in small businesses that served the Mexican American community. The children went to public schools, where they were generally ignored by their European American teachers.

The Mexican Americans were effectively bicultural because they had to be to survive, but the European Americans were effectively monocultural because we owned and controlled pretty much everything from city hall to main street to the newspaper to the potato fields. European Americans were the dominant group, and all others were regarded as outsiders. Looking back, I find that attitude to be ironic; the ancestors of the Native Americans and Mexican Americans had lived in that area and developed their cultures long before the European settlers arrived, so we were really the outsiders.

There was another people group in my little Colorado town, a group of five. They were a Japanese American family who settled there after being released from an internment camp on the eastern prairie of Colorado after the end of World War II, a camp I knew nothing about until long after I left Colorado.

When I was growing up, my parents never told me I was better than anyone else, and they certainly never told me I was superior to anyone. They didn't have to. I learned about "better than" and "superior to" from my circle of friends, teachers and coaches. I learned from observing how I was treated and how Mexican Americans were treated. Whenever I did not perform at a level acceptable to my parents or teachers, I was told that I could do better if I applied myself, that I should want to do better in order to achieve and excel. I was told I could accomplish whatever I wanted if I only worked at it. My teachers never said that to the Mexican American students, at least not in my hearing. On the contrary, throughout my public school education, I frequently heard my teachers say to these students that they were doing the best they could and it was all right if they didn't receive A's and B's; all that was really important was that they pass. Many times I heard teachers tell Spanish-speaking students that their difficulty in speaking English came from the fact that English was not spoken in their home, or that the English spoken there was incorrect. I learned that it was desirable for a student to aspire to do better, and my parents and teachers as well as the school system, police department, churches and business community all worked to encourage the growing fires of my ambition and aspirations; they were all there to nurture me and people like me to responsible adulthood. But I also learned that if a person spoke Spanish, had black hair and dark skin, and a surname like Gallegos, Martínez, González, Suárez, Padilla, Ortega or Rodríguez, he or she was neither expected nor encouraged to achieve by the European American community. Moreover, when a Mexican American did achieve, it was regarded by the dominant group as *unusual*.

That's what I learned growing up in my "monocultural" community, and at the time I just supposed it to be natural and normal. My community didn't have to *tell* me I was better than others; I just absorbed that understanding in the network of relationships and support offered to me by my community. Looking back, I realize that what my community taught me was racism.

My argument in this book is that if it can be shown that race and racism are social constructions, then perhaps a clearer path might be suggested for Christian efforts to deconstruct the world of race and racism. The discussion in this book is occupied primarily with European Americans for two reasons: European Americans are the people group who created and developed "white racism," and the practices of racism have been and still are characteristic of social, economic, political and religious institutions under their influence and control. The crucial element here, then, is focusing not only on what European Americans think about other people groups, how they have related to them, and how their views have shaped a shared world but also on what European Americans think about themselves and how they have made—and made sense of—a world shared with other people groups. The patterns of racism that draw the most attention in this discussion are those found in the history of European American exploitation and domination of Africans and their descendants and the sociocultural worlds built on this basis. These patterns of racism constitute the model or prototype of racism in relation to which European Americans have regarded all other people groups in this country.

Unable to press the indigenous peoples into forced labor, the European colonists and their descendants instead expropriated their lands and either committed genocide against them or forced them to migrate westward away from the centers of European American life, eventually restricting them to "reservations." These practices were certainly "racist," but their effect was largely to acquire the resources of Native Americans' land by eradicating them. Thus the indigenous peoples were never merged into the social and economic fabric of the developing European American context.

Beginning in the early 1600s, on the other hand, European colonists and their descendants found a virtually endless supply of cheap labor in the form of African slaves, who became vital to building European American society and the national economic infrastructure. Ever since, the domestic history of European America has been shaped by the changing patterns of "white" domination and exploitation (racism) and "black" subordination and survival (resistance).

Beginning in the nineteenth century, the immigration of people groups from non-European countries engendered a response from European Americans not all that dissimilar to their view of African Americans. European Americans regarded immigrants from Asian and Latin countries as having few if any social and economic rights, and those they did have were restricted by law and custom. Discrimination was practiced against them with impunity. Indeed immigrants from non-European countries were ineligible to become naturalized citizens of the United States until 1952, when racial restrictions on naturalization were finally removed.

Taking the history of "white" and "black" relations as the prototype of racism, however, should not imply that the *experience* of racism by Asian Americans, Hispanic Americans and Native Americans is identical to the experience of African Americans. What I can say as a European American is that in general my people group has regarded all "persons of color" as foreigners, interlopers or second-class citizens who did not "build" this nation and therefore could be denied an equal share in the freedom, rights and opportunities accorded to members of the majority group. That is clearly racism, the paradigmatic forms and expressions of which are rooted deeply in the almost four-hundred-year history of intergroup relations between the descendants of Europeans and Africans.

It will be helpful here to describe briefly the organization of the book's discussion. Chapter one explores some of the dynamics present in interracial dialogue on race and racism, particularly those that make this conversation difficult, even seemingly impossible. Race discourse has contributed to the construction of a world in which race matters. My concern here is to identify how language is used to both express awareness of and designate what is perceived in the external world. We look closely at the principal terms of this discourse (race, racial, racism and racist) in order to develop an understanding of how this linguistic world both shapes and is shaped by a social world. This chapter lays down some of the basic building blocks for the discussion in subsequent chapters.

The historic and contemporary literature on racism is extensive. Much of this work has been written by social scientists, behavioral scientists, cultural anthropologists, historians, legal scholars and journalists—that is, by specialists for other specialists in specific academic disciplines, and not necessarily as Christians. Chapter two discusses the importance of developing a *theory*, a way of correlating and interpreting the data that make up an area of inquiry. Both race and racism can be viewed as theories, and a major portion of the second chapter reviews some contemporary critical theories on race and racism. The purpose is to identify a range of critical approaches, so we consider theories that focus attention on psychological, social, political and economic dimensions of racism. As models, these critical theories serve as a kind of foil against which the discussion in the following two chapters unfolds. Chapter two closes with an indication of the strengths and weaknesses of these theories for theological reflection.

The attempt to engage race and racism continues in earnest with chapter three, where I begin to develop my notion of race and racism as a social construction of reality. The chapter looks at the world "out there," the everyday world outside of us, aiming to identify and describe some of the major ways in which the notion of race and the manifestation of racism are made objective not only *in* but *as* a sociocultural world dominated by European Americans. I analyze how an everyday social world is built and the contribution of so-called race science to this effort. Attention is given to personal, social and institutional modes of racism as well as the ways this sociocultural world is maintained by the interests of European Americans. In short, this chapter looks at the construction—patterns and structures—of the objective world in which we live.

Chapter four takes a look inward, analyzing the internal or subjective world with focus on the consciousness of self, others and the world in terms of race and racism. The concern here is to examine the phenomenon of racial identity and the ways the external world of race and racism is internalized in the formation of race consciousness. The main contention in this chapter is that European Americans especially function with a false consciousness oriented by the myth of race and the ideology of racism, both of which are described in some detail. To support the argument regarding race consciousness, the chapter examines some of the social-science data on public opinion on race, with particular attention to why European American opinion on matters of racism is so different from the opinions held by other people groups. A subquestion here is whether public opinion measurement itself reflects racism (i.e., whether European American attitudes on race and racism can even be measured). So we look at the factors that go into shaping opinion on race and racism.

Finally, chapter five brings insights from the contextual analysis of the previous chapters to bear on the development of a theological basis for contesting and dismantling race and racism. The theological construction in this chapter is grounded in an engagement with the resources of Christian faith and takes as its point of departure the triune God as expressed in and through the Scriptures. An attempt is made to analyze racism in terms of *sin*, and the principal argument rests on an interpretation of the epistle to the Ephesians with its vision of one new humanity disclosed in Jesus Christ. The chapter seeks to describe what could—or maybe *should*—be the posture of Christian communities in relation to race and racism, grounding this authorization in the biblical emphasis on reconciliation.

Thus this book as a whole moves from an analysis of racism in its objective expressions (context) through an engagement with the consciousness of race (experience) to a theology that calls the church to become active in dismantling both race and racism (Bible/traditions). Each chapter begins with a Jesus saying from one of the four Gospels, followed immediately by a brief modest commentary on the saying. Each chapter also ends with a quotation from one of the New Testament epistles, also with brief commentary. The verses speak for themselves, but my comments are not necessarily an interpretation *of* the text but rather an interpretation *with* the text. The scriptural passages I have selected and the commentary I offer are both intended to position the chapter's discussion within my commitment to Jesus Christ, the sacred literature of our common faith, the strategic importance of Christian communities and my love for all the saints. I ask only that you, the reader, ponder the chapter's discussion in relation to these biblical frames.

Last and probably least, a note on the footnotes: Apart from obligatory citations of the location of a quotation, the footnotes contain several items that may or may not be of interest to the reader. First, they indicate the location of discussions that can help a reader pursue a particular topic at greater length; second, they contain observations that could have been included in the body of the text but would have diverted attention from my main focus and disrupted the flow; third, they express some strong disagreements with other authors; and fourth, in chapter three they contain a running illustration of a rather difficult construction offered by an author whose work I employ.

So—let's get to it!

1

THE LANGUAGE
OF RACE

You spirit that keeps this boy from speaking and hearing, I command you, come out of him, and never enter him again! Mark 9:25

Have you ever been unable to speak because you didn't know what to say? Have you ever realized that what you heard was not what somebody said? Have you ever ignored somebody, tuned them out, just shut down instead of listening? Did you ever imagine that maybe the reason you responded this way was that you were in the grip of the evil spirit of racism?

●　　●　　●　　●

Race. Racial. Racism. Racist.* These are words in the English language that evoke an awareness of ourselves, and of ourselves in relation to those who are different from us, and of how we perceive both these others and ourselves. They are just words, and yet they carry a range of meanings that give comfort to some and great discomfort to others, particularly when the words are spoken in conversation. For some people, the meanings embedded in these words explain much of their experience of the world. For them the words are heavy and burdensome: their meaning limits human lives. For others the meanings are quite different, pointing to something of which they have little conscious experience. For these, the words are light because their lives do not knowingly carry the weight of their meaning.

They are just words, yet they can inflame passions because they draw on centuries-long patterns of inter- and intragroup relations and their social, cultural, economic and political contexts. For some these words relate to personal identity and how environments have challenged and limited the formation of self in relationship with others. Their self-consciousness and awareness of others emerge in a polarized and hostile world, and passions are aroused by the inhospitality of that world and the ways it isolates and subordinates them. But the words bear very little on others' sense of self and pose even less threat to the continuing formation of self. Identity and relationships are possibilities within a friendly and comfortable world, and passions are aroused in the defense and preservation of that world and their place within it.

These words have an extraordinary capacity to obscure communication and understanding. They mean different things to different people. These meanings are related to human experiences and shape the contexts in which they are used. When people encounter each other in situations where the dynamics to which these words refer are at work, there is not merely interpersonal conflict but a collision of experiences and perspectives. The realities and fictions to which they refer are at work as the undercurrents, dynamics, structures, patterns, histories, values, understandings and norms that shape the encounter. When the encounter is itself about these realities and fictions—when interaction is focused on what these words point to—it is not uncommon for participants to become antagonistic and defensive as emotional temperatures rise to a level of considerable discomfort.

Before we move on to consider the function of some of the principal terms of modern race discourse, it will be useful to explore what kinds of difficulties we confront when discussing the thorny and perplexing phenomena to which these words refer. The language in our conversations on race and racism is frequently both ambiguous and alienating, disarming and divisive.

The Dis-ease of Conversation: Talking About Race and Racism

Our conversations about race and racism are uncomfortable. The terms we use, what they mean, what they refer to, what we think and feel, and the social distance between us tend to insulate us from one another. The conversation constantly shifts under pressures of accusation and denial, argument and rebuttal, awareness and ignorance. Americans are fearful in no small part because the conversation is limited by words that require levels of awareness of ourselves, our world and others—awareness that is reflectively painful. We are not just talking *about* race and racism; in our talk we *implicate ourselves* in the meaning of these terms. We are in fact talking about ourselves, and this is no less true even when meanings are slippery and ambiguous. We may think we know the meanings of the words we use to categorize people, but the clarity we assume is actually nonexistent. The goal of clarity and mutual understanding ought to be a prime objective in the conversation rather than an assumption.

Throughout the history of the United States, race and racism have been one of the most difficult subjects of conversation in both church and society. The fact that the conversation is difficult, and an air of discouragement, fatigue and indifference hangs over it, should remind us that many of the issues and prob-

lems we face as a nation are bound up with the legacy of our conduct in matters of race relations and the world this conduct has produced. Whether the
focal point of a conversation is public policy, political viewpoint, institutional
practice, cultural values or personal behavior, lurking within it are matters that
bear either directly or indirectly on race and racism. Such a conversation will
be difficult. On the other hand, what begins, accidentally or intentionally, as a
conversation about race and racism all too frequently degenerates into volatile
exchanges, or aborts into tension-filled silence. Participants leave unshaken in
their understanding of their position and even more convinced that conversation is neither practical nor possible. This pattern of volatile interaction or
numbing quietness in conversation about race and racism has led Bruce Jacobs
to observe: "Increasingly, talk about race carries either the tone of violence or a
sense of sterile, exaggerated civility. . . . Talking about race is, quite literally,
dangerous."[1]

One of the difficulties is that we do not share horizons of understanding
regarding these terms. We use them thinking they mean the same for everybody, yet we have difficulty defining them and describing what they refer to.
European Americans tend to regard "race" as a set of recognizable biological
characteristics of other people groups. European Americans are not particularly
mindful of themselves as a "race" (a contention that will be elaborated more
fully as we move to subsequent chapters). Consequently they tend to regard
"racism" as prejudicial and discriminatory conduct directed against persons
because of their "different race." Those who hold this view tend not to think of
themselves as "racist"; it is behavior of which "others" are guilty. In general,
"race" and "racism" for European Americans are realities peripheral to their
everyday world and experience (and this will be exposed more fully and challenged in subsequent chapters).

Members of other people groups, on the other hand, tend to regard "race" as
a fabrication that governs the worldview, collective identity and sociocultural
structures of European Americans. Indeed, "race" *is* this constructed European
American world. As the worldview legitimating the structure of this sociocultural reality of European Americans, "race" affects members of other people
groups not only in everyday experience but in their sense of their histories as
peoples in America.

Any conversation about race and racism between European Americans and
other peoples is likely to consist in talking at or around one another, since it is
not likely that each will understand what the other means. When the attempt is

---

[1]Bruce A. Jacobs, *Race Manners: Navigating the Minefield Between Black and White Americans* (New York: Arcade, 1999), p. 1.

made conversationally to remember and understand the history of African America and European America, it is evident that, as Norman Hill suggests, "in many ways black and white America are two solitudes, unable to communicate effectively, talking past each other in a language whose common words are no longer comprehensible to the other."[2] The history of "black" America and "white" America, however, is not the only history of peoples on this continent, so "if we look at some recent developments through the prism of race, they diffract into [multiple], often conflicting interpretations of the same realities engendering divergent emotions, attitudes and psychologies."[3]

Little wonder that conversation about race and racism is difficult and painful. Many are willing to converse if the terms of discourse are limited to personal attitudes, behaviors and practices (e.g., prejudice, discrimination, inequality) from which it is possible to distance oneself. There may even be willingness to talk about values such as sensitivity, diversity and fairness. But such a conversation is misguided—a talking *around*—because it does not focus on what gives rise to such alienating and dehumanizing attitudes and behaviors: a world in which race and racism matter. It is a kind of "rhetoric of silencing," an attempt to "deter opposition, perhaps so that we will not have to spend energy refuting it."[4] When we refuse to talk directly about race and racism, we set up a "universe of bounded discourse" or "an arena in which some ideas can be debated and others cannot."[5]

The difficulty and discomfort, however, should not prevent us from staying in the conversation or discourage us from attempting to gain understanding. The greater purpose is *reconciliation.* If a conversation unfolds with indifference or restriction, if our talk of race and racism is unreflective and unconcerned, it may well indicate a capitulation to it or naiveté about it. In either case all that will have been accomplished is the extension of personal and social distance and denial.

Factors inhibiting conversation. One of the greatest inhibitors of conversation, and one of the greatest sources of resistance to the exploration of race and racism, is *fear:* fear of honesty, fear of discovery, fear of confrontation, fear of change, fear of being mistaken and ultimately fear of *truth.* Manipulation, exploitation and dehumanization occur in social, political, economic and cultural realms as well as interpersonal and linguistic realms. When it comes to the

---

[2]Norman Hill, "Race in America—Through a Glass, Darkly," *The Public Perspective* 7, no. 2 (1996): 1.
[3]Ibid.
[4]Stephen L. Carter, *Civility: Manners, Morals and the Etiquette of Democracy* (New York: BasicBooks, 1998), p. 133.
[5]Ibid., p. 134.

conversation on race and racism, all of these realms are involved, as are all the fears. Frustration, inhibition, resentment, shame, guilt, sorrow, anger, rage, anxiety, uncertainty—all of these and countless other human emotions are at work underscoring the sense of fear.

Words like those at the beginning of this chapter carry strong emotional content for both those who use them and those who listen. Ashley Montagu goes so far as to suggest that "the meaning of most, if not all, words [is] to some extent emotionally determined and that humans, are, in large part, creatures of emotion. And because emotions attach to words rather than to ideas, it is important to be aware of the fact that words frequently have an emotional rather than a factual basis."[6] One of the reasons our conversation on race and racism may involve a rhetoric of silencing, inhibited by a bounded discourse, is that the emotions evoked by the words are too strong, perhaps even overwhelming. It seems natural and even easy to deny or ignore the emotions that well up at the prospect of discussing our most difficult topic. But if we suppress or deny our emotions, or "if we all waited until we knew we were right before opening our mouths, allowing ourselves zero risk of misunderstanding or overstatement, then nothing worthwhile would ever get said."[7]

We move toward reconciliation through conversation and the quest for shared meaning and understanding regarding this world of race and racism. This entails not only willingness to talk but willingness to confront, to take risks and to be vulnerable. Regardless of what we may think or feel, racism exists and it will not go away of its own accord. The language we use to hide or disclose it neither renders it powerless nor alters the world in which it is manifest. Whatever or whomever we fear, and however else we feel about it, it is basic to the conversation on race and racism that there will be confrontation. Without it there can be no *dialogue* in any sense of the word. Moreover, we need not merely to identify manifestations of racism but also to recognize its changing shape, adaptability and persistence in a society that at one level has officially repudiated it yet at other levels has more thoroughly embraced it (a distinction to be explored more fully later).

In addition to their fears, participants to the conversation bring their operative and profoundly differing assumptions and perceptions regarding race and racism and the world they have constructed. Anyone who has participated in a productive or abortive conversation on these matters, or read a text by an author from the perspective of another people group, or listened to a conversa-

---

[6]Ashley Montagu, *Man's Most Dangerous Myth: The Fallacy of Race*, 6th ed. (Walnut Creek, Calif.: AltaMira, 1997), p. 359.
[7]Jacobs, *Race Manners*, p. 151.

tion between members of different people groups on the subject of race and racism, or seen the jail-cell dialogue between the lawyer and the defendant—or the final defense summation—in the movie *A Time to Kill,* is at least *aware* that different assumptions and perceptions are at work in the conversation.

Assumptions are the notions that we take for granted; they are the ideas, beliefs or "facts" that are accepted as true and real without proof or demonstration. They make up a fund of common knowledge on which one draws—unreflectively and uncritically—in the course of decisions and actions, and especially interpersonal relations. The word that refers to assumptive conduct and beliefs is *presumptuous,* and the distance from here to *arrogance* is not far. Assumptions are not always true, but they nevertheless serve one reasonably well until they are shown to be false *and one recognizes their falsehood.* Then it is necessary to abandon or revise the assumption—or retain it in spite of the evidence to the contrary, in which case the assumption has become prejudice and the assumer a bigot. The distance between presumption and arrogance has been effectively traversed.

Perception, on the other hand, is both the process and effect, the act and product, of becoming aware of something through the senses, especially eyes and ears. It is the insight gained by seeing or hearing something, the "fact" deposited into the fund of knowledge on which one draws in routine interaction with the world. In one rather narrow sense, perceptions are what is seen. But in a broader, more functional sense, perceptions are what is *thought* or *believed* regarding what is seen. Thus perceptions are interpretive: they embrace the significance discerned in or attributed to what is perceived. Like assumptions, perceptions are not always true, but they tend to serve one well in the course of routine living until they are shown to be false *and one recognizes their falsehood.* What one sees is not always there, and what is there is not always seen. At best, perceptions are fragments just as assumptions are limited. But when perceptions are exposed as untrue or too narrow or incomplete, it is necessary to abandon or revise the perception—or retain it unaltered, in which case it becomes not merely a misperception but a distortion of what is perceived, and the perceiver has become a fool.

Assumptions and perceptions take place within a larger view of the world. They are related to a worldview from which they are derived, by which they are sustained and for which they are building blocks. They are necessary for interaction with the world and for the creation and discernment of meaning and value, conduct and beliefs. They can be flexible or rigid. Everyone has them and functions with them. They help and hinder, bring aid and comfort, and render human life possible. People draw on and deposit into their fund of common knowledge on a regular basis, quite frequently without conscious awareness.

When it comes to the conversation on race and racism, differences in assumptions and perceptions tend to discourage candid discussion. At one level, we are simply afraid to talk with each other about these matters. At another level, the differing assumptions and perceptions on matters of race and racism render us unable to talk with each other. These differences function like a grid through which dialogue passes; some comments pass through in altered form, while others are blocked at the outset. As long as European Americans draw on a fund of "white" common knowledge and experiences to establish the categories by which we organize our views of the world and of others, we will continue to come to the conversation—if we come at all—and to encounters with members of other people groups with reluctance to see, interact and learn in a way that makes a fruitful exchange of common knowledge possible. We won't come in any other way than that which conforms to our existent categories. As long as we are unwilling to examine critically our assumptions and perceptions of ourselves and our context, and to pay close attention to what others are saying, we are not merely bigots and fools, we are not *free*. As Montagu states, "The readiness with which we are prepared to accept others as human beings determines how we perceive them."[8] The freedom of all to think, to choose, to converse, to act, to believe and to behave is supported *and* limited by the fund of common knowledge, and persons are not free to think, choose, converse, act, believe and behave if other possibilities—and change—are precluded or prohibited by social taboo or ignorance.[9]

European Americans constitute a sociologically and demographically identifiable people group alongside other people groups, and European Americans are mindful that there are more—though a proportionally diminishing number—of them than there are of the others. But European America is not just a place and a people. It is also an identity and view of the world, and most of the time European Americans neither question nor challenge it. It is assumed and absorbed as natural and normative. David Wilkins notes that "white Americans

---

[8]Montagu, *Man's Most Dangerous Myth*, p. 341.

[9]This modest discussion of assumptions and perceptions hardly exhausts their role and significance for the conversation on race and racism. The subject will be examined more thoroughly in chapter three and especially in chapter four. For a lively and somewhat populist discussion of the role of assumptions and perceptions in race relations, see Richard J. Payne, *Getting Beyond Race: The Changing American Culture* (Boulder, Colo.: Westview, 1998).

Also, I am mindful that in this discussion of the obstructive nature of assumptions and perceptions, my finger is pointing at European Americans. This should not be read to absolve African Americans from liability to the same degree of obstruction. One who shares this view is George A. Yancey, *Beyond Black and White: Reflections on Racial Reconciliation* (Grand Rapids, Mich.: Baker, 1996). My finger points as it does because European Americans as a group are those who most widely share the patently false assumption that racism no longer exists—a matter to be taken up more fully in subsequent chapters.

rarely see themselves as 'raced' at all. Nor, unlike members of other racial groups, have they been forced to adopt a racial identity in response to systematic state-supported racial prejudice. For most whites, therefore, their culture is 'American culture,' or, even more unselfconsciously, simply the way things are."[10] When the subject of race and racism rises, there is a tendency not to challenge but to defend the European American place, people, identity and worldview. When the subject revolves around euphemistic expressions of matters related to race and racism ("civil rights," "equal opportunity," "integration," "fair housing," "affirmative action," etc.), European Americans are profoundly conscious of "us" and "them," and the fears, assumptions and perceptions make the continuation of the conversation difficult and uncomfortable. The terms of the discourse, in all their ambiguity, require the recognition of responsibility, and given the tone and direction of the conversation and the differing assumptions and perceptions that steer it, European Americans tend to disclaim either personal or communal responsibility for the status of things. In this conversation European American response-ability is diminished by the fearful desire to minimize vulnerability, and this is accomplished by placing responsibility onto others: other *persons* (other European Americans), other *places* ("racism is not a problem here") or other *things* (the impersonal "system"). The assumptions and perceptions that restrict the ability to respond and the denial of personal and communal culpability make the conversation on race and racism difficult and sterile. This leaves the terms of our discourse increasingly alien and vacuous.

The tragedy is that the inability to engage in constructive conversation on race and racism pushes us all toward silence. And the silence preserves and tends to legitimate the status quo of race and racism. When the conversation is abandoned, the funds of common knowledge remain in place, largely confirmed and virtually unchanged. It then becomes exceedingly more difficult to break the silence, to return to or take up another conversation. It is more likely that the silence will be replaced by an intragroup conversation whose objective is neither inquiry nor critical reflection but confirmation of group assumptions and perceptions—and worldviews—as well as an approval of the rhetoric. This phenomenon of intragroup discussion on matters related to race and racism is common; members of one people group learn quickly and easily how to talk about other people groups. In the case of European Americans, it takes place most often in ways that validate the situation as normative, invite its sanction by

---

[10]David B. Wilkins, "Introduction: The Context of Race," in *Color Conscious: The Political Morality of Race,* ed. K. Anthony Appiah and Amy Gutmann (Princeton, N.J.: Princeton University Press, 1996), p. 22.

other group members and distance the discussants from culpability.[11]

Factors to consider in conversation. The chasm that discourages conversation on matters of race and racism and seemingly fosters the alienation between people groups can be overcome, but not without resolve and effort—and not without the recognition of several other factors. Perhaps chief among these is the fact that the conversation must begin within our present situation and draw critically on current notions of race and racism. This is, after all, where we are living and the language we are using. While we may not all share a common horizon of understanding and meaning on these matters, we must work collaboratively from our places and engage each other in a movement toward that horizon. So far as our situation and language are concerned, we are not helped by the illusion of stability and precision. Our assumptions and perceptions are skewed, and while we think we know what we are talking about, our vision is in fact very limited. On the other hand, a refusal to take up the conversation and deal with matters of race and racism leaves the present situation unchanged. This refusal reflects a racism-oriented sensibility in its own way and continues to serve the interests of those most resistant to change. We do not liberate ourselves and each other by refusing to talk about race and racism, and doing so *in race- and racism-oriented language.*

---

[11]This phenomenon has been noted by Raleigh Washington and Glen Kehrein in their book *Breaking Down Walls: A Model for Reconciliation in an Age of Racial Strife* (Chicago: Moody Press, 1993), pp. 146-50. They refer to it as "'Whites know how to talk to whites about blacks' and 'Blacks know how to talk to blacks about whites,' or WWB/BBW for short" (p. 146). They also observe that these intragroup conversations develop "a common body of 'knowledge' . . . about the other race that fortifies the feeling of 'us' versus 'them'" (ibid.). There is, in effect, both a personal and a group fund of common knowledge. Christine E. Sleeter also notes this phenomenon in her article "White Silence, White Solidarity," in *Race Traitor*, ed. Noel Ignatiev and John Garvey (New York: Routledge, 1996), pp. 258-64, except that she uses the language of "white racial bonding," by which she means "interactions that have the purpose of affirming a common stance on race-related issues, legitimating particular interpretations of oppressed groups, and drawing we-they boundaries" (p. 261). For other European American perspectives on inter- and intragroup conversation, see Paul Kivel, *Uprooting Racism: How White People Can Work for Racial Justice* (Gabriola Island, B.C.: New Society, 1996); David K. Shipler, *A Country of Strangers: Blacks and Whites in America* (New York: Alfred A. Knopf, 1997); and a work with explicitly Christian sensibility by Jody Miller Shearer, *Enter the River: Healing Steps from White Privilege Toward Racial Reconciliation* (Scottdale, Penn.: Herald, 1994). From an African American perspective, see Ellis Cose, *Color-Blind: Seeing Beyond Race in a Race-Obsessed World* (New York: HarperCollins, 1997), and *The Rage of a Privileged Class* (New York: HarperCollins, 1993), especially chaps. 1-2; Harlon L. Dalton, *Racial Healing: Confronting the Fear Between Blacks and Whites* (New York: Anchor, 1995); and Michael Eric Dyson, *Reflecting Black: African-American Cultural Criticism* (Minneapolis: University of Minnesota Press, 1993), especially chap. 10. For another work dealing with this phenomenon from a Christian perspective, jointly authored by an African American and a European American, see Spencer Perkins and Chris Rice, *More Than Equals: Racial Healing for the Sake of the Gospel* (Downers Grove, Ill.: InterVarsity Press, 1993).

A second factor has to do with the tendency to hide behind words in order to minimize self-disclosure. Those who monitor public opinion remind us that it is difficult to determine whether people mean what they say and say what they mean when asked about race and racism (something to be considered in chapter four). Equivocation is a form of fence-riding or truth-stretching, or even self-aggrandizement, all intentionally designed to deflect and deceive. In conversation on the matters at hand, honesty, transparency and vulnerability are *at-risk* behaviors, while equivocation and reluctance are *comfort-zone* behaviors.[12] Talk will be cheap if the objective is to conceal rather than to bridge the chasm that divides us as people groups. Honest speaking is related to active listening: it is dishonest to say only what others want to hear or to listen only to those with whom one agrees. This does not mean that there cannot be disagreement; there is always plenty of that in conversations on race and racism.

The objective, as James Waller articulates it, is a commitment "to stay in conversations that are difficult and to disagree in ways that keep a conversation going."[13] A conversation is a language event, but it has not happened merely once one has spoken. It requires for its completion that one has listened, and comprehended, and acknowledged, and responded, *and been altered.* Otherwise the broadcast merely goes out on the airwaves while radios are either off or tuned to another station.

When we engage in conversation with members of other people groups, especially about race and racism, the language is so coded, so loaded with clues that may signal the sentiments of race and racism, that we immediately begin to assemble judgments and arguments and draw conclusions about what we are "dealing" with. Arguably, when it comes to matters of race and racism, we know neither how to speak nor how to listen.

---

[12]Here I must respectfully—but forcefully—demur from the opinion of Orlando Patterson that candor on the part of African Americans and European Americans in conversation on race is "naive, at best" because it engenders "anger and resentment" (*The Ordeal of Integration: Progress and Resentment in America's "Racial" Crisis* [Washington, D.C.: Civitas/Counterpoint, 1997], p. 2). It seems to me that naiveté actually encourages bigotry and foolishness, and as a consequence license is given to presumption and ignorance. Furthermore, to conduct oneself in a manner that avoids or minimizes affective acknowledgment discounts the power and significance of affect in human experience. Am I better off not being honest with others *because* I am angry and resentful? I think not, for silence and repression are extraordinarily destructive. In *Black and White Styles in Conflict* (Chicago: University of Chicago Press, 1981), Thomas Kochman has explored, with penetrating insight and description, the dynamics and differing demeanors among European American and African American participants in race dialogue, offering a perspective that I can confirm from my own involvement in such conversations.

[13]James Waller, *Face to Face: The Changing State of Racism Across America* (New York: Insight, 1998), p. 196. See also Shipler, *Country of Strangers*, p. 447.

A third factor is atmospheric, or perhaps better, environmental. As atomic particles react differently to light depending on their stratospheric location, so the participants in conversations on race and racism react differently depending on the environment. By virtue of the language and the subject, there is already sufficient tension and fear among them. If this level is raised further, the participants will simply check out before any meaningful ground can be covered. It is important that the conversation's environment not inhibit or prevent the conversation. A conducive environment—whether living room, classroom, church room, staff room, board room, union hall or broom closet—is a *virtual place* in which discussants are encouraged to be real and true to themselves and others without fear of prejudgment; a *safe place* in which the movement is toward mutual understanding and away from personal attack; a *sacred space* in which participants can be assured that the gift of their integral self to others in conversation will be respected and hallowed, in spite of the brokenness of the gift. This means, simply, that there must be freedom to talk about race and racism and the issues that affect our lives. There must be freedom to dialogue. That is what environment means here.

A fourth factor is the recognition that our dis-ease in conversation on race and racism stems principally from the fact that the subject goes to the very core of self-identity and our relationships with others. Race and racism have to do with *me* and *you* and *us.* They have to do with who we understand ourselves to be and who we want to become, and who we are not and do not want to become. They pertain to the social, cultural, economic, political and religious worlds we inhabit, worlds we have built as expressions of who we are. Race and racism are related to the choices we make, the actions we take, the places we go, the people we know; they have to do with the God we glorify and the devil we disdain. But fundamentally, they have to do with who, where, when and why we are—our selves. Talking about race and racism is talking about ourselves—our pride, arrogance and condescension, as well as our idleness, humiliation and surrender. And talking about ourselves is difficult, discomforting and distressing. As Ronice Branding has observed: "To be able to talk about racism truthfully and in ways that help us understand each other across the racial divide is the challenge. Arriving at some common understanding about the nature of racism is part of the difficult but necessary work, so that attitudes, practices, and structures identified as racist can be addressed and changed."[14] Challenging, yes. Difficult, yes. But talk about it we must.

But how do we talk and what do we say? What is the significance of the lan-

---

[14]Ronice Branding, *Fulfilling the Dream: Confronting the Challenge of Racism* (St. Louis: Chalice, 1998), p. 45.

guage we use? What happens in the employment of language? What do the terms of discourse on race and racism suggest for a critical understanding of ourselves and our world? With a sense of the dis-ease of race discourse, we need now to turn our attention more directly to the task of sorting through the language.

The World of Language: Building Common Sense

Language is not merely a means of communication in and about the world in which we live. It has a way of shaping that world as well as being shaped by it. We not only use language as a way to communicate with one another. We also live in a world of language, a linguistic world, a universe of discourse. Both language and its context are human social constructs, reflecting the conventions, meanings and referents that constitute a shared world. Human beings invent, construct, revise and refine language as a means of communication and world-building, but human beings as individuals in relation with one another are also developed, changed and enriched by language and the world it expresses. We inherit, adapt to and build our linguistic world—our universe of discourse— even as it works its power upon us. Surely Richard Payne has this in mind when he observes: "Language is a powerful agent of change. It influences perceptions, thoughts, and actions in subtle but potent ways. To a large extent, language plays a pivotal role in one's perception of reality. The language used reflects a society's thinking, its values, and its method of structuring human relations. Language defines us; it signals who we are."[15]

Indeed language is indispensable to the construction, coherence and continuity of social life. Without a world of language there is no society in any meaningful sense of the term. Kevin Vanhoozer asserts that language functions in a twofold way as a medium of relations between persons and their world. This "covenant of discourse" establishes "the inter-subjective bond between speakers" in that "language is the medium in which we relate to others," and it establishes "the objective bond between language and reality" in that "language is the medium in which we relate to and seek to understand the world."[16] Anthony Appiah extends this observation by noting that language facilitates the understanding of social practices and how they work in a shared world: "To share a language is to participate in a complex set of mutual expectations and understandings: but in such a society it is not only linguistic behavior that is co-ordinated through universally known expectations and understandings. People

[15]Payne, *Getting Beyond Race*, p. 12.
[16]Kevin J. Vanhoozer, *Is There a Meaning in This Text? The Bible, the Reader and the Morality of Literary Knowledge* (Grand Rapids, Mich.: Zondervan, 1998), p. 206.

will share an understanding of many practices . . . and will largely share their views about the general workings not only of the social but also of the natural world."[17] Thus the ability to use language assumes a social world.

Beneath this mutuality of social life and language is the fact that, as Molefi Kete Asante reminds us, "all language is epistemic."[18] Language is the medium for human knowledge and understanding, the means by which we access and express ourselves and the world in which we live. Language is like the money we deposit in our fund of common knowledge, without which we have nothing to draw on in engaging the world. But language is also a very powerful instrument because it can be used to create and manipulate reality. Language is used to designate and define, and as such it is a form of power. It not only expresses our understanding of the world but is used to shape it. Kenan Malik draws attention to this function: "The very language we use to describe facts imposes truth or falsity upon those facts. Hence it is the discourse itself that creates the truth about a particular topic and competing discourses create competing truths. Truth lies not in the relationship between discourse and social reality but in the relationship between discourse and power. It is the relationship between discourse and power which decides which one of the many truths is accepted as *the* truth."[19] As Frantz Fanon asserts, one who possess language "consequently possesses the world expressed and implied by that language. . . . Mastery of language affords remarkable power."[20]

Thus language in and of itself may seem to be neutral or innocent, but the uses to which it can be put are hardly such. As an instrument for grasping and shaping personal and social reality, language can ostensibly be social *and* individualist, political *and* partisan, economic *and* utilitarian, jurisprudential *and* antinomian, preferential *and* biased, authoritative *and* dominative, descriptive *and* exploitive, sensual *and* pornographic, ecstatic *and* debilitating, disclosive *and* concealing, inclusive *and* exclusive. The language in the fund of common knowledge can be spent on different things, and differing sums and values can be attached to the currency in the account.

Language in the conversation on race and racism is mired in a pool of differing currencies and denominations. The value of a note in one place is not its

---

[17]K. Anthony Appiah, "Race, Culture, Identity: Misunderstood Connections," in *Color Conscious: The Political Morality of Race,* ed. K. Anthony Appiah and Amy Gutmann (Princeton, N.J.: Princeton University Press, 1996), p. 86.

[18]Molefi Kete Asante, *Afrocentricity,* rev. ed. (Trenton, N.J.: Africa World Press, 1988), p. 32.

[19]Kenan Malik, *The Meaning of Race: Race, History and Culture in Western Society* (New York: New York University Press, 1996), p. 233.

[20]Frantz Fanon, *Black Skin, White Masks,* trans. Charles Lam Markmann (New York: Grove, 1967), pp. 17-18.

value in another, and the exchange rate fluctuates so frequently and wildly that one can never be certain of a fair conversion. The conversation has become so entangled that it is practically impossible to understand what people mean, and efforts at clarification only bring deeper confusion and frustration. In no small part, this is because the subject has itself become embedded in the language. *Race, racial, racism* and *racist*—these hard-core words both express a sense of the matter and shape us and the world. But they are confusing and ambiguous. The soft-core words in which the matter is embedded and that shape our sense of ourselves and the world include *inequality, injustice, discrimination, exclusion, domination, subordination, stereotype, difference, culture, black, brown, white,* to say nothing of "code" words like *welfare, underclass, disadvantaged, deprived, urban, nonwhite.* These words are no less confusing and ambiguous, for as Robert Terry has remarked, "words are not neatly definable; they carry with them multiple meanings which shade off into each other. As such, some words have emotional content that is not always easy to specify."[21] The words in the universe of race discourse also have cognitive content in that they represent and express what we think we know. The merger of the affective and cognitive content constitutes the personal fund of common knowledge.

The work of language in social worlds. But how does it come about that human beings both shape and are shaped by language? How does it happen that our selves and our world—our identities and context—are formed in and by the universe of discourse? Here we may be aided by the scholarship of sociologists Peter Berger and Thomas Luckmann, whose work is a cornerstone in the sociology of knowledge.[22] In their exploration of the basis for human knowledge, Berger and Luckmann draw attention to the fact that our everyday life is presented to us as an *objective reality* which we interpret and find subjectively meaningful. This objective presentation and subjective interpretation make up a coherent world, and our consciousness is always directed toward objectivity and/or subjectivity (i.e., consciousness is never "empty"). Different spheres of everyday life, or objective reality, present different objects to our consciousness—trees, buildings, persons, and books with pictures of trees,

---

[21]Robert W. Terry, *For Whites Only,* rev. ed. (Grand Rapids, Mich.: Eerdmans, 1975), p. 166.

[22]For the paragraphs that follow, see Peter L. Berger and Thomas Luckmann, *The Social Construction of Reality: A Treatise in the Sociology of Knowledge* (New York: Doubleday, 1966), pp. 19-46. In my judgment, this seminal work has been largely overlooked in both the practical and theoretical literature on race and racism, an oversight that the present work intends to correct. The contention that race and racism are socially constructed is commonly found in the literature. What is absent, however, is a critical and constructive analysis of this contention. The literature reviewed in chapter two will provide a framework for understanding this contention, and then chapter three will take up such an analysis under the notion of the "sociality" of race and racism. There I will draw again on Berger and Luckmann.

buildings, persons, and stories about _____ and dreams of _____, all of which we discern and differentiate in their objectivity, but all of which are presented to our consciousness as objects from different spheres. We grasp our everyday life as a multitude of objects, an ordered and coherent constellation of phenomena independent from but imposed upon our apprehension. In this way reality is objectified—out there—as other than and apart from us; it is presented in all its complexity as *there*, and it is taken for granted as self-evident. The everyday world seems to us to be a "stubborn fact," notes Clifford Geertz. "Like Mt. Everest it is just there, and the thing to do with it, if one feels the need to do anything with it at all, is to climb it."[23]

This reality is also presented in what Berger and Luckmann call an *intersubjective world*, by which they mean not only a world shared with others but a world that is *known* as shared with others, a world that is known to be *as real* for others. This intersubjective world is thus the world of common knowledge: I know that you know, and you know that I know; I know what you know, and you know what I know. As our authors put it: "I know that there is an ongoing correspondence between *my* meanings and *their* meanings in this world, and that we share a common sense about its reality. . . . Commonsense knowledge is the knowledge I share with others in the normal, self-evident routines of everyday life."[24] *Common knowledge,* then, is what we presume everyone to know regarding our world, and *common sense* is our presumption that everyone experiences and interprets our world in basically the same ways. As Geertz declares: "What distinguishes common sense as a mode of 'seeing' is . . . a simple acceptance of the world, its objects, and its processes as being just what they seem to be—what is sometimes called naive realism."[25]

Together we share this reality of everyday life, a reality structured by space and time. As Berger and Luckmann tell it, the heres and nows of the reality of our lives are shared to one extent or another, and our physical proximity to one another is the greatest variable. As the prototype of all social interaction, the face-to-face encounter is the most important experience we have with others because it represents the intersection of one's here-and-now with another's. In

---

[23]Clifford Geertz, *The Interpretation of Cultures* (New York: BasicBooks, 1973), p. 111.

[24]Berger and Luckmann, *Social Construction*, p. 23. Doubt, whether of reality as presented, or of intersubjectivity, or of consciousness, is an extraordinary, rather than an ordinary, engagement in and with everyday life. As Berger and Luckmann note, it is easier in everyday life to suspend doubt than to challenge reality (ibid.). This problem of *capacity* to doubt and *unwillingness* to doubt will be taken up in chapter four under the rubric of "consciousness" of race and racism.

[25]Geertz, *Interpretation*, p. 111. In *Invitation to Sociology: A Humanist Perspective* (New York: Doubleday, 1963), Peter Berger maintains that "the commonsense view is actually the grown-up view taken for granted" (p. 67).

this encounter each person is apprehended by the other by means of what Berger and Luckmann call *typificatory schemes* that shape the mode of interaction. Each person sees the other as a manifestation of a type, and the typification involves rules for conduct. For example, typifying a person as friend or foe, foreigner or citizen, businessperson or buyer, employer or employee, physician or patient, or leader, lover, laborer, loser, or astronaut, abuser, addict, adulterer—or even bigot, or fool, or *racist*—is a way to delimit the mode of interaction. Furthermore, these typificatory schemes are reciprocal: not only does each person typify the other, but each person plays out the typified role to one extent or another. The conduct of the one typified as "physician" is interpreted by the one typifying as "patient" as consistent with the typification "physician-patient."

For Berger and Luckmann, the typifications or schemes of social interaction fall along a continuum from face-to-face situations to progressively distant and anonymous situations. The shared world of everyday life is thus crisscrossed with patterns of interaction in which participants draw upon a commonsense knowledge of themselves and their world. The totality of these encounters and typified patterns of interaction thus make up the social structure of everyday life.[26]

In Berger and Luckmann's view, language is a system of vocal signs that objectivate—or *objectify*[27]—human expressivity; language is the verbal means whereby human beings reveal themselves, or bring themselves to objective expression. We objectify ourselves through the production of signs—signification—that express our subjectivity, our consciousness or our inner world. Ver-

---

[26]At this point the reader can—and should—fairly discern that the Berger/Luckmann notion of typificatory scheme goes some distance toward interpreting the phenomenon of "stereotype" as a way of regarding and interacting with others. Significantly, the social, epistemological and behavioral patterns of the typificatory schemes are grounded in the seeming objectivity— the *thereness*—of reality as it is presented to consciousness, and as it is understood in terms of a socially shared, commonsense knowledge. Furthermore, typificatory schemes can be construed as categorizations—organizing and classifying by category—that also contribute to the formation of stereotypes. This is how Thomas F. Pettigrew develops the notion of category in *Prejudice*, ed. Thomas F. Pettigrew et al. (Cambridge: Belknap, 1982), pp. 5-9. We will turn our attention more directly to stereotype in chapter three.

[27]The view Berger and Luckmann are developing draws heavily on two words that will not be found in a dictionary, *objectivate* and *objectivation*. The verb refers to the process in which something is made objective or external. Throughout this discussion I will use the more familiar word *objectify* to refer to this process. The noun *objectivation* refers to the characteristic of being objective or external. I will use the more familiar word *objectivity* to refer to this characteristic. In both cases these words point to something that has been brought to external expression. Thus, for example, to say that something has been objectivated or objectified is to say that it has been expressed into the external world outside oneself. Likewise, to say that something is an objectivation or has objectivity is to say that it is expressed in the external world outside oneself. The verb *express* will also be used to refer to the process of objectifying, and the nouns *expression* and *expressivity* will be used to refer to objectivity as product.

bal signification objectifies our subjective processes, intentions, meanings, conditions and so on, and as products these expressions become indicators or "indices" of subjectivity. Language is not the only system of human objectivity, but for Berger and Luckmann it is the most important system because "the common objectivations of everyday life are maintained primarily by linguistic signification. Everyday life is, above all, life with and by means of the language I share with my [fellow human beings]."[28]

While language begins with face-to-face encounters, it can be detached from these situations, and in fact is to the extent that language as the objective expression of subjectivity is filled with accumulating experiences and the interpretations and meanings we derive from and lay on them. In this capacity language preserves and mediates meaning and understanding across space and time. Even when language is detached from face-to-face encounter it continues to form and re-form the subjectivity that finds both expression and confirmation in the reality of everyday life. Indeed language that can be detached and transported makes the subjective self who is objectified in it even more real (I am here-and-now as I was there-and-then—a self in continuity through space and time).

Because language is grounded in the reality of everyday life and is constituted by shared life with others in that reality, it can be said that language is a "stubborn fact" that acts on the self by squeezing its expressions into the patterns of language. Our sense of ourselves and the world around us and our interactions with others are limited by the universe of our language.[29] But language also makes it possible to name experiences and express their meaning in ways that make them communicable to others who share the same social and

---

[28]Berger and Luckmann, *Social Construction,* p. 36. One might wish for a fuller discussion by Berger and Luckmann of the nonlinguistic systems of signification (e.g., art, music, architecture, clothing, "styling," body painting, tattoos), but my reading of their argument suggests that they would respond to this criticism by saying that all systems of signification (a) are rooted in a socially constructed linguistic world (debatable) and (b) derive their objectivation of subjectivity from a primal linguisticality (also debatable). In any event—and for the present purpose—my interest is in what they have to say about language.

[29]Some will read my words here as an intellectually elitist caricature of ignorance (from Latin *ignorare,* not to know, to disregard, ignore). But ignorance, like knowledge, is socially constructed. In the literature on race and racism I find only caricatures of ignorance and no discussion of the phenomenology of ignorance vis-à-vis the sociality of race and racism. "Ignorant folk" are dismissed as bigots and fools. I say ignorant folk are innocent—not culpable—if they do not "know"; ignorant folk are culpable—not innocent—if they "disregard." Earlier I tried to suggest that how one deals with assumptions and perceptions pushes one in one direction or the other. Here I want to suggest that whether and how one is pushed is correlative to one's sense of and place in the linguistic universe. We will return to ignorance in chapter four, where the consciousness of race is taken up.

linguistic universe. In this way subjectivity is not only objectified but confirmed in everyday life with others who also use language to express similar experiences and meanings. Thus language objectifies the common sense.

Human beings use language to transcend a particular situation and establish connections among other spheres of everyday life, uniting them into a coherent whole. Language that transcends, connects and unites spheres of everyday life is what Berger and Luckmann call *symbolic language*. We develop symbol systems that overlay separate spheres and can be transported from one sphere to another. We interpret and integrate experiences in the various places of our lives by appealing to linguistic symbols. Within a religious sphere, for example, *absolution* is a linguistic symbol, a term that points to something beyond the immediate situation and that can be appropriated to objectify human experience in other arenas. Likewise, in a legal sphere *acquittal* may present itself as the most meaningful way to objectify an experience. While they do not necessarily refer to the same thing, *absolution* and *acquittal* can be used symbolically to name a *similar* experience in another sphere. Symbolic language is thus important for the commonsense apprehension of the complexity of everyday life.

Berger and Luckmann also draw attention to what they call *semantic fields*, or language zones that encompass the particular language and linguistic expressions related to a particular area of everyday life (e.g., occupation, recreation, family). Within a discrete area, semantic fields bring order and structure to activities and encounters that are usual and ordinary, expressing the sense and meanings peculiar to the area. Semantic fields are organized by language in ways that differentiate and classify objects as well as express patterns of action and degrees of social intimacy.

The ability to objectify, retain and accumulate personal experiences is made possible by semantic fields. For Berger and Luckmann, this accumulation of objective expressions in an intersubjective world results in a social stock of knowledge that is transferable from generation to generation and available to the self at any given time. Thus interaction with others is influenced and managed by the common sense, or the mutual participation in the social stock of knowledge. This commonsense knowledge is qualified by what our authors call *relevance structures* that govern the usefulness and appropriateness of semantic fields and their use in objectifying experience across the spheres of everyday life. For example, it is neither useful nor appropriate to tell the salesclerk about your work problems, or the librarian about your salary raise, or the mechanic about your spouse's infidelity, unless of course the salesclerk is also your friend, or the librarian is your brother, or the mechanic is your neighbor, in which case there will be multiple semantic fields at work.

A final helpful observation Berger and Luckmann offer has to do with the notion of the *social distribution of knowledge*. From their point of view, the social stock of knowledge in everyday life is distributed differentially and to varying degrees among different persons. The commonsense or social stock of knowledge possessed by any one person is not shared equally or completely with any other. One does not know everything that is known to all others, just as all others do not know everything known by one. Indeed the social distribution of knowledge issues in "exceedingly complex and esoteric systems of expertise"[30] that, in turn, affect social and epistemological stratification in everyday life. Thus language as objectified human expressivity ultimately imposes a certain structure on the reality of everyday life, aiding the objectivity and legitimation of the social order and rendering it discernible, durable and predictable.

Our tendencies with language. There remain three distinguishable but interrelated linguistic phenomena that require attention before we consider the terms of the discourse of race and racism: abstraction, categorization and reification. One of the ways language lends itself to the development, apprehension and preservation of human expressivity in social worlds is through abstraction. As an act of cognition, abstraction is the process of separating out inherent qualities or characteristics from the actual entity to which they belong, and drawing attention to those qualities or characteristics apart from the entity from which they are derived. An abstraction is a word or idea that has been stripped of concreteness and its actual referents, moving some distance away from objectivity and immediate or remembered experience. As one can remove this limb from this tree, so one can abstract limb from tree; or better, one can abstract from this limb and these limbs to the notion or concept of "limb." As a word, *limb* is an instrument for linguistically objectifying this thing growing out of the side of this tree, but as an abstraction, *limb* can be thought of, analyzed and stated apart from—and without reference to—the concrete existence of this specific limb. *Limb* does not exist except as a word, an abstraction, the meaning of which is deposited in the fund of common knowledge and withdrawn on occasions when an object perceived to conform to the abstraction needs to be named or objectified, or when one thinks about limbs in the aggregate, or when one wants merely to ponder limbness, or when one wants to do any or all of these things with *limb* abstracted from human- or animal-body appendages. Thus it is from existent entities that abstractions emerge to become usable means for apprehending and managing spheres and worlds and, drawing on the common sense, enabling meaningful self- and world-expression. But the abstraction does not exist except as a linguistic device for the apprehension, management and expression of a self with others in a world.

---

[30]Ibid., p. 46.

Second, the act of abstracting and the use of abstractions tend toward categorization, that is, the act of separating, organizing and classifying phenomena with the application of criteria external to the phenomena themselves. Categories are structural or organizational units of cognition, the way we distinguish and objectify this thing in relation to that thing. They are definitional in that they delimit and determine the meaning or signification of a phenomenon and its characteristics. They are reasonable to the extent that phenomena placed within them conform to criteria established by the categorizer(s) and are validated as such by the common sense.

A category can superordinate and subordinate its phenomena in relation to criteria. For example, one category is "piano," with the criteria being (1) stringed instrument (2) with keyboard and (3) sound made by hammers striking the strings. The category can be subdivided according to size (concert grand, baby grand) or shape (upright, spinet) or sound, manufacturer, cost, materials, color and the like. Harpsichords and electronic keyboards cannot be included in the category because they do not meet all the criteria: the strings of a harpsichord are struck with a plectrum, and an electronic keyboard has no strings. To include harpsichords and electronic keyboards in the category "piano" would require a revision of the criteria. If we limited the criteria to one—instruments whose sound is made with the use of a keyboard—we could include pianos, harpsichords and electronic keyboards, but we would also have to include computers, and common sense would probably resist the notion that computers are pianos! Yet through the processes of abstraction and categorization, a computer can be apprehended as a piano.[31]

Jung Young Lee is correct in stating that "defining is often merely a process of categorization. Human knowledge is conveyed mostly in categories pre-established by social conventions."[32] Edward Hall maintains that this tendency to classify phenomena by categories "is an excellent example of how the majority of Western peoples have been trained to think. . . . The result has been, how-

---

[31]Here I take issue with Gordon Allport's declaration in *The Nature of Prejudice* (Reading, Mass.: Addison-Wesley, 1954) that "to be rational a category must be built primarily around the *essential* attributes of all objects that can be correctly included within the category" (p. 171, emphasis his). I would agree with him if he removed the italicized word *essential*, acknowledged that "attributes" are user-defined—objectified—according to extraneous criteria, and either removed the word *correctly* or exegeted it in terms of the "common sense." The point is that "essential" and "attributes" are social-epistemic constructions in categorizations, and their usability is related to the criteriology of the common sense. What Allport does not address, and what I have yet to account for, is whether and under what conditions a common-sense category can be challenged—a matter to be addressed in chapter three.

[32]Jung Young Lee, *Marginality: The Key to Multicultural Theology* (Minneapolis: Fortress, 1995), p. 29. See also Waller, *Face to Face*, pp. 174-81.

ever, that whichever way we Westerners turn, we find ourselves deeply preoccupied with specifics . . . to the exclusion of everything else."[33] Nevertheless, without categorization human cognition, affect and conduct are disintegrated, and our engagement with reality is chaotic. Our categories may be thoroughly arbitrary, or they may be rational, but naming and classifying the objects in our world "are the first steps for reducing nature to order and for systematizing the chaos of the available material."[34]

Third, when we move from abstraction and categorization to reification, we have crossed a threshold from ordinary processes of cognition and apprehension to *extra*ordinary processes. We have moved from apprehension, conceptualization and organization to attribution, transformation and fixation. In reification we attribute concrete existence to an abstraction, transforming it from an idea to something that exists, thereby objectifying it in reality. In addition to abstractions, we reify categories, concepts and ideas; they are regarded not merely as fixed ideas but as concrete material entities, existing apart from but expressed in real particularities.

Reification is the objectifying of human cognition to the extreme; we might call it the thingification of ideation. Indications of reification surround us in everyday life. When a criminal trial reaches its end, we might say that "*justice* has been served," or we buy a particular automobile because the manufacturer tells us that "*quality* is our most important product," or we hear a newscaster remark that "the *market* declined today," or "late this afternoon, the *White House* announced that . . ." A physician might say that "AIDS is the greatest threat to *public heath*," or a professor might preface a lecture by saying that "*postmodernity* has thrown *history* into the *backwater* of *sociology*." Now while most of us would probably admit that the referents of the italicized words do not exist except as abstractions or categories or concepts, they are nonetheless useful in communication because the common sense discerns a meaning to the words in their linguistic context. A modest amount of critical reflection will enable us to apprehend that these "things" are not real in themselves but rather linguistic devices for objectifying something.

But that is precisely the problem with reification: the absence of critical reflection, modest or otherwise, produces a linguistic device that effectively takes on a life of its own. The common sense may discern a meaning to the words, but the common sense is both *common* (intersubjective) and *sense* (apprehension) because as abstractions the terms have become reified—that is,

---

[33]Edward T. Hall, *Beyond Culture* (New York: Anchor, 1976), p. 123.
[34]Julian S. Huxley and A. C. Haddon, *We Europeans: A Survey of "Racial" Problems* (New York: Harper & Brothers, 1936), p. 85.

objectified at the extreme. The more critical reflection is brought to bear on reified terms, the further one moves from the common sense and the usability of
the terms as linguistic objectivity.[35]

Building Race: How to Make Things with Words

Now, having developed a perspective on the nature and function of language,
we can consider the principal terms that constitute the linguistic world of race
discourse—the first four words in this chapter. (You should be dissuaded from
turning to a dictionary at this point, for you are not likely to be helped by what
you read there. Rather the deposit of race-discourse currency in your fund of
common knowledge is likely to be confirmed, and that may result in an
obstruction of critical understanding. The entries you will find are merely
expressive of the common sense. Besides, we will turn in due time to a dictionary for illustrative purposes.) And we shall begin—colloquially—with . . .

   Race. Imagine this conversation between a high school student and an
English teacher:
"Race." Is it a useful word?
Yes!
Noun?
Yes . . . at least I think so. Mrs. Prentice said that a noun was a person, place or
thing.
Phenomenon?
Ummm . . . are we talking common sense or philosophy here?
What difference does it make?
Well . . .
Don't start a sentence with "well"!
Sorry! Common sense says "yes," 'cause everybody can see that there are dif-
ferent kinds of people.
Everybody? That's a bit of a generalization, isn't it?

---

[35]Very important discussions of the phenomenon of reification can be found in Stephen Jay
   Gould, *The Mismeasure of Man*, rev. ed. (New York: W. W. Norton, 1996), where the focus
   of attention is the reification of "intelligence" (esp. pp. 56, 280-82, 350). This book was orig-
   inally published in 1981, but Gould felt compelled to revise and republish it in the wake of
   the controversy surrounding the publication of *The Bell Curve: Intelligence and Class Structure in American Life* (New York: Free Press, 1994), in which Richard J. Herrnstein and
   Charles Murray argue that intelligence is heritable and largely determines one's "life chances"
   and that this "fact" ought to have implications for social policy. Another discussion of reification worth reading is Berger and Luckmann, *Social Construction*, pp. 80-91, where the focus
   in general is on the reification of the social world and in particular on institutions and roles.
   Finally, there is a lively discussion of the reification of symbols as a kind of "verbal realism"
   in Allport, *Nature of Prejudice* (pp. 178-89), where he draws attention to the reified "we" and
   "they" in in-group/out-group dynamics.

OK, *we* see that . . .
Ah-ah-ah! You can speak for others?
Well, no . . .
Ah-ah!
No, ma'am, I guess I can't . . . but *I* see there are different kinds of people!
You see! So, your "common sense" is empiricism?
Yeah, OK . . . I call 'em as I see 'em!
And "kinds"?
Yeah—you know . . . *races.*
So a "race" is a kind of people?
Yeah, sure.
You're aware that "kind" is a classifying noun?
Well—oops! Sure, "race" is a word we . . .
Ah-ah!
OK, *I* use to classify different kinds of people. But I use it only because every-body . . .
Backup there!
. . . we . . .
Ah!
I believe that "race" refers to different kinds of people.
Somebody taught you that "race" refers to different "kinds" of people?
Yeah, Mr. Swartz in biology class says that there's, like . . .
Do not use that word!
Sheesh . . . Well . . . Anyway, yeah, he said there's this *genus* stuff—like—ah—such as mammals, and then you got your . . .
You "got"?
Ah, you *have* your *species,* you know, like . . .
"Like" is fine here, but lose the "you know"!
Ah, OK . . . Anyway, he says that humans are a "species" of mammals, a sub-group or what*ever* . . .
And "races"?
Races? I think they're . . . su . . . subspecies? You know . . . Ugh! . . . Man! How come you're on my case about frickin' words!
Frickin'? Are you talking about the nineteenth-century steel manufacturer Henry Frick? What does his name mean as a participial adjective?
As a what?
What does "fricking" mean?
Oh, wow! I don't know . . . Hey, everybody knows what "frickin'" means!
Everybody? I don't. Tell me!
Hey! you gotta be there, you know . . . it's gotta . . . it's gotta work for you. It's a

word, man—it's just a frickin' word! Nobody knows what it means!

I beg your pardon.

Oops! Sorry! It's just a word . . .

. . . that "everybody" knows and uses, but you can't tell me what it means. And I am not a "man."

Oh, give me a break. Why you jerkin' me around?

Number one, I haven't touched you; number two, there should be an "are" in that question; and number three, I just want to know what you understand "race" to mean.

Race refers to different kinds of people . . . Black people, white people, yellow people, red people, brown people . . .

. . . purple people, green people, puce people, chartreuse people . . .

There are no "purple" or "green" people!

Ah, so philosophically you're not an empiricist but a phenomenologist.

Say it again!

You're really into stuff that appears real but hasn't been shown to exist. You're into virtual reality.

Yeah, I can do virtual. So what! But people colors are real, *ma'am!*

So you're saying that "kind" is in fact determined by "color."

Yeah . . . Right!

Do you know a "black" person?

Yeah, Mustafa here.

And do you know a "yellow" person?

Sure, Hwang Hee.

And do you know a "red" person?

No—but Mr. Swartz says they're the Indians.

The people who live in India?

No . . . ugh! The people who were here when the settlers came over.

"Were" here?

Yeah, they were all over the place, but now you don't see 'em much anymore, 'cause there ain't that many of 'em and besides, they all live on reservations and get drunk and run casinos.

Excuse me!

Oops! There *aren't* that many of them—sorry!

Uh-huh! Just so I understand: you believe that "race" refers to different kinds of people, and that the difference is notable by "color." Right?

Yup, that's it! Bingo! You win!

So tell me, what does the fact that Mustafa here is "black" tell you about him?

Well . . . huh! That he's . . . you know . . . he's . . . he's *BLACK!* . . . Ah, man— we all know what it means.

Sam, can you say "re-i-fi-ca-tion"?

My contention is that *race* is an abstraction and a category, both of which have been reified in and by the common sense and transmitted from one generation to the next. As such, *race* is an extraordinary example of the social construction of reality. In the remainder of this volume I will seek to lay out this contention, showing how this is so.

The word *race*—as Sam correctly observed—is a noun, an abstract noun, an abstract classifying noun, a word that is useful because it has been deposited in and drawn from the fund of common knowledge. It is used not merely to name but to *objectify* consciousness and apprehension(s) as well as what is apprehended, and thus to objectify a fragment of experience in relation to a fragment of the social reality of everyday life within which it occurs. The reification is indicated, for example, when Sam declares that *race* as a word is a noun because it is a *thing*, a linguistic device that has a life of its own. When pressed to indicate whether this "thing" race is indeed a phenomenon, Sam acknowledges that it is so because differing "kinds" of people are apprehended. When denied access to the funds in the *common* knowledge—*everybody, we*—and pushed to make a withdrawal from his own account of *personal* knowledge, Sam nevertheless proceeds with confidence because he "knows" that his funds have value and stability all the way up the line. "Race" objectifies his consciousness and apprehensions as well as the world in which he lives *because* the social construction of the common sense assures him that race is . . . *real*.[36]

---

[36]Because I believe it is an important mechanism for understanding the historic and contemporary situations vis-à-vis race and racism, I am somewhat surprised that analyses of the reification of race are not all that frequent in the literature. One does find the use of the term, but usually as a declaration *that* race is reified, as though the statement served adequately to explain this phenomenon. There are, however, three critical studies wherein the authors, in different ways and from different perspectives, attend to this matter of the reification of race. In *Racial Subjects: Writing on Race in America* (New York: Routledge, 1997), David Theo Goldberg explores the ways the U.S. census has contributed to the reification of race; he argues that census taking is a profoundly racialized act. In light of the addition of a new "category" in the 2000 U.S. census, Goldberg's work is worth reading (especially chaps. 3-5). On the other hand, Ian F. Haney López argues in *White by Law: The Legal Construction of Race* (New York: New York University Press, 1996) that jurisprudence in the United States has been instrumental in the reification of race, principally through federal and state court decisions that define—categorize—race to establish eligibility for naturalization (I will turn more directly to his arguments in the next chapter). Finally, Victor Anderson argues in *Beyond Ontological Blackness: An Essay on African American Religious and Cultural Criticism* (New York: Continuum, 1995) that African Americans have reified a particular race identity that he calls "ontological blackness," the corrective to which is a "postmodern blackness" that nevertheless remains grounded in "race" as a permanent "category" for identity formation. In this respect Anderson shares the opinion of such critics as Derrick Bell (see, e.g., *Faces at the Bottom of the Well: The Permanence of Race* [New York: BasicBooks, 1992]) and Bell Hooks (see, e.g., *Killing Rage: Ending Racism* [New York: Henry Holt, 1995]).

Howard Winant argues that "if race is so much a part of 'common sense'; if it is so involved in the production of person, culture, state, and nation; if racial identity is so recognizable, so palpable, so immediately obvious, then in practical terms at least, it becomes 'real.'"[37]

Historians and critics of race and race discourse have noted that *race* as a term referring to differing people groups was initially introduced into common discourse by way of the scientific lexicon of natural history in general and physical anthropology in particular.[38] A quartet of seventeenth- and eighteenth-century scientists is typically credited with appropriating the term as a category within which to include groups of people differentiated by criteria associated with physical (i.e., presumed "biological") characteristics. Each successive scientist built on and refined the categories and criteriology of his predecessor(s).

French physician François Bernier (1620-1688) undertook the first classification of all the varieties of humankind; his work, published in 1684, identified four classifications: Europeans, Far Easterners, "blacks" and Lapps. Carolus Linnaeus (1707-1778), a Swedish professor of botany, appropriated

---

[37]Howard Winant, "Racial Dualism at Century's End," in *The House That Race Built*, ed. Wahneema Lubiano (New York: Vintage, 1998), p. 89. In his essay in the same volume ("What Is Black Culture?"), David Lionel Smith argues that "our reliance on 'common sense' racial notions subverts our ability to produce accurate theoretical or even descriptive accounts of our social and cultural circumstances. This is not to imply, however, that we can simply dismiss racial categories. Spurious or not, they continue to inform our consciousness" (p. 181).

[38]The reader will find useful discussions of the emergence of race as an organizing category in the following critical literature: Lucius Outlaw, "Toward a Critical Theory of 'Race,'" in *Anatomy of Racism*, ed. David Theo Goldberg (Minneapolis: University of Minnesota Press, 1990), pp. 62-63; Robert E. Hood, *Begrimed and Black: Christian Traditions on Blacks and Blackness* (Minneapolis: Fortress, 1994), pp. 10-12; Kivel, *Uprooting Racism*, pp. 17-18; Montagu, *Man's Most Dangerous Myth*, pp. 68-69, 77-79, 100; Michael Omi and Howard Winant, *Racial Formation in the United States from the 1960s to the 1990s,* 2nd ed. (New York: Routledge, 1994), p. 63; Cornel West, *Prophesy Deliverance! An Afro-American Revolutionary Christianity* (Philadelphia: Westminster Press, 1982), pp. 53-59; and in Cornel West's essay "Toward a Socialist Theory of Racism," accessible on the Internet at <http://eserver.org/race/toward-a-theory-of-racism.html>. For discussions in the *historical* literature, see Thomas F. Gossett, *Race: The History of an Idea in America*, new ed. (New York: Oxford University Press, 1997 [first published 1963]), pp. 32-39; Gould, *Mismeasure of Man*, pp. 401-12; Ivan Hannaford, *Race: The History of an Idea in the West* (Washington, D.C.: Woodrow Wilson Center Press, 1996), pp. 187-88, 203-11; Malik, *Meaning of Race*, pp. 38-100; Audrey Smedley, *Race in North America: Origin and Evolution of a Worldview* (Boulder, Colo.: Westview, 1993), pp. 36-39; and Winthrop D. Jordan, *The White Man's Burden: Historical Origins of Racism in the United States* (New York: Oxford University Press, 1974), pp. 100-106. And for perspectives grounded in the *contemporary situation*, see Cose, *Color-Blind*, pp. 4-26; Kenneth R. Manning, "Race, Science and Identity," in *Lure and Loathing: Essays on Race, Identity and the Ambivalence of Assimilation,* ed. Gerald Early (New York: Penguin, 1994), pp. 317-25; and Payne, *Getting Beyond Race*, pp. 33-37.

the Aristotelian categories of *genus* and *species* to aid in the construction of a classification system that, when published in 1735, showed four groupings: Europeans, Asians, Africans and Americans. Linnaeus was the first to use and emphasize *color* as a part of the criteria, so we also have in the same order white, yellow, black and red people. George Louis Leclerc Buffon (1707-1788), a French natural historian, developed a sixfold classification system in which—for the first time—humanity was formally classified into *races*.[39] In a 1778 publication Buffon described six such races: Europeans, Lapps, Tartars, South Asians, Ethiopians and Americans. Following Bernier, Linnaeus and Buffon, a German professor of medicine, Johann Friedrich Blumenbach (1752-1840), developed a classification system that evolved from four to five races as his published work, first appearing in 1775, moved toward a third and final edition in 1795. To Blumenbach is credited the scheme that dominated the physical-anthropological classification of human "races": Caucasian, Mongolian, Ethiopian, American and Malaysian. He was the one who created a category that entered and shaped scientific and common discourse to the present—the term *Caucasian*. He chose this label for the classification of the European "race" because he found a skull from the Caucasus region of Russia most aesthetically pleasing.[40]

All of these scientists pursued their observations, investigations and meas-

---

[39]Hannaford has convincingly shown that the term *race* entered the commonsense vocabulary of the West in the sixteenth century (*Race*, pp. 147-84) but that its usage reflected a wide variety of meanings, none of which—obviously—could be considered "scientific." This usage is significant in that it clearly suggests that "race" was part of the fund of common knowledge *prior to* its co-optation by the developing natural sciences in seventeenth-century Europe. For divergent views on whether Bernier or Buffon was the first to use the term *race* as a category in classifying human beings in natural science, see (for Bernier) West, *Prophesy Deliverance*, pp. 55; Hood, *Begrimed and Black*, p. 10; and Gossett, *Race*, pp. 32-33; and (for Buffon) Montagu, *Man's Most Dangerous Myth*, pp. 68, 100. Regardless of the outcome of this debate, it remains that the term *race* objectified apprehensions in everyday life, and for this reason it could be serviceable, refined and stipulated as a "technical" term in natural science, where it became a dominant—and practically uncontested—category in the nineteenth century with the work of Blumenbach.

[40]See Johann Friedrich Blumenbach, *On the Natural Varieties of Mankind [De Generis Humani Varietate Nativa]* (New York: Bergman, 1969), which contains both the first and third editions. Blumenbach first used this system of classification in the third edition of his book (1795). There he stated: "I have taken the name of this variety from Mount Caucasus, both because its neighbourhood, and especially its southern slope, produces the most beautiful race of men, I mean the Georgian; and because all physiological reasons converge to this, that in that region, if anywhere, it seems we ought with the greatest probability to place the autochthones [i.e., earliest] of mankind. For in the first place, that stock displays . . . the most beautiful form of the skull, from which, as from a mean and primeval type, the others diverge by most easy gradations on both sides to the two ultimate extremes (that is, on the one side the Mongolian, on the other the Ethiopian)" (p. 269).

urements with an inquisitive mind, firm in the belief that they were contributing to a stock of scientific knowledge that was grounded in and descriptive of the world as it was. With the development of categories and criteriology they described and classified the data they encountered. But while they construed their work as describing and organizing objective phenomena, each of these scientists was also objectifying his own perceptions and experiences, drawing on and contributing to both his own and the fund of common knowledge. Over time, with colleagues and disciples continuing and refining areas of investigation and inquiry, and with scientific "knowledge" becoming increasingly usable in and applicable to everyday life, objective knowledge that floated on a sea of objectified perceptions became assumption, then presupposition and eventually a priori contention. Voilà! A world is objectified and a category reified.

This can be seen nowhere better than in the sociocultural uses to which this scientific "knowledge" was put. Each of these scientists, in subtle or blatant ways, showed a preference for the European "race(s)," in no small part because the socially constructed—objectified—world of Europe was the point of reference. To one extent or the other, the European peoples and worlds were given normative status in the classification schemes.

Now, classifying according to category and criteria can be an innocent enough activity. We do it all the time. For example, the category is "tree," defined as woody plant with single trunk and multiple stems, and the criteria are height, circumference of trunk, color of trunk and foliage. Based on this category and these criteria, and from observation, I can classify all the plants outside my window. My research results in the following classifications: (1) tree: tall: wide: tannish-cream: leaf, and (2) tree: short: narrow: brown: needle. To trees in category 1 I give the name *aspen*, and to those in 2 the name *fir*. Now I see that some firs are taller than some aspens, and some aspens are narrower than some firs. This means at least two things: first, that no single tree conforms to all criteria, and second, that the objects variously classified are *relative* to each other and to the criteria. But with observations, measurements and words I have linguistically objectified and differentiated the trees outside my window. Innocent? Yes, until I ascribe meaning and valuation to the objects classified. I *like* tall and *prefer* the changing colors of leaves in the fall over the ever-green needles. Granted, I *enjoy* the aroma of burning fir in the fireplace, but a log of aspen is *more desirable* because it burns longer and gives greater heat. Thus for several reasons I think some trees are *better* than others, and when I present and interpret the results of my research, I will find it difficult to keep from saying, "Aspen trees are different from, *and better than*, fir trees." Innocent? Hardly, for not only have my classifications linguistically and categorically objectified the trees in my world, but they have likewise objectified my consciousness, perceptions and valuations.

Furthermore, in this little exercise the trees did not self-classify or self-differentiate. *I did that!* In the face of a multitude of trees, I defined the category, developed the criteriology and differentially classified the trees. And in so doing I created—and invaded—a realm of trees for the purpose of knowing, differentiating, organizing and managing its citizens. In short, I objectified treedom, and to the extent that my category, criteria and classifications are linguistically and objectively shared by others (intersubjectivity), it can be said that I have contributed to the fund of common knowledge, and thus to the construction of the reality of everyday life.

So it was with our quartet and their peers and followers. Perceptions structured reality. Categories, criteriologies and classifications objectified the human realm. And when this organized and structured realm was accompanied as it always is by interpretation of the *data*, the result was an objectivity of the meaning and value of perceptually differentiated people groups relative to the norms of the point of reference. Linguistically objectified consciousness, perception and knowledge led to differentiation, criterialization and classification that, when bathed in valuation and the attribution of meaning, issued in a hierarchy of superordination and subordination that was construed to legitimate *discrimination, violation, isolation and extermination.*

And with time, the category and all that followed from it as deposited in and withdrawn from the fund of common knowledge have been reified: *race exists and everybody knows it!* Race and its indicators have become so established in the fund of common knowledge that practically anyone can use a classification scheme to categorize the race of practically everyone. As Malik declares, "In popular language, 'race' is usually synonymous with 'colour.' . . . Virtually everyone can distinguish between the physical characteristics of the major racial groups. . . . This universal ability to distinguish between different human groups has given credence to the idea that races possess an objective reality."[41]

Abstracting. Categorizing. Differentiating. Classifying. We need them and *do* them accidentally and purposefully, with naiveté and with sophistication. They aid us as we live in and come to know a social world we organize with the help of language. The discourse of race and racism, like the "world" it linguistically objectifies, is ordered by assumptions and perceptions and influenced by categories and classifications. It is a discourse and a world structured by rules and

---

[41]Malik, *Meaning of Race*, p. 2. See also Amy Gutmann, "Responding to Racial Injustice," in *Color Conscious*, ed. Appiah and Gutmann, pp. 113-14.

norms deeply embedded in a common sense. Thus race constitutes a semantic field with its own relevance structure.

To reject the notion that race exists is to dereify the category; it is an act of denial. But it is not yet a denial of a linguistically objectified, socially constructed world infused with *race*. To reject such a world is to dereify the social order; it is an act of deconstruction, and ultimately—from a theological point of view—an act of subversion.

For an indication of the extent to which the common sense has been shaped by the race-world discovered and linguistically objectified and reified by the science of the seventeenth and eighteenth centuries; and for an indication of the ambiguity that surrounds the terminology of popular discourse on race and racism, one need only look in a dictionary, a repository for the linguistic fund of common knowledge. As a definition for *race*, mine says:

> 1. A local geographic or global human population distinguished as a more or less distinct group by genetically transmitted physical characteristics. 2. A group of people united or classified together on the basis of common history, nationality, or geographic distribution: *the German race*. 3. A genealogical line; a lineage. 4. Human beings considered as a group. 5. *Biology.* a. A population of organisms differing from others of the same species in the frequency of hereditary traits; a subspecies. b. A breed or strain, as of domestic animals. 6. A distinguishing or characteristic quality, such as the flavor of a wine.[42]

What then follows as apparently *subsequent* or *derivative* meanings are entries delineating definitions that refer to competitions of speed, political campaigns, moving water and so on. That is "race," and its context.

Now we are in a position to consider the remaining principal terms of the discourse of race and racism.

Racial. Given the reification of race as a category and an abstraction, it is not inappropriate to consider the term *racial* as an ascription that preempts other meanings, the fundamental purpose of which is to draw attention to a peculiar objectivity. When used as an adjective or adverb, the term is understood in the common sense as a categorization that moves whatever it refers to into the

---

[42] *American Heritage Dictionary of the English Language*, 3rd ed. (1992), s.v. "race." More-than-casual readers may be interested to note that under the word *color*, the definitions—following the physics stuff—are as follows: "2. A substance, such as a dye, pigment, paint, that imparts a hue. 3.a. The general appearance of the skin; complexion. b. A ruddy complexion. c. A reddening of the face; a blush. 4. The skin pigmentation of a person not *classed* as white" (ibid., emphasis mine). This last definition has been changed since 1969 when the first edition of the dictionary was in print. Then it said: "The complexion of a person not *classed* as a Caucasian [Blumenbach?], especially that of a Negro" (emphasis and brackets mine).

world of race. In this way the referent is objectified in terms of race and becomes itself a race term, a constitutive element in the linguistic universe of race. Whether explicitly stated or merely implied from its linguistic context, the term delimits the range of meanings that might otherwise be attached to its referent, because they are now embroiled in the tangled web of race discourse. Because practically any noun or verb can be co-opted into the linguistic world of race, any noun or verb can contribute to objectifying and reifying race. All that is necessary is that the common sense discern the meaning of the word now qualified by the term *racial*. Assumptions and perceptions, real or imagined, true or untrue, are not merely linguistically objectified when brought to speech and qualified by this ascriptive term. There occurs at the same time an objectifying of race.

Consider for example the notions of "group," "preference" and "relations," all of which are suitable for use in a variety of ways and contexts, and all of which contribute to linguistically objectifying consciousness and the spheres of everyday life. We can qualify the meanings and referents of the words with an adjective such as *community*, in which case we have objectified aspects in one sphere of everyday life—the interactive population in a common location. Or we can use the word *institutional*, thereby objectifying yet another sphere—the practices and structures of an organization. We might also use the word *international*, or *educational*, or *fundamental*, all of which objectify both consciousness and a sphere of everyday life. Or we might accentuate the illustration, focusing on cognitive and affective dimensions of consciousness as well as the imaginative construal of the objectified referents, by using the adjective *sexual*, so we could talk about and thereby objectify an aspect of human subjectivity and social expressivity with sexual *group*, sexual *preference*, sexual *relations*, and because of the common knowledge we share we have a sense of what we are discussing. In any case, the use of a qualifier delimits not only the referent but also its meaning and the sphere within which it is located. More important, it contributes to objectifying the referent, meaning and sphere in the fund of common knowledge.

So it is with *racial*. When used as a qualifier, the term not only linguistically objectifies what is construed as a sphere of everyday life but also contributes to the linguistic objectivity and legitimation of *race*. *Racial group*, *racial preference* and *racial relations*—all of these and many other words have value in the fund of common knowledge because they are understood to be related to and interpreted in terms of the category of *race*. Identifying a group by race, preferring an individual or group because of race, and the conduct of interaction between or among persons on the basis of race—these are but fragments in the mosaic of ways by which consciousness and social world *and race* are objectified in everyday life.

We can consider the term *racial* to be an ascription that preempts other meanings because, as Gordon Allport has observed, "there is a curious air of finality"[43] about the term when it is used as a qualifier. In the fund of common knowledge, the category of race is reified in part because it is understood as having to do with heredity, and thus the transmission of indelible traits sufficient to characterize a distinct human group. The hereditary traits generally associated with race are deposited in the common fund as permanent and immutable, and this is no less true when the traits are limited to the physical or enlarged to include intelligence, character, demeanor, acumen or aptitude. The process of reification, based as it is on assumptions, perceptions, classifications and criteriologies, moves easily from the heritable through the natural to the essential. It moves from the transmission of traits through their determination by nature to an ontology of race (i.e., race is a determination of being). By invoking the permanent and essential as over against the mutable and accidental, the term *racial* draws attention to qualities and characteristics that define and objectify in terms of race, preempting all other ascriptions and enclosing our language, assumptions and perceptions in the reified sphere of race essentialism.[44]

To reject race essentialism is to dereify the category; it is an act of denial. But it is not yet an act of deconstruction. For that it is necessary to displace the preemptive meanings that have contributed to objectifying both consciousness and the world of everyday life.

Without foreclosing further discussion on what the term *racial* signifies, we need to turn our attention to what is perhaps the most ambiguous and inflammatory of terms in race discourse.

Racism. The next chapter will contain a more thorough discussion of the contours and textures of racism. At this point it is important to develop an understanding of *racism* that is correlative with the terms we have already con-

---

[43]Allport, *Nature of Prejudice*, p. 107.

[44]Race essentialism is associated with the reification of race and for purposes of the present argument can best be understood as the view in which race is the singular and irreducible core of all that constitutes humanness, or the fundamental determinant of all concrete expressions of human particularity. Race is thus "essential" to human existence. For critical discussions of essentialism, see Anderson, *Beyond Ontological Blackness*, pp. 11-19, 51-52; Dyson, *Reflecting Black*, pp. xiii-xxxiii; Kwame Anthony Appiah, "Racisms," in *Anatomy of Racism*, ed. Goldberg, pp. 3-17; Omi and Winant, *Racial Formation*, pp. 53-75; Patterson, *Ordeal of Integration*, pp. 72-77; Pat Shipman, *The Evolution of Racism: Human Differences and the Use and Abuse of Science* (New York: Simon & Schuster, 1994), pp. 225-33; and Manning Marable, *Beyond Black and White: Transforming African-American Politics* (New York: Verso, 1995), pp. 117-28.

sidered. The first observation is that, despite its having been deposited in the fund of common knowledge, the term remains slippery and rather elusive in its evincibility. It can be a basket that holds nothing ("racism no longer exists") or everything ("racism is ubiquitous").

In part, the ambiguity of the term derives from the fact that the concept of "race" and its uses have undergone change historically. But virtually all the meanings of the term can be found in the contemporary situation. Typically, discussions of racism draw initial attention to one, two or all of three possible descriptive approaches.

First, racism is understood to be a belief or set of beliefs regarding the phenomenon of human variability and its significance. The focus here is on the ideas, attitudes, values, assumptions and perceptions held by persons in one people group regarding persons in other people groups, with attention drawn to stereotype, prejudice, bigotry and disdain. This approach can be called *ideological*.

Second, racism is viewed as the particular conduct or actions of persons in one group related to or directed toward persons in another on the basis of the perception and valuation of human variability. The focus here is on intentions, roles, expectations and patterns of relations between and among persons in different people groups, with attention to animosity, antipathy and bias. This approach can be called *behavioral*.

Third, racism is construed as a structural phenomenon in which human variability is thought to be the warrant for the differential and exclusionary customs, policies, practices and norms that are embedded in social infrastructures. Here the focus is on institutions, organizations and social systems, with attention to hierarchy, stratification, advantage, privilege, domination, discrimination and ethnocentrism. This approach can be called *sociocultural*.[45]

Through each of these descriptive approaches there is a potent current that carries the effect of the manifestation of racism: the oppression, exploitation,

---

[45]The notion that racism is primarily beliefs and attitudes tends to overlook the ways in which beliefs and attitudes authorize and come to expression in behavior and sociocultural phenomena. Likewise, the notion that racism is primarily actions tends to discount the ways in which ideas reflect personal and social needs and aspirations. Furthermore, the notion that racism is primarily sociocultural tends to ignore the ways in which structures and systems are developed and managed by real believers and behavers who have vested self- and group-interests. In an analysis of racism, belief, action and culture need to be held together dialectically as a constellation of expressions, mutual determinations and supports. How this is the case will become clearer as we move along, especially in chapter two. In the meantime, see relevant discussions in Goldberg, *Racial Subjects*, pp. 17-26; Omi and Winant, *Racial Formation*, pp. 53-76; and Andrew Hacker, *Two Nations: Black and White, Separate, Hostile, Unequal* (New York: Ballantine, 1992), pp. 20-34.

Discerning readers will note that lurking around the edges of this discussion is a tripartite

segregation, degradation, dehumanization and violence perpetrated by one people group upon others.

Fundamentally, racism has to do not merely with the real or perceived differences between people groups but with the value and significance of these differences. It has to do with the presumption of superiority over other people groups and the conduct of personal and social life that manifests this presumption in personal, communal and sociocultural ways. Racism has to do with beliefs, actions and structures that centralize some by marginalizing others on the basis of supposed differences. The value placed on various physiological, psychological, intellectual, social or cultural characteristics then tends to legitimate this center/margin structure. In short, racism is the linguistically and socially objectified world of *race*, a world crafted with a worldview that nourishes and sustains ideology, behavior and sociocultural systems.

There are two predominant strands of racism that can be identified, the first having largely given way to the second in the twentieth century, though it is not without its contemporary adherents. Each is characterized by particular assumptions regarding the basis and value of human variability. The first strand, which can be labeled *bioscientific* racism, assumes that human variability is determined by genetic factors and that people groups can be classified according to criteria that reflect the moral and social value of the manifest differences in physiology, cognitive function and cultural expression. More specifically, it is assumed that character, personality, physical characteristics and mental/intellectual abilities, as well as group social and cultural development, are genetically based and that one group is superior in all these regards to all other groups

---

classification of racism as "individual, institutional, cultural." My problem with this scheme of the "forms" or "types" of racism is that it tends to fragment, inhibit and occasionally truncate and exonerate the expressivity of racism. For this reason, I prefer—at the moment—to speak of *approaches* to the phenomenon rather than the *forms* of the phenomenon of racism. For analyses that depend heavily on this tripartite classification of forms, see especially Joseph Barndt, *Dismantling Racism: The Continuing Challenge to White America* (Minneapolis: Augsburg Fortress, 1991); Christopher Bates Doob, *Racism: An American Cauldron,* 2nd ed. (New York: HarperCollins College, 1996); William Julius Wilson, *Power, Racism and Privilege: Race Relations in Theoretical and Sociohistorical Perspectives* (New York: Free Press, 1973); and Terry, *For Whites Only.* Other analysts use bipartite schemes, sometimes instead of, other times alongside of, the tripartite classification. E.g., "overt/covert" in Shearer, *Enter the River;* "direct/indirect" in Barndt, *Dismantling Racism;* "minimal/maximal" in Wilson, *Power, Racism and Privilege;* "intrinsic/extrinsic" in Appiah, "Racisms"; and "overt/institutional" in Gertrude Ezorsky, *Racism and Justice: The Case for Affirmative Action* (Ithaca, N.Y.: Cornell University Press, 1991). Payne in *Getting Beyond Race* speaks of racism as "redneck, aversive, modern," but this is a popularized variation of racism as "dominative, aversive, metaracism" in Joel Kovel, *White Racism: A Psychohistory,* reprint ed. (New York: Columbia University Press, 1984), to which we shall turn in the next chapter.

that can be ranked on a hierarchical scale. From this genetic model flow expressions of racism, including the warrant for differential treatment of persons and groups, without regard to the fact that it has never been demonstrated that genes connect physiology, intellectual capacities and cultural expression.[46]

The second strand, which can be called *envirorelational* racism, assumes that human variability is rooted not so much in the human genome—though this can explain the most perceptibly obvious physical differences—as in qualitative classification, differentiation and valuation of intellectual, social and cultural achievement. This strand works with the categories of superior/inferior and dominant/subordinate and assumes the viability of the classification of nongenetic phenomena. On the basis of this criteriology, individual, communal and cultural expressions are judged as congruent or incongruent with the norms established by the predominant group, and intergroup relations are evaluated as consistent or inconsistent with values embedded in the social structures developed by the predominant group. In this strand, racism is the demarcation of structures and relationships with the implicit or explicit intent of maintaining a degree of exclusion and inequality between groups, or of preserving the hegemonic prerogative of what is thought by the predominant group to be historically and culturally their own by virtue of their group initiative and ownership. From this cultural model flow expressions of racism, including the warrant for differential treatment of persons and groups, without regard to the fact that it establishes a structure oppositional to the social order, or a dualist worldview in which there exist those who are judged essential and therefore valuable to the constituted world and those who are judged extraneous and therefore superfluous.[47]

As the linguistically and socially objectified world of race, racism is constituted by typificatory schemes that limit and determine roles and manners in interaction of persons and groups in communal settings. Racism is also consti-

---

[46]I call it *bio*scientific because the differences across the board are judged to be inherently and irreducibly biological and therefore transmissible, and bio*scientific* because it has been advanced under the aegis and authority of science. See, e.g., F. James Davis, *Who Is Black? One Nation's Definition* (University Park: Pennsylvania State University Press, 1991), pp. 23-27; Mark Nathan Cohen, *Culture of Intolerance: Chauvinism, Class and Racism in the United States* (New Haven, Conn.: Yale University Press, 1998), pp. 11-110; Franz Boas, *The Mind of Primitive Man*, rev. ed. (New York: Collier, 1963), pp. 45-99; Martin Barker, "Biology and the New Racism," in *Anatomy of Racism*, ed. David Theo Goldberg (Minneapolis: University of Minnesota Press, 1990), pp. 18-37; Montagu, *Man's Most Dangerous Myth*, pp. 41-97, 111-54; Payne, *Getting Beyond Race*, pp. 2-4; Gould, *Mismeasure of Man*, pp. 176-263, 351-64; Shipman, *Evolution of Racism*, pp. 225-61; and Wilson, *Power, Racism and Privilege*, pp. 32-40.

[47]It is called *enviro*relational because it recognizes the influence of sociocultural environments on the expressivity of human ideation and conduct, and enviro*relational* because it discerns

tuted as a semantic field in that it consists in linguistic expressions that point to a particular structure and order to human encounters as well as the settings in which they occur. Racism is the peculiar expression of these relations bounded by a constellation of beliefs, actions and sociocultural contexts. As a relevance structure racism makes possible the appropriation and control of meaning across a range of everyday situations by suggesting points of reference and rationalizations to legitimate belief and conduct and preserve sociocultural structures. In short, racism objectifies a social world inhabited by various people groups.

It matters little whether one's participation in and contribution to this world is conscious or unconscious. What matters is that this world has been and continues to be objectified in ways that sanction some and disfranchise others by linguistic and social ascriptions of difference and preference.

To reject racism is to dereify the category; it is an act of denial. But it is not yet an act of deconstruction. For that, it is necessary to dismantle the ideological, behavioral and sociocultural infrastructures in and through which the world of race is objectified.

And finally, we can turn our attention to the last of our terms.

Racist. In the common discourse on race and racism, this term is also

the patterns, structures and practices of the interaction between and among persons and groups. See, e.g., Louise Derman-Sparks and Carol Brunson Phillips, *Teaching/Learning Antiracism: A Developmental Approach* (New York: Teachers College Press, 1997), pp. 2-10; Joe R. Feagin and Melvin P. Sikes, *Living with Racism: The Black Middle-Class Experience* (Boston: Beacon, 1994), pp. 3-4; Joe R. Feagin and Hernán Vera, *White Racism: The Basics* (New York: Routledge, 1995), pp. 2-18; Lerone Bennett Jr., *The Shaping of Black America*, rev. ed. (New York: Penguin, 1991), pp. 223-25; Charles W. Mills, *The Racial Contract* (Ithaca, N.Y.: Cornell University Press, 1997), p. 2; Manning Marable, *Black Liberation in Conservative America* (Boston: South End, 1997), pp. 185-94, and *Beyond Black and White*, pp. 118, 186; Shelby Steele, *The Content of Our Character: A New Vision of Race in America* (New York: HarperCollins, 1991), p. 4; Asante, *Afrocentricity*, p. 95; Doob, *Racism*, pp. 4-5; Omi and Winant, *Racial Formation*, pp. 70-71; Montagu, *Man's Most Dangerous Myth*, pp. 27-100; Haney López, *White By Law*, pp. 165-67. Goldberg, *Racial Subjects*, p. 21; Kivel, *Uprooting Racism*, pp. 123-73; and Wilson, *Power, Racism and Privilege*, pp. 29-33.

Implicit here is the truncated formula expressed as "racism = prejudice + power." Apart from the fact that it is too simplistic, this formula should be discouraged because it is misleading: neither those with power but without racial prejudice nor those with racial prejudice but without power are implicated in the expressivity of racism. In discussions of the significance of this formula as a mechanism for apprehending racism, far too many qualifications, equivocations and disclaimers are needed to carry its meaning and delimitation. For analyses that draw on this formula, see especially Barndt, *Dismantling Racism;* Ronice Branding, *Fulfilling the Dream;* Susan E. Davies and Sister Paul Teresa Hennessee, eds., *Ending Racism in the Church* (Cleveland, Ohio: United Church Press, 1998); Derman-Sparks and Phillips, *Teaching/Learning Anti-racism;* Feagin and Sikes, *Living with Racism;* Feagin and Vera, *White Racism;* Shipler, *Country of Strangers;* Shearer, *Enter the River;* and Judith H. Katz, *White Awareness: Handbook for Anti-racism Training* (Norman: University of Oklahoma Press, 1978).

shrouded in ambiguity and confusion. For some it comes easily and all too quickly to the lips. It is used as an assumption and a description as though its meaning were clear in the common sense. It can be pressed by analysts to describe a wide range of phenomena, but the referents it qualifies are not always recognized as such by an equally wide range of observers. The term *racist* can be used as either an adjective or a noun, but its meaning as a noun is derived from the ascriptive function of the adjective. When used as a noun, *racist* represents a linguistic conversion of the adjective into an entity. So we might say, "A racist is one who . . ." or "The racist said . . ." or "Racists designed . . ." when what is really meant is "Racist *person(s)* . . ." When used as a noun, the term refers to persons who effect race and racism.

Its use as an adjective is more flexible because it can specify not only persons but places, things, qualities and actions. Like *racial, racist* is a preemptive ascription that categorizes its referent in the world of *race*. But unlike *racial, racist* is understood in the common sense as related primarily to *racism*. Whether used as a noun or an adjective, *racist* refers to the objectivity of racism in the sphere(s) of everyday life. Any*one* and any*thing* can be "racist" insofar as he, she or it objectifies racism. More specifically, the term *racist* designates expressions of racism as the ideology, behavior or sociocultural systems that objectify the world of race. Thus *racist* indicates the linguistic and social expression of *racism*. An entity is racist to the extent that it objectifies racism in a race-world.

It is not the case that one must only think or believe disparaging things about, or act in rancorous ways toward, other people groups in order to be considered racist. Neither is it the case that a sociocultural system must practice discrimination in order to be regarded as racist. All that is necessary is that a person, group or institution collaborate in, acquiesce to or be the beneficiary of the objectivity of racism. It is reductionist to contend that racism is limited to certain beliefs, attitudes and actions.[48] We are misled if we suppose that racism is equivalent to racial prejudice, bias or antipathy, or—more frequently heard— an irrational or deviant view or behavior. To the contrary, these are *engendered*

---

[48]Thus I could not disagree more with the disingenuous caricature of the "racist" offered by Dinesh D'Souza in *The End of Racism: Principles for a Multiracial Society* (New York: Free Press, 1995). Early in his discussion, he offers the following as an interpretation of *racist* culled from several definitions of *racism:* "In order to be a racist, you must first *believe* in the existence of biologically distinguishable groups or races. Second, you must *rank* these races in terms of superiority and inferiority. Third, you must *hold* these rankings to be intrinsic or innate. Finally, you typically *seek* to use them as the basis for discrimination, segregation, or the denial of rights extended to other human beings" (p. 28, emphasis mine). This definition convicts few and exonerates most. In my view, consent with, capitulation to or capitalizing from racism renders a racist, for each of these is a contribution to its linguistic and social objectivity.

by the linguistic and social objectivity (i.e., typificatory schemes, semantic fields, relational patterns, meaning and value systems, relevance structures and so on) of the world of race, within which a range of racist views, behaviors and structures are *legitimated* as rational and normal. Equating racism with racial prejudice, hatred and irrationality inhibits critical discernment because, as David Theo Goldberg has noted, this equation tends to "make racist expression turn on a psychological disposition, an emotive affect(ation), a dis-order—and so as ab-normal and un-usual."[49] The structure of racist sensibilities, whether benign or malevolent, is grounded in the assumptions and perceptions we have about ourselves, others and the world, as well as the patterns of conduct and relation by which these are objectified. Indeed racism has been shown in both its prototypal and developed expressions to have emerged concurrently with—and with the assistance of—a scientific rationality and worldview that progressively normalized racial categories, criteriologies, classifications, differences, structures and hierarchies.[50] Racist expression, far from being driven only by animus and deviance, is made possible by the rationalization and normalization of racism embedded in the linguistic and social objectivity of the spheres of everyday life.[51] As Christian Delacampagne has noted, racism "developed in the midst of a system of thought that strove to be rational; it progressed hand in

---

[49]Goldberg, *Racial Subjects*, p. 18.

[50]In this vein, David Theo Goldberg has commented that "classification is central to scientific methodology; and scientific method, in turn, was taken to furnish the ideal model of rationality," and that "classification, order, and value are fundamental to the forms of rationality we have inherited" ("The Social Formation of Racist Discourse," in *Anatomy of Racism,* ed. Goldberg, pp. 302-3). Furthermore, he declares that "racisms are not unusual or abnormal. To the contrary, racist expressions are normal to our culture, manifest not only in extreme epithets but in insinuations, and suggestions, in reasoning and representations, in short, in the microexpressions of daily life" (*Racial Subjects*, p. 20). These and my own contentions merit further elaboration, and I will endeavor to provide this in the chapters that follow. For historical analyses that pertain to the "rationality" and "normalcy" of racism, see Hannaford, *Race*, pp. 187-324; Bennett, *Shaping of Black America*, pp. 207-29; Gossett, *Race*, pp. 32-122; Malik, *Meaning of Race*, pp. 38-70; Shipman, *Evolution of Racism*, pp. 85-141; Jordan, *White Man's Burden*, pp. 99-133; George M. Fredrickson, *The Black Image in the White Mind: The Debate on Afro-American Character and Destiny, 1817-1914* (Hanover, N.H.: Wesleyan University Press, 1971), pp. 71-96, 228-55, and *The Arrogance of Race: Historical Perspectives on Slavery, Racism and Social Inequality* (Hanover, N.H.: Wesleyan University Press, 1988), pp. 189-205; and Richard Hofstadter, *Social Darwinism in American Thought*, rev. ed. (Boston: Beacon, 1955), pp. 3-50.

[51]Having said this, I must nevertheless contend against D'Souza's notion regarding "rational discrimination." He supposes that "most of us take for granted that what we call 'racism' is based on irrational hostility, that its sources are 'prejudices' and 'stereotypes,' and that their consequence is unwarranted 'discrimination'" (*End of Racism*, p. 246). Note the reference to—or withdrawal from—the fund of common knowledge. Since he believes that "racism and discrimination are fundamentally different now than in the past" (ibid.), he suggests there are

hand with the very foundations of Western rationalism."[52]

A racist is one whose beliefs, attitudes, values, language, conduct and worldview are formed under the influence of, contribute to and are sustained by the objectified world of race. To reject racist expressivity is to dereify the category; it is an act of denial. But it is not yet an act of deconstruction. For that, it is necessary to disestablish the consciousness of race and racism and engage in acts of contestation and resistance in the spheres of everyday life.

Race, racial, racism and *racist*—these are the principal terms of the discourse we use, not only in our conversation but also in the construction of our social world. They are firmly yet fluidly deposited in the fund of common knowledge, and the conversation must utilize them in ways that objectify but seek also to deconstruct the race-world. It is necessary that we become mindful of this language, its contribution to objectifying our world and its role in the expression of consciousness. With this understanding of the importance of the linguistic world of race and racism as a resource, and following some explorations of other critical theories of race and racism, we will proceed to a more focused examination of the contention that race is a social construction.

●   ●   ●   ●

Let no evil talk come out of your mouths, but only what is useful for building up, as there is need, so that your words may give grace to those who hear. And do not grieve the Holy Spirit of God. . . . Put away from you all bitterness and wrath and anger and wrangling and slander, together with all malice, and be kind to one another, tenderhearted, forgiving one another, as God in Christ has forgiven you. E p h e s i a n s 4 : 2 9 - 3 2

Have you ever said something that offended another? Have you ever been offended by something someone said? Do you even care about language and the effect it has on others? Maybe you've heard the saying "Sticks and stones will break my bones, but words will never hurt me." Do you suppose, for one minute, that this saying is true? Does what you say express love to those who hear you?

---

circumstances in which discrimination is rational. By this he means that it is warranted, or justifiable, largely because he discerns an element of truth in the European American stereotypes of African Americans. This is far from what I am contending here. What D'Souza is talking about is illustrative of what I am describing as *rationalized* discrimination, or the rationalization and normalization of the objective expressions of racism.

[52]Christian Delacampagne, "Racism and the West: From Praxis to Logos," in *Anatomy of Racism*, ed. Goldberg, p. 83.

2

THEORETICAL CONSTRUCTIONS OF RACE AND RACISM

You are from below, I am from above; you are of this world, I am not of this world. I told you that you would die in your sins, for you will die in your sins unless you believe that I am he. John 8:23-24

You hypocrites! You know how to interpret the appearance of earth and sky, but why do you not know how to interpret the present time? Luke 12:56

The fact of our worldliness underscores the fact of our sinfulness. Together these point toward our death in a way of life that prefers this world over its Lord. If we do not wish to die in our sin, would it not be prudent to ask about the extent to which we are of this world? By holding certain beliefs and clinging to certain facts, we practice certain ways of life that call into question our claim to faith in Jesus Christ. We find a way to make sense of practically everything in order to live in the present moment, but we neglect to do the one thing necessary: to ask whether the present is true. If we do not wish to die in our sin, would it not be prudent to look again at the way things are and how they have come to be this way?

• • • •

People who think about race and racism need tools to help them take hold of these complex phenomena. For European Americans especially, the movement from unreflective awareness to critical discernment does not take place easily or naturally. Indeed it does not take place at all unless there is some catalyst to get it started and some mechanism to help it along. As noted in chapter one, conversation on these matters with partners from differing people groups is one means to facilitate this, inasmuch as the dialogue draws attention to the fears, assumptions and perceptions that are at work among participants. The encounter with others invites reflection on what we feel and believe and how we interpret what we see and hear. It also stimulates reflection on what we have learned, endured, condoned and disregarded, and how our perspectives and frames of reference have been formed and established for better and for worse. But most important, dialogue with others surfaces *how* and *what we think* about matters of race and racism; it exposes the contours and content of racial- and racist-oriented thinking and the ways these come to expression in the formation of personal identity and demeanor on the one hand and the sociocultural environments and systems that cultivate and sustain them on the other. The fact is that attending to and interacting with the perspectives of others are necessary for the formation of critical discernment of race and racism.

But there is little or no hope for engaging, resisting and deconstructing race and racism from any frame of reference without analyses that explore the rationales, legitimations and expressions of race and racism in our context. So we have to think about thinking about racism. We need to have and use thinking tools in order to identify, describe, interpret and assess the phenomena of race and racism. As Christians, it is particularly important that we begin the development of our critical discernment with regard for Paul's contention that thinking differently can effect transformation, but aware that the discipline of humility and the exercise of "sober judgment" are required (Rom 12:2-3).

It will serve us to give some consideration to what other disciplined thinkers have thought about race and racism. Our task in this chapter will be to explore several theories of race and racism, each of which represents a different approach to comprehending these phenomena. This review will provide resources for later analysis and construction for the purpose of developing a theology of racial reconciliation.

A theory is a cognitive tool used to organize, correlate and explain the data that constitute a sphere of reality or a body of knowledge related to reality. Theories work with assumptions, perceptions, observations, principles and rules, all of which are intended to assist in the analysis and explanation of a phenomenon; they are constructions that facilitate comprehension and judgment and suggest courses of action. On the other hand, a theory may be limited to assumptions and perceptions when there is a lack of knowledge or disregard for evidence. In this case the theory amounts to a conjecture that may be unreflective and unsubstantiated but nonetheless is used to organize and explain phenomena.

A theory can be said to be "critical" when it forms and expresses discriminating judgments in its analysis and evaluation regarding the significance, value and truth of the phenomena under disciplined investigation. So our interest in this chapter is with critical theories as "tools" and the theorists as "voices" to assist us in the engagement with race and racism. As Kenan Malik says, "racial theories are an expression of the way that a particular society views humanity, and in particular views the relationship between humanity, nature and society."[1] I am contending that race and racism are linguistic and social constructions, so we will inquire into the ways these theorists' accounts of race and racism attend to the ideological, behavioral and sociocultural dimensions we have begun to uncover. We will observe that racism cannot be reduced to a singular problem or admit of an unqualified solution, any more than a solitary theory can capture the complexity of its expressions. "The problems that fall under the category of race, the variety of racisms, are wide-ranging, dynamic, multiple, and numerous. So any claim to having a single solution to '*the* race problem' or '*the* problem of racism,' just like any claim that we have come to '*the* end of racism' . . . is necessarily misleading."[2]

In this review of race theories, we will find it useful to keep in mind what Michael Eric Dyson calls the context, subtext and pretext of race: "Race as context helps us to understand the *facts* of race and racism in our society. Race as subtext helps us to understand the *forms* of race and racism in our culture. And race as pretext helps us to understand the *function* of race and racism in America."[3] We seek

---

[1]Kenan Malik, *The Meaning of Race: Race, History and Culture in Western Society* (New York: New York University Press, 1996), p. 5. A growing body of literature known as "critical race theory," written mostly by legal scholars from people groups other than European American, explores and contests the ways the American legal system has contributed to racial domination and social stratification. From a variety of perspectives for understanding and strategies for change, this group of legal scholars interprets and critiques the correlation between democratic legal ideals and the development of a free society under the rubric of race- and racist-oriented legal-political power and public policy. In its engagement with the legal culture in particular and American society in general, this movement is noted for its disillusionment with conventional civil rights thinking and strategies for racial integration. As such, it represents not only a significant critique of American jurisprudence but also a contribution to our constellation of theoretical constructs of race and racism. (We shall consider two such critical race theorists in the present chapter: Mills and Haney López.) For collections of articles in this emerging field, see Steven Gregory and Roger Sanjek, eds., *Race* (New Brunswick. N.J.: Rutgers University Press, 1994); Kimberlé Crenshaw et al., eds., *Critical Race Theory: The Key Writings That Formed the Movement* (New York: New Press, 1995); and Richard Delgado, ed., *Critical Race Theory: The Cutting Edge* (Philadelphia: Temple University Press, 1995).

[2]David Theo Goldberg, *Racial Subjects: Writing on Race in America* (New York: Routledge, 1997), p. 12. The tendency in thinking about race and racism is to focus on one expression of the problem—beliefs, behaviors, sociocultural systems and institutions, etc.—to the exclusion of others, and contend that a solution oriented by that expression will bring an end to racism. In conversation, what frequently happens is that differing understandings of the "problem" and its "solution" compete with each other, usually out of the concern to "manage" the problem and apply its solution to limited spheres. Responses to racism must follow from analyses and judgments of its multifaceted expressivity, and they must engage, resist, contest and alter the conditions and processes that make this expressivity possible.

[3]Michael Eric Dyson, *Race Rules: Navigating the Color Line* (New York: Vintage, 1997), p. 33. Dyson develops this theoretical construct to analyze and interpret the differing responses to the verdict in the O. J. Simpson criminal trial. After exposing misconstrual and ignorance regarding

not only to explore the ways these theorists construe—linguistically and socially—the facts, forms and functions of race and racism, but also the extent to which racism can be seen in their theories to be the objectivity of consciousness, common sense, conduct and context.

Rational Dimensions of Race and Racism

The first area of theory we shall consider has to do with the logic or rationality of race and racism, and in particular the question of the relationship between what is believed or thought about the phenomenon of race on the one hand and the implications that have tended to follow from this on the other. This pathway into theoretical constructions leads us into what I previously referred to as the ideological approach (a set of beliefs regarding the phenomenon of human variability and its significance).

Extrinsic and intrinsic racism. Kwame Anthony Appiah suggests that there is a certain kind of structure and movement of thought—a logic—at work in racism, one that works with and from a particular presupposition that warrants two distinct but related forms of racism.[4] He indicates that because racism can be construed as having a rationality of its own, it should be possible to contend against racism on rational grounds; the strategy for engaging expressions of racism could utilize reason to expose the flaws in racist thinking, since one aspect of the dilemma is what and how one thinks. In this construct, the fundamental presupposition that underlies racism is what Appiah calls "racialism," or the notion that "there are heritable characteristics, possessed by members of our species, that allow us to divide them into a small set of races, in such a way that all members of these races share certain traits and tendencies with each other that they do not share with members of any other race."[5] This presupposition—or *assumption*—

---

our racial history, the variety of ways arguments are used to obscure the forms of racism, and the ways racial ideas and interests are legitimated, he acknowledges that this theoretical construct cannot unearth what lies in the human heart: "We don't know what intentions or motivations people have apart from the behavior we can observe" (p. 44). Interpreting behavior gives insight, but not with certainty, into personal and social beliefs, attitudes, values and so on. This suggests all the more reason to explore the ideological—subjective and intersubjective—dimensions of race and racism, inasmuch as these intersect with the behavior and sociocultural dimensions.

[4]On the paragraphs that follow, see Kwame Anthony Appiah, "Racisms," in *Anatomy of Racism*, ed. David Theo Goldberg (Minneapolis: University of Minnesota Press, 1990), pp. 3-17.

[5]Ibid., pp. 4-5. The word *heritable* here means that these characteristics are capable of being transmitted genetically from one generation to the next. Elsewhere Appiah has described "racialism" with greater precision, indicating that it is the belief that members of a certain group or race share "certain fundamental, heritable, physical, moral, intellectual, and cultural characteristics with one another that they did not share with members of any other race" ("Race, Culture, Identity: Misunderstood Connections," in *Color Conscious: The Political Morality of*

functions as a kind of first principle by acknowledging not only *that* there are differences among races but that the phenomena thus differentiated are *constitutive* of each particular race.

The first of the two forms of racism that flow from this presupposition is "extrinsic racism," by which Appiah means the notion that each "race" has its own heritable essence whose expressions and qualities have moral significance. These expressions and qualities are distributed differently across the races, and members of a given race can be distinguished on the basis of the extent to which they have or do not have, express or do not express, certain moral attributes. "Racism" in this form has to do with the practice of treating people of another race differently because the characteristics and qualities exhibited by people of that race are judged to be morally deficient; different moral sensibilities and expressions warrant differential treatment. The logic here is that (1) the differences between races are genetically based, (2) each race has different moral aptitudes and expressions, and (3) therefore morally differential treatment of persons of another race is legitimated. In short, *the expressions of racial essence is a moral category.* An extrinsic racist might say, "I treat you differently because you act in ways that I consider to be less honest [or trustworthy, or decisive, or disciplined], and the explanation for your acting this way is that you are a member of a different race. So my treating you differently is appropriate, inasmuch as we are of different races."

The second form is "intrinsic racism," which builds from the belief that each race has a different moral status irrespective of the characteristics and qualities that express its racial essence. In this form the notion of "race" itself bears moral significance, apart from the ways a particular racial group expresses itself behaviorally or morally. It is the *fact* of differences that substantiates the practice of valuing and preferring members of one's own racial group over members of another. To put it another way, there is an inherent—genetic—moral interest in valuing and preferring members of one's own "kind," those with whom one shares certain characteristics and qualities, and this *fact* legitimates the differential treatment of persons from a different race. The logic here is that (1) the differences between races are genetically based, (2) these differences themselves have significance inasmuch as they accrue to each race on a moral basis, and (3) therefore differential treatment of persons of another race is morally legitimated. In short, *racial essence is itself a moral category.* An intrinsic racist might say, "I prefer and treat you differently

---

Race, ed. K. Anthony Appiah and Amy Gutmann [Princeton, N.J.: Princeton University Press, 1996], p. 54).

because you are a member of my race, and I treat you this way because our race is inherently morally superior. So my treating you differently is appropriate, inasmuch as we are of the same race."

Both forms of racism, according to Appiah, presuppose that racial differences across a range of behavioral and sociocultural expressions are genetically heritable. The warrant for differential treatment in both cases has to do with moral significance attributed to differences thought to be genetically based. In the case of extrinsic racism, the moral judgment is directed to the *differential expressions* of racial essence, and in the case of intrinsic racism, to the *fact* of different racial essences, regardless of different expressions.

Appiah suggests that what is needed to dissuade extrinsic racists of their belief is a presentation of evidence that shows there is no connection between genetics and moral expressiveness. Rational arguments, supported by evidence, ought to persuade rational people that their belief and conduct are in error. The fact that extrinsic racists do not abandon their beliefs and alter their conduct in the face of reason and evidence indicates that they are afflicted with what Appiah calls "cognitive incapacity" and "ideological resistance" that characterize a "systematically distorted rationality."[6] It is not so much that they are unwilling to think critically and differently as that they are unable to do so for reasons having to do with the vested interests, advantages and privileges they enjoy by virtue of being members of a dominant racial group.

Intrinsic racists, like extrinsic racists, are just as incapacitated, resistant and afflicted with distorted rationality, except that in their case scientific evidence and reason do not address the belief that race itself is inherently morally relevant; there is no "evidence" sufficient to warrant a change in either belief or demeanor, because the flaw is not in science but in the moral judgment by which one makes distinctions between races and prefers one's own because it is one's own. As Michael Polanyi has observed, "Moral judgments are appraisals and as such akin to intellectual valuations."[7] Both extrinsic and intrinsic racism are manifestations of a race thinking that appeals to the notion of racial essence, assigning moral significance either to different characteristic expressions of racial essence or to

---

[6]Ibid., pp. 6-8.

[7]Michael Polanyi, *Personal Knowledge: Towards a Post-critical Philosophy* (New York: Harper & Row, 1964), p. 214. In this study Polanyi seeks to demonstrate the conditions entailed in knowing and believing, especially how he may "achieve a frame of mind in which I may hold firmly to what I believe to be true, even though I know that it might conceivably be false" (ibid.). He argues that belief is the source of knowledge, and that both entail trust in and commitment to what is held (pp. 266-68).

the different racial essences themselves.[8]

Ascribing differences. Extending this reflection on the rationality of race and racism a step further, David Theo Goldberg suggests that racism can be understood as a "field of discourse" that encompasses the range of racist expressions in beliefs, actions and institutions, as well as texts that seek to explain the development and rationality of racism.[9] Goldberg's approach is suggested by the observation that "the social abuse we have come this century to call 'racism' mirrors in some respects the linguistic and conceptual abuse perpetrated under the banner of race."[10] Beliefs and descriptions are central in this approach, and in his view, racists can be identified on the basis of their beliefs: "Racists are those who explicitly or implicitly *ascribe racial characteristics* of others that they take to differ from their own and those they take to be like them. These characteristics may be biological or social. The ascriptions do not merely *propose racial differences;* they *assign racial preferences*, and they express desired, intended, or actual inclusions or exclusions, entitlements or restrictions."[11] The actions that follow from these ascriptions are racist to the extent that they involve discrimination against persons *because* they are consid-

---

[8]In *Race Matters* (New York: Vintage, 1994), Cornel West has similarly addressed the problems in "racial reasoning" that appeals to the notion of "racial authenticity," noting that "racial reasoning discourages moral reasoning. Every claim to racial authenticity presupposes elaborate conceptions of political and ethical relations of interests, individuals, and communities. Racial reasoning conceals these presuppositions behind a deceptive cloak of racial consensus—yet racial reasoning is seductive because it invokes an undeniable history of racial abuse and racial struggle" (pp. 39-40). For other discussions of the correlations between race thinking and racial essences, see especially Gordon Allport, *The Nature of Prejudice* (Reading, Mass.: Addison-Wesley, 1954), pp. 110-14, 175, 196; Victor Anderson, *Beyond Ontological Blackness: An Essay on African American Religious and Cultural Criticism* (New York: Continuum, 1995), pp. 51-53, 78-79, 142-47; Franz Boas, *The Mind of Primitive Man*, rev. ed. (New York: Collier, 1963); Mark Nathan Cohen, *Culture of Intolerance: Chauvinism, Class and Racism in the United States* (New Haven, Conn.: Yale University Press, 1998), pp. 11-59, 127-32; George M. Fredrickson, *The Black Image in the White Mind: The Debate on Afro-American Character and Destiny, 1817-1914* (Hanover, N.H.: Wesleyan University Press, 1971), pp. 1-15, 71-75, 305-6; Stephen Jay Gould, *The Mismeasure of Man*, rev. ed. (New York: W. W. Norton, 1996), pp. 105-8, 181-90; Ivan Hannaford, *Race: The History of an Idea in the West* (Washington, D.C.: Woodrow Wilson Center Press, 1996), pp. 57-58; Robert E. Hood, *Begrimed and Black: Christian Traditions on Blacks and Blackness* (Minneapolis: Fortress, 1994); Malik, *Meaning of Race*, pp. 95-96, 109, 201; Ashley Montagu, *Man's Most Dangerous Myth: The Fallacy of Race*, 6th ed. (Walnut Creek, Calif.: AltaMira, 1997), pp. 76-77; William Ryan, *Blaming the Victim*, rev. ed. (New York: Vintage, 1976), pp. 3-8; Pat Shipman, *The Evolution of Racism: Human Differences and the Use and Abuse of Science* (New York: Simon & Schuster, 1994), pp. 107-21, 146-54, 225-33; and Naomi Zack, *Thinking About Race* (Belmont, Calif.: Wadsworth, 1998), pp. 2-7.

[9]See David Theo Goldberg, "The Social Formation of Racist Discourse," in *Anatomy of Racism*, ed. Goldberg, pp. 295-311.

[10]Ibid., p. 295.

[11]Ibid., p. 296, emphasis mine.

ered to be from a different racial group. Language expressing beliefs about and descriptions of others constitutes the discourse of racism, and to these beliefs and descriptions Goldberg adds the language of moral decisions in relation to others, regulations that structure and manage institutions of various kinds, and articulated norms for personal and social behavior.

The rationality or logic embedded in and expressed through this discourse is premised on the perception of human physical and sociocultural variability and takes its principal form in the tendency to classify and value what is perceived. Goldberg regards this tendency as the precursor to the formation of a racist temperament. The rationality involved here is not the *fact* of human variability but the *method* of identifying and classifying. He states that "classification is central to scientific methodology; and scientific method, in turn, was taken to furnish the ideal model of rationality."[12] Thus the ordering and assignment of people groups to various human-contrived categories was construed to be a rational, scientific enterprise, one that led inexorably to a race hierarchy. To the extent that this project of classifying and ordering was based on differing physical characteristics, it was possible to defend the hierarchical classification as both *rational* and *natural*.

The entire system of classification, however, presumed not merely difference but *racial* difference. Goldberg argues that racial differentiation is not racist in itself and that, indeed, "classification, order, and value are fundamental forms of rationality we have inherited."[13] What makes this rationality of classification racist is the progressive movement from racial differentiation that defines otherness to differential exclusion of the other, or from the ascription of racial differences to the assignment of racial preferences. When wedded to social, political and economic powers of enforcement, the fundamental claims that emerge from this rationality become the warrant for differential treatment. Thus belief in racial differences—biological and/or sociocultural—that admit of linguistic description and methodological classification is the rational foundation of racism as a field of discourse, and thereby the supposed moral foundation for the practice of differential exclusion. When the discourse of racism is internalized, it functions as the personal and social definitions of self and other ("I *am* different from you; you *are* different from me").

In different ways, Appiah and Goldberg both draw attention to racism as a set of beliefs regarding the phenomenon of human physical-sociocultural variability and the ways significance and value are imputed to this taxonomy of differences. They uncover the kinds of rationality at work in the formation of the

---

[12]Ibid., p. 302.
[13]Ibid., p. 303.

ideational content of racism, each with an eye toward what I have called the bioscientific strand of racism. The fact that the scientific community no longer holds to a hierarchy of races does not mitigate the fact that such a hierarchy remains ingrained in the common sense. People believe in and ascribe value to supposed racial differences, and the fact that these differences can be described in ways thought to warrant both belief and behavior indicates the need to assess critically the linguistic and sociocultural expressions of race and racism.

What Appiah and Goldberg do not address in their exploration of the logic of race and racist belief is the psychological dynamics of race thinking and racist expressivity, especially as these dynamics influence the human imagination and the ways people who are "different" are regarded. We now turn to a theory that addresses this dimension of racism.

Psychological Dimensions of Race and Racism

Underneath the personal and sociocultural expressions of racism lie the beliefs that have come to be associated with racism, and underneath the beliefs—and the assumptions, perceptions and reasons that support them—lies the fluid and malleable human psyche, the forms and operations of which correlate the affective, cognitive and behavioral expressions of human physical, personal and social existence.

Fantasy and symbol of race. In his critical analysis, Joel Kovel has developed what he calls a psychohistorical approach for exploring the emergence of racism in Western culture and the ways racism is not merely a part of but actually constitutive of the culture's fabric.[14] He understands culture as "a *system of*

---

[14]The discussion that follows is based on Joel Kovel's book *White Racism: A Psychohistory* (1970; reprint, New York: Columbia University Press, 1984). While Allport's *The Nature of Prejudice* remains a classic text in the psychology of racism, its principal focus is on the psychological and sociocultural formation of prejudice as a personality *dis*order directed toward any number of different types of groups (including, but not limited to, "racial" groups), and his analysis attends only infrequently to the historical development of racist behavior and racism as a worldview. Kovel, on the other hand, is not concerned with personalities that might be assessed psychologically as aberrant, deviant or atypical; such an approach regards racism and racist expressivity as grounded in psychological pathology. Quite to the contrary, Kovel seeks to lay bare the extent to which racism is indigenous to our culture, and thus his interest—psychologically, historically and socioculturally—is in ordinary people and the emergence of their common, everyday racism (see Kovel, *White Racism*, pp. 45, 94). For useful discussions that concern psychology of racism, see Franz Boas, *Race, Language and Culture* (Chicago: University of Chicago Press, 1940), pp. 247-59; Boas, *Mind of Primitive Man*, pp. 124-79; Goldberg, *Racial Subjects*, pp. 17-25; Montagu, *Man's Most Dangerous Myth*, pp. 225-79; Paul M. Sniderman and Thomas Piazza, *The Scar of Race* (Cambridge, Mass.: Belknap/Harvard University Press, 1993), pp. 35-64; James Waller, *Face to Face: The Changing State of Racism Across America* (New York: Insight, 1998), pp. 25-67, 100-140. Histori-

shared meanings, an organized structure of symbols, made by [persons] in order to define their world and regulate their mutual relations."[15] Thus culture is both an ordered worldview and a means for coordinating human experience and action. It is with attention to the way our culture develops as a "system of shared meanings" that Kovel launches his analysis, challenging the conventional wisdom that "racism" follows from the notion of "race." Quite provocatively, he sets out to demonstrate not only that racism is endemic to our culture but that racism created the *category* of "race."

The historic phenomenon that draws first attention is the institution of slavery. Kovel contends that as early North American culture developed, two aspects emerge interactively and simultaneously: the attitude toward property and the formation of a national identity. Property is regarded as material in the external world, other than the self, that can be acquired and managed as an extension and expansion of the self. Not only did slave owners acquire and own slaves as their property, but they had to justify or rationalize this ownership of other human beings *as* property. This was done by reducing the slave first to only a *body,* and then to a *thing,* an economic tool and commodity useful for enlarging other forms of wealth and property. This process of dehumanization, or "thingification,"[16] produced in the slave owner's psyche an extraordinary ambivalence, a mixture of attraction and repulsion. On the one hand, to own and manage property, especially income-producing property, was appealing, meaningful and contributive to personal and social progress. On the other hand, owning and managing enslaved human beings as property was itself a constant and horrific reminder of dehumanization, and the presence of slaves regarded as subhuman was a source of disgust. Kovel argues that this attraction-repulsion toward slaves "became the basis in *culture* of the *idea* of the black [person], and it has consequently become the historical nucleus of our present-day racism."[17]

---

cally oriented discussions that address the psychological dimensions of racism can be found in Fredrickson, *Black Image,* pp. 1-41, 256-311; and Winthrop D. Jordan, *The White Man's Burden: Historical Origins of Racism in the United States* (New York: Oxford University Press, 1974), pp. 3-25, 69-86. For a superb study of the historical and psychological formation of resistance and response among enslaved African Americans, see John W. Blassingame, *The Slave Community: Plantation Life in the Antebellum South,* rev. and enl. ed. (New York: Oxford University Press, 1979).

[15]Kovel, *White Racism,* p. 4.

[16]Ibid., pp. 20, 185. Kovel contends that "dehumanization is a twofold process, involving first, the formation of an idea of another living person as less than a person, as a living or even inanimate *thing;* and second, an *action* upon that person so as to sustain one's dehumanized conception of him. Obviously these two aspects—the idea and the action—are utterly necessary to each other" (p. 36).

[17]Ibid., p. 19. Kovel's discussion of the other aspect—formation of national identity—takes us through the following stages: (1) the formalization of the slave status as simultaneous with

In Kovel's view, the institutionalization and enculturation of a practice require that it be affective and meaningful for people; a behavior or way of doing something becomes validated, stabilized and normalized when it is shared and affirmed by a significant number of people. Thus from the enculturation of slavery and the affective ambivalence of the slaver toward the enslaved come three types of racism which Kovel labels *dominative, aversive* and *metaracism.* The first two types have been present throughout America's history, and all three are rooted not in scientific fact or empirical data but in fantasy. Herein lies the psychology of racism: racist belief rests not on objective and rational "truth" but rather on subjective and arational needs and desires.[18] These three types of racism can be associated to one degree or another with discrete phases in our national history: dominative racism is associated primarily with the physical and sexual oppression of Southern slavery, aversive racism with the separate coexistence and restrictive intergroup relations characteristic of the Northern states and the period of legal segregation, and metaracism with the evolution of a highly impersonal, complex and technological sociopolitical economy. Herein lies the history of racism: racist practice has undergone a series of transmutations through historic periods, but no mutation has disappeared from the stage of history.

To get a clearer picture of what Kovel is contending with the psychohistory of these three types, we need to note briefly his view of the relevance of "symbolization." Symbols are means for expressing and conveying meaning; they capture, correlate and communicate the rudiments of the human self and its experience in a world. From a psychological perspective, Kovel suggests that symbols are created in order to correlate the content of the ego's repressed wishes and needs with the corresponding activity of repressing in the external world (e.g., my need to enlarge my self and the ways my actions inhibit enlargement). Consequently symbols take two forms, abstract and concrete, or *primary* and *secondary.* A primary symbol refers to an abstract idea, feeling,

---

evolving notions of freedom and bondage, (2) the formation of the nation in the Revolutionary War, spurred by the ideas of the Enlightenment, (3) the North-South struggle and American expansionism, (4) the reunification of European Americans North and South, the national development of industrialism, and the segregation of African Americans, and (5) the consolidation and expansion of capitalist America as a nation-state. Throughout each of these stages, the aspect of property fuels and refines the development of cultural relations and institutions (see pp. 21-26).

[18]Kovel defines fantasy as "a *form of knowing based upon wish and desire*—i.e., upon the internal mental state of a person" (p. 47). I qualify his definition with the word *needs* because I interpret his discussion of fantasy to reflect not only something that is desired or wanted but also something that is required or necessary. I think this will become clear as we progress in Kovel.

value or action that does not refer to an actual object (freedom, anger, precious, playing); a secondary symbol materializes when a primary symbol is associated with an external object, in which case the secondary symbol takes on a new form. For example, "property" is a primary symbol for my need to enlarge my self. "This particular piece of property" is a secondary symbol in that it is a tangible, meaning-bearing expression of my need. In this way objects in the external world take on symbolic value.

Now the acquisition of this property does not enlarge my self actually, but it does so symbolically, and to this extent the acquisition of this property is the "symbolization" of my need. To the extent that the practice of acquiring property is socially affective and meaningful, over time this practice becomes validated, stabilized and normalized—institutionalized and enculturated—as a part of human consciousness and the sociocultural environment. In short, for Kovel, culture is created to maintain the world in such a way that it conforms to and supports the inner needs and desires—and fantasies—of human beings.[19]

The predominant fantasy that underlies the dominative type of racism has to do with the symbol of blackness. Kovel and others have observed that even before their encounter with Africans, *black* symbolized for Europeans all that was diabolic, depraved, dirty, deathly and disgraceful.[20] What was extraordinary in the wake of the encounter was the birth of the "black" African as a secondary symbol for the primary symbol of "blackness as evil"; with its application to "black" Africans, the primary symbol is fixated as a secondary symbol. But it was not only the color of the Africans' skin that caught the attention of the Europeans, it was also their manner of dress, their way of life and their religion, all of which were "different" from those of the Europeans. "Blackness seemed to confirm a sense of radical difference between peoples, a difference that, combined with the

---

[19]The thrust of Kovel's argument here regarding symbolization is expressed in his observation that "culture itself is established to maintain the world in a shape that conforms to the symbolic needs of the ego's activity" (p. 99). He also argues for an aggregate of personal egos as a "Cultural Ego" with a "Cultural Unconscious," understood as "the summation, on a mass level, of the unconscious mental processes of the people in a social group" (p. 104).

[20]See ibid., pp. 62-63, where Kovel draws on the previous scholarship of Jordan, *White Man's Burden*, pp. 3-10. Frank M. Snowden Jr. has examined the symbolizations of blackness in ancient Greco-Roman culture and the early centuries of Christianity, and though he has isolated symbolizations that associate the color black with sin and evil and the color white with goodness and holiness, he judges there is little evidence to support the association of these symbols with the color of skin pigmentation and the nature of intergroup relations in a way that might suggest an ancient construal of "race" and an ancient form of "racism." See his *Blacks in Antiquity: Ethiopians in the Greco-Roman Experience* (Cambridge, Mass.: Belknap/Harvard University Press, 1970), especially pp. 196-215, and *Before Color Prejudice: The Ancient View of Blacks* (Cambridge, Mass.: Harvard University Press, 1983), esp. pp. 58-108.

African's evident heathenism, gave the Europeans a sense of awe. The fantasy of blackness immediately became elaborated: these people were black; they were naked; they were unchristian: ergo, there were the damned."[21] Given the sense of fear, guilt and vulnerability in this fantasy of evil, symbolized primarily in "black" and secondarily in the darker-skinned African—to say nothing of the fantasies related to sexuality, both that of the repressed European and that of the supposed-to-be uninhibited African—it is not a long step to the subjugation and enslavement of "black" Africans as a desire- and need-repressing activity.

The dominative racist is one who acts out these fantasies and beliefs, tinged with the polarity of attraction and repulsion. In Kovel's view, there is a structure to the personality of dominative racists that contributes to the transformation of fantasy into action, requiring that they seek out objects to which they can direct their intolerance and over which they can exercise their power. The dominative racist is inextricably tied to these objects for reasons that have to do with the fantasy needs and desires; the racist needs the "black" man and the "black" woman to conquer the racist's own struggle with evil, fascination with sex and inability to assuage guilt. Thus from this psychological perspective, American slavery emerges paradigmatically as the institutionalization of the fantasized need for power, control and dominance over evil and sexuality.

The predominant fantasy that underlies the aversive type of racism has to do with dirt, and in particular moral symbolizations associated with the state of being dirty or filthy. Here "dirt" is a moral primary symbol, and here again there is a tensive polarity of attraction and repulsion. People play in dirt, do things with it and make things out of it; they try to stay away from it, but get it on themselves, and then wash it off.[22] But in the fantasy, dirt symbolizes personal

---

[21]Kovel, *White Racism*, pp. 62-63. It should be apparent that this fantasy of "blackness" entails also a fantasy of "whiteness"; they presuppose and require one another. To the extent that the primary symbol of blackness takes on particularity as a secondary symbol in its application to Africans and other dark-skinned people, so the primary symbol of whiteness becomes a secondary symbol when applied to light-skinned Europeans and European Americans. Kovel correctly observes: "The West is a white civilization; no other civilization has made this claim. White emblemizes purity, but purity implies a purification, a removing of impurities. This is indeed part of the meaning of white; for, though scientifically the sum of all colors, to the symbolizing mind it becomes the absence of color, that which remains when color has been removed. And it is upon this symbol of whiteness that the psychohistory of our racism rests" (p. 107). I will address the construction of whiteness more directly in chapter four.

[22]This last sentence came to my mind after I walked through a construction site on my way to get a cup of coffee. *Immediately* after I passed the threshold of the dirt path through the site and came onto a concrete sidewalk, I said to myself, "I must remember to wash my new shoes before I return so I don't bring dirt into my host's condo." My next thought was a recollection of Psalm 51, especially verse 2: "Wash me thoroughly from my iniquity, and cleanse me from

moral uncleanness, unacceptability and unworthiness, a moral defilement that cannot be cleansed or removed by the physical act of washing. When the primary symbol was applied to darker-skinned Africans, they were regarded—in fantasy and in effect—as dirty and smelly, and thus to be avoided lest one become unclean. To focus this point, Kovel remarks: "The nuclear experience of the aversive racist is a sense of disgust about the body of the black person based upon a very primitive fantasy: that it contains an essence—dirt—that smells and may rub off onto the body of the racist. Hence the need for distance and the prohibition against touching."[23]

The aversive racist is the one who believes in the moral superiority—the purity and cleanness—of his or her race and seeks to preserve this superiority by maintaining physical and social distance from the "darker" races thought to be morally inferior. One major characteristic of aversive racists that distinguishes them from dominative racists, according to Kovel, is that the former do not conspicuously act out their racist fantasies and beliefs; they ignore, avoid contact with, appear disinterested in and act condescendingly toward the despised other, all the while in the grip of a psychic struggle between their symbolic projection and their yearning to disavow this projection. More often than not this struggle immobilizes aversive racists, rendering them quiescent and deferential as the only way to relieve the inner struggle. Still, having given up the prospect of physically dominating the other, aversive racists need "dirty" persons to alleviate and clarify their own sense of moral ambiguity; they need a baseline in relation to which they can measure their moral righteousness and purity, much like the Pharisee in Jesus' parable in Luke 18:9-14. Thus from this psychological perspective, the period of legal segregation—American apartheid—emerges paradigmatically as the enculturation of the fantasized need for moral purity.

When Kovel turns to the third type, metaracism, he speaks of an expres-

---

my sin." Knowing that the plea "wash me, and I shall be whiter than snow" (v. 7) was in this psalm, I resolved to read the entire psalm upon my return. This I did, with clean *black* shoes, but hardly a clean heart, mindful of both a racist reading of the psalm and the truth of Kovel's contentions at this point.

[23]Ibid., p. 84. Kovel goes on to discuss the symbolization of human defecation, contending that "the root symbol between the idea of dirt and the blackness of certain people is that highly colored, strongly odored, dispensable and despised substance which the human body produces so regularly" (p. 87). While I see the sense—and the offensiveness—of this contention, I am unpersuaded that this is a "root" symbol. Nevertheless, since he engages this symbolization in his discussion—it is, after all, a theoretical construction—it is appropriate to note it here, even though the weight of his discussion can be carried by the symbol of "dirt" alone. Cornel West's discussion in his Internet article ("Toward a Socialist Theory of Racism" <http://eserver.org/race/toward-a-theory-of-racism.html>) clearly shows the influence of Kovel's opinion on this matter.

sion of racism that both embraces and transcends the previous two types. Psychologically and historically, metaracism incorporates the fantasies, symbols and expressions of dominative and aversive racism—power over and avoidance of—into a sociocultural system that no longer requires that each individual act dominatively or aversively toward a despised people. "Racist psychology is a prerequisite of racist institutions, and racist institutions engender a racist psychology."[24] The fantasies and symbolizations of racism give birth to sociocultural structures whose purpose is to embody, authenticate and mediate the psychodynamics of the human group that collectively owns and manages them. Those who participate in and derive benefit from these structures—institutions and their culture—find a world that is experienced as valid, stable and normal. But this world is created and established in such a way that those who are excluded, avoided or tolerated experience it as threatening, dehumanizing and self-alienating. Metaracism is a continuation of racial degradation, but in a virtually transcendent form: absent the conduct of overt physical-sexual domination and covert aversion, the metaracist need only capitulate to the sociocultural, economic and technological systems created by the expressions and acceptance of the earlier types of racism.

Racial prejudice and racist conduct are no longer needed to be racist. Metaracism avoids both blatant and veiled racist conduct precisely in order to advance the larger cultural and institutional interests. Because racial fantasies and symbolizations have become institutionalized, one need only participate in and condone the status quo of a historically dominative and aversive culture; one need only serve as a means toward the ends ordained by a fantastically racist culture. As Kovel declares, "Metaracism—the illusion of non-racism coexisting with the continuation of racism's work—exists wherever, in this subtle balance of human and anti-human forces, destructivity predominates no matter what the gains in 'racial equality.'"[25]

Thus metaracism, absent a direct human agent, is the most impersonal and dispassionate form of racism expressly because it constitutes the warp and woof of a sociocultural world. It is the type of racism that characterizes our present situation, years after slavery when dominative (and to a lesser extent aversive) racism prevailed, and legal segregation when aversive (and to a lesser extent dominative) racism prevailed, and the advent of civil rights when both forms went underground, only to return in transmuted forms of degradation and violence regarded by a metaracist society as aberrations.

---

[24]Kovel, *White Racism*, p. 44.
[25]Ibid., p. 218.

By drawing attention to the fantasies of race and racism, Kovel's theoretical construction clearly opens a horizon not only on the psychology involved but also on the intersections of belief, behavior and sociocultural expression. Furthermore, his psychohistorical approach makes it possible to recast the notion of racial prejudice: rather than seeing prejudice as the presupposition of racism, or the same as racism, Kovel argues that it is the *product* or *expression* of a pre-existent racism rooted in psychogenic fantasies that are symbolized in dark-skinned peoples and validated in sociocultural practices and institutions. Thus since racism gives rise to race prejudice, dealing only with prejudice—in either its bigoted or veiled form—will not be a viable strategy for combating racism. One must look not only to behavior but also to the beliefs, emotions, needs and desires that come to expression in behavior on the one hand and to the sociocultural realities that embody and express them on the other. Having considered some theories regarding the former to this point, we turn in the next section to some theoretical perspectives on the latter.

Sociopolitical Dimensions of Race and Racism

When any group of people live together, there soon emerge not only certain patterns of relationships and practices that characterize and distinguish their common life but also mechanisms for ordering and regulating their common life. The former can be said to be their "society" and the latter their "politics." In broad strokes, we can understand culture as the totality of the patterns of belief, behavior and institutions engendered by a society, but with the question of how a society's life is organized and administered—especially with regard to principle, policy and precept—we enter the political realm. The theories we shall examine in this section are generally *sociocultural* in that their frame of reference is the contextual environment of the common life of a people. But in particular these theories draw attention to the political dimensions of this common life, and so I am labeling these socio*political* theories. They will take us further in the exploration of the ways human subjectivity gives rise to, and in turn becomes expressed in and through, sociocultural institutions, thus highlighting the envirorelational strand of race and racism.

The racial contract. With exceptional analytical skill, Charles W. Mills has crafted a theory of race and racism that draws on political theory as well as the history of the United States.[26] His central contention is that "racism . . . is *itself* a political system, a particular power structure of formal or informal rule, socio-economic privilege, and norms for the differential distribution of material

---

[26]For what follows, see Charles W. Mills, *The Racial Contract* (Ithaca, N.Y.: Cornell University Press, 1997), esp. pp. 1-40.

wealth and opportunities, benefits and burdens, rights and duties."[27] As the title of his book *The Racial Contract* suggests, his construction works principally with the notion of a "social contract," a concept in eighteenth-century European social and political theory that locates the foundation of society in the voluntary decision of a populace to establish a civil and governmental order. But for Mills the notion of a social contract is not merely a theory—or even a metaphor—for the exploration of race and racism. Rather, as a tradition in sociopolitical thought, the social contract is an explanation of the social and political origins of a particular self-selecting aggregate of people, the Anglo-Saxons. To the extent that this people identifies and distinguishes itself from non-Anglo-Saxon people in the formation of their social and political order, their social contract presupposes a *racial contract*. So Mills argues throughout the book that the Racial Contract as a social and political theory is not a variation on the social contract theory but rather prior to, and foundational for, the social contract. As such, it constitutes a kind of *meta*theory within which the social contract operates. It exposes the ideology of racism—white racial domination—and the ways this ideology shaped and determined the social and political order of the United States.

In developing his construct, Mills advances three arguments, the first of which is that the Racial Contract is inherently political, moral and epistemological. As *political*, it accounts for the origins of society and civil government and the ways individuals are constituted as members of society and citizens of the state. In this case, the Racial Contract was among the European descendants to the exclusion of non-Europeans. Mills regards the Racial Contract as "a set of formal and informal agreements" whereby Europeans who self-identified as "white . . . full persons" consented to categorize all other people groups as "nonwhite . . . subpersons" with "a different and inferior moral status" and thus having "a subordinate civil standing in the white or white-ruled" social-political order.[28] With such agreements there emerges a sociopolitical order premised on a distinctively *racial* state that separates humanity into "white" and "nonwhite" and excludes from this order those who fail to meet the criteria of whiteness. Mills goes on to state that "the 'consent' expected of the white citizens is in part . . . a consent, whether explicit or tacit, to the racial order, to white supremacy, what could be called Whiteness."[29] In effect, according to Mills, this explicit or

---

[27]Ibid., p. 3. In Mills's work here, "racism" is construed as "global white supremacy" and the means whereby "race" is constructed. Thus "race is sociopolitical rather than biological, but it is nonetheless real" (p. 125).

[28]Ibid., p. 12. Mills's assertion at this point is particularly cumbersome, but with the quoted phrases I think the salient features of his statement are retained.

[29]Ibid., p. 14.

tacit consent to a contract that socially and politically includes some and excludes others on the basis of culture- and color-criteria is itself the creation of "race."[30]

As *moral*, the Racial Contract accounts for the creation of a peculiar set of rules that rests on a preexisting moral foundation, the philosophical and theological notion of "natural law." Thus the freedom and equality of all persons are established by either the (philosophical) "state of nature" or the (theological) "purpose of the Creator." However, the Racial Contract is an agreement to restrict "natural" freedom and equality to *white men*. An extraordinary philosophical-theological contradiction is present here: the self-evident "truth"—that "all *men* are created *equal*, and endowed by their Creator with certain inalienable rights, and among these are life, *liberty*, and the pursuit of happiness"—is neither self-evident nor universal in scope. It is, rather, inclusive of all "white" *men* and exclusive of all "nonwhite" *men* and of women. As Mills observes, "Nonwhites are appropriately relegated to a lower rung on the moral ladder. . . . They are designated as born *un*free and *un*equal."[31]

As *epistemological*, the Racial Contract is the basis of the "norms and procedures for determining what counts as moral and factual knowledge of the world."[32] By this Mills construes the Racial Contract in all its formality and informality as prescribing a way of thinking and knowing—of correctly seeing and interpreting the world—that validates one as a legitimate participant in the sociopolitical order. Because of the discontinuity between the principles and the facts, however, this epistemological consensus entails an agreement to misapprehend and misinterpret the world, both intellectually and morally. The contract is, surreptitiously, the promotion of an "*epistemology of ignorance*," the warrant for a "consensual hallucination" and the legitimation of a constellation of "cognitive dysfunctions," all of which are "psychologically and socially functional."[33]

The second of Mills's three arguments is that the Racial Contract is factual

---

[30]Ibid. He later notes, "'White' people do not preexist but are brought into existence as 'whites' by the Racial Contract—hence the peculiar transformation of the human population that accompanies this contract. The white race is *invented*, and one becomes 'white by law'" (p. 63).

[31]Ibid., p. 16. I have italicized the word *men* in this paragraph to draw attention to the fact that, contrary to the principles embedded in the sociopolitical theory and originative documents of our nation, the facts of our national history indicate that the word was neither generic nor socially neutral but rather reflective of the social and political construction of gender (i.e., the exclusion of women, who have been—and in no small measure, still are—regarded as less equal and free, irrespective of "race").

[32]Ibid., p. 17.

[33]Ibid., p. 18.

and historical, and therefore *real.* While there was no physical contract and no particular time and place where it was formally approved as such, the European social, political and ecclesiastical debates, decisions and laws that sanctioned the European encroachment into the "new world," as well as the establishment of legal processes and structures during and following the conquest, together constitute a series of actions that, over time, can be regarded as the "conceptual, juridical, and normative equivalent" of a contract and its ratification.[34] Through all these actions there is a bifurcation of the world on several fronts— European and non-European geography, civilized and savage culture, Christian and non-Christian religion—all of which merge into the dichotomy of "white" and "nonwhite," that is, the classification of superior and inferior *races.* Furthermore, Mills distinguishes three subcontracts within the Racial Contract: the "expropriation contract" that endorsed the acquisition of lands and resources for Europe, the "slavery contract" that legitimated the enslavement of the indigenous people of Africa and North America, and the "colonial contract" that authorized the rule of Europeans over other nations whose territory they came to inhabit.[35]

The last of Mills's three arguments is that the Racial Contract is an agreement to establish economic domination by the exploitation of the "nonwhite" world for the benefit of Europeans. This economic dimension of the contract is its driving force and its ultimate objective: "The whole point of establishing a moral hierarchy and juridically partitioning the polity according to race is to secure and legitimate the privilege of those individuals designated as white/persons and the exploitation of those individuals designated as nonwhite/subpersons. There are other benefits accruing from the Racial Contract . . . but the bottom line is material advantage."[36] Thus through all its stages and expressions, the "Racial Contract" can be seen as the European engagement with non-European peoples for the purpose of acquiring and enlarging lands, material resources and wealth (property!).

Mills contends that in spite of the abolition of slavery, decolonization and the emergence of so-called developing nations, the legacy of the Racial Contract has been bequeathed to the European descendants of its subscribers in the form of global economic hegemony, an economic "white supremacy." The economic objective of the contract has effectively been achieved. The stability of its structures and the normalization of its advantages presuppose the preservation of the ethos of the Racial Contract at local,

---

[34]Ibid., p. 21.
[35]Ibid., pp. 24-29, 72-76.
[36]Ibid., pp. 32-33.

national, regional and global levels: the ethos of *racism*.

Legal construction of race. Another sociopolitical theory that continues the trajectory developed by Mills can be found in the scholarship of Ian F. Haney López, whose work takes us more directly into the world of American jurisprudence and, in particular, the ways the law and formal court decisions have contributed to the formation of race and racism.[37] The court cases he examines have to do with petitioners seeking to become naturalized U.S. citizens, and the decisions reviewed are those handed down by both lower courts (state and federal) and the U.S. Supreme Court. The decisions in these cases all turned on whether the petitioner was judged to be "white" as laid down in statutes and interpreted by the court. More significant, however, these decisions included the explanations on the basis of which "whiteness" was legally delimited and thereby legally constructed.

As important background for his review of these cases, Haney López surveys the history of racial restriction in citizenship law, noting that at the time it was first ratified in 1789, the U.S. Constitution did not address the question of who was or was not a citizen. Continuing the tradition of English common law, persons born in the United States were citizens. However, our nation's history indicates that only descendants of Europeans were accorded the birthright of citizenship; the descendants of Africans, whether slave or free, living in the country at the time of the ratification of the Constitution, or subsequently born in the United States, were disfranchised as citizens, a practice formally legalized in the *Dred Scott v. Sanford* decision handed down in 1857 by Chief Justice Roger Taney. Birthright citizenship came to the descendants of Africans only with the adoption of the Civil Rights Act of 1866 and the Fourteenth Amendment in 1868. Still, this did not include citizenship for the indigenous peoples living within the territory of the United States; their citizenship was not granted until 1924, and only in 1940 was birthright citizenship granted to children born to indigenous peoples. Thus Haney López notes that "the basic law of citizenship, that a person born here is a citizen here, did not include all racial minorities until 1940."[38]

The concern to preserve citizenship only for European descendants is apparent in laws stipulating eligibility for *naturalized* citizenship. Haney López draws attention to the fact that by an act of Congress in 1790, qualifications for naturalized citizenship were limited to "any alien, being a *free white person* who shall have resided within the limits and under the jurisdiction of the United

---

[37]For the discussion that follows, see Ian F. Haney López, *White by Law: The Legal Construction of Race* (New York: New York University Press, 1996).

[38]Ibid., p. 41.

States for a term of two years."[39] Thus whiteness was legally established as a prerequisite for naturalized citizenship. Furthermore, as Haney López observes, "though there would be many subsequent changes in the requirements for federal naturalization, racial identity endured as a bedrock requirement for the next 162 years. In every naturalization act from 1790 until 1952 [when racial restrictions were removed], Congress included the 'white person' prerequisite."[40]

His research indicates that the history of the role played by racial prerequisites in naturalized citizenship can be divided into two periods: first, from 1790 when only "whites" were eligible to 1870 when the prerequisite was besieged in the wake of the Civil War and the increasing effort to vacate the *Dred Scott* decision; and second, from 1870 until 1952, when the prerequisite laws were abolished. Haney López is interested in this latter period, inasmuch as all fifty-two of the prerequisite cases were handed down in the this time frame, the first coming in 1878. More particularly he is interested in the twenty-seven cases handed down between 1878 and 1923 because it is during this period that "whiteness" achieved its legal definition.

Haney López's review of these cases suggests that the fundamental issue before the courts had to do not merely with whether a petitioner was eligible for citizenship but with how to determine the petitioner's racial identity, since this was a prerequisite for eligibility. Given the legal prerequisite of "white person," the courts had to adjudicate the litigant's petition by first interpreting what "white" meant (establishing a criteriology) and then ascertaining the extent to which the litigant gave evidence of meeting this prerequisite (classifying the phenomenon). Beyond the language of the statute, there was no codification of the legal meaning of "white," so—arguably—the logic of the decisions as well as the decisions themselves go a long way toward the legal definition of who satisfies the prerequisite. Thus the meaning of "white" is constructed through the legal sanction of court opinion.

Clearly the principal matter before the courts was the determination of the racial identity of the petitioner. In order to achieve this, however, the courts had to have some basis, some source or criterion, some rationale to authorize its legal—and in the case of the U.S. Supreme Court, its unimpeachable—decision on the matter. In Haney López's analysis, the courts found this authority in four areas: common knowledge, scientific evidence, congressional intent and legal precedent. Of particular interest to us here, and to Haney López, are the first two. He notes that both appear in the first case in

---

[39]Cited in ibid., p. 42. Emphasis mine.
[40]Ibid., p. 43.

1878, and that in fact both work together to authorize decisions to deny all but one of the twelve petitioners' requests for naturalization in the period 1878-1909. On the other hand, decisions in thirteen lower-court cases between 1909 and 1923 show a divergence of court opinion on the authority: seven courts based their determination on scientific evidence (with all petitions granted), and six courts based their determination on common knowledge (with all but one petition denied), with no single court decision based on both authorities.

In 1922 and 1923 the U.S. Supreme Court decided two cases, and in both the authority was common knowledge. Haney López interprets the decisions in these cases to signify that the Court "abandoned scientific explanations of race in favor of those rooted in common knowledge when science failed to reinforce popular beliefs about racial differences. The Court's eventual embrace of common knowledge confirms the falsity of natural notions of race, exposing race instead as a social product measurable only in terms of what people believe."[41] In effect the Court chose as its authority not science (there is no such thing as "race") but popular "white" opinion (everybody knows there are "races" and which one they belong to).

Thus Haney López argues that the legal construction of race commences with the statutory racial restriction on eligibility for birthright and naturalized citizenship, continues with juridical, statutory and constitutional modification based on racial classification, and reaches its zenith with the U.S. Supreme Court's appeal to the common sense of the meaning of race. Ultimately the courts' definition of who is not—and by implication, who is—"white" reflects the original sense of the nation's founders. The fact that "nonwhites" are now eligible for both birthright and naturalized citizenship does not mitigate the fact that these rights were first excluded on racial grounds and later granted on the same grounds. The law presupposed, privileged, codified and legitimated racial differences, with "whiteness" as the norm.

Racialized society in conflict. The final theory to be considered in this section is one that approaches the subject in terms of the way race shapes, and is shaped by, the structures of our state and civil society. The joint work of

---

[41]Ibid., pp. 79-80. In its decision in *United States* v. *Thind* the Court stated, "What we now hold is that the words 'free white persons' are words of common speech, to be interpreted in accordance with the understanding of the common man, synonymous with the word 'Caucasian' only as that word is popularly understood" (cited in ibid., p. 90). For discussions concerning the evolution of the social and legal definitions—the "common knowledge"—of "black" (i.e., the "one-drop" rule), see especially F. James Davis, *Who Is Black? One Nation's Definition* (University Park: Pennsylvania State University Press, 1991), and Lawrence Wright, "One Drop of Blood," *New Yorker,* July 24, 1994, pp. 46-55.

Michael Omi and Howard Winant addresses the primacy and dominance of race in American political affairs and social life. They are interested in the political sphere not so much as government and its management of civil affairs but more as a social and civil polity racially constructed and characterized by contestation. They set out to show that we do not merely have a politics of race, as one kind of situation politics alongside other kinds of situation politics in our civil society, but rather that all our politics—and therefore our sociopolitical order—is essentially and thoroughly *racialized.*[42]

To advance this contention, Omi and Winant undertake an exploration of the interconnectedness of racial identity, politics and social structures, arguing that "race" needs to be understood as "an autonomous field of social conflict, political organization, and cultural/ideological meaning."[43] In their construct, race is viewed neither as a biologically determined essence with an objective reality (external fact) nor as a mentally produced fabrication that is entirely subjective (internal image). Rather for them, race is "a concept which signifies and

---

[42]For what follows, see Michael Omi and Howard Winant, *Racial Formation in the United States from the 1960s to the 1990s* (1986; reprint, New York: Routledge, 1994). See also Howard Winant, "Racial Dualism at Century's End," in *The House That Race Built*, ed. Woheema Lubiano (New York: Vintage, 1998). For discussions that bear on the politics of race and what has come to be called "identity politics," see Appiah and Gutmann, eds., *Color Conscious*, pp. 76-80, 109-77; Stephen L. Carter, *Reflections of an Affirmative Action Baby* (New York: BasicBooks, 1991), pp. 197-211, and *Integrity* (New York: BasicBooks, 1996), pp. 210-30; Harlon L. Dalton, *Racial Healing: Confronting the Fear Between Blacks and Whites* (New York: Anchor, 1995), pp 27-49; Andrew Hacker, *Two Nations: Black and White, Separate, Hostile, Unequal,* rev. and exp. ed. (New York: Ballantine, 1992), pp. 241-45; Manning Marable, *Beyond Black and White: Transforming African-American Politics* (New York: Verso, 1995); Orlando Patterson, *The Ordeal of Integration: Progress and Resentment in America's "Racial" Crisis* (Washington, D.C.: Civitas/Counterpoint, 1997), pp. 15-81, 113-32; Richard J. Payne, *Getting Beyond Race: The Changing American Culture* (Boulder, Colo.: Westview, 1998), pp. 2-29; Sniderman and Piazza, *Scar of Race,* pp. 16-33, 88-109; Paul M. Sniderman and Edward G. Carmines, *Reaching Beyond Race* (Cambridge, Mass.: Harvard University Press, 1997), pp. 1-12, 100-154; and Thomas Sowell, *Race and Culture: A World View* (New York: BasicBooks, 1994), pp. 118-30. An important historical study of the politics of race in the formation of legal segregation in the South can be found in C. Vann Woodward, *The Strange Career of Jim Crow,* 3rd rev. ed. (New York: Oxford University Press, 1974). Jennifer L. Hochschild has analyzed the political strategies involving school desegregation in *The New American Dilemma: Liberal Democracy and School Desegregation* (New Haven, Conn.: Yale University Press, 1984). Two different approaches in assessing the current state of racialized politics can be found in Tom Wicker, *Tragic Failure: Racial Integration in America* (New York: William Morrow, 1996), and Jim Sleeper, *Liberal Racism* (New York: Viking, 1997). A defense of European American centrality and normativity in social-political affairs can be found in Jared Taylor, *Paved with Good Intentions: The Failure of Race Relations in Contemporary America* (New York: Carroll & Graf, 1992).

[43]Omi and Winant, *Racial Formation,* p. 48.

symbolizes social conflicts and interests by referring to different types of human bodies," the characteristic features of which are selected arbitrarily by a "social and historical process."[44] Thus race is a socially contrived depiction of human beings that structures and expresses a sociocultural world in inherently conflictive ways. A racialized society is not one that accommodates race as one of its many dimensions or features but one whose very foundation, infrastructure and edifice are infused with race as the signifier of difference and the arbiter of social, political and economic conflict.

For Omi and Winant, this means that the process of "racial formation" involves the invention, application and modification of racial categories through a series of historic and sociocultural events in which there is a continuing mutual determination between the depiction and valuation of human differences on the one hand and the design of social structures on the other. The specificity of this process at any given time is indicated for them by the term *project,* connoting the correlation between the meaning of these depictions and the design of social structures that together mediate human experience and its interpretation. A *racial* project is defined as "simultaneously an interpretation, representation, or explanation of racial dynamics, and an effort to reorganize and redistribute resources along particular racial lines."[45] Thus attention is given to the racial dimensions of social design and structure, as well as to the social dimensions of racial depictions and their meanings; the way we understand racial signification is correlative to social structures, and the way we develop social structures is expressive of racial signification. As Omi and Winant observe, "Racialized social structure shapes racial experience and conditions meaning" at the same time that "our ongoing interpretation of our experience in racial terms shapes our relations to the institutions and organizations through which we are imbedded in the social structure."[46] What we have here is a socially constructed, structurally embedded and

---

[44]Ibid., p. 55.

[45]Ibid., p. 56. In principle I concur with the Omi-Winant definition of a *racial project.* However, I am unable to agree completely with their articulation of this understanding when later they qualify the definition: "A racial project can be defined as *racist* if and only if it *creates or reproduces structures of domination based on essentialist categories of race*" (p. 71). Essentialism is one of several differing construals of "race" and the criteriology employed for differentiating and classifying human variability. If a racial project can be judged to be racist only to the extent that it is based on essentialism, this tends to validate essentialism and exonerate the "structures of domination" that are based on sociocultural criteriologies and taxonomies. In my judgment, racial *essence* is spurious, especially if defined as Omi and Winant define it: "real, true human essences, existing outside or impervious to social and historical context" (ibid.). Belief in racial essence (i.e., "essential*ism*") does not make it real or true.

[46]Ibid., pp. 59-60.

project-mediated understanding of race that is self-perpetuating; it is the *common sense.*[47]

Omi and Winant locate the origins of the process of racial formation and the modern understanding of race in the European conquest of the Americas. This "discovery" (conquest) of the "new world" (habitat), the "encounter" (subjugation) with the "natives" (indigens), and the "migration" (deployment) of Europeans to "claim" (expropriate), "develop" (arrogate) and "use" (exploit) the land's "abundant riches" (natural resources) for the "leaders" (ruling commercial and political aristocracy) of Europe together constitute the paradigmatic racial project. With this history, the "distinctions and categorizations fundamental to a racialized social structure, and a discourse of race, began to appear."[48]

Following a review of the racial-project history and the evolution of religious, scientific and sociocultural schemes for justifying such projects, Omi and Winant argue that "race" needs to be seen in this history as fundamentally politicized: "For most of its existence both as European colony and as an independent nation, the U.S. was a *racial dictatorship.*"[49] This dictatorship meant that the social, legal and cultural definition of American identity was "white," society was demarcated into racial partitions, and the host of indigenous and expropriated nations were stripped of their own national identities and homogeneously classified by labels defined by the "white" dictatorship.[50] Over time this dictatorship evolved into a "hegemony" maintained by "coercion and consent," whereby rule was established by the political powers and agreed to

---

[47]The authors' contention at this point is no less definitive: "Everybody learns some combination, some version, of the rules of racial classification, and of her [or his] own racial identity, often without obvious teaching or conscious inculcation. Thus are we inserted in a comprehensively racialized social structure. Race becomes 'common sense'—a way of comprehending, explaining, and acting in the world. A vast web of racial projects mediates between the discursive and representational means in which race is identified and signified on the one hand, and the institutional and organizational forms in which it is routinized and standardized on the other. These projects are the heart of the racial formation process" (p. 60). The concern here, as in our previous discussion of the logic or rationality of racism, is what I will call—and analyze more thoroughly in chapter four—the social and epistemological formation of false consciousness.

[48]Ibid., p. 61. Except for *discovery, conquest* and *natives,* the words in quotation marks and parentheses in the preceding sentence are my own. I write this sentence to illustrate the vagaries of both an "innocent" and a "critical" reading of history. For an insightful discussion of the phenomenon of "innocent" reading, see Justo González, *Mañana: Christian Theology from a Hispanic Perspective* (Nashville: Abingdon, 1990), pp. 75-87.

[49]Omi and Winant, *Racial Formation,* p. 65.

[50]"Just as the conquest created 'native' [or 'Indian'] where once there had been Pequot, Iroquois, or Tutelo, so too it created the 'black' [or 'Negro'] where once there had been Asante or Ovimbundu, Yoruba or Bakongo" (ibid., p. 66). See also Scott L. Malcomson, *One Drop of Blood: The American Misadventure of Race* (New York: Farrar Straus Giroux, 2000), pp. 100-14.

by the citizenry, or submitted to in the case of subjugated peoples.[51] Eventually the hegemony of racialized rule functioned by the incorporation of its opposition within itself; a place was made within the hegemonic sociopolitical order for those who previously had been coercively excluded, and thus their opposition could be more efficiently managed.

When they turn their attention to the state, Omi and Winant contend that the institutions and organizations of government became racialized through a series of confrontations between racial groups or movements and the civil and political institutions. The outcomes of such conflicts and confrontations have ranged from violent suppression to compromise to accommodation on the part of the established civil-political authorities. In any case, this series of racially suffused confrontations, and the adjustments made by the state in response, have determined the continuing formation of the racial state. Throughout most of its history, the racial policy of the United States has been a racial project in itself: the suppression and exclusion of non-Europeans and the establishment of structures of domination to preserve this situation. When this has been contested by the subject peoples—through rebellion or revolt, or defense against armed encroachment, or other forms of resistance such as nonviolent direct social action—the state had mechanisms and legal authority to respond and enforce its claim in one way or another. Thus through the formation of policies, rules, regulations and laws as well as the administrative agencies responsible for enforcing or modifying them, the state has effectively perpetuated itself in racialized forms. Whether, for example, it was legitimating discrimination (as it did up to the 1950s) or enforcing anti-discrimination laws (since the 1960s), the state was conducting its business of governing by attending to differentiation and inequality articulated in racial terms, thereby securing itself as a racial state.

The authors touch the heart of their construct of the racial state when they endeavor to analyze the racial politics of the present. History shows that the relations among differing people groups in the United States have been precarious and variable. Relations between the state and groups historically subordinated by the European American social, political and civil structures have also been variable. Omi and Winant describe the variable nature of race relations this way: "The racial order is equilibrated by the state—encoded in law, organized through policy-making, and enforced by a repressive apparatus. But the equilibrium thus achieved is unstable, for the great variety of conflicting interests, encapsulated in racial meanings and identities can be no more than pacified—at best—by the state."[52] Between the "equilibrium" side and the "insta-

---

[51]Omi and Winant, *Racial Formation*, pp. 66.
[52]Ibid., pp. 84-85.

bility" side there is a constant shifting, sometimes continuous and sometimes discontinuous; both the racial state and racial groups/movements undergo change, from one time to another, from one expression of activity to another, from one degree of engagement to another.

In this historic and current intersection of the racial groups/movements and the state, a pattern of initiative-and-response is discerned, and the codependence of the groups/movements and the state is manifest: "Racially based political movements as we know them are inconceivable without the racial state, which provides a focus for political demands and structures the racial order. The racial state, in its turn, has been historically constructed by racial movements; it consists of agencies and programs which are the institutionalized responses to racial movements of the past."[53] What Omi and Winant are suggesting is that in any given period of unstable equilibrium there is a marked absence of racial conflict, and the racial order operates unimpeded. At some point, however, suppressed or subordinated racial groups/movements emerge to resist and oppose the existing order and press for change. There then follows a period of crisis or disequilibrium. The state responds to this situation in one of two ways: either the demands are mitigated by being adopted in modified form, in which case they have been *absorbed,* or the state relegates the demands to a sphere where its fundamental interests and essential project are not at risk of change, in which case they have been *insulated.* In either case, a modicum of equilibrium—unstable as it may be—has been reestablished.

But more important, both the state and the racial groups/movements have been ever-so-slightly altered in definitively racialized ways, and thus the racial order has effectively been changed. "Change in the racial order, in the social meaning and political role played by race, is achieved only when the state has initiated reforms, when it has generated new programs and agencies in response to movement demands. Movements capable of achieving such reforms only arise when there is significant 'decay' in the capacities of pre-existing state programs and institutions to organize and enforce racial ideology."[54]

---

[53]Ibid., p. 86.

[54]Ibid., p. 88. Examples include the Civil Rights Division of the U.S. Department of Justice, the Equal Employment Opportunity Commission, President Johnson's "war" on poverty, etc. Co-opting the agenda of racial groups/movements by *absorption* or mollifying them by *insulation* was addressed by Kwame Ture (Stokely Carmichael) and Charles V. Hamilton in their book *Black Power: The Politics of Liberation* (New York: Random House, 1967), when they contended that "the basic goal is . . . the inclusion of black people at all levels of decision-making," and that "any federal program conceived with black people in mind is doomed if blacks

Thus with this theory Omi and Winant contend for an understanding of race and racism that has been and continues to be sociopolitically constructed, one that emerges from the fact that "race" is deeply embedded in the structure of the American political system, forged from the outset by the interaction between racially defined groups/movements and a racialized state. Racialization takes place in the unfolding stages of racial domination and resistance, opposition and conflict, crisis and turmoil, and absorption and insulation, all of which together engender the continuing formation and modification of racialized identity, politics and social structures. We have here a peculiarly mutable but nonetheless recognizable interrelation between the facts, forms and functions of race and racism, an indication that the patterns of *inter*group relations are nurtured and modified—but essentially sustained—by the sociopolitical opposition and conflict that has formed *intra*group identities.

With the theoretical constructions of Mills, Haney López, and Omi and Winant, we can discern the ways beliefs regarding race and behavior oriented by racism both shape and are shaped by the civil or political structures that order and regulate a common life. We can observe, with varying emphases, the interface of cognitive, behavioral, social and political dimensions in sociocultural environments. Needed, however, is an integration of economic dimensions into these theoretical constructions—dimensions that can also be viewed as contributing to the construction of race and racism. Accordingly, we will turn our attention now to two theories that address this dimension.

Socioeconomic Dimensions of Race and Racism

A social and political order is also an economic order, given that the common life of a people and its regulation require material resources that can support their development and assure the continuation of their way of life. Economics has basically to do with the production, development and management of these material resources for the well-being of the members of a society. It also has to do with the ownership, distribution and consumption of the goods and services needed or desired by a people, and the commodity or medium of exchange—"money"—that makes this acquisition possible.

Like those in the previous section, the theories now to be considered are generally *sociocultural* in that they attend to the context of a society's common life. At the same time, however, these theories are concerned with the economic aspects of this common life, so I will regard them as socio*economic* theories of race and racism. Once again we will observe some of the

---

do not control it. The fact is that the government will never 'give' blacks everything they need economically unless they have the power to threaten enough in order to get enough" (p. 183).

ways human subjectivity generates and becomes manifest in sociocultural structures and institutions, underscoring the envirorelational strand of race and racism.

Working to be white. In the European American fund of common knowledge, there is an awareness of the history of American slavery. Typically this history is pictured as the tyranny of violent and dehumanizing slave owners over the Africans they considered to be their legal property. Approaches to the history of Africans in America focus on this *institution* of slavery in its social, political and economic dimensions in the antebellum South, the *practices* of exclusion and discrimination of free Africans in the North, and *policies* of segregation and inequality in both regions in the post-Civil War period. Paralleling and intersecting this history of Africans in America is the history of European American labor—the emergence of the "white worker."

David R. Roediger is interested in the ways the American economic system has contributed to the formation of personal and social race-identity, and thus the construction of race and racism. In analyzing the link between race and class, he contends that the evolution of the working class and the formation of a "white" self-identity and social identity are phenomena occurring simultaneously and interactively through the history of this country, but especially in the nineteenth century.[55] In this framework he develops the notion that "white" is the formation of a kind of counter-identity, or over-against-identity, among the European American working class: We are *not* slave but free; we are *not* black but white. Thus one of the fascinating aspects of Roediger's theory is the role of language in shaping and expressing identity and sociality, or the linguistic construction of race and racism.

As a term differentiating Europeans from non-European peoples, *white* was used even prior to the establishment of the colonies in North America. As Roediger and others point out, the first "workers" to be brought to North America were both "white" Europeans and "black" Africans, and they were brought under similar circumstances: indentured servitude.[56] However, these similar circumstances quickly became dissimilar with the profitability of the African slave trade. Roediger notes that among early European workers there were varying

[55]On the following, see David R. Roediger, *The Wages of Whiteness: Race and the Making of the American Working Class* (London: Verso, 1991). Roediger has also published a collection of essays on these and related themes in *Towards the Abolition of Whiteness: Essays on Race, Politics and Working Class History* (New York: Verso, 1994).

[56]See Roediger, *Wages of Whiteness,* pp. 19-27; Jordan, *White Man's Burden,* pp. 3-54; and Lerone Bennett Jr., *Before the Mayflower: A History of Black America,* 6th rev. ed. (New York: Penguin, 1988), pp. 28-53, and *The Shaping of Black America,* rev. ed. (New York: Penguin, 1993), pp. 7-57.

degrees of "unfreedom" which nonetheless distinguished them from their African counterparts: "Indentured servitude, impressment, apprenticeship, convict labor, farm tenancy, wage labor and combinations of wage labor and free farming made for a continuum of oppression among whites. Of course . . . that continuum did not extend to the extreme of chattel slavery as was inflicted on people of color."[57] Indentured whites and enslaved blacks were both referred to by the term *servant,* but over time the permanence of black slavery took it in a different direction from white servitude. Roediger states that "indentured servitude was not chattel slavery" and that "the differences remained and mattered both for how ordinary whites saw slaves and how they saw themselves. Indentures were part of a late colonial population that was sometimes careful to claim rights as 'freeborn *British White* subjects.' They would soon again be free. Slaves were born Black, not British, and were often born in chains."[58]

With the victory of the colonialists in the American revolution, the economic and political bonds that had kept the colonies tied to Britain were severed, and with the dawn of republican liberty, indentured servitude quickly became ineffective and insignificant as a means of recruiting and managing a labor force. The corps of white indentured servants became the working class of wage laborers for whom political and economic independence would be only partially fulfilled; the growing mass of African laborers would be more thoroughly ensconced in the increasingly important and expanding institution of slavery.

For Roediger, the peculiar notion of "whiteness" among the working class emerged following the Revolutionary War as a response to their concerns about having to rely on only seasonal labor as a source of unpredictable income in the shifting economy of the newly independent nation. The workers' depen-

---

[57]Roediger, *Wages of Whiteness,* p. 25. In *Before the Mayflower* Bennett observes that "the first black immigrants were not slaves. . . . They came, these first blacks, the same way that most of the first white immigrants came—under duress and pressure. They found a system (indentured servitude) which enabled poor whites to come to America and sell their services for a stipulated number of years to planters. Under this system thousands of whites—paupers, ne'er-do-wells, religious dissenters, waifs, prisoners and prostitutes—were shipped to the colonies and sold to the highest bidder. Many were sold, as the first blacks were sold, by the captains of ships. Some were kidnapped on the streets of London and Bristol, as the first blacks were kidnapped in the villages of Africa" (pp. 34-35).

[58]Roediger, *Wages of Whiteness,* pp. 31-32. In commenting on the commonsense construal of *servant* and *slave,* and the tendency to confound the meaning of the former by collapsing it into the latter, Roediger states: "There was good reason for such confounding, dating from the early imprecisions of colonial usages of *slave* and *servant* right through Noah Webster's inconsistent distinctions between the two terms in his dictionary of 1828 and the tendency in the South to apply *servant* overwhelmingly to slaves in the antebellum years. Yet another complicating factor was that free blacks often worked as domestic servants, with the result that the degradation suffered by slaves, by Blacks generally and by domestics all came to be associated with the heading *servant*" (pp. 47-48).

dence on labor for wages seemed to diminish their recently acquired political independence. For European American workers living and seeking to survive in such a young and tenuous economic system, the counter-indication of their situation was not the capital-owning economic and political elite but rather the enslaved Africans. While they sought to *climb* to the status of self-employed, resource-owning, wealth-producing capitalists, and so achieve a greater degree of economic independence, they also sought to keep from *falling* to a kind of "white" bondage and servitude similar to what they saw in chattel slavery, and so protect a modest degree of economic independence. With their economic status hanging precariously between independence and dependence, European American workers who had nothing but their own labor to sell gauged their dependent and debased condition with reference to the situation of enslaved Africans. As Roediger observes, "Racial formation and class formation were thus bound to penetrate each other at every turn."[59]

A certain status accrued to European American laborers by virtue of their "race," and while this status at the time did not necessarily cash out into full political and economic independence, it did bring with it some intangible compensation: personal and class identity as "white" workers, counterformed in relation to "black" slaves. As a class, European American wage laborers were exploited by their employers with little that could be done to improve their conditions. At the same time, their capacity to draw a living wage was diminished by the possibility that they could be replaced by nonwage slaves. Caught in this precarious situation, so Roediger argues, they found comfort in and forged status from the fact that they were white; they paid themselves the "wages of whiteness."[60] Thus the European American wage laborer became a "hireling," a "hired man" willing to work at tasks considered menial or offensive, offering labor as a commodity, becoming not a *slave* but a *white worker,* a *freeman,* an economic self-description that took its counterpoint in the unfreedom and degradation attached to the black slave who had neither economic nor political rights.[61]

In the aftermath of the Civil War and emancipation, one might expect the

---

[59]Ibid., p. 20.

[60]Thus the title of Roediger's book. See also ibid., p. 13.

[61]Ibid., pp. 27, 33, 45-50, 55-59. Roediger states, "Webster's 1829 dictionary gave as its first definition of *freeman* 'one who enjoys liberty . . . one not a slave or a vassal,' and as its second 'one who enjoys or is entitled to a franchise'" (p. 56). A superb study of social stratification that attends to the class relations in ancient, agrarian and industrial societies can be found in Gerhard E. Lenski, *Power and Privilege: A Theory of Social Stratification* (New York: McGraw-Hill, 1966; University of North Carolina Press, 1984). Lenski's discussion of the socioeconomic stratification in agrarian societies (pp. 190-296) is particularly helpful in developing an understanding of the economic status and identity formation of wage laborers, though he does not address this matter, as Roediger does, in terms of race.

economic interests of European American and African American working classes to converge, bringing them together into a labor force united against the exploitive, oppressive, and propertied class that had kept both groups in subjection. However, while the freedom of the slaves meant it was no longer possible for European American laborers to self-define as "not slave," there was enough entrenched meaning to "white" that it remained possible—and important—to continue to self-identify as "not black." The freedom of African American slaves took on an altogether different threat: direct competition for jobs. The sense of economic superiority that had sustained the European American class of free laborers was consequently diminished, but the sense of *racial* superiority began to flourish and frustrate the convergence of economic interests in the laboring class on all fronts. The occasional convergence of mutual interests and the fomenting of resistance to and organization against oppressive labor conditions that did occur episodically from the time of early colonization remained the exception rather than the rule in labor relations with landowners and industrialists well into the twentieth century.[62]

Economic power and racial stratification. Another analytical approach to uncovering the socioeconomic dimensions of race and racism, with particular regard to the connection between the acquisition and distribution of resources and racial and class stratification, is the theoretical work undertaken by William Julius Wilson.[63] This construct is not as focused on the historical development of race and racism per se but rather on the extent to which socioeconomic power fosters and shapes intergroup relations in ways that presuppose, manifest and construct differing forms of racism. Wilson's contention is that an understanding of race relations—and thus of the racisms that shape them—must be oriented by

---

[62]For chronicles of some of these joint actions of resistance, see Danny Duncan Collum, *Black and White Together: The Search for Common Ground* (Maryknoll, N.Y.: Orbis, 1996). For discussions of the economic conditions of African Americans following the Civil War, see W. E. B. Du Bois, *The Souls of Black Folk* (1903; reprint, New York: Vintage/Library of America, 1990), pp. 16-35, 120-36; Fredrickson, *Black Image*, pp. 171-86; and Gunnar Myrdal, *An American Dilemma: The Negro Problem and Modern Democracy* (1944; reprint, New Brunswick, N.J.: Transaction, 1996), 1:205-424. Two works attending to socioeconomic conditions contributing to the development of race and racism that deserve attention because of the way they are framed are Christopher Bates Doob, *Racism: An American Cauldron*, 2nd ed. (New York: HarperCollins, 1996), where the phenomena of racism are interpreted in terms of "internal colonialism," and Roy L. Brooks, *Rethinking the American Race Problem* (Berkeley: University of California Press, 1990), who argues that contemporary racism is patterned along the lines of *intra*group economic stratification more rather than *inter*group racial polarization.

[63]For what follows see William Julius Wilson, *Power, Racism and Privilege: Race Relations in Theoretical and Sociohistorical Perspectives* (New York: Free Press, 1973).

a theory of socioeconomic power and its differential use by and between groups. His analysis is only secondarily concerned with expressions of undisguised antagonism between groups and personal bigotry or prejudice. Rather it focuses on the structures and uses of power that provoke this racial antagonism and bigotry by engendering racial and socioeconomic class stratification.

Without power and resources, one group is not in a position to oppress, discriminate or otherwise dominate another group. Thus in Wilson's view, oppression, discrimination and other forms of domination are to be construed as presupposing and exhibiting power. To put it another way, *power over* assumes and expresses *power to*. The guiding assertion for Wilson here is that, as a concept, "power . . . can be used to help account for group oppression per se and to explain the continued association of certain racial groups with certain class or caste positions. Class or caste membership develops from historical contact in which groups possessing a power advantage have been able to place themselves in superior positions by solidifying a social structure that features a racial stratification system."[64] He develops this assertion by examining first the intergroup dimensions of power and then the ways these dimensions foster racial stratification.

There are three dimensions of power that, when correlated with intergroup relations and demeanor, reveal the seeds of stratification. According to Wilson, there is first "active power," by which he means the actual exercise of power by one group over a second group in such a way that the behavior of the second group is made to conform to the expectations of the first group (i.e., one's exercise of power over elicits the desired behavior from the other). Second, there is "power ability," or the capacity of one group to exercise power for the purpose of controlling or influencing the behavior of a second group, regardless of whether the second group's behavior has actually been influenced (i.e., the possibility—or threat—of exercising power over is sufficient to elicit the desired behavior). Third, there are "power resources," or the physical and material as well as social, political and economic assets that determine the extent of one group's ability to affect the behavior of another group (i.e., one's exercise of power over is correlative to the resources at one's disposal [variation of the Golden Rule: the one who has the gold makes the rules]). "Power resources" may be deployed directly by "active power" or indirectly by "power ability" in any number of ways to engender the desired behavior, but Wilson describes these ways generally as coercion (force a behavior), inducement (encourage a behavior) and persuasion (choose a behavior).[65] Commenting further on the

---

[64]Ibid., p. 7.
[65]Ibid., p. 15.

confluence of these dimensions of power, he states: "In the final analysis, the greater the scope and the higher the liquidity of a group's resources, the greater is the group's power ability. In the study of racial-group power, the focus of analysis shifts from power ability to active power to the extent that the group's resources become mobilized to exert influence."[66]

When these three dimensions of power are brought to bear in *interracial* group relations, the differences in power between dominant and subordinate racial groups are correlative to the extent of domination exercised by one group over another. Wilson observes that it is largely the circumstances in which the two groups first come into contact that determine the basis for any existing power relation between them. The initial contact between racial groups historically has taken one of three possible configurations, which Wilson calls slave transfers, colonization and voluntary migration: "In each instance, the dominant racial group assumes a certain degree of control over the subordinate population, with the most rigid control and greatest power discrepancy occurring in slave transfers, followed by colonization and voluntary migration in descending order."[67] The onset of power relations between racial groups through the agency of slave transfers has by definition issued in extreme differential power, with virtually absolute power in all three of its dimensions in the hands of the dominant group and virtually no power held by the subordinate group. To the extent that initial power relations are situated in colonization wherein the colonizers seek control of indigenous peoples, and in voluntary migration wherein the dominant group seeks control of immigrant peoples, the three dimensions of power are proportionately diminished for the dominant group as they rise for the subordinate group.

Wilson maintains that whatever the forms of domination that emerge from the first contact between dominant and subordinate racial groups, there follows the development of structures and institutions effectively creating systems of racial stratification that not only endure but function as means for expressing and consolidating the threefold dimensions of power. What prompts one racial group to dominate and oppress another, he contends, is essentially economic in nature: the desire to control scarce resources through the removal of competition, and the maximization of profit through the exploitation of the subordinate group as labor. The three dimensions of power are oriented toward these ends, and in both cases power relations between the dominant and subordinate racial groups lead to an institutionalized structure of social and economic stratification. Differential power in its three dimensions establishes, preserves and

---

[66]Ibid., p. 17.
[67]Ibid., p. 19.

extends the socioeconomic interests of the dominant group at the expense of, and through the powerful control of, the subjugated group.[68] In this way, argues Wilson, the stratification of racial groups into a class—or caste—system can be seen to have originated in a paradigmatic initial contact shaped by the economic interests of a racially different power group.

What is needed to maintain this socioeconomic stratification and power differential is a warrant, or authorization, a basis on which to legitimate both its structure and the socioeconomic interests of the dominant power group. This Wilson finds in *racism*, which he defines as "an ideology of racial domination or exploitation that (1) incorporates beliefs in a particular race's cultural and/or inherent biological inferiority and (2) uses such beliefs to justify and prescribe inferior or unequal treatment for that group."[69] Whether in latent form at the time of initial contact or emerging over time as power relations become more fully demarcated, racism as the ideological legitimation of domination develops into a worldview that eventually feeds into and normalizes exploitive socioeconomic structures. As such, racism prescribes the patterns of interaction between dominant and subordinate racial groups in ways that come to be accepted as normal by the dominant group. Normalizing racism supports differential power and engenders new expressions of domination and exploitation. In Wilson's analysis, these prescribed patterns and exploitive structures constitute the institutionalization of racism: "When the ideology of racial exploitation gives rise to normative prescriptions designed to prevent the subordinate racial group from equal participation in associations or procedures that are stable, organized, and systematized . . . institutional racism exists. Institutional racism therefore represents the structured aspect of racist ideology."[70]

---

[68]Ibid., pp. 22-25. In a comment that echos Roediger's argument, Wilson says, "Although it is true that the nonslaveholders derived some psychic benefit from identifying with a 'superior' caste, the motivation for the system of slavery initially came from the privileged classes, whose desire to maximize their own resources led to the permanent servitude of blacks" (p. 25).

[69]Ibid., p. 32. Wilson argues at this point that there is a difference between biological and cultural racism: "a rationale or justification for racial domination is implicit in assumptions about inherent biological inferiority," but "a rationale for minority subjugation is not logically implied in beliefs of cultural inferiority, because there it is not assumed that the minority race is biologically incapable of achieving equality with the dominant group" (p. 33).

[70]Ibid., p. 34. Wilson delineates two other levels of racism, both of which are less structured than the institutional level: "collective" and "individual." "Collective racism connotes the existence of informal societal or group norms that specifically reinforce sporadic collective acts of racial discrimination, exploitation and suppression . . . whereas individual racism refers to a given person's set of attitudes . . . 'derived from' or influenced by racist norms and ideology" (ibid.). It is apparent that Wilson's theoretical interest is in the institutional forms of racism,but this should not be construed as disinterest in the other two forms. Indeed he states that "the development of racism in society is ultimately a collective process" and that "racism can

A closer inspection of the racial stratification that emanates from differential power in its three dimensions reveals that the economic interests and position of the dominant group contribute to the continuation of racial group subjugation. Wilson argues that "the more that dominant-group members identify with their group position, the greater the likelihood that they will strive to perpetuate their position."[71] The dominant group must control not only resources but also the means whereby the subordinate group may seek to develop and strengthen their own power. Thus it is necessary that the dominant group employ its threefold dimensions of power to limit or prohibit access to such things as formal education, certain occupations, open housing and a range of goods and services.

Wilson notes that as racial group relations have developed historically, a transition from one form of power structure to another has moderated the capacity of the dominant group to maintain its level of control. At the outset the groups were characterized by *paternalistic* power relations, with the differences in socioeconomic power being extreme and the subordinate group having little or no power to resist or contend against the structures of domination. In the situation of slavery, for example, practically all that could be done was to refuse to work, flee or revolt, and in all these cases the actual or potential use of superior power on the part of the dominant group put life at risk or induced compliance. But to the extent that slaves worked under duress, restrained themselves from fleeing or actually engaged in revolt, there are indications of their repudiation of the system institutionalized by the socioeconomic interests and power of the dominant group. Over time, however, domination and subordination have taken on the expression of competitive power relations, wherein the differences in socioeconomic power are narrowed because the capacity of the subordinate group to resist and contend is augmented by the acquisition of power resources. Among other things, access to education and occupations contribute to the development of socioeconomic power resources within the subordinated group, putting them in a more competitive position.

This shift in the power differential is perceived as a threat by the dominant group, whose response may be a heightened sense of competition leading to a more sophisticated deployment of its power resources for restricting the development of the subordinate group, or a sense of indignation and rivalry leading to varying degrees of violence, or both.[72] In any case, group relations in a socio-

---

only be understood as a product of collective action" (p. 35). Thus racism as a justificatory ideology is constructed through individual, collective and institutional expressions.
[71]Ibid., p. 42.
[72]Ibid., pp. 52-56.

economic structure characterized by competition and diminishing differences in power resources move to both more subtle and more explicit expressions of race conflict, and contribute more insidiously to the sanction of racism as an ideology among members of the dominant group. As race relations change and the forms of racism become more varied, dominant group members may moderate or even surrender beliefs regarding the inferiority of the subordinate group.

But in itself this change does not issue automatically in the evacuation of institutionalized racism. It may simply occasion an alteration of existing forms or transmigration into altogether new forms. For example, mere compliance with antidiscrimination laws does not make an institution nonracist. An institution built on the expressivity of Wilson's three dimensions of power does not become nonracist simply by declining to use the power it has. To the extent that an institution retains "active power," "power ability" and "power resources" that have been acquired and developed on the basis of racism—the ideology of domination and exploitation—it remains racist, both potentially and actually, paternalistically and competitively.[73]

With their particular approaches, both Roediger and Wilson expose some of the camouflaged ways that economic factors give rise to the construction of race and racism. Arguably both are contending that "racism" engenders "race," but in ways that differ from the argument laid down by Kovel. For Roediger, the keynote is the economic basis for fabricating and inculcating a counter-identity under the rubric "white." For Wilson, it is the economic basis for institutionalizing structures of racial stratification in power relations. Their focus on the socioeconomic aspects of racism underscores the need to attend to the manner in which economic resources and their control have contributed to the formation

---

[73]As pertinent as I think Wilson's construct is to the present situation, it should nevertheless be noted that he has subsequently—and quite controversially—argued that "race" is no longer the decisive factor in social and economic stratification that it once was. In his book *The Declining Significance of Race: Blacks and Changing American Institutions*, 2nd ed. (Chicago: University of Chicago Press, 1980), he argues that continuing class stratification in the African American community is more related to economic factors than to racial ones, more related to the development of an industrial economy than to a racialized one. Social and economic stratification remains, but socioeconomic mobility and quality of life depend less on one's race and more on one's economic class position. In this more recent book, Wilson's contention is that "one's economic class position determines in major measure one's life chances, including the chances for external living conditions and personal life experiences" (p. ix). In his latest work, *The Bridge over the Racial Divide: Rising Inequality and Coalition Politics* (Berkeley: University of California Press, 1999), he argues that the continuing racial divisions in the United States mitigate the potential of our political system to work effectively for equality and that a multiracial political coalition could bring focus to the interests and concerns shared across people groups.

of both racialized identity within and between people groups and racializing structures that have directed the development of our national economy. Both approaches—white economic identity and white economic power—are important to an analysis of the economy of racism.

The Significance and Limitations of Constructive Theories

Despite its brevity, this review of constructive theories opens a horizon onto the multilayered and cross-sectional dimensions of race and racism along the range of ideological, behavioral and sociocultural expressions. It should be apparent that while the facts, forms and functions of race and racism are open to interpretation from a variety of perspectives and approaches, there is no single theory that can capture and address all of their dimensions and expressions. Certainly none of these theorists can be accused of being disinterested or unfocused; all of them have an agenda, and all of them suggest or imply strategic measures for undermining the work that race and racism have done. But they do so largely within the province of their respective investigations. Singly and together, these theories seek to account for the matter but not to absolve it; they seek to make sense of it but not to sustain it. In the end, the purpose of their analytical and theoretical work is not merely to enable others to gain a deeper understanding of the world in which they are formed and to which they contribute. For these theorists it is important to interpret and comprehend how our world works, but this knowledge has little value if it is not used to effect change.

Singly and together, these theories can not only evoke an awareness of racism but also engender consternation and undergird discontent; we may find ourselves implicated—to one degree or another—by these constructs, as though seeing ourselves "in a mirror, dimly" (1 Cor 13:12), a mirror that reflects back to us our own consciousness, common sense, conduct and context. Mirrors have a way of reflecting back, just as theories have a way of rearranging and re-presenting our understanding of reality and our interpretation of its meaning.

However, the significance of these theoretical constructions lies less in what they may evoke in us or mirror for us—important as this is—and more in the analytic and historic profiles of racism they place before us. They are the foil that makes it possible for us to engage in critical reflection on the phenomena of race and racism, the whetstone that stimulates and hones our skills in discernment, the panorama that makes it possible to recognize the contours, contortions and contradictions in the topography of human personal and social life. They are, in short, indicative of the principal parameters in relation to which this book will seek to formulate a critical understanding of racism, and the purpose of this is ultimately to contend against it by participating in its deconstruction. For the moment, however, it may be useful to articulate in broad strokes the parameters

gained in this review, for we will seek in the remaining chapters to engage these and other theorists in the development of our own understanding.

There are five such parameters that should be kept in mind as we proceed. First of all, each of our theorists is concerned with the *genesis* of racism, its origins in the arena of human history. There was a time when race and racism were not, and then there came a time—and a place and a people—when they were. The interest in origins has to do with attribution of the spatiotemporal beginnings of the phenomena of race and racism; they are not eternal. Our theorists differ in locating a particular place and time for this origin, and they differ in the historic constellation of circumstances and events in relation to which they appear, but they are agreed that these phenomena are peculiarly and particularly not ex nihilo. They were, rather, exhaled from the minds and hearts of human beings, exhibited in the formation of new human communities and expanded to fill the nooks and crannies of social worlds.

Second, our consideration of the constructs of these theorists has given evidence of the *exodus* of racism, not only its migration from place to place, and time to time, but also its extraordinary ability to undergo transformation or—better—transmutation into new forms and appearances, leaving old expressions strewn like litter on the landscape of history. This interest in transmutation has to do with the changes in racism's expressions, the fact that it lived there in that form, then embarked upon a journey to a new place and in the passage became yet again something different—though not altogether different. Racism is remarkably stable even as it has passed through the instability of its appearances. Our theorists may not all agree on the insidious expressions of racism, but they are agreed that racism is not transcendent, lying beyond the limits of human perception and experience, independent of the stuff of our macro- and micro-worlds. Rather the expressions of racism are transactions of the human mind and heart with others, tranquilizers of personal and social discomfort, and transitions from one stage of life's journey to another.

Third, there is consideration for the *leviticus* of racism, its rules, regulations and restrictions, what it permits and what it forbids, as it forms and fragments a community into classes of rulers and ruled, advantaged and disadvantaged, included and excluded, centralized and marginalized. The interest of our theorists here has to do with the ways racism has generated its own justification and thereby embedded itself with authority in personal and social life; it defines a view of self, others and the world that becomes normalized in life's structures. Our theorists do not all agree on the particular ways that racism governs, shapes and validates a social world, or on the priests who superintend and exonerate the observance of its statutes, but they are agreed that racism is not regal, decreed from above, entitled to legitimation on its own terms, worthy of adoration and gratitude. Instead the hegemony of racism is the regent of the human mind and heart over against others, the refraction of human community into vested interests and polarizations, and the recompense for giving up accountability and giving in to the status quo.

Fourth, we find among our theorists a sense of the *numbers* of racism, the manifold dimensions within which personal, behavioral and sociocultural expressions of racism hide and disguise themselves, accumulating layers of language and meanings that indicate the connectivity of personal belief and conduct in sociocultural environments, and communal practices that nurture and sustain them. Their interest here has to do with the collective, the masses, the aggregate that is required to support and inculcate ideology and demeanor, the formation of a sense of groupness that makes it possible for one to identify with the many, and the social foundations for a homogeneous plurality. While the theorists may not agree on the particular intersections of racism's many aspects, they do agree that racism is not singular in its warrant or expression, a monolithic phenomenon whose presence is always discernible in human relationships and community, a monologue whose message is separable from the media that bear it along. Rather, racism is multifarious in its influence on minds and hearts, multilayered in its venues for personal and social formation, and multidirectional in its cultivation of a collective understanding and support for its personal and social world.

Finally, consideration is given to the *deuteronomy* of racism, the recapitulation of its story for the purpose of empowering an adjudication of its claims, a pause in the trajectory to render again or anew the decision to follow after or to abandon its lead, the call for an opportunity in new circumstances to reread, reinterpret and revalue the past with an awareness of the present and an eye toward the future. The interest our theorists have here is related to the moral decisiveness that is required in the encounter with the truth and untruth of race and racism, the acknowledgment of a junction in the path and the necessity to choose either love or hate, initiative or withdrawal, solidarity or hostility, life or death. They may not all agree on the particular alternatives, but they are agreed that racism is not equitable, offering impartial and straightforward possibilities from among which choices may be made with moral impunity, charting a course from past to future with safety and neutrality as landmarks; instead it obscures the dissimilar circumstances that make choosing difficult if not seemingly impossible. Rather, racism is equivocal in minds and hearts where it weakens decisiveness, equivalent to the desolation of self and the devastation of others, and the equation of a preferred way of passage with the least difficult way of passage.

These, then, are the parameters I will seek to incorporate into this book's framework. But there is yet one other parameter that we need to keep in mind.

Unlike our theorists, we seek a *theological* perspective for understanding racism and initiating measures toward its abrogation; we seek to participate in and extend God's reconciliation in Jesus Christ in a racialized personal and social context. To cooperate in God's reconciling work, we need to understand the interpersonal and sociocultural dimensions of the world we have inherited and continue to build, and for us in our place and time, this means that we must understand the phenomena of *race* and *racism*. If we believe that God seeks reconciliation with us, in our situation, and that this reconciliation is to be lived out in the world in relationship to God and others, then it is necessary that we understand and contend against all that hinders the realization of this reconciliation, and this means understanding and contending against race and racism.

To move ourselves toward this end, we will need to do some self-reflection, considering our attitudes, perceptions, beliefs, the ways we think, and how we have been influenced in these by the ideology of racism. We will need to reflect critically on our conduct, exploring our intentions, expectations, roles and patterns of relationship, and how these have been shaped by the behavioral manifestations of racism. And we will need to analyze the systemic ethos of life together, assessing the bases and structures of our common life and the ways in which they presume and develop the sociocultural dimensions of racism. So to these tasks we now turn, with attention to the construction and deconstruction of race and racism.

●   ●   ●   ●

Do not seek your own advantage, but that of the other.   1 Corinthians 10:24

For by the grace given to me I say to everyone among you not to think of yourself more highly than you ought to think, but to think with sober judgment, each according to the measure of faith that God has assigned. . . .

Let love be genuine; hate what is evil, hold fast to what is good; love one another with mutual affection; outdo one another in showing honor. Do not lag in zeal, be ardent in spirit, serve the Lord. Rejoice in hope, be patient in suffering, persevere in prayer.
Romans 12:3, 9-12

In a world where not everyone obtains what is needed or desired for life, it seems only normal to seek advantage and look out for ourselves. Stepping on and stepping over others is the way to success in our competitive world. In a culture that values individualism, looking out for others means protecting oneself from others, and thinking highly of oneself is a way to put others down. The way of love, however, seeks the other and sees in him or her the reflection of God's own image. Genuine love in all circumstances honors and intends the well-being of the other.

3

THE SOCIALITY
OF RACE

*How hard it is for those who have wealth to enter the kingdom of God! Indeed, it is easier for
a camel to go through the eye of a needle than for someone who is rich to enter the kingdom
of God.* Luke 18:24

*If the wealthy can't make it, what hope is there for the rest of us? Isn't their prosperity a
sign of God's blessing? No, it isn't. The wealth of some comes by the exploitation of
others; the poverty of many preserves the comfort of the few. One cannot enter the reign
of God by oppressing others, and resources gained by depriving others are ill-gotten gain.
Is it possible that one reason Jesus told the rich ruler to sell his possessions and give the
proceeds to the poor was that this ruler had come by his wealth by exploiting the poor? If
so, then how he came by his wealth is most assuredly a moral issue. How are the rich
related to the poor, and how has it happened that in our country some have become
comfortable at the expense of many who have been excluded?*

• • • •

I n the present chapter we turn our attention to the development of a critical
understanding of the social construction of race and racism. The themes introduced in chapter one will be developed further: the ways language expresses
consciousness and what is perceived. In particular we will inquire into the
sociocultural configurations and structures that express consciousness and
apprehension and mediate beliefs and knowledge as well as personal and communal identity and relations.

The word *sociality* in this chapter's title refers to the human inclination to form
societies and communities; it reminds us that we are social persons who live
together in a shared world that we have inherited and continue to develop. Our
task is to analyze some of the ways society has engendered race and formulated a
social world and a worldview oriented by it. We are interested not merely in the
origins of a racialized society but also in the aspects of life in community that pro-

duce, express and perpetuate the notion of race and the worldview of racism. This is what is meant by the sociality of race: the social formation of race and racism as evidenced in our beliefs, behaviors and institutions.

A Trip to the Library, a Look at People

Before proceeding further, however, I want to pose a little thought experiment as a metaphorical interlude. This will serve not only as a transition to the primary task of this chapter but also as a modest explication of what is meant by "social construction" of race.

Imagine a library full of books. There are big thick books and little thin books. Some stand tall on the shelf, others are almost hidden because they are short. There are a good many books that are hardbound and sturdy, and others are softbound and almost flimsy. A few still have their paper dustjacket, though it has been wrapped in plastic to preserve it. There are even some books that are now hardbound after having been published as softbound (you can spot these because the hardbound cover has a cutout of the original paperback cover taped to it). There are books that are so new that they creak when you open them, others so used that they practically open themselves, and a few so old that they crack when opened. The titles of some books are short, in some cases just a single word; these can be read horizontally on the shelf. Other books have long titles, including some with subtitles; these are read vertically by tilting the head to the right (or left, if it is a foreign publication). There are a few books that do not have a title on the spine; these you have to pull off the shelf to read the front cover or the title page. The covers of the books come in all different colors; most of the hardbound covers seem to be monochrome in color (though a few have a different color for just the spine), while the softbound covers are multicolored, many with illustrations.

And of course, the library is organized and laid out in such a way that one can find a particular book without having to browse all of them; the books are cataloged according to subject and author, and consulting the catalog will provide the location of a particular book. As different as all these books are, they have these things in common: size and shape, colorful covers, titles, pages with printing or writing (and maybe pictures), and of course the library's bookplate on the inside, and probably the call number stamped or written on the spine and backside of the title page.

Why is the library catalog organized by subject and author? Why are the books shelved by subject? This seems rather arbitrary, given the fact that there is more to a book than its subject and author. Why not organize and lay out a library by book size, from biggest and thickest to smallest and thinnest? Why not use type of cover as the criterion, with hardbacks here, paperbacks there, and in between the books with dustjackets and those converted from soft to hardcover? It would also be feasible to organize the library by the age of the book (newest to oldest) or title (short to long, or maybe vertical to horizontal reading). Why not organize the library's books by their color, or by whether they are monochrome or multicolored, or both? Instead of subject and author, why could not all these other criteria be used to organize and lay out a library? ("Big old hardcover books with green covers are in the southwest corner of the first floor!")

The answer is that it would not be practical, because people do not come to a library to access books according to these criteria; they seek books according to subject and author. Libraries are organized and laid out to be useful, and it so happens that usefulness is defined in terms of accessibility by subject and author. But libraries *could* be organized and laid out according to these other criteria. There is nothing inherent in "library" that requires a collection of books to be classified and shelved according to *any* criteria, with the possible exception of usability. Even if a library were to be organized and shelved according to size, cover, color, age or title, individual books could still be cataloged according to subject and author to ensure that they can be located with ease.

Fundamentally, it is usefulness and accessibility, qualified by patrons' interest in particular subjects and authors, that have determined the conventional organization and layout of libraries. A collection of books differing from one another across a wide range of characteristics needs to be organized to render it accessible and usable, and a catalog listing the holdings is needed to render the books easily locatable. The organization of the catalog determines the organization of the books, and the catalog is structured by criteria chosen to maximize usability and accessibility.

So libraries are conventionally constructed in terms of the needs and interests of patrons. To put it another way, libraries as collections of differing books, and catalogs as indices of the holdings, are socially constructed. And now, the question: Does a collection of differing books necessarily imply a particular scheme for organizing and shelving the holdings, or is the scheme developed according to criteria extraneous to the collection as a whole?

Now let us imagine ourselves as a collection of people. How did we come to see ourselves as white, black, brown, red or yellow, and what do these words mean? Why do we tend to view the world in terms of these colors and live in a world that is structured along the lines of color? If "nature" can be generally understood as the essential characteristics and qualities of something—that which is necessary for a thing to be what it is—how do we understand *human* nature? Does human nature come in colors, and if so, does this imply that there is one nature with colorful variations on a theme, or do variations in color imply that there are multiple natures? Is it meaningful to talk not only about a static constitution of humanness but also a dynamic production of humanness? How did it come about that variations among human beings became distinctions between human beings? Are variations natural or accidental? Are distinctions natural or accidental? Do variations have significance, and if so, on what basis? What do distinctions mean, and how are they to be assessed? What is the relationship between human nature and the formation of individual and social life? Questions, questions and more questions.

It would be impertinent to say that racism is the answer to these questions, even if the notion of race is acknowledged to be a human innovation. But it would not be impertinent to say that racism is involved in these questions, either as the soil out of which they grow or the direction in which they lead. There is such a thing as "racism" because we have organized and laid out a world in terms of "race." Human biology and variability do not require or necessarily imply "race," any more than a particular human characteristic—like skin pigmentation or hair texture—must function as a criterion in a classification of human variability. To the extent that it is apprehended by human consciousness, this variability exists and is real. But the issue is not the phenomenon of human variability as such but rather what we make of this variability. The issue is not *what* we see but *how* we see it, and in seeing it, objectify—or real-ize—it in consciousness and impute significance to it. The issue is what we make of it in cognitive, attitudinal, behavioral and sociocultural ways.

It is human consciousness that transforms variability into races; the mind takes certain observable human characteristics and traits—or phenotypes—and ascribes objectivity, immutability and meaning to them. This "fact," then, objectifies both consciousness and what is apprehended. There is a bioscientific basis for human variability in the human genome. This is to say that biological variations and their distribution in a population are related to genes, and thus certain physical characteristics and traits are heritable (transmissible from one generation to the next). The configuration of genetic composition within a group of people—or genotype—can be identified, but these configurations are obviously malleable rather than fixed, both within a genotype and between genotypes; some characteristics or traits are not always transmitted within a genotype, and intermixture of genotypes alters the composition of both in subsequent generations. Caution is called for when we seek to group people into a circumscribed "type" on the basis of shared physical characteristics.[1]

---

[1]In his book *Anthropology and Modern Life* (1928; reprint, New York: Dover, 1986), cultural anthropologist Franz Boas expressed just such a caution: "We are easily misled by general impressions. . . . The more uniform a people the more strongly are we impressed by the 'type.' Every country impresses us as inhabited by a certain type, the traits of which are determined by the most frequently occurring forms [i.e., phenotypes]. This, however, does not tell us

But there is no bioscientific basis for "race"; it is neither a natural nor a biological phenomenon. Rather it is a notion that objectifies and ascribes meaning to phenotypes, the physical characteristics and traits that we observe. Bioscience draws attention to the genetic basis of human variability, but we create and re-create race by apprehending, distinguishing and signifying variability and embedding this objectivity in the structures of sociocultural life. We do not merely sort people according to their phenotype. Rather the very act of identifying phenotypes—objectifying consciousness and apprehension—sorts people into aggregates. After they were defined, assessed and ordered, phenotypes were used to distinguish one group from another and to limit and prescribe possibilities and opportunities. Thus people were sorted into social aggregates, not on the basis of biological variability but on the basis of ascribed differences and the value and ranking assigned to them. In general, this is what has come to be known as the production of race: the human invention of a category that defines, differentiates and evaluates people groups.

When a social order emerges in relation to these ascribed differences and their supposed significance, you have a *racial origin* of society, and when a social order is developed, structured and refined on this basis, you have a *social construction* of race, that is, the cultivation and perpetuation of "races" as the fabric and form of a social world, lines of demarcation that distinguish and allocate kinds and qualities of life. The ideology or worldview that guides and legitimates this reality is "racism," and the personal and social practices that embody and express this worldview are "racist."

Race as a Social Construct: The Objective Reality of Race

How did race come to play such an important role in the development of our society, and why do we think and act in terms of race? Many have put their minds and hearts to the task of answering these questions. The previous chapter surveyed the work of some who came to these questions from different approaches and perspectives (reason, psychology, political science, economics). Others have focused on physical and cultural anthropology, history, philosophy, social science, cultural criticism or the contemporary situation across a range of sociocultural fronts.

My approach to engaging these questions, while drawing on these and other

---

anything in regard to its hereditary composition and the range of its variations [i.e., genotype]. The 'type' is formed quite subjectively on the basis of our everyday experience.

"We must also remember that the 'type' is more or less an abstraction. The characteristic traits are found rarely combined in one and the same individual, although their frequency in the mass of the population induces us to imagine a typical individual in which all these traits appear combined" (pp. 22-23).

perspectives, is focused on the ways race and racism have been formed both subjectively and objectively. To put it another way, we will focus on the process whereby race and racism have become—and continue to be—constitutive of our subjective and objective reality, our internal and external world.

In order to advance our discussion, we need first to consider how objective reality is formed, and for this we will return to the work of Peter Berger and Thomas Luckmann. I will then bring these perspectives to bear on an analysis of some of the pronounced features of race and racism as these have emerged operationally in our shared world.

Building a social world: Institutionalization. We live from day to day assuming that the external world exists; we encounter and interpret the world outside ourselves as an objective reality, a constellation of persons, places and things held together in space and time by a web of interconnected spheres. This external reality strikes us as a given; it is there, presenting itself to our consciousness in all its micro-details and macro-complexity. We interact with it through its spheres, sometimes shaping it and other times being shaped by it. This world outside ourselves is an ordered world. Some of its structures and boundaries are endemic to what we refer to as God's creation: mountains, valleys and plains; creeks, rivers and oceans; comets, stars and planets. Others are made by us: sidewalks, streets and highways; cabins, houses and buildings; businesses, organizations and institutions; governments, nations and borders. These structures and boundaries contribute to the objectivity of the world, or they objectify the world outside ourselves. But what is involved in the process of structuring our world of everyday life, and why is it structured the way it is? In what sense is our shared world a world that we have created and objectified?

Berger and Luckmann address these questions by noting first that human beings live in and interact with an environment that is both natural and social, or God-given and human-made.[2] While acknowledging that human beings are biological organisms and that a particular natural environment influences and shapes human life, their concern is with the sociocultural environment and its role in the formation of human individual and communal identity. They reject the notion that human biology determines sociocultural development, so when they speak of "human nature," they have in mind our adaptability and capacity to interact with the world as the fundamental qualities that give rise to sociocultural developments. In their view "humanness is socio-culturally variable," and

---

[2]For what follows, see Peter L. Berger and Thomas Luckmann, *The Social Construction of Reality: A Treatise in the Sociology of Knowledge* (New York: Doubleday, 1966), pp. 48-128. The discussion I am summarizing is conceptually quite thick, so the notes will contain a series of modest illustrations at appropriate points to help clarify the principal points and stimulate the reader's imagination.

the particular shape that this humanness takes in any given time and place is determined by, and relative to, a sociocultural environment and its own variations.[3]

Berger and Luckmann do not sever the connection between humans' physical nature as biological organisms and humankind's sociocultural formation. They simply oppose the contention that the former is the sole or primary ground and condition for the latter. By denying the biological determination of sociocultural development and variability, it is possible for them to argue that human beings manufacture themselves and that they cannot be understood without attention to the sociocultural environment in which they are formed.

In a manner of speaking, human beings construct themselves in relation to their environment, and this is by definition a social enterprise. Human beings construct the totality of their sociocultural environment together. Thus it appears that an individual's development as a biological organism is preceded by a particular sociocultural environment into which he or she enters, an environment situated in a particular natural environment. Because this human-made environment is not derived from or determined by a natural or biological foundation, it is not appropriate to regard the social order as a given, or as itself "natural," or generated from the "laws of nature," however these may be construed. Rather the "social order exists *only* as a product of human activity. No other ontological status may be ascribed to it. . . . Both in its genesis (social order is the result of past human activity) and its existence in any instant of time (social order exists only and insofar as human activity continues to produce it) it is a human product."[4]

---

[3]Ibid., p. 49. The interest is in the formation of humankind's *social* nature (what we make of ourselves and our shared environment) and not in an intrinsic human *nature* that is given and shared by all human beings.

[4]Ibid., p. 52. The rejection of a biological or "natural" determination of sociocultural environments does not imply that there is no connection between natural and sociocultural environments, or that a given natural environment does not influence and in some ways limit the formation of a social order. Humanly constructed habitats and social orders may reflect their natural environment, as when one finds fishing villages alongside seacoasts, or farmers on the plains, or skiers in the mountains. Socioeconomic structures and the cultures that support them may seem "naturally" indigenous to an environment, but they are hardly necessary to or determined by such environments. Human beings who choose to fish the oceans develop fishing villages and cultures; oceans do not make fishers out of human beings. Franz Boas made this argument: "Environmental conditions may stimulate existing cultural activities, but they have no creative force. The most fertile soil will not create agriculture; navigable water will not create navigation; a plentiful supply of wood will not create wooden buildings; but where agriculture, the art of navigation and architecture exist they will be stimulated and in part moulded by geographical conditions" (*Race, Language and Culture* [Chicago: University of Chicago Press, 1940], p. 266). See also Franz Boas, *The Mind of Primitive Man*, rev. ed. (New York: Collier, 1963), pp. 173-79.

For Berger and Luckmann, the social order emerges and continues as a human construction in that it is a basic means for expressing—or objectifying—both the self and the self-with-others. As human beings express themselves and act with others, they *externalize* themselves in these activities. In time, this externalization involves forming an environment suitable for social coexistence. This environment then becomes a world into which human beings may enter and continue to express or externalize themselves. Human activity takes on habitualized patterns; actions done a certain way over time become routine and familiar, and it becomes easier to repeat them because they become habit. Actions done in habitualized ways not only express the one acting but *typify* the actor and the actions to the extent that one's self is embodied and represented in the action.[5]

At this point the authors introduce the notion of institutionalization: when a habitualized activity involves multiple actors, each engaged in an aspect related to the activity and interacting with each other, these actors and actions together constitute the typification, and every typification is an *institution*. "The typifications of habitualized actions that constitute institutions are always shared ones. They are *available* to all the members of the particular social group in question, and the institution itself typifies individual actors as well as individual actions."[6] Furthermore, institutions manage human behavior by their established patterns of activity. While there may be variations in style or manner of expressing oneself in an institutionalized activity, there are some behaviors that are regarded as normal and expected and others that are unacceptable or inappropriate to the institution.[7]

Individuals come into and experience an institution as an objective reality

---

[5]One who glides down a snow-packed slope with two long flat runners attached to the feet over time—habitually—becomes a *skier* who *skis*, and thus one who expresses one's self in *skiing*. Skier is a *type* of actor, and skiing is a *type* of activity.

[6]Ibid., p. 54. To the extent that skiers, ticket agents, chairlift operators, ski patrol, medical personnel, maintenance staff and shelter-house employees do what they do relative to the activity of gliding down snow-packed slopes, they and their actions constitute the ski institution. Thus (like politics) all institutions are essentially local, and the interconnectivity of institutions moves out from there. In the case of my example, a local ski area with its patrons and support staff is itself an institution. When to this is added the manufacturing of lift and ski equipment, the ownership and financing of ski areas, the restaurants, accommodations, and after-hours entertainment associated with them, and the (occasional) government lease that makes the mountain available for this activity, you have exposed the infrastructure of the ski *industry*, or a thoroughly entangled web of ski institutions. No *one* skis unless some*one* does some, many or all of these things. The skiers (actors) who ski (activity) engender the institutionalization of skiing (typification). Thus *skiing is a social institution.*

[7] For example, cutting into lift lines, swinging or jumping off the chairlift too soon, skiing out of a trail's marked bounds, skiing over fallen skiers all fall into this category.

that has its own history. They come to it after it began, and they will undoubtedly leave it before it ends. The individual's interaction with the institution is a convergence in space and time of the individual's life and the institution's life. But the institution is regarded and experienced as larger and other than the individual; it is simply there—external and objective—as a means for expressing the self.

For Berger and Luckmann, this institutional objectivity does not diminish the fact that the institution *in its totality* is a human construction. Indeed, because it emerges and continues as an externalization of human life in activity, an institution is basically the objectivity of humanness, that is, the sociocultural expression of human life. The externalization of the self by an activity in a world is a world- (or institution-) building activity, and the world thus built, existing as it does outside the self, is regarded and engaged as an objective reality. The authors contend that the relationship between human beings and their sociocultural environment is dialectical in that they act upon and influence each other: the producer acts to produce a social world as a product, and the product acts upon its producer.[8]

Common knowledge. Because institutions are objectified human activity involving multiple actors, they tend toward integration. Individuals engage in the particular "typical" actions that express the institution, but these actions are not disconnected from one another. They are components that contribute to the meaning of the institution and the formation of an ethos that is not confined to the particular activity of a specific individual but expressed and shared by all. This integration consists in the actors' knowledge of the institutional order and the meanings that give rise to and sustain it. It is the common sense of an institution, the awareness that what one knows—institutional stories, beliefs, values, ways of doing things and so on—is knowledge shared by others. It is an unreflective sense of how things work, who does what and why, rather like an intuitive discernment of what is appropriate conduct.

Berger and Luckmann contend that this common knowledge shapes the

---

[8]See ibid., pp. 60-61. It may be difficult to imagine how a "world" can "act upon" an individual or a collective. What Berger and Luckmann have in mind here is the way patterns and structures of institutions stimulate, designate, guide, manage, modify and balance actors/activity in self-expression. For example, skiers can ski anywhere they want to, including outside the bounds of a marked trail. But they know that by doing so they not only break a rule and put themselves in physical danger but may also have their lift ticket revoked. The rule against skiing out of bounds is a way to manage the institution of skiing. A skier cannot break the rule and still be "typical." Thus the institution that emerged as the externalization of self imposes limits on self-expression, and crossing the limits disqualifies the "typical" skier: "I am a skier; I cross the bounds; I am *no longer* a 'skier.'"

roles played by actors and defines, motivates, controls and predicts institutional conduct. "Since this knowledge is socially objectified *as* knowledge, that is, as a body of generally valid truths about reality, any radical deviance from the institutional order appears as a departure from reality."[9] This knowledge is produced with the emergence of the institution as an externalization of humanness, so it aids the apprehension of the objectivity of the institutional order. It also manages the ways externalization continues to shape this order. At the same time, this knowledge is itself embodied and expressed—objectified—in the structures, practices and rules of the institution, so that it is possible to say that this knowledge contributes to the continuing construction of the institution's objective reality. This body of knowledge is what everyone who participates in the institution's typifying activities "knows." It is passed on to the next generation as objective truth, and it is the basis for the socialization and integration of new "typical" actors. But it is, and remains, a knowledge that is socially produced and socially objectified.

Role-playing. At this point in their delineation of institutions, Berger and Luckmann introduce the concept of "roles" as the way individuals exemplify and actualize an institution. It is by "playing" roles that individuals share in a social world, and to the extent that such role-playing is internalized, the individual finds the social world to be a subjective reality. Roles emerge in the habitualized and objectified activities that constitute an institution. By way of the common knowledge, these roles are standardized and available to any who may participate in the institutional order. "Roles appear as soon as a common stock of knowledge containing reciprocal typifications of conduct is in process of formation, a process that . . . is endemic to social interaction and prior to institutionalization proper. . . . *All* institutionalized conduct involves roles. Thus roles share in the controlling character of institutionalization."[10]

Playing a role embodies and objectifies it, at the same time that it expresses the institution's ethos of behavior and the common knowledge. Thus the institu-

---

[9]Ibid., p. 66. Skiers and lift operators know what each other does, and each is (practically) useless without the other. They do not think a lot about what each does, and they probably do not know each other, but they do know what each is *supposed* to do. When a skier falls down, or a lift operator misses a chair as it comes around for the skiers, all recognize that there has been to some extent a departure from the reality of skiing.

[10]Ibid., p. 74. *Roles* is another way of describing what it is that actors do in relation to both the other actors and the institution as a whole. They underscore the interconnections of an institution's defining activities. For example, members of the ski patrol monitor the safety of the slopes and the skiers and when necessary come to the aid of an injured skier. Skiers who hurt themselves are met by role-playing ski patrol members. You cannot have ski patrol without skiers, because the patrol's role is auxiliary to the activity of skiing.

tional order is realized in all the roles played by actors to the extent that these roles depict an institution's definition of them. Each role objectifies a portion of the common knowledge and contributes to the total ethos that characterizes an institutional order.

Explanation and legitimation. Orientation to and participation in an institutionalized social order involve the transmission of the common sense or the objectified knowledge. Eventually institutions require explanation. There comes a time when persons who were not involved with the origin of an institution come into contact with it, and these actors are unaware of the meaning and circumstances in which the now-institutionalized self-externalizing activity emerged. The institution has a history and a tradition embedded in the memory of the originators, but this must be told and interpreted to succeeding generations in order that they may embrace and ultimately embody (i.e., typify in their own selves and activities) the institution as an externalization of self and the objectivity of a social world.

Institutions develop many different ways to present and interpret themselves to new generations, and these self-promotional activities are constant.[11] These explanations or interpretations are, for Berger and Luckmann, an institution's *legitimations* and *justifications*. Explaining an institution involves retrieving its original circumstance and meaning, either from memory or from tradition, and adapting these to the present circumstance in order that a newcomer can find a place within it for self-expression.

With each succeeding generation, not only is there further temporal distance from the point of origin, but the process of legitimation results in the accumulation of layer upon layer of explanation and interpretation. The authors contend that this "edifice" of institutional legitimations "is built upon language and uses language as its principal instrumentality."[12] This is to say that language not only expresses and objectifies the shared experiences but makes these experiences accessible to others. By orienting and objectifying new experiences, language assimilates new actors into the meanings objectified by the institution, and thus into the common sense. Thus language serves to legitimate an institutionalized social order and contribute to what Berger

---

[11]Ski areas are presented and interpreted, for example, in ways that underscore the distinctiveness of their operations, equipment, slopes, auxiliary support systems, communities, public service functions and so on. Public relations and advertising are very important to the fiscal health of a ski area, especially in a competitive environment.

[12]Ibid., p. 64. Ski areas are described in language, frequently with superlative adjectives (*latest, biggest, longest, widest, highest, deepest, most scenic, fastest growing,* etc.). Saying you are "the biggest" does not make it so, but it certainly leaves an impression—an objectivity—in the mind of the hearer/reader.

and Luckmann refer to as "the socially available stock of knowledge."[13]

Legitimation also adds to this common knowledge because it is a process of reflecting on the meanings objectified in an institutional order for the purpose of making them comprehensible and available to others. Thus legitimation is a secondary objectivity of meaning that makes the originative or primary objectivity of meaning more accessible and plausible—that is, it *makes* sense *for* others. The authors contend that "legitimation 'explains' the institutional order by ascribing cognitive validity to its objectified meanings. Legitimation justifies the institutional order by giving a normative dignity to its practical imperatives. . . . Legitimation not only tells the individual why he *should* perform one action and not another; it also tells him why things *are* what they are."[14]

There are several different levels of legitimation, from prereflective discernment expressed in the common language, to basic explanations of how things are, to theories regarding a particular activity or role, to a more comprehensive articulation that embraces and integrates the many aspects of the institutional order into a coherent whole. This latter level is what Berger and Luckmann call an institution's "symbolic universe," which embraces the past by establishing a shared memory and points to the future by providing a perspective in relation to which individuals can locate themselves as participants in the ongoing life of the institution. It is, in a manner of speaking, a worldview that "provides a comprehensive integration of *all* discrete institutional processes. The entire society now makes sense. Particular institutions and roles are legitimated by locating them in a comprehensively meaningful world."[15] For any particular institutional order to be meaningful as a whole, it must be situated in a symbolic universe.

---

[13]Ibid., p. 64. Among other things, the institutionalization of skiing entails that "skiing" becomes deposited in the common sense (the social stock of knowledge) as a typical activity in the ski institution. Explaining and interpreting what a skier does and how a skier does it, as well as how and why the activity of skiing began as a human self-expressive activity, tends toward the validation or authentication—legitimation—of what any particular skier is and does. Thus not only does a person learn what skiing is and what a skier does historically, but he or she can assess whether he or she (or someone else) is actually—legitimately—a skier who is skiing. For Berger and Luckmann, the basic instrumentality for this process is language.

[14]Ibid., pp. 93-94. The legitimation of skiing entails explaining how and why skiers ski and what is involved in the act of skiing (both the physics and the athletic skill). It also involves articulation of the ways skiing as an industry (or at a particular ski area) contributes to the economy of a community or region (jobs, tax revenue, etc.). It might even include attention to the aesthetics of skiing (adrenaline rush, sense of accomplishment, being outdoors). Thus as an institution that typifies a particular form of recreation, skiing can be legitimated in a variety of ways.

[15]Ibid., p. 103. Skiing has a world all its own, a kind of symbolic universe, in that it has its own history as a sport, standards of excellence established by the accomplishments of its "stars," directions for the development of ski-related technology, and a set of beliefs, values and practices that are situated in a meaningful framework that gives them *sense*.

This "situation" is an institutional order's ultimate legitimation or validation; it is the outermost boundary of an order's structure and meaning, within which all are placed and in relation to which all find their place.

The extent of the holistic institutionalization of a social order is related to the extent to which its relevance structures are widely shared and its objectivity is apprehended as factual reality. The more objectified a social order becomes to its members, the greater the likelihood that its objectivity will assume a life of its own. This opens a horizon on the *reification* of the social order. Berger and Luckmann state that "reification is the apprehension of the products of human activity *as if* they were something else than human products. . . . Reification implies that [one] is capable of forgetting his own authorship of the human world, and further, that the dialectic between [humankind], the producer, and [humankind's] products is lost to consciousness."[16] When the members of a social order encounter its externalized structures, it is as though they encounter an "objective reality" outside themselves, and the link between "we made that" and "that exists" is severed. The social order as a whole, and in its constituent parts, may be regarded not only as "real" in itself but as "natural" or coterminous with the natural order. Particular institutions and roles can become reified as members assign being to them or assume that they have a status entirely separate from the human actors and activities that objectify them.

The fact that one comes to an "existing" institution, or into an "existing" social order, tends to support viewing them as virtually self-existent and permanent. They cease to be regarded as the product of human externalizations and become "fixated as a non-human, non-humanizable, inert facticity."[17] Over time the institutions and roles, as well as the social order they constitute and the symbolic universe that justifies them, become *real-ized* in extraordinary ways.

Maintaining the universe. According to our authors, a symbolic universe needs to be maintained if it is to contextualize and justify the reified social order. This is particularly important when a problem arises, such as an alterna-

---

[16]Ibid., p. 89.

[17]Ibid. Skiers go to the mountain where slopes are groomed and bounded by trees. They sit in chairlifts that carry them up the mountain. They arrive at the top and ski down one of many different slopes, each of which requires a certain level of skill to negotiate successfully. They do this over and over again all day long. At the end of the day they leave the mountain ski area, tired and hopefully uninjured. They are not aware of the activities of others that made their day possible, or where they came from, or how and when they learned their job. They are unaware of all the people and activities that have been required over time to produce a place where they could ski. For all they know or care, skiing simply exists because there are skis, boots, poles and ski areas; the ski industry has become reified. In fact, however, ski areas exist because there is skiing, a self-expressing, externalizing typical activity that constructs an institution.

tive construal of the social order or a variant rendering of the symbolic universe itself. When a differing construal or rendering emerges among a growing number of a society's members, it poses a challenge—a threat—to the social reality constituted in relation to the symbolic universe. When one social order encounters another social order that has its own network of social institutions and universe of meaning, this is equivalent to acknowledging that one's own network and universe are less real, or stable, or certain, perhaps even less ultimate. In short, reality is threatened.

At this point, it is the task of the custodians of the symbolic universe not only to press its justification but also to establish its *superiority*. The mechanisms for maintaining a symbolic universe are themselves products of social activity, and their effectiveness in their task is contingent upon the use of power to define, sustain and enforce the practices that constitute a social order and its institutions. In this regard Berger and Luckmann declare that "the success of particular conceptual machineries is related to the power possessed by those who operate them. The confrontation of alternative symbolic universes implies a problem of power—which of the conflicting definitions of reality will be 'made to stick' in the society. Two societies confronting each other with conflicting universes will both develop conceptual machineries designed to maintain their respective universes. . . . [The one] who has the bigger stick has the better chance of imposing [the] definitions of reality."[18] At the conceptual level, the symbolic universe is defended and refined by the machinery of mythology, theology, philosophy and science, each of which—to varying degrees—contributes to the formation of the social world as an institutional order in its own right.

The machinery of universe-maintenance in a social order will operate either to absorb and control its variants, keeping them in check as inferior within the social order, or to reject its variants, denying their construal and construction of "reality" and assimilating the variant order into the established superior social order, thereby obliterating the variant rendering. "If the symbolic universe is to comprehend all reality, nothing can be allowed to remain

---

[18]Ibid., pp. 108-9. As a group, skiers share not only a common outlook and mutual interests but also a symbolic universe that orients and gives meaning to the many activities that make up the ski industry. People who glide down ski slopes with only a single runner attached to the feet, a wide board shaped like a skateboard (but without wheels) with the feet set across the width of the board, are known as snowboarders. In general, skiers dislike snowboarders (and vice versa) because their demeanor and style are different from those of skiing. Furthermore, the emergence of a snowboarding culture expresses an alternative set of activities, values and meanings. Some ski areas allow skiers and snowboarders to share certain slopes as long as snowboarders obey certain rules of conduct (absorb and control), other ski areas provide some slopes exclusively for snowboarders (segregate), and still others prohibit snowboarding altogether (reject and exclude).

outside its conceptual scope."[19] The coherence of any given social order ulti-mately depends on the coherence of its symbolic universe and its mainte-nance.

The institutionalization of race. Now in order to develop an understanding of the social construction of *race*, we need to approach it in terms of the Berger-Luckmann articulation of the institutional order as the human construction of social reality. This is to say that we need to understand race as an *institution* in the sense in which our authors amplify it: habitualized and reciprocal typifica-tions of actors and activities that engender a shared reality whose objectivity over time is reified. This is not to suggest that race can be viewed as an "institu-tion" alongside other institutions—for example, a race institution alongside an education institution (school) or a finance institution (bank) or a politics institu-tion (party) or a health institution (hospital). These latter institutions are exam-ples of particular institutions, established organizations with a location (usually in a building), and of course they are all human products (social constructions) with all the marks and dynamics of the Berger-Luckmann understanding of institution. Rather race can be viewed as a defining set of beliefs, values, cus-toms, practices, relationships and behaviors, as well as social patterns and structures that are made relevant to the life of a community or society. This implies that race is an institution in some ways similar, for example, to the "institution" of marriage or the family, or education, finance, politics, health care and so on.

In terms of the work of Berger and Luckmann, viewing race as an institution points us to the spheres of everyday life in which human self-expression is externalized in habitualized and typified ways. It points to the emergence, structure and ethos of the established institutions that objectify our shared world as well as the integration of this social order in the intersubjectivity of our common knowledge about reality. Furthermore, it underscores the ways the roles we perform and the typification schemes that organize and arrange them exemplify and actualize race. There is also a profound sense in which the insti-tution of race gives rise to, and is then itself legitimated by, a symbolic uni-verse—*racism*—in which the origins, history and meaning of the "institution" are validated through both its persistent and modified forms.

Language as the objective expression of consciousness has shaped this insti-tution and continues to shape it as a work in progress, a linguistic world that expresses and governs objective reality and our common knowledge of it. The institution of race—the "racial order"—has symbol systems that connect the separate spheres of everyday life (e.g., "discrimination," "integration"), seman-

---

[19]Ibid., p. 116.

tic fields that are linguistic expressions specific to a particular sphere (e.g., "equal opportunity," "affirmative action"), and relevance structures that manage the usefulness and appropriateness of language in a certain sphere ("black," "white").

To the extent that the institution of race has formed our social order and found its legitimation at all levels, including its maximal level in our symbolic universe, it is a *meta*-institution, a *totalizing* institution that precedes, encloses and is expressed concretely (or "externalized") in the particular institutions that make our objective sense and make up the reality of the social order.

In the remaining sections of this chapter I will develop these contentions more directly by focusing on the ways race has been institutionalized to become the objective reality of our sociocultural world. Then in the next chapter we will look more closely at the construction of the subjectivity of race—the formation of identity and the appropriation and internalization of the common knowledge of race.

Making Sense of Difference: The Science of Race

Many years ago Michael Polanyi observed that human thinking has the remarkable capacity to be self-validating, and that whether such thinking endures and develops socially depends on whether it is a *passionate* thinking that is shared by many and embedded in a society's cultural institutions.[20] For Americans, thinking about race is certainly passionate thinking, and it tends easily to self-validation; no one is disinterested or neutral, and there is a wealth of evidence that can be summoned to "prove" a point of view. It is also a thinking that is broadly shared and deeply embedded in the structures of our social order; not only is it the common sense, but there are linguistic and social structures that constantly authenticate our race-thinking.

But fundamentally it is a belief that there are races and that every individual is a member of one. Americans think this belief is true, but there is no empirical or rational evidence that it is so, except evidence that has been fabricated out of passionate and partisan views of reality, views that draw more on the institutionalized common sense than on a critical and competent engagement with what presents itself as reality. In a remark that anticipates Berger and Luckmann by a few years and sounds strangely like a theological definition of faith current in some Christian communities, Polanyi declared that "we must recognize belief . . . as the source of all knowledge. Tacit assent and intellectual passions, the sharing of an idiom and of a cultural heritage, affiliation to a like-minded

---

[20]Michael Polanyi, *Personal Knowledge: Towards a Post-critical Philosophy* (New York: Harper & Row, 1962), p. 215.

community: such are the impulses which shape our vision of the nature of things on which we rely for our mastery of things."[21]

The existence of human cultural and biological variation is not the cause of racism, any more than the existence of fish is the cause of fishing. Rather racism has emerged when the phenomena of human variation are linguistically objectified as "differences" to which meaning and value are assigned, and people come to believe that there are real, objective differences that have significance for sociocultural life.

Variations or differences. A good many Americans believe in race and hold to the truth that racial differences are objectively real. Whether by assent or under duress, we are initiated into the racial order by what psychologists and sociologists refer to as the process of socialization; not only are we introduced to an objective social order that precedes us, but we are oriented to that world and trained to find ourselves and our way in it. We are taught what it means to be "white," "black," "red," "brown" and "yellow," if not explicitly in the formal arenas of our socialization (family, school, church and so on), then implicitly from the activities and relationships that constitute the social order. It is not necessary to be *told* that one group is inferior or superior to another in order to believe in race and racial differences. The objectified world of race is linguistically and socially patterned in such a way that one can infer the inferiority or superiority of a particular group from actual social locations, conditions, attitudes and relationships. Explaining this racial and social stratification as "natural" (that is, rooted in biology) or "cultural" (rooted in a particular way of life) contributes to the development of a rationale for the way things are in the objective world.

One of the most discernible aspects of this objective world is that there are people groups who vary from each other along the lines of physical characteristics and sociocultural expressions. The idea of race objectifies these variations by conceiving them, then classifying them and ascribing social significance to them. The variations are real enough, but thinking about and naming them objectifies them as *differences,* and it then becomes easy not only to know them and believe in them but to recognize them when they are encountered in social reality. Variation is the fact of being varied or the condition of being various. As such, variation carries no value judgment; it is neutral (these individuals are variations of "human"). But difference is comparative and normed; it is the quality or condition of being unlike or dissimilar in nature, quality or form. As such, difference carries a value judgment because there is a criterion by which something is judged to be a departure from the norm (those people are different

---

[21]Ibid., p. 266.

from me). Race is less about the phenomenon of human variation and more
about what people believe about differences. As Ian Haney López has stated,
"Racial categories exist *only* as a function of what people believe."[22] Ideas and
beliefs have consequences, and categorically, race is a social relationship
marked by inequality that has become institutionalized.

    A drop of blood. Many scholars have analyzed the history of race thinking
and the classifications and social expressiveness that it produced. I cannot
undertake a review of that history here,[23] but we can discern the making of dif-

---

[22]Ian F. Haney López, *White by Law: The Legal Construction of Race* (New York: New York
University Press, 1996), p. 103. For pertinent discussions of the belief in the fact of race, see
Ellis Cose, *Color-Blind: Seeing Beyond Race in a Race-Obsessed World* (New York: Harper-
Collins, 1997), pp. 11-12; Joe R. Feagin and Hernán Vera, *White Racism: The Basics* (New
York: Routledge, 1995), pp. 7-15; George M. Fredrickson, *The Black Image in the White
Mind: The Debate on Afro-American Character and Destiny, 1817-1914* (Hanover, N.H.:
Wesleyan University Press, 1971), pp. 331-32, and *The Arrogance of Race: Historical Per-
spectives on Slavery, Racism and Social Inequality* (Hanover, N.H.: Wesleyan University
Press, 1988), pp. 189-205; Lucius Outlaw, "Toward a Critical Theory of 'Race,'" in *Anatomy
of Racism*, ed. David Theo Goldberg (Minneapolis: University of Minnesota Press, 1990), pp.
58-62; Andrew Hacker, *Two Nations: Black and White, Separate, Hostile, Unequal*, rev. and
exp. ed. (New York: Ballantine, 1992), pp. 4-8; David Lionel Smith, "What Is Black Culture?"
in *The House That Race Built*, ed. Wahneema Lubiano (New York: Vintage, 1998), pp. 179-
82; Kenan Malik, *The Meaning of Race: Race, History and Culture in Western Society* (New
York: New York University Press, 1996), pp. 70, 121-30; Manning Marable, *Black Liberation
in Conservative America* (Boston: South End, 1997), pp. 96-97, 185-94; Richard J. Payne, *Getting Beyond Race: The Changing American Culture* (Boulder, Colo.: Westview, 1998), pp. 31-
37; and Cornel West, *Prophesy Deliverance! An Afro-American Revolutionary Christianity*
(Philadelphia: Westminster Press, 1982), pp. 20-21, 97-98.

[23]In addition to the works cited in the previous note, readers should consult the following as
substantive treatments of the history of race thinking: Gunnar Myrdal, *An American Dilemma:
The Negro Problem and American Democracy*, 2 vols. (1944; reprint, New Brunswick, N.J.:
Transaction, 1996); Frantz Fanon, *Black Skin, White Masks* (New York: Grove, 1967); Thom-
as F. Gossett, *Race: The History of an Idea in America*, new ed. (1963; reprint, New York: Oxford University Press, 1997); Stephen Jay Gould, *The Mismeasure of Man*, rev. ed. (New York:
W. W. Norton, 1996); Ivan Hannaford, *Race: The History of an Idea in the West*, 1996);
Richard Hofstadter, *Social Darwinism in American Thought*, rev. ed. (Boston: Beacon, 1955);
Robert E. Hood, *Begrimed and Black: Christian Traditions on Blacks and Blackness* (Minne-
apolis: Fortress, 1994); Ashley Montagu, *Man's Most Dangerous Myth: The Fallacy of Race*,
6th ed. (Walnut Creek, Calif.: AltaMira, 1997); Pat Shipman, *The Evolution of Racism: Human
Differences and the Use and Abuse of Science* (New York: Simon & Schuster, 1994); and
Thomas Sowell, *Race and Culture: A World View* (New York: BasicBooks, 1994).

    Dinesh D'Souza has defended racial classification, thereby justifying race thinking, by say-
ing, "Of course racial classifications are variable in that they involve a human decision to categorize in this way rather than that, but it does not follow that these classifications do not
describe real differences in genetic composition (genotype) or its manifestations (phenotype).
Clearly human beings do differ biologically and it is difficult for scholars to avoid some system
of classification. Categorization is the link between sense perception and cognition" (*The End
of Racism: Principles for a Multiracial Society* [New York: Free Press, 1995], p. 449). Un-

ference and the construction of race in the socialization of the so-called one-drop rule.[24] This rule has functioned as the basis for racial classification in the United States, but only for persons of African descent. Quite simply, the rule stipulates that one's racial classification as "black" is determined solely by whether there is any known African ancestor anywhere in one's lineage. As the rule's name implies, all it takes for a person to be considered "black" is the presence of a drop of "black blood." Human biological science in the early eighteenth century knew nothing of genes, so this blood-myth of racial determination developed as the explanation for the biological transmission of race; it reflects what Itabari Njeri has called "the little-dab'll-do-you school of genetics."[25] European Americans defined and applied this rule at a time when they were deeply concerned to preserve the homogeneity and cohesiveness of their group over against the enslaved Africans and their descendants.

But the situation addressed by this rule of definition was a problem situation, one that called into question certain habitualized activities and had the potential to threaten the symbolic universe that legitimated slavery. The activity was the sexual intercourse between European Americans and African Americans that resulted in the birth of offspring, and the problem was the status of these children. In order to maintain the institution of slavery, legitimated as it was by the ascribed inferior status of the African American slaves, these children could not be regarded as either "white" or a mixture of "white"

---

knowingly, I think, D'Souza here has begged rather than countered the question of the social construction of race. What is the basis and significance for such a "human decision"? Are differences in genotype "real" in the same way that differences in phenotype are "real"? What moves scholars to adopt a classification system? If categorization connects perception and cognition, then does not categorization shape—objectify—what is perceived and known? In other words, D'Souza assumes that the human decision involved in classifying human beings is disinterested, without motive and neutral, that racial differences have objective reality apart from the viewer, and that human perception and knowledge is frameless or without perspective and context.

[24]The most definitive discussion of this "rule" appears in F. James Davis, *Who Is Black? One Nation's Definition* (University Park: Pennsylvania State University Press, 1991), but one can also consult Kathy Russell, Midge Wilson and Ronald Hall, *The Color Complex: The Politics of Skin Color Among African Americans* (New York: Anchor, 1992). More modest but nonetheless insightful discussions of a historical-critical nature can be found in Haney López, *White by Law*, pp. 27-28; Winthrop D. Jordan, *The White Man's Burden: Historical Origins of Racism in the United States* (New York: Oxford University Press, 1974), pp. 84-85; Payne, *Getting Beyond Race*, pp. 41-43, 136-37, 161-64; Kenneth M. Stampp, *The Peculiar Institution: Slavery in the Ante-bellum South* (New York: Vintage, 1956), pp. 193-96; James Waller, *Face to Face: The Changing State of Racism Across America* (New York: Insight, 1998), pp. 44-45; and Naomi Zack, *Thinking About Race* (Belmont, Calif.: Wadsworth, 1998), pp. 5-7.

[25]Itabari Njeri, "Sushi and Grits: Ethnic Identity and Conflict in a Newly Multicultural America," in *Lure and Loathing: Essays on Race, Identity and the Ambivalence of Assimilation*, ed. Gerald Early (New York: Penguin, 1993), p. 23.

and "black." In either of these cases, a claim—legal or otherwise—might be made on the European American parent, a claim for freedom, property, rights or privileges.

The children were thus ruled by custom and by law as "black," and if they were born to an enslaved mother, they were unquestionably slaves. To classify them otherwise would ultimately threaten the status of "white" racial identity and blur the distinctions between European Americans and African Americans, especially with regard to the economic and social benefits amassed by European Americans on the basis of their "race." The social status of the "black" parent was conveyed to the offspring, and because this was a racialized social status, the offspring was accordingly assigned to the "black race." The benefit of this assignment went only to the assigners; such children increased the number of slaves and abrogated any possibility of socioeconomic advantages for the children. For the European American slavers who dominated and controlled the social order, this assignment made sense.

In itself, the notion that one's social position and identity are conveyed from one's ancestors is not difficult to accept. Everyone enters the world in a particular social place and draws from one's forebears—even if only a single parent— a sense of familial identity. But conveyance and assignment are not the same; one can appropriate and alter a conveyed position and identity, but one can only live out or resist an assigned position and identity. The "one-drop rule" emerged as part of a universe-maintenance scheme that assigned social position and identity based not merely on ancestry but on the socially constructed status of a subordinate group. This rule presupposed the notion of racial purity and that social status as such was heritable. By defining who was and who was not "black," and by implication who was and who was not "white," the rule linguistically and socially objectified the heritability of social and racial status; the offspring of persons from different racial groups hypodescended (i.e., inherited the status of the parent from the subordinate group). To put it crudely, if European American men were not bedding African American women as a social practice, there would be no problem[26] in the institutionalized social order and its symbolic universe.

---

[26]The "problem" was multilayered. On the one hand there was involuntary sexual intercourse between "white" slavers and "black" slave women and (less frequently) intercourse between "black" male slaves and "white" females. Such conduct was illegal but rarely punished. Rather it was conventionally tolerated, if not socially condoned. On the other hand there was the evidence of this illegal activity: the birth of children. Putting aside for the moment the other layers of intrafamily relations and roles, including the "sanctity" of marriage and the "purity" of "white" women among European Americans and the unstable and ephemeral family life of African Americans resulting from slavery and the domination of slavers, the "problem" that occupied the custodians of the dominant culture was, what do we do with the kids?

What sociologists call "miscegenation," or race mixing,[27] was then in fact an institution: an externalization of humanness through habitualized activity with multiple actors and reciprocal typification. The "one-drop rule" was created precisely as an authorization for, and legitimation of, the practice of sexual intercourse between persons from the dominant and subordinate social groups. The problem was solved, and the worldview remained unchanged.

What is most remarkable about this "one-drop rule" is not that it validated a social practice or that it continued to legitimate the social subordination of African Americans during the post-Civil War era of segregation (commonly referred to as the Jim Crow era). Nor is it the fact that it assumed the objective reality of "races" and was intended to preserve racial "purity" by homogenizing one group and variegating the other. Rather what is most remarkable is that people *believed* that an African American anywhere in one's lineage made one "black."

In the application of this rule, race took on a new objectivity and became incorporated into the common sense and passed on from generation to generation. The rule was illogical and absurd. Because the child of a "black" parent and a "white" parent *looked* more like the "black" parent, the child was assigned the social and racial status of that parent. But looking "more like" is not looking "the same as." The child could just as easily have been assigned the status of the other parent. The rule meant that a "black" woman can give birth only to a "black" child, but a "white" woman can give birth to either a "black" or a "white" child. A child who had two "white" parents but one "black" grandparent and three "white" grandparents (a "quadroon"), or one "black" great-grandparent and seven "white" great-parents (an "octoroon"), was nevertheless

---

[27]Miscegenation is the mixture of different races through cohabitation, sexual relations or marriage. The conventional—commonsense—definition has to do with both interracial marriage and the production of racially mixed offspring. The term *miscegenation* entered the lexicon of race discourse only in 1864, when the word was literally created by two New York journalists to discredit the Republican Party (see Fredrickson, *Black Image,* pp. 171-74; David R. Roediger, *The Wages of Whiteness: Race and the Making of the American Working Class* [London: Verso, 1991], pp. 155-56; and Montagu, *Man's Most Dangerous Myth,* p. 538). Up to that time the term used to refer to interracial marriage was *amalgamation.* Etymologically, "miscegenation" is constructed from the Latin *miscere* (to mix) and *genus* (race). *Miscegenation* has clearly superseded *amalgamation* in the common sense; dictionary definitions of the former are exclusively about "race mixture," while one will look in vain for a dictionary definition of the latter that has anything to do with "race." But what is more significant is the fact that a word was *created* to objectify linguistically the activity of "race mixing." Naming and describing authenticates reality! For discussions of beliefs and attitudes regarding miscegenation (and its predecessor "amalgamation"), see Franz Boas, *The Mind of Primitive Man,* rev. ed. (New York: Collier, 1963), pp. 240-42; Jordan, *White Man's Burden,* pp. 74, 133; Myrdal, *American Dilemma,* 1:53-60, 102, and 2:586-87; Fredrickson, *Black Image,* pp. 89-90, 121-23, 131-32, 171-74; Montagu, *Man's Most Dangerous Myth,* p. 538; and Stampp, *Peculiar Institution,* pp. 350-61.

designated "black."[28] A "drop of black blood" overwhelmed and contaminated all the "drops of white blood," so racial descent was exclusively unidirectional; no amount of "white blood" made an African American "white."

The practice of miscegenation typified its practitioners and their offspring, all playing their respective roles. It was institutionalized as a sphere of everyday life, complete with its objectivity and legitimation through its rule. It constituted a semantic field with its peculiar language that signified and objectified human expressivity, and its relevance structure circumscribed the sense and meaning of its reality. In short, the "one-drop rule" contributed to the social construction of the "objective" reality of race.

It is also remarkable, and an indication of the ways "race" continues to be socially objectified, that Americans continue to hold to this rule that defines who is "black," and by implication who is "white." This is something of an irony and a paradox. On the one hand, the rule was formulated and imposed by slavers and segregationists to keep the races separate and maintain the status of an exploited, oppressed and marginalized group. One would expect that the abolition of slavery, the disassembling of legal segregation and the legal establishment of equality and civil rights for African Americans would result in the abandonment of the rule. But this has not happened. Among those who are committed to preserving the "one-drop rule" as a determination and objective expression of racial identity are those who now *appropriate* what was once *assigned.* What once served the exclusive interests of "whites" now serves the inclusive interests of "blacks." Granted that historically African Americans came to define themselves according to the rule as a means for establishing intragroup solidarity against oppression (you aren't one of them, they've rejected you; but you are one of us) and consolidating the development and boundaries of a distinctive sociocultural world (preserving our humanizing way of life in contradistinction to their way of life that dehumanizes us), the fact remains that this belief in the rule and the identity-forming and sociocultural

---

[28]Persons born of a "white" parent and a "black" parent were referred to as "mulatto," whose root meaning in Spanish is "hybrid." Eventually, the offspring resulting from the sexual intercourse between a "white" and a "black" of *any* mixture came to be called "colored," "Negro," or "black," and the fractionalized terms (mulatto, quadroon, octoroon, etc.) fell out of use. Lawrence Wright notes: "For most of the nineteenth century, the census reflected an American obsession with miscegenation. The color of slaves was to be specified as "B," for black, and "M," for mulatto. In the 1890 census, gradations of mulattos were further broken down into quadroons and octoroons. After 1920, however, the Census Bureau gave up on such distinctions, estimating that three-quarters of all blacks in the United States were racially mixed already, and that pure blacks would soon disappear. Hence-forth anyone with any black ancestry at all would be counted simply as black" ("One Drop of Blood," *The New Yorker,* July 24, 1994, pp. 47-48). See also Payne, *Getting Beyond Race,* pp. 169-72.

activities emanating from it are an objective expression of social reality—the social construction of race.

The paradox is that "blood" and "culture" remain inextricably linked. Biology is thought to determine, or at least influence, sociocultural expression; biological *variation* has been objectified into sociocultural *difference.* F. James Davis has observed that "although whites invented and have determinedly enforced the one-drop rule, both by custom and by law, the rule is now strongly reinforced by social controls within the black community. . . . The rule has come to be considered essential to maintaining pride in the black ethnic community."[29] The totality of those who self-identify as African Americans in the United States today does not constitute either a biologically or socioculturally homogeneous lineage, and the same is true for the totality of European Americans. Rather there is extraordinary mixture of genetic lines in all people groups in this country. It has been estimated that 70 to 90 percent of the current African American population have non-African ancestors, while estimation of non-European ancestors in the European American population runs from 6 to 21 percent.[30] Furthermore, it has been estimated that 20 to 30 percent of the genetic material distributed in the African American population has its origin in non-African populations.[31] Given the fact that genes are randomly distributed in

---

[29]Davis, *Who Is Black?* p. 168. See also p. 139; Orlando Patterson, *The Ordeal of Integration: Progress and Resentment in America's "Racial" Crisis* (Washington: D.C.: Civitas/Counterpoint, 1997), pp. 69, 71; Payne, *Getting Beyond Race,* pp. 43-44, 136-37, 161-63; Russell, Wilson and Hall, *Color Complex,* pp. 14, 74.

[30]See Lerone Bennett Jr., *Before the Mayflower: A History of Black America,* 6th rev. ed. (New York: Penguin, 1988), p. 325; Davis, *Who Is Black?* pp. 21-22; Myrdal, *American Dilemma,* 1:132-33; and Zack, *Thinking About Race,* p. 6.

[31]See Amy Gutmann, "Responding to Racial Injustice," in *Color Conscious: The Political Morality of Race,* ed. K. Anthony Appiah and Amy Gutmann (Princeton, N.J.: Princeton University Press, 1996), p. 115. Gutmann states: "Scientists calculate that the average genetic difference between two randomly chosen individuals is .2 percent (two *tenths* of one percent!) of the total genetic material. Of that genetic diversity, 85 percent can be found between neighbors. Nine of the remaining 15 percent can be found between ethnic or linguistic groups. Six percent represents differences among geographically more separate groups, such as Europeans and Asians. If Europeans and Asians are considered separate races, only .012 percent—.00012!—of their genetic differences is accounted for by their 'race.' And those genetic differences that can be accounted for have little or no scientific, let alone moral, importance" (ibid.). See also Malik, *Meaning of Race,* p. 4; and Mark Nathan Cohen, *Culture of Intolerance: Chauvinism, Class and Racism in the United States* (New Haven, Conn.: Yale University Press, 1998), pp. 11-59. Cohen has observed that "given all the genes that make a person and the amount of known (and unknown) variation in those genes, the small number that make any visible trait seem a poor basis for a 'racial' classification. Even skin color, which is widely accepted as the primary basis for 'racial' divisions, is determined by only an estimated 6-10 gene pairs out of 50,000-100,000 gene pairs that make up a human being, so it hardly seems a rational basis for classification" (p. 45).

populations, it is possible that the offspring could phenotypically inherit none or all of the genes of one of the parents.[32]

The differences that we note between and among people groups simply do not correspond to a race gene, and it is not genetic science that stipulates that human beings must be categorized according to a perceived characteristic like skin color, or hair texture, or shape of facial features. The paradox is that for those who self-identify as African Americans the rule now legitimates "black" as an institution, with self-externalization, habitualized activity, roles, typificatory schemes, common sense, symbol systems, semantic fields, relevance structures and a reified symbolic universe that needs maintenance. "Black" is an objectified social order, bounded by a selective lineage, perceived and valuated characteristics and sociocultural expressivity.

But the same can and must be said for "white." It too is an institution with all these accouterments. More important, it is indicative that the rule is believed and followed when European Americans regard as "black" someone with *any degree* of the physical characteristics or traits associated with persons of African descent and relate to that person in ways that externalize racist attitudes, beliefs, values and perceptions. It matters little how African Americans identify themselves, or how varied their skin tone may appear, or however present or absent other supposed characteristics may be. European Americans will visually, categorically, socially and racially classify *anyone* with *any* such features as "black" and more often than not relate to them on this basis. European Americans notice "shades of black," but the persons so perceived are still classified in consciousness as "black"; lighter skin tone and the relative absence of putative African features do not make one "more white" but rather "less black." By so defining persons, and *making sense* of them, and relating to them in a way oriented by this definition and sense, European Americans continue to objectify a social order they produced, albeit with less overt forms of domination and oppression. There has been, and there remains, a "white" institution.

Biological determinism. The science of race, or theorizing about racial "types," followed the institution of slavery in the seventeenth century and sought to demonstrate that biological differences were the basis or cause of sociocultural differences. Scientific inquiry in the eighteenth and nineteenth centuries was thought to be empirical and impartial (what you see is what you get). Indeed it is part of the common sense in our social order that science is the

---

[32]Both my mother and father had thick black hair, but only one of their six children has black hair. I am the only one to inherit my mother's brown eyes, which she inherited from her father and mother. Four of my siblings have blue eyes, inherited from our father; we don't know where the other sibling's eye color came from. None of us have complexions that resemble either of our parents' (though two of us have been generously gifted with Mother's freckles).

most accurate and credible source of knowledge concerning the physical or "natural" world. In terms of "races" as the "natural varieties" of humankind, race scientists like Carolus Linnaeus (1707-1778), Johann Friedrich Blumenbach (1752-1840) and Joseph Arthur de Gobineau (1816-1882) claimed that human morphology (form and structure) determines human abilities and temperament. This view, known as biological determinism, amounts to the belief that particular physical characteristics as well as mental ability, behavior and the capacity to develop sociocultural life are biologically heritable (i.e., genetically transmitted).[33]

Race science collected morphological features and behaviors and categorized them in a hierarchy of "natural" types. Under the influence of Charles Darwin's theory of evolution and its application to social worlds, this view presumed a continuum of the human and animal world in such a way that the formation of human community was governed by "natural" law; the supposed difference between humans and animals was a matter of degree and not of kind. By contending that social development is rooted in biological development, the social world of any particular racial type could be viewed as "natural," subject to the evolutionary law of natural selection and categorized according to its position on the evolutionary scale.

What resulted from this science was the conviction that human morphology is indicative of ability and that differences in characteristics and sociocultural expressivity are explained by biology.[34] This "science," in effect, theoretically created and practically legitimated a racial and social stratification by locating the hierarchy not in society but in "nature." Superior racial types develop superior culture, *naturally.* Social Darwinism, as this view is known, explained differences not only in morphology and physiology but in culture as well. The biological world of nature, including humankind, was seen as having evolved from the most elementary to the more sophisticated forms, and some "types" of humans remained (or were arrested) in earlier stages of the evolutionary scale. Scientists

---

[33]On biological determinism, see, e.g., Montagu, *Man's Most Dangerous Myth,* pp. 31, 117; Gould, *Mismeasure of Man,* pp. 26, 52, 355; and Payne, *Getting Beyond Race,* p. 45.

[34]A story abroad in my family, told by my maternal grandfather and mother, remained an enigma to me until I did the research for this book. The gist of the story was that each of my mother's suitors had to present themselves to her father for approval, and it was not until my father so presented himself that a suitor gained the desired approval. The criterion for approval, confessed by my grandfather, was the shape of the suitor's head; he believed that there is a correlation between the shape of a head and the owner's character. The science that posited and developed this belief is known as "phrenology," a subdiscipline of race science, now thoroughly discredited. Though I can find no books in my grandfather's library that deal with phrenology, I remain discomfited by his declaration that "everyone knew this to be so" (i.e., this "fact" was common sense).

and social theorists linguistically designated those whom they judged to be slower or aborted in their physical-cultural development as "primitive," while those (like themselves) who had advanced to higher levels were "civilized."[35]

The "one-drop rule" and the objective expression of race science have so effectively shaped our construal of reality that we believe the "facts" of race have been established beyond dispute. If not explicitly, then certainly at an intuitive level, followers of the rule tend to interpret the phenomenon of human physical and cultural variability in terms of a link between biology and culture. Rarely does it occur to them that a position in, and commitment to, an existing racial order may have conspired to move these scientists to develop a universe-maintaining legitimation for that order (what you get is what you *want*). As Payne has noted, "Science often functions to consolidate and institutionalize ideas that are consistent with society's dominant interests."[36]

What I am calling "race science" or theorizing about racial "types" is not merely passé as a field of research in the scientific community but has been utterly repudiated by the vast majority of biological, anthropological, physiological and genetic scientists. Few are they who continue to argue for biological determinism in any of its conceivable forms.[37] Because the refinement of theo-

---

[35]The application of Darwin's theory of evolution (natural selection, struggle for existence, survival of the fittest, etc.) to sociocultural development is also unidirectional: from nature to culture. The stage of any particular sociocultural world is therefore construed as "natural," and as such subject to evolutionary development from lower to higher forms. But these sociocultural forms are related to the evolution of physical—racial—types. No physical or sociocultural form evolves of necessity; it is rather a "struggle" in which only the "fit" survive. No better analysis of social Darwinism exists than Hofstadter's *Social Darwinism*. But see also Ivan A. Beals, *Our Racist Legacy: Will the Church Resolve the Conflict?* (Notre Dame, Ind.: Cross Cultural, 1997), pp. 123-35; Gossett, *Race*, pp. 144-75; Shipman, *Evolution of Racism*, pp. 92-133; Malik, *Meaning of Race*, pp. 90-100; and Hannaford, *Race*, pp. 277-368.

[36]Payne, *Getting Beyond Race*, p. 44. I do not think Payne's use of the words *consolidate* and *institutionalize* here is fortuitous, though he may not necessarily have the work of Berger and Luckmann in mind. Nevertheless, his contention that science can both create and reflect popular social construals (i.e., the common sense) draws attention to the ideological agenda of "science."

[37]Franz Boas was the first to lay down the requirement that biological determinism would have to meet in order for its theory to be proved true. He declared in 1938, at the beginning of the end for such race theories, "If the defenders of race theories prove that a certain kind of behavior is hereditary and wish to explain in this way that it belongs to a racial type they would have to prove that the particular kind of behavior is characteristic of all the genetic lines composing the race, that considerable variations in the behavior of different genetic lines composing the race do not occur. This proof has never been given and all the known facts contradict the possibility of uniform behavior of all the individuals and genetic lines composing the race" (*Mind of Primitive Man*, p. 227). The most recent attempt to meet Boas's challenge was the work of Richard Herrnstein and Charles Murray, published as *The Bell Curve: Intelligence and Class Structure in American Life* (New York: Free Press, 1994). Their attempt failed to persuade critics of biological determinism, but for those who already held to it their attempt was

ries of racial types followed the institutionalization of slavery and the social domination of African Americans, and because no link between biology and human expressivity and culture has ever been established, we can only regard the "one-drop rule" and the ideology of biological determinism (and the science that spawned it) as "pseudo-science," or social philosophy, but in any case as preeminently a universe-maintenance scheme legitimating the racialized social order.

Typifying Actors and Activities: The Habit of Race

Our lives unfold from day to day in our interactions with others. The spheres of our everyday life involve people, places and activities. Some of these are familiar and comfortable, others less so. For the most part, however, the spheres that make up our everyday life are experienced as stable, if not always tranquil. Occasionally there is some dissonance, and maybe even change, but basically the spheres endure; they are there, and we experience them as real. We have no contact or interaction with others outside some kind of "sphere," involving activities of one sort or another. Indeed it is difficult to imagine a human experience or mode of living that does not occur in relation to a sphere. These spheres are the "institutionalization" of our lives, the expression of our humanity and our sociocultural world, and as such they organize and structure both the interaction with others and the activities that take place. This happens primarily through what Berger and Luckmann have called "typificatory schemes," and just as there is no human interaction outside a sphere, so there is no sphere without a typificatory scheme. In fact, any given sphere with its persons, places and activities will be layered with several schemes, some of which complement one another, others of which conflict and compete with one another. This phenomenon is what we need now to explore, because the layers of complementary and conflictive typificatory schemes not only form and objectify the sociocultural order but—more important—constitute the social construction of race and racism in the spheres of everyday life.

The logic of stereotypes, their construction and use. In the conversations and literature on race and racism, it is not at all uncommon to find discussions of stereotype, prejudice and discrimination. In the lexicon of race discourse, *prejudice* and *stereotype* are often used interchangeably, and *discrimination* is viewed as prejudicial or preferential behavior. It is unusual to find agreement on what these terms signify and how and where they originate; everyone seems to have his or her own definition. Part of the problem is that these varying definitions are really linguistic expressions that objectify

---

most successful—it was a legitimation of a symbolic universe.

differing experiences and their significance. Nevertheless, it will be useful to delineate how these terms are understood and used so that we can then develop an alternative rendering, one that reframes them in relation to typificatory schemes to show more directly how they contribute to the social construction of race and racism. In other words, I want to show how "stereotype," "prejudice" and "discrimination" are intrinsic and necessary to the typificatory schemes that objectify—organize, structure and thereby real-ize—the spheres of everyday life, including the objective expression of race and racism.[38] I will go beyond the Berger-Luckmann construal of typificatory schemes, taking our analysis more directly into the arena of race and racism as social constructs in ways they have not.

A stereotype may be considered a set of beliefs one holds about a particular group. For example, Italians love pasta, truckers work long hours, lawyers are unscrupulous, doctors are rich, judges are impartial, teachers are patient, Native Americans are drunks, cabdrivers are racist, roses are red—huh? yup!—apples are sweet. We recognize that these beliefs are overgeneralized and exaggerated, but they nonetheless are illustrative of the fact that we do have images or pictures—beliefs—in our minds when we think about the particular group. Because we have learned or developed a stereotype, these images or beliefs enter consciousness as a result of a variety of stimuli: seeing or interacting with a group member, reading or hearing about the group or a group member, remembering an encounter or something previously learned, read or heard.

---

[38]Much of the literature simply does not give a definition of these terms, as though their meaning were "common knowledge." Other works do offer a shorthand definition, but for the most part these focus only on the negative aspects of stereotypes, prejudices and discrimination, and then exclusively in terms of their application to so-called ethnic or racial minorities. Still other works provide disciplined analysis of the phenomena, especially in relation to their rational and psychological (i.e., irrational and dysfunctional) dimensions. But here again, these are assessed *only* negatively and in terms of their application by members of one people group to members of other people groups. Furthermore, they leave unanswered the prior question of whether and to what extent these are useful, important and necessary functions in our engaging with and constructing—objectifying—the spheres of our shared world—that is, whether they are *normal,* or *regular,* or—as I contend—typical. I am going to argue for a quite different understanding of these phenomena, one that moves away from conventional race discourse but certainly not toward D'Souza's notion of "rational discrimination" and the legitimacy of stereotypes and prejudice (see his *End of Racism: Principles for a Multiracial Society* [New York: Free Press, 1995], pp. 24, 156-59, 245-87, 525-70). Nevertheless, the most significant analyses can be found in Gordon Allport, *The Nature of Prejudice* (Reading, Mass.: Addison-Wesley, 1954), pp. 165-204; Thomas F. Pettigrew, introduction to *Prejudice,* ed. Thomas F. Pettigrew et al. (Cambridge, Mass.: Belknap/Harvard University Press, 1982), pp. 1-29; Paul M. Sniderman and Thomas Piazza, *The Scar of Race* (Cambridge, Mass.: Belknap/Harvard University Press, 1993), pp. 25-65; Montagu, *Man's Most Dangerous Myth,* pp. 225-52; and Waller, *Face to Face,* pp. 25-42, 171-89.

But notice that there are two aspects to the stereotype. First there is the *category* that identifies the group (e.g., Italians, truckers, lawyers); then there is the *attribution* that associates a particular behavior, characteristic, condition or quality with the group (e.g., love pasta, work long hours, are unscrupulous). To hold that persons in category *X* express attribution *Y* is to believe a stereotype; there must be both a category and an attribution. The stereotype is then *localized* when the attribution is applied and used to interpret—make sense of—a particular member or members of the category group. The stereotype is *activated* when one's demeanor and actions toward a group member or members are shaped or influenced by the presumed truth of the stereotype. One can believe a stereotype without localizing and activating it, and one can believe and localize a stereotype without activating it.

Now stereotypes are quite useful. In fact, like assumptions, we need them and use them all the time. Overgeneralized and exaggerated as they may be, stereotypes are important imaginative and cognitive tools that help us deal with the complexity of our world by simplifying and managing the data we take in. They are a way of homogenizing an aggregate or group, what Gordon Allport calls a "cognitive shortcut"[39] and what bell hooks calls a "form of representation."[40] Thus they entail what Gunnar Myrdal describes as a "restriction and distortion of knowledge."[41] (I do not and cannot know every Italian and every lawyer, but I can know something about Italians and lawyers.) To the extent that a stereotype is broadly shared among or believed by people, it can be said that the stereotype is common knowledge (i.e., part of the common sense).

But notice also that there is another aspect to a stereotype. The examples above reflect attributions that are generally regarded as *positive* (love, impartial, patient), *negative* (unscrupulous, drunks, racist) or *neutral* (rich, work, red, sweet). This third aspect is the implicit or explicit moral, aesthetic or social *judgment* regarding the attribution. To the extent that these judgments reflect the common sense or what is taken to be common knowledge, they can be said to be grounded and expressed in the beliefs, attitudes and values

---

[39]Allport, *Nature of Prejudice,* p. 28.

[40]In her article "Representations of Whiteness in the Black Imagination" in *Black on White: Black Writers on What It Means to Be White,* ed. David R. Roediger (New York: Schocken, 1998), bell hooks goes on to say: "Like fictions, [stereotypes] are created to serve as substitutions, standing in for what is real. They are there not to tell it like it is but to invite and encourage pretense. They are a fantasy, a projection onto the Other that makes them less threatening. Stereotypes abound when there is distance. They are an invention, a pretense that one knows when the steps that would make real knowing possible cannot be taken or are not allowed" (p. 44).

[41]Myrdal, *American Dilemma,* 1:42.

of a culture.[42] When a stereotype is localized and activated, this judgment is passed on the individual, just as it is passed on the group as a whole in the stereotypical belief, but from a greater distance and with greater anonymity.

Please allow—and forgive—this illustration: If I judge that drunks are morally repugnant, I am likely to regard any particular drunk as immoral. If I believe that Native Americans (category) are drunks (attribution), I will *judge* them as a group to be immoral (judgment). If I encounter a Native American and localize and activate the stereotype, I have not only judged him or her as immoral, based on attributions associated with the group, but I have *objectified* my sense of moral repugnance, regardless of whether he or she is actually drunk. Here I have erred, with repression, on the side of disparagement.

On the other hand, if I judge drunks to be morally repugnant but *disbelieve* the stereotype, then being morally repulsed by a drunk Native American is not the localization and activation of the stereotype; I am not repulsed by a drunk Native American *because* he or she is a Native American but rather because he or she is *actually* drunk (i.e., individual-specific behavior). Additionally, if I disbelieve the stereotype, I will not be surprised when I encounter a sober Native American (it is only believers in the stereotype who are amazed—and sometimes dismayed—when they meet a group member who doesn't "fit" or objectify the stereotype).

There is, nevertheless, a stereotype at work in this latter illustration. But the stereotype to which I am subscribing is "drunks are repugnant," and I subscribe to it because I have been socialized (conditioned) to think and believe (judge) that inebriation is a character flaw, socially unacceptable and not in the interest of the public welfare. In this case, my judgment and sense of repugnance are objectified by the *fact* of drunkenness, a condition in which *anyone* can be by choice or addiction.

On yet another hand, if I judge patience to be a positive virtue, then when I encounter a teacher I am likely to localize and activate a stereotype ("teachers

---

[42]While he does not discuss "stereotype" in his book *No Place for Truth: Or, Whatever Happened to Evangelical Theology?* (Grand Rapids, Mich.: Eerdmans, 1993), David F. Wells offers a definition of *culture* that illustrates how stereotypes are cultural phenomena and become embedded in the common sense. He uses the term "to signify the set of values, the network of beliefs that are institutionalized in a people's collective life and that govern their behavior. Culture, then, is the outward discipline in which inherited meanings and morality, beliefs and ways of behaving are preserved. *It is that collectively assumed scheme of understanding that defines both what is normal and what meanings we should attach to public behavior.* It is what reveals eccentrics for their eccentricity, rebels for their rebellion, no-gooders for not doing good. *It is what tells us what owning a Cadillac means, what significance being gay has, how we can measure someone whom we learn is a doctor, an engineer, a street artist, or homeless.* It is what gives us our inner coordinates, the markers beside the trail that, from infancy onward, slowly leads us to civilized life" (p. 167, emphasis mine).

are patient") in such a way that I objectify my sense of patience, regardless of whether the teacher is in fact patient. Here I have erred, with aggrandizement, on the side of generosity. Thus the stereotype functions because an evaluative judgment has been formed prior to its association with a category and its attributions.

Here we meet with the phenomenon of prejudgment or prejudice. The undercurrent of a stereotype is the prior social, moral and/or aesthetic judgment passed on a behavior, characteristic, condition or quality. Consider drunkenness and patience. Neither of these exist as such. Rather they are abstractions from concrete expressions; we abstract drunkenness from the condition and behaviors of inebriated people, and patience from that of persevering people. Or, to use Joel Kovel's notions, drunkenness and patience are *primary* symbols, and as such they do not refer to an actual object. But when drunkenness and patience are associated with, attributed to or expressed by actual persons, they become materialized *secondary* symbols (objective expressions of primary symbols). It can then be said that the judgment passed is a *symbolic* judgment, because it is passed on both the primary symbol (abstraction—"drunkenness") and the secondary symbol (its concrete expressivity or objectivity—"this drunk").

But note that categories are also abstractions, artificially defined classes of objects, and as such they are also primary symbols. "Native Americans" and "teachers" do not exist as such; rather they are primary symbols. Thus any particular Native American or teacher can be viewed as a secondary symbol, the concrete expression of Native Americanness or teacherness. When a symbolic judgment is passed, for example, on a characteristic, *and* that characteristic is then attributed to a category, what you have is a twofold symbolization (abstraction and concretion of both category and attribute) to which a twofold symbolic judgment applies. It is rather like a syllogism that can be expressed this way:

> Patience is good (judgment of characteristic/primary symbol).
>
> Teachers are patient (characteristic attributed to category/primary symbol, or *stereotype*).
>
> Ergo, teachers are good (judgment of category/primary symbol).

This twofold symbolic judgment is the *pre*judgment embedded in, and carried by, the stereotype, and this symbolic judgment can be favorable or for something (positive), unfavorable or against something (negative), or indifferent (neutral). Stereotypes are symbol complexes, the symbolization of a category and its attributes that contain symbolic judgements (both the category and the attributes are judged symbolically). Thus stereotypes are *inherently* prejudicial, in that they already have attached a moral, aesthetic or social judgment to an attribute and a category.

Now when a stereotype is localized (i.e., attribution is applied and used to interpret a member or members of the category group), it will flow something like this:

Teachers are patient (attribution of prejudged characteristic to a category, or *stereotype*).

You are a teacher (attribution of prejudged category to an individual).

Ergo, you are patient (attribution of prejudgment to individual).

The localization and activation of a stereotype amounts to the realization or objective expression of both the category and the attribute. When I believe a stereotype, I assent to its twofold symbolic judgment (I judge patience as good and attribute patience and goodness to teachers as a group). When I encounter a teacher, I apply this stereotype, not because he or she is patient (I do not know this) but because he or she is a teacher (i.e., member of a category group, or *one* of a *kind*). I will distinguish, regard and act toward this teacher as though he or she is in fact patient because I have prejudged him or her as a way of making sense of him or her; I will exercise discriminating judgment and express discriminating behavior.

If over time I discover that this teacher is in fact patient, the stereotype and its symbolic judgments will have been confirmed. On the other hand, if I do not find the teacher to be patient, then I have four options: (1) I can continue to believe the stereotype and think that this person is not really a teacher but only feigning teacherness. (2) I can grant that this teacher is an exception to the rule, thinking that he or she is not a "typical" teacher, thereby continuing to believe the slightly modified but still-ruled stereotype. (3) I can disbelieve or abandon the stereotype altogether, in which case I am left with no cognitive or imaginative way to make sense of teachers as a group. (4) I can formulate a new stereotype such as "teachers are *im*patient," in which case I have strayed from the common sense. There are two things I cannot do: (1) believe an inherently contradictory stereotype (teachers are patient and impatient) or (2) subdivide a stereotype (some teachers are patient, and some teachers are impatient). Both of these options are excluded because the first one makes no sense and the second begs the question of which one will in fact prevail in the encounter with a teacher.

Thus what goes by the name of "prejudice" is a belief in and attitude toward the symbolically judged attributes assigned to a category group. Stereotypes are inherently prejudicial and discriminatory in that they reflect moral, aesthetic and/or social judgments of behavior, characteristics, conditions and qualities that are not individual- or group-specific but are expressed in many ways by many people in many situations. When a previously judged behavior is assigned to an aggregate group (stereotype), localized to group members so as to define them (application of prejudgment) and activated by attitudinal and behavioral expression that corresponds to the judgment (discrimination), it can be said that one has not only manifested prejudice and discrimination but *objectified* the category, its assigned attributes and the symbolic judgments in a sphere of everyday life. In short, one has real-ized the stereotype.

The schemes in everyday life. Let us now turn our attention to typificatory schemes, analyzing their components to discern the ways they contribute to the social construction—institutionalization—of race and racism by the convergence of schemes that are complementary and conflictive. All social interaction takes place in spheres of everyday life, and the basic model of social interaction is the face-to-face encounter in which persons have immediate experience of others. This interaction, as has been noted, entails the execution of a typificatory scheme of one kind or another. Perhaps a list of such schemes, by way of illustration, will stimulate thought to construct their everyday sphere and imagination to lay out the sorts of roles, conduct and rules that express them: student—teacher, patient—doctor, wife—husband, child—parent, employee—supervisor, customer—salesclerk, tenant—landlord, borrower—loan officer, home buyer—real estate agent, friend—friend, neighbor—neighbor. Each of these is a type of role in a particular typificatory scheme that shapes interaction in a sphere of everyday life.[43]

All stereotypes, their prejudices and discriminations, take place only in a sphere, and thus only as components of typificatory schemes that objectify human consciousness, interaction and social reality. There are literally thousands of stereotypes, and they all work—that is, have a function and serve a purpose. None of them are literally or universally true. Some of them are positive, others negative, and still others neutral. The function of *all* of them is to enable us to apprehend and make sense of objects or persons by grasping and interpreting the particular in terms of the general. As such, they are guides to

---

[43]What Berger and Luckmann call "typificatory schemes" Edward Hall refers to as "situational frames." He describes them this way: "There are hundreds if not thousands of different situational frames in cultures as complex as our own. These frames are made up of situational dialects, material appurtenances, situational personalities, and behavior patterns that occur in recognized settings and are appropriate to specific situations. Some common settings and situations are: greeting, working, eating, bargaining, fighting, governing, making love, going to school, cooking and serving meals, hanging out, and the like. The situational frame is the smallest viable unit of a culture that can be analyzed, taught, transmitted, and handed down as a complete entity. Frames contain linguistic, kinesic, proxemic, temporal, social, material, personality, and other components" (Edward T. Hall, *Beyond Culture* [New York: Anchor, 1976], p. 129).

discerning and engaging spheres of everyday life and the roles and rules of their typificatory schemes, thus shaping our anticipations, expectations and conduct. Again, there is no human interaction outside a sphere, and there is no sphere without a typificatory scheme. Stereotypes are intrinsic to these schemes, and their purpose is to objectify social reality. We need now to look more closely at typificatory schemes to clarify how and to what extent they construct race and racism.

Generally speaking, there are seven components that constitute the structure of a typificatory scheme: sphere, types, roles, protocol, apprehension, interpretation and power.

1. *Sphere.* A sphere is not a place, though it may have spatial dimensions. It is, rather, a distinctive set of conditions and circumstances that surround, characterize and affect human life and interaction. In this sense a sphere can be viewed as a bounded environment with a characteristic ethos, demarcated by the nature and extent of the exhibition of particular attitudes, values, knowledge and practices thought to be appropriate for interaction. Typificatory schemes are situated in a sphere. Indeed they are sphere-specific; one might consider a scheme as an event that takes place in a sphere. Because schemes are transportable, migrating from place to place, spheres can be duplicated; the student—teacher scheme can be eventuated in a classroom, log cabin, bus terminal, mountainside, chairlift, in which case the sphere has been "placed," or incarnated in a physical space. But a sphere is not identical with its setting, even though there are many physical spaces that have been designed to accommodate a particular sphere (such as retail store, physician's office, schoolhouse).

Yet even within these accommodating places, any number of spheres may also be engendered when different typificatory schemes characterize the social interaction (for example, student—teacher scheme takes place in a retail store). In short, a sphere is an environment and ethos that make possible the expressivity or objectivity of social interaction. But note: spheres are the occasions and places for expressing behaviors, characteristics, conditions and qualities that are influenced by and correlative to the particular scheme that takes place.

2. *Types.* Types are the characteristic actors and activities that distinguish a particular sphere. They refer to the doers and what is done. "Student" is a type of actor, and "reading" is a type of activity that students do. To the extent that a person is doing this, it can be said that he or she is an actor typified as "student," engaged in an activity typified as "reading." Or to put it another way, a student typically reads, because the activity of reading typifies an actor as student.

Now obviously not everyone who "reads" is a student; neither does every "student" read. But the point here is that typical actors do certain things, and typical things characterize certain actors when these are shaped by a typificatory scheme and eventuated in a sphere. If a person is reading because a teacher assigned it, that person typifies "student." If a person is reading for enjoyment or personal interest, that person cannot be said to typify "student," though he or she may be typifying an actor and activity in another sphere (e.g., the sphere of entertainment or personal enrichment, both of which are growth industries). Doing an activity makes an actor anywhere, but doing a *typical* activity makes one a *typical* actor when both are situated in a sphere and its typificatory scheme. In short, typical activities objectify actors as types in social interaction. But note: types of actors are *categories* and types of activities are *behaviors*.

3. *Roles*. We can describe roles quite simply as the characteristic and expected behaviors that are associated with types of actors and activities.[44] Roles are particular, and they are delineated in relation to each other. Allowing for variations in style and expressiveness, roles nevertheless are the "parts" we "play" as actors in a sphere; the role of "mother" as a type, for example, can be played in a variety of ways. Just like actors on the stage or cinema, we each have an understanding not only of our part but of the parts played by others. We know what to say and do, and we anticipate saying and doing our part. We know what the other is expected to say and do, and we anticipate the other's saying and doing his or her part. In other words, our interaction is scripted by our roles and our participation in the scheme is oriented by cues.

Roles delimit the range of possibilities for actors and activities. The person playing the student role in the student—teacher scheme can play this role in many ways, but he or she cannot simultaneously play the teacher role. Nor would it make any sense for that person to play a tenant role in the student—teacher scheme. While a person may play many roles in various schemes (doctor at clinic, customer at service station, member at church, spouse at home) and various roles in the same scheme (person is doctor, supervisor, businessperson, office tenant at clinic), roles are nevertheless sphere-specific in that a particular role can be played only in a particular sphere.

Furthermore, as Mark Nathan Cohen has noted, roles are either *achieved* through one's playing of other roles in other schemes, as when the role of "senator" is achieved through the role of "candidate" in the political sphere, or

---

[44]In his book *Invitation to Sociology: A Humanist Perspective* (New York: Anchor, 1963) Peter Berger states: "A role . . . may be defined as a typified response to a typified expectation. Society has predefined the fundamental typology. To use the language of the theater, from which the concept of role is derived, we can say that society provides the script for all the *dramatis personae*" (p. 95).

ascribed by birth or social status, as when the role of "man" is ascribed by being born male, "sister" by having siblings or "expert" by peers.[45] Roles can also be appropriated *voluntarily* or *involuntarily*, as when a person signs a rental agreement and takes on the role of "tenant," or when an automobile accident produces a "victim."

Because roles have to do with characteristic and expected behaviors, they lend themselves quite easily to reification. This occurs especially when a person elects to self-define as a particular role. One not only *identifies with* the role but identifies oneself as having *become* the role: "I am not just *playing* a doctor; I *am* a doctor." Such reification is evident in the inability to vacate the role in other schemes and spheres, as when a person says to a person playing a "cashier" role, "Hurry up! I am a physician, and my time is too important for you to waste it by dillydallying around!" Or a person recovering from substance abuse tells the person playing the "counselor" role after having been found to be using again, "But I am a *victim,* so I can't be blamed!" Generally reification has occurred when one particular role dictates a person's expressiveness in multiple spheres and schemes. In short, roles are delimited and objectified in the interactive behaviors that are expected by players in schemes and spheres. But note: roles are *categorical,* and behavior consistent with the interactive roles in a scheme is both anticipated and expected and as such *prescribed* by the role played.

4. *Protocol.* Each typificatory scheme is structured by a protocol, or rules of conduct and etiquette. There is a sense of ceremony that is built into a sphere's scheme: You are ushered by a nurse to the examining room, where you wait patiently for the doctor to come to you; you bought this book before you read it, but you bought your restaurant meal after you consumed it; the salesclerk asks, "May I help you?" when you enter the store; not only do you sign a lease before you move into the apartment, but you pay the rent on time afterward; the teacher gives the examination after you have read the assignment.

This protocol warrants the expectations of each role player in the interaction and governs the behaviors in the particular situation. It is constituted by a set of rules that are either implicit and somewhat intuitive or explicit and codified in regulations, but in any case protocol stipulates what is acceptable and appropriate behavior and, by implication, what kinds of behaviors are otherwise. I expect my physician to be attentive and inquisitive and to demonstrate competence in dispensing medical advice; he can ask me anything as a "doctor" as long as it is related to my health. On the other hand, he expects me to be honest and responsive and to be compliant in taking his advice; I can say or ask any-

---

[45]Cohen, *Culture of Intolerance,* p. 84.

thing as "patient" as long as it is health-related. If either of us acts differently, we have broken the rules of the patient—doctor scheme; our behavior is unacceptable or inappropriate to the scheme.

In short, protocol establishes the customary patterns and boundaries of interactive behavior through which the role players express or objectify themselves in particular ways in a sphere of everyday life. But note: protocol is a *judgment* on behavior to the extent that it limits, encourages or prescribes particular behaviors.

5. *Apprehension.* A scheme is initiated by apprehension. Each person perceives, becomes conscious of and understands the other as a type playing a role in the scheme. Immediately the curtain opens, the play begins, and the interaction unfolds along scripted lines and actions. The actors are mindful of what they say and do as they play out their roles in the interaction, and each regards the other as a manifestation of a type. Not only does each person expect the other to play his or her role, but in the interaction each also perceives the conduct of the other as typifying that role. There is, in a sense, a double perception in the scheme's apprehension: the other is perceived as a type (you are "doctor"), and the other's conduct is perceived as typical (what you say and do is "doctored"). In other words, the sphere and its scheme authorize and prescribe the particular perceptions each has of the other.

It is possible to apprehend the other as several types simultaneously, but the scheme designates which type is to prevail. For example, when the person enters the examining room wearing a lab coat and carrying a folder, I immediately apprehend this one as *doctor* because I know doctors wear and carry these. I may also apprehend this one as a *supervisor, manager* and maybe even *golfer,* but I do not interact with this person as a manifestation of these types because they are not the *typical* role in this scheme; my apprehension of this actor is delegated by the scheme at work in this sphere, and these other apprehensions are irrelevant to the scheme.

But in addition to apprehending the type and its characteristic expressions in typified conduct and actions, one apprehends the *person* who is playing the role and whose conduct typifies the role. One apprehends the behaviors, characteristics, conditions and qualities of the person who is acting, and these are the means whereby a particular person manifests the typified role. I notice that the "doctor" is a woman with short hair, writes left-handed, half-closes one eye when listening, and raises her voice inflection at the end of a sentence or question. Thus the process of apprehending the other as a type in a scheme requires prior experience, knowledge or opinion regarding the type and its typical behaviors. It also entails apprehending the particularity of the person who typifies the role.

In short, apprehension involves recognizing a typifying actor and typified activities as the manifestation or objectivity of a role expressed idiosyncratically by a particular person. But note: apprehension of the other as a type assumes prior familiarity with the type, and this assumption functions as a prejudgment that shapes and influences the construal of the person playing the role as well as the role itself and how it is played.

6. *Interpretation.* In apprehending a type, one is necessarily engaged in the interpretation of the conduct by means of which the other expresses his or her role. Again, allowing for a variety of stylized behaviors in a type, one nevertheless experiences and interprets what the other is doing and saying in order to determine whether and to what extent it is consistent with and appropriate to the typification. Linguistic and behavioral expression are sphere-oriented, and even to some degree sphere-specific. This means that some things can be said and done in a certain sphere because the scheme allows, calls for or requires them; they are relevant, appropriate and expressive. These same things cannot be said and done in a different sphere, because there they would be inconsistent and inappropriate. It is appropriate for a doctor to ask about one's sexual activity, no matter how uncomfortable it may be to discuss this. But it is not appropriate for the salesclerk so to ask, regardless of how comfortable one may be. Thus the act of interpretation in a sphere's typificatory scheme involves discerning and assessing behaviors relative to a scheme's types, role-playing and protocol.

But interpretation also involves discerning and assessing the person whose conduct expresses the role. Stylized and sphere-oriented as behavior may be, it is nonetheless expressed by *someone* who brings the totality of his or her individuality to the role. This means that the role player's personal behaviors, characteristics, conditions and qualities are the material out of which a typified role is constructed and expressed; this is true of both stage actors and sphere actors. Anyone can play the role of customer, but "customer" does not exist except as it is embodied in and expressed by a person in a customer-oriented scheme. Furthermore, just as one interprets the particular behavior of the other relative to its consistency and appropriateness to the sphere's scheme, so each actor interprets his or her own role in the scheme by means of the way one understands and expresses it. Thus each person self-interprets in the manner of expression, and each interprets the other's manner of expression.

In short, interpretation involves the recognition and evaluation of the behaviors by means of which particular persons embody and express—objectify—themselves in social interaction. But note: interpretation of the self and the other entails an *explanation and legitimation* of the meaning of behaviors as typified and characteristic self-expression.

7. *Power.* Finally, typificatory schemes are permeated with and structured by power. Like types and roles, power as such does not exist. Rather it is expressed behaviorally and structurally in a sphere through its modes of interaction. This is to say that power is expressed as a relation, more specifically as a *social relation*, and the interaction moderated by typificatory schemes is constantly criss-crossed with power relations and their expressions. Generally speaking, any given scheme will be characterized by the expression of three levels of power: the capacity (1) to perform a typified role effectively, (2) to exercise influence, control or authority consistent with the roles and rules of the scheme, and (3) to effect change in oneself, the other and/or the situation of the sphere itself.

Without unnecessarily complicating the matter, it is nevertheless important to point out that the capacity to express power is derived from a variety of sources and manifests itself in distinguishable degrees. First of all, there is *personal* power, which we might understand as the inherent physical, psychological, emotional and spiritual resources available to capacitate a person; and there is *social* power, referring to capacities that are acquired by endowment (given) or assumption (taken), accomplishment (earned) or exemption (excused). Then there is *absolute* power, understood as unlimited and unaccountable capacity; and there is *relative* power, qualified and subject to challenge in its expressions. There is also power that is *negotiable,* or capacities that are transferable from one to another; and there is power that is *nonnegotiable,* or capacities that cannot be mediated or yielded to another.

Typificatory schemes, played out in a particular sphere of everyday life, are situations that eventuate power relations. Indeed some schemes are characterized primarily if not exclusively by a power relation (e.g., athletic competition, employee evaluation for wage increase, applying for mortgage loan). In any scheme, the interaction of the role-players will be structured in such a way that the scheme presupposes, establishes or alters the personal-social, absolute-relative and negotiable-nonnegotiable power relation (for example, power relations are *presupposed* in prisoner-jailer and soldier-officer schemes, *established* in tenant-landlord and customer-retailer schemes, and *altered* in voter-public official and labor-management schemes; and maybe all three in the wife-husband scheme!). Furthermore, as a consequence of one's capacities in the power relation, one's status or position relative to the other may be presupposed (child), established (home buyer becomes home owner) or altered (employee is promoted).

In short, a scheme is patterned by power relations in that power as a capacity to act effectively, exercise influence and effect change is expressed or objectified in the stylized behaviors, characteristics, conditions and qualities that are brought to or derived from the interaction between persons as role players in a scheme. But note: to the extent that a scheme is patterned by presupposing, establishing or altering power relations and status, it legitimately or illegitimately objectifies *equality and inequality* (i.e., dominant and subordinate capacities, and a hierarchy of social status).

Racialized schemes and stereotypes. Perhaps by this point the reader has begun to recognize the ways inherently prejudicial stereotypes operate in the spheres of everyday life, and how their eventuation—localization and activation—through typificatory schemes contributes to the construction of social reality. Situated as they are in schemes, stereotypes have to do with the assumptions, beliefs, judgments, anticipations, expectations, practices, relationships and behaviors that are expressed in the social interaction of persons in any given sphere. More important, they point to the patterns, structures and dynamics that shape and objectify this social interaction.

Most of the time, people are not mindful that stereotypes are operative in themselves or in a sphere. This is largely because the common knowledge and patterned behaviors and interactions have become habit. Stereotypes, spheres and schemes are our sociocultural world of human interaction, and we know how this world works and how to function within it. It is a familiar world because it is an institutionalized world: the patterned, habitualized and mutually interactive behaviors in its spheres eventuate a shared reality that is stable and predictable.

Inherently prejudicial stereotypes operate in the typificatory schemes that take place within and express the spheres of everyday life. This is the sociocultural world in which race has been institutionalized through the habit of racism. Racism has become institutionalized because actors in spheres have judged, perceived, interpreted and related to each other in terms of race. When the category is a racial group to which prejudged attributions are assigned, you have a racial stereotype that qualifies a scheme by localizing and activating—objectifying—racial types and roles through the protocol, apprehension, interpretation and power that characterize social interaction. Persons are typified as "black," "white," "red," "brown" or "yellow," and to such typifications are attributed prejudged behaviors, characteristics, conditions and qualities. It is anticipated and expected that persons so apprehended will express in their demeanor the prescribed and judged behaviors attributed to the group. The conduct of such persons is interpreted as consistent with or deviating from their type, and the mutual interaction is shaped by power relations.

In other words, for example, "black" and "white" have become typified roles played by persons in typified ways (there is a *kind* . . .). In intra- and intergroup relations, persons apprehend each other as types whose roles are played out according to rules and patterns that prescribe conduct and limit the range of expressions according to what has been judged as consistent and appropriate to the typified role (. . . and you are one of that kind . . .). And stylized personal expressivity is interpreted in such a way that power relations and status are formed and realized (. . . and your kind does not deserve or merit the same consideration or treatment).

These racialized typificatory schemes, when played out in the spheres of everyday life, bring about the continuing real-ization of race and racism. But they do so only because the enactment of any given scheme presupposes and expresses positive, negative and neutral racial stereotypes. When the actors in a sphere apprehend each other as members of different people groups, in that same moment the scheme becomes encumbered with race, and this eventuates in playing out the scheme in potentially or actually conflictive modes. An everyday sphere becomes *racialized* when actors apprehend themselves and each other as racial types, such as "black" customers and "white" salesclerks, or "black" employees and "white" supervisors, or "black" voters and "white" candidates, or "black" students and "white" teachers. To the extent that the scheme is played out, in one way or another and to one degree or another it will occasion self-expressions, mutual interpretations and social interaction along the boundaries, assumptions and expectations of race.

Such schemes become conflictive because there are likely to be two levels to the types, roles, rules, apprehensions, interpretations and power relations at work. There are, in effect, two typificatory schemes unfolding: the conventional scheme that is characteristic of the particular sphere and the scheme that is characterized by race. More often than not, the race scheme supersedes the conventional scheme, and it is indicative of the institutionalization of racism that the race scheme has itself become the conventional scheme in many spheres.

It should come as no surprise that any sphere can be the occasion for eventuating more than one scheme. A customer and a salesclerk may be friends, in which case their social interaction in a store may by characterized by both schemes. Or a child may be a doctor whose patient is a parent, or vice versa. Or a client may be a member of the same church as the architect who is developing the plan for a new business facility or home. Or a client may be a friend and a teacher of the lawyer who is doing legal work for the client when he or she is not socializing in the friend's home or preparing for the teacher's class. In any single sphere, these various schemes may be present and played out with ease of movement in the transitions, though only one scheme can be primary at any given moment.

Such schemes can be described as complementary in that they are layered and fluid. But they can also become conflictive, as when a friend-customer presumes a favor from a salesclerk-friend but does not receive it; or when a parent-patient is resistant to the medical advice of a doctor-child; or when a husband-employee is evaluated by a supervisor-wife. Primary and secondary roles can coexist as long as the players play along and by the rules, but when the demeanor and behavior of one is interpreted as inconsistent with the scheme at the moment, there is conflict. Tension rises as attitudinal, cognitive, behavioral and linguistic expressions appropriate in one scheme are manifest in another. The expression of a role is then apprehended and interpreted as out of sync with the scheme, as when a person is apprehended and interpreted as *wife*, and dealt with accordingly, while the wife is self-defining and executing the role of *student*. In this situation, *mis*apprehension and *mis*interpretation become characteristic of the interaction, and following competing rules may result in power relations characterized by struggle and competition. Conflictive schemes are thus oppositional and rigid.

Race and racism are brought to objective expression in social worlds when schemes are overlaid with racially oriented typifications. Such schemes are inherently conflictive because they express not only misapprehensions and misinterpretations but also illegitimate restrictions in the capacity of one or the other to act effectively, exercise influence and effect change. As we have seen, schemes entail categories, attributions and judgments by which the participants orient their apprehension of self and other to a sphere, and they are the means for localizing and activating the stereotypes that shape our anticipations and expectations and guide our conduct. But when one apprehends and interacts with the other as a *racial* type in a scheme, the conventional interaction is abrogated by race. The scheme is bifurcated into a race scheme and a conventional scheme, and it makes no difference whether the actors play out the scheme as racial or as conventional, or whether one plays out the race scheme while the other plays out the conventional scheme; it will be inherently conflictive to the degree that one or the other—or both—consent to, or are perceived and interpreted as, playing out the racial type. In either case the scheme will have objectified race and racism in the attitudes, beliefs, behaviors and power relations that are implied or expressed in the interaction.

Institutionalizing the Social Order: The Culture of Race

Situated as they are in the spheres of our everyday lives, typificatory schemes constitute the modes and structures of the social interactions that make up a shared world. Infused as they are with stereotypes, these schemes are nonetheless the fundamental ways we externalize ourselves in activity and express our humanness, our knowledge, beliefs, attitudes, values and judgments; they are the arena of our conduct and the authorization for the ways we practice ourselves.

But schemes are also the principal way in which we dominate, exploit, humiliate and dehumanize; they are the means whereby we prevent others from expressing themselves in ways they deem necessary or appropriate. Historically, some schemes and the spheres in which they are situated have been constructed precisely to do just that (the master-slave scheme in the slavery sphere comes immediately to mind). But as the Berger-Luckmann analysis indicated, the spheres and schemes of everyday life are the basic building blocks for the institutionalization of the social order; habitualized activity involving multiple actors over time eventuates in the development of an institution in and through which persons externalize themselves and by which an objective world is constructed. This external world or *social order* consists, then, in a multitude of everyday schemes and spheres or *institutions*, the totality of which is construed as objective reality, a web of interconnected spheres constituting the *sociocultural environment.*

For advancing the notion of the social construction of race and racism, it will be helpful now to explore more closely the phenomenon of institutionalization. This will open a horizon of understanding on the ways our sociocultural world has been developed largely for the benefit of one people group, namely European Americans, and why this world has been so resistant to change by the inclusion of other people groups.

The structure of institutions and systems. The common sense defines an institution as an established organization, but a more sociologically oriented definition, such as we have encountered in the work of Berger and Luckmann, construes an institution as an intentionally structured composite of actors engaged in particular actions undertaken through time for a purpose. By this definition, an institution may be either informal or formal, simple or complex, private or public; it may be local, regional, national or international. But in any case its objectivity will have most if not all of several distinguishing features.[46] It will have

□ a purpose that stipulates the reason for its existence and the range of its activities, whether expressed in a formal statement or implied in the conduct of its participants

□ a constitution, charter, license or articles of incorporation that formally—and

---

[46]I am indebted to Joseph Barndt and Crossroads Ministry in Chicago for this construal of institutions. I have adapted it somewhat for the purposes of the present discussion. Nevertheless, this delineation identifies a baseline of the phenomenon of institutions and can thus serve as a point of access to analysis of the simplicity or complexity of any given institution. It also suggests the possibility of forming evaluative questions regarding the way any given institution actually conducts its affairs.

often legally—grant authority to conduct its affairs and prescribe the nature, function and limits of its organization and ownership, as well as several of the other features to follow

☐ a leadership structure, generally organized as a hierarchy, with lines of authority, responsibility and accountability

☐ an organizational structure that reflects the function and contribution of various entities or departments

☐ financial resources such as revenue generated as income, assets earned through investment or acquired through contribution, and real property, including physical plant

☐ established policies, procedures and practices that stipulate and manage how the organization carries out its various activities on a daily and long-term basis

☐ personnel with particular areas of function and responsibility that contribute to the execution of the organization's purpose

☐ programs, projects and services, for internal or external implementation, designed to meet a perceived need

☐ clientele or customers, those who seek the services of and are in turn served by the organization

☐ a constituency, those on whose behalf the organization functions, or whose support of or investment in the organization reflects a vested interest

All together, these features constitute the objectivity of any particular institution; they give shape and texture to a sphere of everyday life and indicate the range of schemes that unfold from day to day.

The aggregate of similar and auxiliary institutions constitutes a complex whole that can be called a "system," a network of interrelated, interacting and interdependent institutions. No matter how local or autonomous an institution may appear to be, it will in fact be part of a system, and as such dependent on other institutions to execute its purpose effectively. All together the institutions that make up a system contribute to its objectivity in the sociocultural world. Consider this list of illustrative local institutions (and the systems of which they are a part): bank (financial), pet food store (commerce), light bulb factory (industry), real estate agency (real estate), insurance agency (insurance), local headquarters of the Democratic Party (political), police headquarters (law enforcement), drivers license bureau (government), courthouse (judicial), mental health center (social/human services), train station (transportation), electric company (public utilities), library (public services), college (education), hospital (healthcare), union headquarters (labor), radio station (communications), golf course (recreation), movie theater (entertainment), charity headquarters (philanthropy) and church (religion).

It should also be observed that there are intersystem relations that connect one institution to others: the pet food store borrows money from the bank for expansion, buys light bulbs, pays rent and electric bills, buys insurance and advertises on the radio; the light bulb factory employs union labor and contributes to local charity; the hospital contracts with the college for in-service training; the court refers defendants to the mental health center. Together these intra- and interconnected systems constitute *the System*, one grand metasystem, the social order whose objectivity consists in the extraordinary interrelatedness and variation of spheres and schemes that structure social interaction.

Institutional power. An institution effectively executes its purpose through the exercise of its power, particularly through its human and financial resources. But this power should not be construed as essentially different from the power discussed previously in connection with typificatory schemes. This is to say that an institution's power consists in its *power relations*, and more specifically the capacity of its human agents up and down the line to perform their roles effectively; exercise influence, control or authority consistent with the roles and rules of the scheme; and effect change in themselves, others and/or the situation itself. This capacity to express power is derived from personal and social, absolute and relative, and negotiable and nonnegotiable sources, and the effective use of this capacity presupposes, establishes and/or alters the power relation.

An institution as such does not exercise power; rather human agents who engage in habitualized activity in particular spheres and schemes for particular purposes exercise power *in and on behalf of* the institution. This does not mean that every person in a particular institution has the same capacities or that any person can play any role in any scheme. What it does suggest is that institutional power is expressed through the integrated activities of its agents as they discharge their function—play their roles—in the various interrelated schemes that structure the institution's objective reality. To the extent that any particular agent plays his or her habitualized role effectively within an institution's structure, it can be said that a dimension of institutional power has been externalized. The capacity of agents to function within the boundaries of their prescribed role and the effective discharge of their function relative to the characteristic features of an institution together constitute the objectivity of institutional power.[47] Absent this attention to institutional

---

[47]The same is somewhat true of systems as networks of similar institutions. However a system may be organized or structured (the patterns of institutional interconnectivity), and regardless of whether a system is administered hierarchically by a human agent or collegium or exists as a network of reasonably egalitarian institutions with varying size and complexity, the system's power is neither more nor less than the capacities of human agents who function on behalf of the system (network of institutions). In this sense it is possible to speak of "systemic power" as the capacity of a system to objectify itself in and through its interrelated institutions.

agents, an institution's power remains abstract and largely invisible.[48]

American society is made up of systems and their institutions, some of which have their beginnings in ages past and places distant, others of which are indigenous to developing American society with beginnings more recent. Whether transplanted or home-grown, these systems and their institutions contributed to the formation of the social, economic, political and religious world on this continent's soil. As ways of living, making and doing things, expressing shared beliefs, values, meanings, understandings, perspectives, customs and so on, they contributed to the formation of a *culture,* a human-made social environment, a sociocultural world.[49] All of these institutions have undergone change—some more, some less—as we have developed historically from a predominantly agrarian society to an industrial and now technological society. But it remains the case that, as Joel Kovel has observed, "[human beings] draw

---

[48]John Searle's analysis of institutional power parallels the present discussion, with somewhat different terms to describe its nature and function. In his book *The Construction of Social Reality* (New York: Free Press, 1995), he summarizes his presentation in this way: "The structure of institutional facts is a structure of power relations, including negative and positive, conditional and categorical, collective and individual powers. . . . Everything we value in civilization requires the creation and maintenance of institutional power relations through collectively imposed status-functions. These require constant monitoring and adjusting to create and preserve fairness, efficiency, flexibility, and creativity, not to mention such traditional values as justice, liberty, and dignity. But institutional power relations are ubiquitous and essential. Institutional power—massive, pervasive, and typically invisible—permeates every nook and cranny of our social lives, and as such it is not a threat to liberal values but rather the precondition of their existence" (p. 94). See ibid., pp. 80-126, for a superb discussion of the social phenomena of institutions that diverges from the trajectory taken by Berger and Luckmann. Another helpful discussion of institutional power, construed as an "impersonal" and more "socially acceptable" form of power than "force," can be found in Gerhard E. Lenski, *Power and Privilege: A Theory of Social Stratification* (New York: McGraw-Hill, 1966; University of North Carolina Press, 1984), pp. 56-58.

[49]In his book *The Interpretation of Cultures* (New York: Basic Books, 1973) Clifford Geertz discusses the matter of "the cultural and social aspects of human life." He notes: "One of the more useful ways—but far from the only one—of distinguishing between culture and social systems is to see the former as an ordered system of meaning and of symbols, in terms of which social interaction takes place; and to see the latter as the pattern of social interaction itself. On the one level there is the framework of beliefs, expressive symbols, and values in terms of which individuals define their world, express their feelings, and make their judgments; on the other level there is the ongoing process of interactive behavior, whose persistent form we call social structure. Culture is the fabric of meaning in terms of which human beings interpret their experience and guide their action; social structure is the form that action takes, the actually existing network of social relations. Culture and social structure are then but different abstractions from the same phenomena. The one considers social action in respect to its meaning for those who carry it out, the other considers it in terms of its contribution to the functioning of some social system" (pp. 144-45). This distinction and interrelation of culture and social structure are carried within the *sociocultural world* or *sociocultural environment,* specifically for the purpose of distinguishing it from a *natural* world or environment.

themselves together in a culture through the various structures upon which it rests: the institutions of society; church, state, systems of economics and work, systems of technology, systems of belief about other people, and so forth. Each institution has a distinct and differentiated structure, yet all are symbolically related in culture."[50] In the institutionalization of our social, economic, political and religious life, we have developed a culture that is formed as the external-ization of our humanness, an extension that expresses the self and in turn con-tinues to form our humanness. This intersection of our humanity with the self-expressive institutions of culture has led Clifford Geertz to contend that "there is no such thing as a human nature independent of culture."[51]

The beneficiaries of sociocultural development. In light of this sense of cul-ture and the institutionalization of the sociocultural world, the question that now needs to be raised is this: For whom was this institutionalization of the social order developed, and what peculiar feature(s)—beliefs, attitudes, values, behaviors, practices—did this institutionalization embed in the sociocultural environment? Many have observed that culture as the institutionalization of human social existence is learned and passed on from one generation to the next. As such, it represents the patterns and possibilities for living from day to day. It expresses and influences human identity and interaction by providing the roles we play, the rules by which we play and the statuses we thereby obtain. Institutionalized spheres and schemes are principal means for exercis-ing power and generating personal and institutional wealth. Moreover, culture delineates the boundaries both within and between people groups; and as the grand totality of the manifold spheres and schemes, it constitutes an objective world that is perceived and experienced as *there.* Thus the question: Whose purposes, aspirations, interests, norms, memories, meanings and worldview

---

[50]Joel Kovel, *White Racism: A Psychohistory* (1970; reprint, New York: Columbia University Press, 1984), p. 5.

[51]Geertz, *Interpretation,* p. 49. This observation is made in the context of Geertz's discussion of the influence of culture on a modern social-scientific understanding of humanity, that is, an-thropology (pp. 34-81). In his book *Beyond Culture* Hall echoed the same sentiment, if only more starkly, by suggesting that "it is not man who is crazy so much as his institutions and those cultural patterns that determine his behavior" (p. 11). It should be apparent here that we are working with such a modern *cultural* anthropology in laying out the significance of insti-tutions. For discussions treating the history and meaning of *culture* as an anthropological term, see Kathryn Tanner, *Theories of Culture: A New Agenda for Theology* (Minneapolis: Fortress, 1997), pp. 3-37; Audrey Smedley, *Race in North America: Origin and Evolution of a World-view* (Boulder, Colo.: Westview, 1993), pp. 14-35; George W. Stocking Jr., *Race, Culture and Evolution: Essays in the History of Anthropology* (New York: Free Press, 1968), pp. 72-75, 199-264; Montagu, *Man's Most Dangerous Myth,* pp. 311-29; Boas, *Mind of Primitive Man,* pp. 149-79, and *Anthropology and Modern Life,* pp. 104-46; Hall, *Beyond Culture,* pp. 9-24, 27-40; and Cohen, *Culture of Intolerance,* pp. 60-126.

have been externalized, established, interrelated and integrated into a sociocultural reality? If "culture is [humanity's] medium" as Edward T. Hall notes, and "there is not one aspect of human life that is not touched and altered by culture,"[52] then who has been and is intended to participate in and benefit from this medium, and who can presume to be favorably altered by its touch?

The answer to this question is the immigrants from Western Europe and their descendants. Practically every institutional system operating in the United States today was created or adapted, developed and enlarged, for the benefit and advantage of European Americans. These institutional systems externalized European American selves, expressing their purposes, aspirations, interests, norms, memories, meanings and worldview. The systems of American government, politics, economics, property, education, transportation, healthcare, labor and a host of others—including religion—were created or adapted *by* European Americans *for* European Americans.

Furthermore, the evolution of *the System* was made possible by the genocide of the indigenous peoples, the expropriation of their lands and the development of race-based chattel slavery, a "peculiar institution" in which millions of Africans were bought and sold by slavers to provide low-cost labor in the emerging agrarian economy. Apart from their role in the particular schemes and spheres to which they were restricted by European Americans and which they did not devise, African slaves and their descendants were not allowed to participate in, or benefit from, the institutionalization of the social order. As a people, they were denied their humanity and excluded by custom and by law from taking advantage of the rights, opportunities, benefits and privileges accorded to the European American builders of the sociocultural order.

This is not to say that Africans and their descendants made no other contribution to the institutionalization of the sociocultural order, but it is to observe that such contributions were made against extraordinary odds and with uncommon initiative to institutional systems they did not design or control but into which they entered as contributors largely against the resolve and intent of European American society. Nor is it to deny the emergence and development of a distinctively African American culture, a counterculture of profound measure and vitality, itself an externalization of selves and institutionalization of a sociocultural order. Rather it is to acknowledge that this culture was bounded by the domination, oppression, exploitation and exclusion by the European American society and characterized by the solidarity of bondage, suffering, struggle and resistance. The "strivings" of African Americans were "the dogged determination to survive and subsist, the tenacious will to persevere, persist,

---

[52]Hall, *Beyond Culture,* p. 16.

and maybe even prevail" as a response to "the vicious attacks on black beauty, black intelligence, black moral character, black capability, and black possibility" in an environment in which "every major institution in American society . . . attempted to exclude black people from the human family in the name of white supremacist ideology."[53]

One avenue of approach to this emergence of the dominant sociocultural order might be characterized as follows.[54] This nation's history spans a period of roughly five hundred and ten years. The period from 1492, when Christopher Columbus landed on the North American continent, to 1865, when the Civil War ended and the institution of slavery was abolished, represents a span of 373 years—73 percent of our history—during which virtually all of our institutional systems evolved. This period includes the establishment of the first British colony at Jamestown in 1607, the 1619 Jamestown offloading of the first twenty Africans who were pressed into indentured servitude, the colonization of the continent's eastern seaboard, the African slave trade, the Revolutionary War, the formation of the United States with the adoption of the Constitution containing the clause that Negroes would be considered as three-fifths of a person for purposes of apportioning representation and taxes (simultaneously "human" and "property"), the Supreme Court decision in *Dred Scott* v. *Sanford* (1857) that denied citizenship and civil rights to the descendants of Africans, the nation's expansion through purchase or war, and the immigration of Chinese to the West Coast. This period can be characterized as "for whites only."

The period from 1865 until 1964-1965, when federal legislation secured the civil and political rights of African Americans, represents a span of one hundred years—20 percent of our history—during which our institutional systems were

---

[53]Henry Louis Gates Jr. and Cornel West, *The Future of the Race* (New York: Vintage, 1996), pp. 79-80. For historical treatments of the development of African American culture in an environment of domination and struggle, see especially John Hope Franklin and Alfred A. Moss Jr., *From Slavery to Freedom: A History of African Americans,* 7th ed. (New York: Alfred A. Knopf, 1994); Paul R. Griffin, *Seeds of Racism in the Soul of America* (Cleveland, Ohio: Pilgrim, 1999); Lawrence W. Levine, *Black Culture and Black Consciousness: Afro-American Folk Thought from Slavery to Freedom* (New York: Oxford University Press, 1977); Albert J. Raboteau, *Slave Religion: The "Invisible Institution" in the Antebellum South* (New York: Oxford University Press, 1978); Sterling Stuckey, *Slave Culture: Nationalist Theory and the Foundations of Black America* (New York: Oxford University Press, 1987); Bennett, *Before the Mayflower,* and *The Shaping of Black America,* rev. ed. (New York: Penguin, 1991); John W. Blassingame, *The Slave Community: Plantation Life in the Antebellum South,* rev. and enl. ed. (New York: Oxford University Press, 1979); Jordan, *White Man's Burden;* and W. E. B. Du Bois, *The Souls of Black Folk* (1903; reprint, New York: Vintage, 1990).

[54]Again, I am indebted to Joseph Barndt and Crossroads Ministry for this construal. Granted, it is somewhat misleading in that it takes a rather untextured macro-view of our history. Nonetheless, it does represent an alternative perspective to those more commonly encountered in the history of European America.

further developed. This period includes Reconstruction; the passage of the Civil Rights Act (1866) and the adoption of the Fourteenth Amendment, granting birthright citizenship to African Americans; the Chinese immigration exclusion acts; the immigration of Japanese to the West Coast, and southern and eastern Europeans to the East; the U.S. Supreme Court decision in *Plessy* v. *Ferguson* (1896) establishing the doctrine of "separate but equal"; further territorial expansion through purchase, conquest or expropriation; industrialization; foreign colonization; two world wars; the internment of Japanese Americans; and the U.S. Supreme Court decision in *Brown* v. *Board of Education* (1954) overturning the doctrine of "separate but equal." This period can be characterized as "legal segregation, exclusion and discrimination."

The period from 1965 to 2002 (date of this book's publication) is a mere thirty-seven years—7 percent of our history—during which many have struggled to include and embrace in all the sociocultural systems not only African Americans but the remarkable waves of immigrants from all continents of the world, and thus to express—externalize—"the entire American Creed of liberty, equality, justice, and fair opportunity for everybody."[55]

In short, for 93 percent of this nation's history, its developing European American sociocultural environment has been marked effectively by either total exclusion of African Americans (slavery, with no civil or citizenship rights or claims)[56] or restricted inclusion (legal segregation and discrimina-

---

[55]Myrdal, *American Dilemma*, p. lxxx. In this massive study of the racial situation in the United States, published in 1944, Myrdal organized his presentation of the social, economic, political and religious data around what he termed the "moral struggle" of America to live out this creed, the origins of which he correctly traced to Enlightenment thought and Western Christianity, both of which were peculiarly European "institutions."

[56]The definitive expression of this denial of rights came in the Supreme Court decision in *Dred Scott* v. *Sanford* (1857). There Chief Justice Roger Taney opined on behalf of the majority that African slaves were to be regarded "as beings of an inferior order, and altogether unfit to associate with the white race, either in social or political relations; and so far inferior, that they had no rights which the white man was bound to respect" (cited in George F. Curry, introduction to *The Affirmative Action Debate*, ed. George F. Curry [Reading, Mass.: Addison-Wesley, 1996], p. xiii). In commenting on and quoting from this opinion, C. Eric Lincoln in his *Race, Religion and the Continuing American Dilemma*, rev. ed. (New York: Hill and Wang, 1999), contends that

> Taney's conclusions were based on the theory that "the class of persons described in the plea [i.e., Negroes] whose ancestors were imported into this country and sold as slaves" were not "constituent members of [American] sovereignty" and that "they were not included, and were not intended to be included, under the word 'citizen' in the Constitution. . . ." This language has never been applied to any other American "*minority*." (p. 213, emphasis and bracketed text in the original)

For discussion of the *Dred Scott* decision in the context of birthright and citizenship law in the United States, see Haney López, *White by Law*, pp. 38-41. The full text of the opinion can be found on the Internet at <http://laws.findlaw.com/US/60/393.html>.

tion as citizens, with limited civil, political and social rights).

White privilege. This construal of the emergence and development of our sociocultural order—our institutional systems—at the hands of and under the control of primarily European Americans is the background in relation to which it is possible to discern the meaning of "white privilege," a constellation of advantages, benefits, immunities, permissions and opportunities that accrue to European Americans as means for objectifying themselves in our institutionalized social order. References to this phenomenon of white privilege or white advantage recur constantly in the literature on race and racism, as one would expect given our history of excluding or restricting the civil and human rights of people groups other than those with European ancestry.[57] Those so marginalized historically have always perceived the advantages assumed by members of the dominant culture; the struggle *against* the oppression of slavery and segregation was always at the same time a struggle *for* freedom and opportunity to participate as full members in the sociocultural order, to engage in unfettered self-externalization in "life, liberty and the pursuit of happiness." The practices of social, political and economic exclusion and restriction—habitualized activity involving multiple actors over time—contributed to the institutionalization of the sociocultural world, engendering spheres and schemes designed for members of one group.

Perhaps one indication of white privilege is that European Americans are so deeply inculturated in their institutionalized systems that they do not have to think about "race" or themselves as "white" on a frequent basis if at all. As Peggy McIntosh observes, "As a white person, I realized I had been taught about racism as something which puts others at a disadvantage, but *had been taught not to see* one of its corollary aspects, white privilege, which puts me at an advantage."[58] The obverse side of this sentiment is represented in the comment of an African American who responded to a query by saying, "[One problem with] being black in America is that you have to spend so much time thinking about stuff that most white people just don't even have to think about."[59] European Americans have the privilege of regarding themselves as

---

[57] One particularly helpful and illustrative treatment of white privilege that is occasionally cited in the literature is Peggy McIntosh, "White Privilege: Unpacking the Invisible Knapsack," *Peace and Freedom,* July/August 1989, pp. 10-12. This article was excerpted from her working paper "White Privilege and Male Privilege: A Personal Account of Coming to See Correspondences Through Work in Women's Studies" (1988). This essay can be found in Margaret L. Anderson and Patricia Hill Collins, eds., *Race, Class and Gender: An Anthology,* 2nd ed. (Belmont, Calif.: Wadsworth, 1995), pp. 76-87.

[58] Ibid., p. 10.

[59] Joe R. Feagin and Melvin P. Sikes, *Living with Racism: The Black Middle-Class Experience* (Boston: Beacon, 1994), p. 67.

individuals first and members of a racial group second, because all the systems in and through which they move are the historic expressions of their culture; they are not obligated to consider whether an institutional sphere and scheme will be favorable or unfavorable toward them *because* of their race. For the most part, their race and its significance are invisible to them. Barbara Flagg uses the word "transparency" to refer to this invisibility of race for European Americans, and attributes it to white privilege: "There is a profound cognitive dimension to the material and social privilege that attaches to whiteness in this society, in that the white person has an everyday option not to think of herself in racial terms at all. In fact, whites appear to pursue that option so habitually that it may be a defining characteristic of whiteness: to be white is not to think about it. I label the tendency for whiteness to vanish from whites' self-perception the transparency phenomenon."[60]

European Americans may very well self-identify as a member of an "ethnic" group (e.g., Italian, English, German, Polish). But in spite of the cultural variability among such groups in their countries of origin, in the United States all such persons are regarded as "white" and are de facto members of the dominant culture. Harlon Dalton reports that "many of my White friends readily embrace their ethnic identity, or define themselves by religion, geographic region, or profession. But few spontaneously think of themselves in racial terms. In part, that is because in settings where Whites dominate, being White is not noteworthy."[61]

There are several dimensions of this phenomenon of white privilege that need to be uncovered and clarified.

1. *Dominant status.* First of all, privilege is located in the context of social relations. As a special prerogative not available to everyone, it expresses a kind of status stratification of superordination and subordination. Thus privilege correlates to hierarchy and dominance. Now privilege can be earned or unearned, conferred or arrogated, but in any case its possession is relative to a structure of dominance; its acquisition either creates dominance or is the result of dominance. Privilege as a form of power or of capacity in a power relation is a means for establishing dominance. One possesses a privilege in relation to the structure of stratification, and the exercise of privilege objectifies dominance.

---

[60]Barbara J. Flagg, "'Was Blind, but Now I See': White Race Consciousness and the Requirement of Discriminatory Intent," *Michigan Law Review* 91 (March 1993): 969. See also Haney López, *White by Law,* pp. 19-34, 155-94; David K. Shipler, *A Country of Strangers: Blacks and Whites in America* (New York: Alfred A. Knopf, 1997), pp. 5-18; and Beverly Daniel Tatum, *"Why Are All the Black Kids Sitting Together in the Cafeteria?" and Other Conversations About Race,* rev. ed. (New York: BasicBooks, 1999), pp. 93-113.

[61]Harlon L. Dalton, *Racial Healing: Confronting the Fear Between Blacks and Whites* (New York: Anchor, 1995); p. 6. See also Spencer Perkins and Chris Rice, *More Than Equals: Racial Healing for the Sake of the Gospel* (Downers Grove, Ill.: InterVarsity Press, 1993), pp. 102-15.

As a prerogative of status or position, privilege may be exercised for the benefit of oneself, and it may be exercised for the welfare and enhancement of others or for the exclusion and detriment of others.

White privilege is the unearned advantage conferred on European Americans by their institutional systems—the network of integrated spheres and schemes structured by power relations that externalize stratification and constitute the sociocultural order. In short, white privilege is the product of a culture of dominance. The dominant culture in the United States is European American; they are the people group who developed the social, economic, political and religious institutions that express their beliefs, values and attitudes. This sociocultural order was built as an exclusive and restrictive world in which one exploited and dehumanized group was dominated and another was effectively exterminated. The notion of "race" and the ideology of "racism" emerged as a means to distinguish one people group from another, legitimate a stratification of superiority and inferiority, and authorize practices of exclusion and oppression. The advantages, benefits, rights and opportunities created by European Americans were denied to members of other people groups, and to the extent that these became embedded in the developing sociocultural order under European American control, they could be passed from—conferred by—one generation to another. So a race-oriented people developed a racist culture, and white privilege amounts to "the social power to name, decide, and enact as reality what it considers to be culturally normal, correct, acceptable, or desirable."[62]

Fumitaka Matsuoka has said, "Because the dominant values are predictably the values of the dominant class, those who have these monopolies also come to have a monopoly of legitimacy and virtue, land and property, and in the end a monopoly of imagination. They control not only every benefit in the present but every imaginable prospect for the future. The monopoly is not just a monopoly of power but has come to be a monopoly of society's norms."[63] In our culture of dominance, privilege is not only implied, it is also institutionalized—a feature of habitualized activity involving multiple actors over time.

2. *Access.* Privilege manifests itself in the form of access to the sociocultural world—its networks, resources and opportunities. To be sure, access admits of varying degrees or levels, but privilege as access nonetheless locates an individual or a group within reach of what the sociocultural world has to offer: education, employment, money, commerce, property, healthcare, recreation, justice—in short, the

---

[62]Ronice Branding, *Fulfilling the Dream: Confronting the Challenge of Racism* (St. Louis: Chalice, 1998), p. 50.

[63]Fumitaka Matsuoka, *The Color of Faith: Building Community in a Multiracial Society* (Cleveland, Ohio: United Church Press, 1998), p. 76.

institutions that objectify the sociocultural order. The accessibility of all institutions, patterned as they are by particular spheres and schemes, is managed by decision-makers who rightfully or wrongfully have the capacity to make the institution available to its clientele. These are the institution's gatekeepers. In order for there to be access, a gatekeeper must mediate the purposes and interests of both the institution and those seeking access. Where there are competing or conflicting interests, access will likely be denied because the purposes and interests of the institution, and those whose beliefs, attitudes and values are externalized in it, will be preferred. By definition, gatekeepers serve the interests of the institution. Access thus entails the presumption of preference and the practice of discrimination.

In our culture of dominance, white privilege amounts to taking advantage of resources and opportunities that are denied to others on the basis of race; it amounts to a level of access to the sociocultural world that is refused to others because they are perceived as racially different from those by and for whom that world was constructed. White privilege trades on the presumption of preference. The health and cohesiveness of a society are dependent on its "social capital," its shared values, norms and experiences as well as cooperative relations between persons that engender trust and respect.[64] But the question of access has to do with whose values and norms are externalized in the sociocultural arena, who controls the social relations and adjudicates cooperation, and who is presumed worthy of trust and respect. In an environment dominated by the social capital generated in one group by the exclusion of another group, social privilege will remain the prerogative of the dominant group.

In a sociocultural world built on preference and exclusion, the accumulation of advantages for one group necessarily results in a corresponding accumulation of disadvantages for the other. As Melvin Oliver and Thomas Shapiro observe, "Practically, every circumstance of bias and discrimination against blacks has produced a circumstance and opportunity of positive gain for whites. . . . The cumulative effect of such a process has been to sediment blacks at the bottom of the social hierarchy and to artificially raise the relative position of whites in society."[65] Through the historic practices of preference for European Americans and discrimination against other people groups, white privi-

---

[64]See Francis Fukuyama, *The Great Disruption: Human Nature and the Reconstitution of the Social Order* (New York: Free Press, 1999). In this book Fukuyama argues that the dissolution of the social order in the United States in the second half of the twentieth century resulted from the erosion of the nation's "social capital." While his arguments are insightful and germane to the present discussion, they neglect to account for the fact that one can also argue—as I do—that the social capital that has eroded was generated largely in a culture of domination constructed by and for European Americans.

[65]Melvin L. Oliver and Thomas M. Shapiro, *Black Wealth/White Wealth: A New Perspective on Racial Inequality* (New York: Routledge, 1995), p. 51.

lege has been institutionalized. But more important, in the development of our culture of dominance, racial preference and racial discrimination have been institutionalized in privileged access to the sociocultural order

3. *Merit and inequality.* Privilege as a feature of power relations entails the presumption of merit and inequality. As noted in the discussion of typificatory schemes and their power relations, a social interaction may presuppose, establish or alter power relations and status, bringing about the objectivity of either equality or inequality. When schemes are structured hierarchically, the advantage goes to the superordinate participant(s) by design. Dominance is institutionalized in roles and rules and objectified as these are played and followed by the participants. Privilege in such schemes comes as a result of position or status in the institutional order; the dominant one has earned or acquired his or her position and has the capacity to exercise the privileges that come with it. But position and status in a stratified institutional environment both presuppose and produce inequality. Privilege as a prerogative of position and status is precisely what demarcates the levels in a social or institutional order; it contributes to the objectivity of inequality to the extent that position and status are restricted to some by virtue of the structure of sociocultural order.

Furthermore, the presumption that position and status are earned or achieved on merit is simply indicative of the inherent inequality of the order's structure. In the institutionalized system of spheres and schemes, a person may legitimately aspire to and work toward achieving a "higher" position and status in order to acquire the privilege that comes with them. But such aspiration is tantamount to an assent to the inherent structure of inequality; one aspires to be more equal than others, and therefore one must be able to compete in order to acquire. The indication of this "more equal than" is the acquisition of position and status in the sociocultural order.

But in our culture of dominance, built on the fabrication of race and the practice of racism, white privilege as racial privilege entails racial position and therefore *racial inequality.* In our culture of dominance, where virtually every nook and cranny of the institutionalized world is structured along the lines of superordination and subordination, where some have been excluded or restricted on the basis of putative differences in race, and where merit and the capacity to compete are preferentially given to others also on the basis of race, *the System* can hardly be said to foster the attainment of sociocultural equality for all.

The capitalist economic system in the United States not only produces economic disparity but is itself the institutionalization of inequality. Furthermore, the notion that persons can achieve their life's goals and succeed in this world by initiative and hard work, with reasonable expectation of reward and recognition, and that in the end one's character and merit will be the basis for assessment and advancement has itself become institutionalized. It is a European American belief externalized into the culture of dominance. In this regard, Michael Eric Dyson has noted that "the dominant belief that legitimates the central place of achievement in U.S. culture and explains the distribution of goods and privileges is that all things being relatively equal, one gets what one merits, based upon intelligence, industry, and a host of other American character traits."[66] In such a sociocultural environment, white privilege is the presumption of the capacity to achieve merit, to be upwardly mobile, in an environment that is structured to make this possible. In our culture of dominance, white privilege is a limit situation that separates the equal ones from the unequal ones, the ones for whom the advantages were designed from the ones for whom the advantages were never intended.

Even within the European American community, social and economic stratification prevails; there are very, very rich *and* very, very poor European Americans, whose situation has resulted from the presence or absence of opportunity, resources, initiative, education and so on. The presence of this stratification has engendered the belief that one can achieve and advance if one seeks out and takes advantage of opportunities. It has also engendered the belief that the reason some people do not achieve and advance is that they do not want to, or are unable to, because of some inherent character—or genetic—flaw, or because "their" culture doesn't value initiative and hard work. This argument, spurious as it is, is nonetheless significant if only because it reveals that any given culture is the externalization of selves and their beliefs, values and norms, and in this case the beliefs, values and norms embedded in the dominant culture constitute the basis for comprehending those who are judged to be unmerited and unequal. In our culture of dominance, built on the presumption of merit and inequality, white privilege "derives its power from the psychological feelings and institutional realities of the superiority, social privilege, economic position, and political power . . . of European Americans."[67]

---

[66]Michael Eric Dyson, *Reflecting Black: African-American Cultural Criticism* (Minneapolis: University of Minnesota Press, 1993), p. 138. This belief is known as the Horatio Alger myth. In *Racial Healing* Dalton discusses the fallacy of this myth and notes that it "suggests that success in life has nothing to do with pedigree, race, class background, gender, national origin, sexual orientation—in short, with anything beyond our individual control" (p. 128).

[67]Susan E. Davies and Sister Paul Teresa Hennessee, eds., *Ending Racism in the Church* (Cleveland, Ohio: United Church Press, 1998), p. 1. See also Kwame Ture (Stokely Carmichael) and Charles V. Hamilton, *Black Power: The Politics of Liberation* (New York: Random House, 1967), p. 8; bell hooks, *Killing Rage: Ending Racism* (New York: Henry Holt, 1995), pp. 270-71; and a provocative treatment of "whiteness" as a property protected by law in Cheryl Harris, "Whiteness as Property," in *Critical Race Theory: The Cutting Edge,* ed. Richard Delgado (Philadelpia: Temple University Press, 1995), pp. 276-91.

Human beings live in a sociocultural environment of their creation, and this means that one's interests and goals can be achieved only in relation to others. It also means it is necessary that there be convergence between an individual's interests and goals and those of the larger society. In all likelihood it is the goals of the larger society that will prevail. Gerhard Lenski observed that "the goals of a given society [are] *those ends toward which the more or less coordinated efforts of the whole are directed—without regard to the harm they may do to many individual members, even the majority.* This means, in effect, that in those societies controlled by a dominant class which has the power to determine the direction of the coordinated efforts of society, *the goals of the society are the goals of this class.*"[68] When convergence is not present or possible, or when persons and groups cannot participate in the sociocultural order, inequality and marginalization of varying kinds result. When our culture of dominance institutionalizes white-race privilege, only those who are *allowed* to compete have any prospect of achieving a level of equality.

4. *Presumed right.* I have previously noted that privilege is an advantage, benefit, immunity, permission or opportunity. In common discourse it is understood to be a *special* prerogative, one that is not commonly enjoyed and therefore peculiar to some in a way that distinguishes them from others. The English word *privilege* comes from Latin, where *privus* (alone, single) and *lex* (law) combine to form *privilegium,* meaning "a law that applies to or affects one person." Additionally, *privus* is the root of the English word *private,* and its opposite is *public,* from *publicus.* Thus in its original usage, *privilege* as a law affecting only one person was distinguished from *public law* affecting everyone. By definition, then, privilege is what it is because it is not granted to or acquired by all; it is in fact, now as then, a prerogative of position and status, linked inexorably with power capacities in social and economic relations.

In the ancient world, power and privilege were wielded almost exclusively by the aristocracy, the ruling elite who accumulated wealth and property, and therefore position and status, by the exploitation of the artisan, merchant and peasant classes. As institutionalized in the sociocultural order, power and privilege brought certain rights, among which was the right to pass on one's wealth and property, as well as one's position and status, to one's children. Thus the privileges of a socioeconomic class were held and passed from one generation

---

[68]Lenski, *Power and Privilege,* p. 41. This argument is developed at considerable length in C. Wright Mills, *The Power Elite,* new ed. (New York: Oxford University Press, 1999 [original edition 1956]), where Mills contends that the ruling class that determines the goals and direction of the United States has been and continues to be made up of the corporate, governmental and military elite. It is notable that this economic, political and military class has been and remains almost exclusively European American.

to the next among a very limited number of people. Those who inherited their wealth, property, position and status did so "by right."[69] Theirs was also a culture of dominance.

In our culture of dominance, white privilege as a prerogative is held by all European Americans, in both private and public, because it is conferred by the sociocultual order. All Americans have the right of inheritance, and acquired economic wealth and social status are passed on to the next generation. But white privilege consists in the fact that European Americans believe themselves to be *due* certain opportunities and advantages that have been held and passed on almost exclusively by their own group. Over an extended period of time, immigrant and U.S.-born European Americans have had the opportunity to develop financial and social resources and status because the institutionalized systems worked for them by excluding others. As Kwame Ture and Charles Hamilton have observed, "*there is a strong tendency for* [European Americans] *to feel that these benefits are theirs 'by right.'* The advantages come to be thought of as normal, proper, customary, as sanctioned by time, precedent and social consensus."[70] White privilege is thus the presumption of right that had been conferred by our culture of dominance, "a set of advantages one receives simply by being born with features that society values especially highly."[71] It is the willing or unwilling, conscious or unconscious acceptance of advantages and benefits conferred by power relations that have been institutionalized as preference for European Americans, preference that is neither earned nor merited but presumed.

5. *Normal and natural.* As an indication of position and status and a capacity in power relations, privilege is not easily relinquished. Persons in a superordinate position, especially one institutionalized in a sociocultural order, come to identify themselves with their position; they become the role they play (remember: "I am a doctor!") and come to assume that the status and privileges are theirs because of their superior moral character, acquired knowledge and skill, or some inherent characteristic. As C. Wright Mills has observed, "People with

---

[69]See Lenski, *Power and Privilege,* esp. pp. 219-31. In this study of social and economic stratification in ancient societies, Lenski describes the relationship between power and privilege by noting: "If privilege is defined as possession or control of a portion of the surplus produced by a society, then it follows that *privilege is largely a function of power, and to a very limited degree, a function of altruism.* This means that to explain most of the distribution of privilege in a society, we have but to determine the distribution of power" (p. 45). He later observes that "*with the shift from the rule of might to the rule of right, power continues to be the determinant of privilege, but the forms of power change.* Force is replaced by institutionalized forms of power as the most useful resources in the struggle between individuals and groups for prestige and privilege, though force still remains in the picture as the ultimate guarantee of these more genteel forms" (p. 56). That is, institutionalized power structuralizes privilege.
[70]Ture and Hamilton, *Black Power,* p. 8.
[71]Dalton, *Racial Healing,* p. 110.

advantages are loath to believe that they just happen to be people with advantages. They come readily to define themselves as inherently worthy of what they possess; they come to believe themselves 'naturally' elite; and, in fact, to imagine their possessions and their privileges as natural extensions of their own elite selves."[72]

Persons with privilege may very well choose not to exercise it, but they are generally most unwilling to give it up. Indeed it is extraordinarily difficult to abdicate privilege, precisely because it has been institutionalized as one of the boundaries separating status positions. Privilege is so identified with position and status in the common sense that vacating one is tantamount to vacating the other. When privilege is exercised, it is presumed to be a natural extension of one's position and status. When challenged, however, privilege requires legitimation, and apart from the default positions of "that's the way things are" or "it comes with the territory," the legitimation of privilege amounts to contending that one has earned it or is otherwise entitled to it, so that it becomes in effect a "right," a prerogative owed a person by law, tradition or custom.

In our culture of dominance, white privilege is difficult to abandon because it is largely invisible to its possessors; it is built into the racialized sociocultural order, and it is legitimated by the assumptions, beliefs, attitudes and values of the supposed superiority of European Americans that have been externalized in structures. European Americans who cannot distinguish themselves as *producers* from the sociocultural order as their *product* are unable to distinguish nature from society. Those who have constructed and reified race by externalizing themselves in the development of a culture of dominance believe that their world is not only *there* but *natural*. The institutional systems built on exclusion and restriction serve their interests and needs "naturally" because they have been designed and developed with only them in mind. Over time the spheres and schemes, roles and rules established by and for them have become objective reality, a European American world that objectifies European American identities. Thus the core of white-race identity in a preferentially white-racial world is relative to the advantages that differentiate whites from others.

As an advantage gained through institutionalized inequality and dominance, white privilege cannot be legitimated; it can only be construed as an ideological defense of the racialized status quo. In an institutionalized system of inequality that advantages some and disadvantages others, it cannot be argued that the reason the disadvantaged fail to achieve and prosper is that they lack the requisite abilities, have poor values, or lack initiative and discipline. But this is precisely the reason given by the advantaged to explain and justify the inequal-

---

[72]Mills, *Power Elite,* p. 14.

ity and deflect criticism from the benefits of white privilege.[73] The fact of inequality does not legitimate advantage any more than the fact of difference legitimates superiority. Rather the conditions of inequality produce advantage, and the exercise of advantage eventuates in inequality, and on the cycle goes.[74]

When the things that tend to contribute to personal and social fulfillment—character, ambition, perseverance, education, competence, religious beliefs, moral values, opportunity and competition—are linked with race, and when the sociocultural environment in which they are fostered and expressed is structured along the lines of race to the advantage of one people group over against others, the situation that results sullies and diminishes the achievements of all. As a nation, we are not likely to abrogate our culture of race so long as the institutionalization of a culture of racial dominance remains intact and the benefits of racism that accrue to the dominant group outweigh its personal and social costs.

Maintaining the Universe: The Problem of Race

In the final section of this chapter, we need to consider the basis on which European America has sought to establish and justify the dominance of its sociocultural order and the strategies that have been employed to preserve it. This takes

---

[73]The points now completed are, in broad strokes, my attempt to respond to the perspectives and explanations of the racial situation in the United States laid out and argued by Jared Taylor in *Paved with Good Intentions: The Failure of Race Relations in Contemporary America* (New York: Carroll & Graf, 1992). In this book Taylor endeavors to refute the position that European Americans are responsible for the situation of African Americans. Specifically, he argues against the position that "whites are responsible for the problems blacks face. Black crime, black poverty, black illegitimacy, black difficulties of all kinds can be traced to a heritage of slavery and to inveterate white racism. In other words, it is the malevolence of whites that causes blacks to fail" (p. 14). His argument attempts to expose, among other things, the "double standards that permit much to blacks that is denied to whites," claiming that "the doctrine of white racism excuses blacks even when they are guilty of what is least tolerated in whites: racism itself" (p. 17).

[74]For discussions analyzing the manifold patterns of "institutional racism," see especially Joseph Barndt, *Dismantling Racism: The Continuing Challenge to White America* (Minneapolis: Augsburg Fortress, 1991), pp. 74-100; Branding, *Fulfilling the Dream*, pp. 43-57; Ture and Hamilton, *Black Power*, pp. 4-55; Christopher Bates Doob, *Racism: An American Cauldron*, 2nd ed. (New York: HarperCollins, 1996), pp. 2-9, 103-60; Gertrude Ezorsky, *Racism and Justice: The Case for Affirmative Action* (Ithaca, N.Y.: Cornell University Press, 1991), pp. 9-27; Feagin and Sikes, *Living with Racism;* Feagin and Vera, *White Racism;* David Theo Goldberg, "The Social Formation of Racist Discourse," in *Anatomy of Racism*, ed. Goldberg, pp. 295-311; Hacker, *Two Nations*, pp. 23-32; George D. Kelsey, *Racism and the Christian Understanding of Man* (New York: Charles Scribner's Sons, 1965), pp. 19-35; Kovel, *White Racism*, pp. 13-41, 177-228; Robert W. Terry, *For Whites Only*, rev. ed. (Grand Rapids, Mich.: Eerdmans, 1975), pp. 1-7, 40-66; Waller, *Face to Face*, pp. 43-54; William Julius Wilson, *Power, Racism and Privilege* (New York: Free Press, 1973), pp. 29-43; George A. Yancey, *Beyond Black and White: Reflections on Racial Reconciliation* (Grand Rapids, Mich.: Baker, 1996), pp. 26-48; and Zack, *Thinking About Race*, pp. 43-46.

us to the "worldview" or "symbolic universe" in relation to which the patterns
and practices of individual and institutional life have meaning and legitimacy.
In a sense it takes us to the racial ideology of European America, the constellation of beliefs that have been used to rationalize the social, economic, political,
and religious interests and practices of one group in our culture of dominance.
We will endeavor to discern this universe of meaning and the ways it has been
maintained in response to challenge and resistance. But first let's ask some
basic questions to find a way into this arena.

From how to why. How is it that we come to know the things we know?
How do we come to understand and interpret the world presented to us the
way we do? And how have we learned to function in this world we see? The
simplest answer is *we have been taught by others.* More particularly, we have
been taught, directly or indirectly, by the explanations, interpretations and practices of others in the world we have come to know, and this teaching has
always occurred in a sphere with its schemes. We learn in school from teachers, at home from parents or guardians, at work from coworkers and bosses, in
church from fellow Christians and pastors. We learn by being told things,
observing things and experiencing things. Explicitly or implicitly, we are taught
in all the spheres of our everyday lives by the persons we encounter and the
activities that take place there. We acquire factual knowledge about things,
practical knowledge about how to do things, personal knowledge about others
and ourselves. We learn values, attitudes and behaviors and how to name,
express and judge them. And we learn how to live by putting knowledge,
observations and experiences to use in our day-to-day lives.

Furthermore, we acquire our view of the world from the sociocultural order
that prevails in our environment. The roles and rules we learn in order to express
our identity in the world are given their value and significance by society. This
orientation to the world around us, our ability to perceive and make sense of it,
and the ways we interpret our own experience and location are related to society's symbolic universe of meaning. The agency that mediates this connection is
what sociologists refer to as a "reference group." Peter Berger has defined this
term this way: "A reference group . . . is the collectivity whose opinions, convictions and courses of action are decisive for the formation of our own opinions,
convictions and courses of action. The reference group provides us with a model
with which we can continually compare ourselves. Specifically, it gives us a particular slant on social reality, one . . . that will in any case be part and parcel of
our allegiance to this particular group."[75] Situated in a reference group, we come
to share in a common knowledge and hold a common sense about the world.

---

[75]Berger, *Invitation to Sociology,* p. 118.

But let's ask a somewhat different set of questions. *Why* do we know the things we know? Why do we understand and interpret the world that is presented to us the way we do? Why have we learned to function in this world we see? Indeed why are things the way they are? We are now asking about not the manner but the purpose or rationale of our learning; we are asking for explanation and justification.

As initiation into a shared world, our education and socialization take place in ways both direct and indirect, explicit and implicit, formal and informal, intentional and unintentional, involving others who speak and act in the spheres of our lives. By the guidance of others or on our own initiative, we become acclimated to and knowledgeable of a shared world. The answers to the *how* and *what* questions are relatively straightforward; the answers to the *why* questions are more complex.

For example: What is a hamburger? How is it made? You learned what a hamburger is and how it is made from someone, either by instruction or by observation. In answer to the question "Why is it made?" you probably would say that the reason you make hamburgers is to consume them as food. But there are other levels to the answer, and they have to do with inter- and intrarelated institutional systems. Why are there hamburgers and why are they made? To provide income for grocery stores, which buy meat and buns from distributors, who buy from suppliers, who buy from ranchers and farmers (who are probably corporate rather than private enterprises), who purchased and raised their commodity by capitalization from a bank that is in the banking business to make money. You would probably not say that the reason you make hamburgers is to keep the bank (and the others) in business, but that's what you're doing. Why does McDonald's make hamburgers? To feed a hamburger-hungry public. People want and eat hamburgers, and McDonald's exists to fill that need. It also exist to provide jobs, low-paying and high-paying up the line. But ultimately the reason McDonald's makes hamburgers is to make money for its stockholders; McDonald's is a corporate business.

Most people enter into existing institutions and systems and participate in their spheres and schemes without giving much thought to the why questions. Students go to school, employees go to work, patients go to clinics or hospitals, voters go to polling places, hungry people go to grocery stores, and borrowers go to banks without giving much thought to the complex network of activities and interactions that make these institutions function and that are largely invisible. We have learned, either by being instructed or by observation, intuition or experience, what the roles and rules are and how to play and follow them; we share in the common knowledge and the common sense of the situation. We blend in and play our part because we know—and we expect others to know—that's the way it is.

We tend not to think about *why* that's the way it is until we perceive or experience the others, the interaction or the environment as problematic. There is some aspect of the situation that becomes what Stephen Brookfield has called a "negative trigger" that stimulates uneasiness, confusion or doubt.[76] When this occurs, we begin to ask the *why* questions that have to do with explanations and justifications. We ask about what is known and assumed and why the situation is legitimate. The answers that are given are usually variants of the following: (1) that is the policy as I/we interpret and apply it here, (2) that is the procedure that I/we have been instructed to follow, (3) that is what the boss/owner(s) wants, or (4) that is the customary practice we observe. All of these are variations on the "that's the way it is" or "that's the way we do things around here" theme; they are indicative of *habitualized* roles, rules and activity.

Such explanations only invite further questions: *Why* is there this policy or procedure, and why is it followed? *Why* does the boss/owner(s) intend this? *Why* is this the customary practice around here? This spiral of questions seeking explanation and justification ultimately takes one up through the scheme, sphere, institution and system to *the System* and the symbolic universe that legitimates it all.

In need of explanation. As we saw earlier, institutions require explanation and legitimation. As objective expressions of habitualized activity expressing human values, attitudes, beliefs and practices, institutions need to be explained and interpreted—legitimated and justified—to those who enter into their spheres as clients, customers or employees. Explanations amount to a retrieval of the original circumstances and meanings and their adaptation to the present situation. The comprehensive articulation that encompasses the many interrelated aspects of an institution, including its history as embedded in documents and memory as well as its future as expressed in its vision and goals, is the institution's symbolic universe, or worldview, in relation to which it has meaning and individuals can find themselves in its life. Just as a particular sphere and its schemes are situated in an institution with its peculiar symbolic universe of meaning, so an institution is situated in an institutional system, and an institutional system in *the System,* and all together these manifold expressions of sociocultural life are bounded by a variegated symbolic universe that is constructed to legitimate the sociocultural order.

At all levels, symbolic universes need to be maintained, especially when

---

[76]See Stephen D. Brookfield, *Developing Critical Thinkers: Challenging Adults to Explore Alternative Ways of Thinking and Acting* (San Francisco: Jossey-Bass, 1987), pp. 6-14, 26, 31-32.

they meet and conflict with an alternative. When variant patterns and practices—institutions and their universes of meaning—emerge, it becomes necessary not merely to defend but to justify superiority—or to change. Effectiveness in maintaining the symbolic universe will depend on the use of power to define and enforce the dominant patterns and practices.

Our culture of dominance, developed along the lines of racial exclusion and restriction, is an institutionalized order set in relation to a symbolic universe that periodically has required maintenance because of contestation. Each encounter between the dominant group and a subordinate group has engendered a conflict, a challenge, a struggle; and having established control over the subordinate group, the dominant group must find ways to preserve and justify its hegemony. The task of the guardians of the universe of meaning that legitimates a sociocultural order is to develop strategies by which its dominance and superiority can be asserted.

Racialized ethnocentrism. In European America, the symbolic universe of meaning that has been maintained to legitimate the sociocultural order is the ideology of racism. Because the beliefs about race and behaviors and practices of racial exclusion and restriction emerged with the origin and development of our sociocultural order; because these beliefs and conduct are embedded in and externalized by the sociocultural order; and because they in turn have served to legitimate the institutionalization of the sociocultural order, we can identify the ideology of racism as this order's symbolic universe of meaning. Moreover, because race does not exist except as the socially constructed inequality between European Americans and other people groups, an inequality maintained by stratified power relations and privileges institutionalized in the sociocultural order, it is possible to identify the universe of meaning more particularly as European America's racialized version of *ethnocentrism*. This is to say that because "race" has been constructed by a dominant ethnic group in and with its development of a sociocultural order characterized by—among other things—the oppression, exclusion and restriction of a subordinated ethnic group, we can use the sociological-anthropological term *ethnocentrism* to label the worldview of the dominant group.

Sociologists and anthropologists define *ethnicity* as a sizable group of people who share a common history, geography, language, religious tradition and way of life that are transmitted as learned behaviors from generation to generation. In short, ethnicity is a *cultural* phenomenon, not a biological one.[77] Because the

---

[77]In popular usage, *race* and *ethnicity* have become virtually synonymous, with the preference for the latter in common discourse growing mostly out of a desire not to offend in the use of the former. However, scholars make a distinction between the two terms: *race* as unequal

European American *ethnic* group constructed *race* by claiming and institution-alizing dominance and superiority over other *ethnic* groups, the symbolic universe of meaning can be called the ideology of *ethnocentrism*, i.e., the unassailable belief that one's own ethnic group is superior to all others. In the words of William Graham Sumner (1840-1910) who coined this neologism, it is "the view of things in which one's own group is the center of everything. Each group nourishes its own pride and vanity and boasts itself superior and looks with contempt on outsiders."[78] Ethnocentric beliefs are based on the presumed superiority of one's culture, so that the evaluation of other cultures that are viewed as "different" always results in their relegation to an inferior status. Using the idealized cultural norms and standards of one's own "reference group" to evaluate another culture invariably issues in the disparagement of the other. In the case of European America, the evaluation eventuated in the ideology of racialized ethnocentrism.[79]

Universe-maintenance strategies. This symbolic universe of meaning has been maintained principally by the use of three strategies, one of which has been predominant at any given time, but all of which have been employed concurrently to varying degrees. These strategies have functioned at conceptual, convictional, institutional and systemic levels to defend and preserve the socio-cultural status quo of the European American group legitimated by the ideology of racialized ethnocentrism. As these strategies are described, keep in mind that they were utilized because the encounter between dominant and subordinate groups was primarily a "problem" of control, a "conflict" between ethnic groups that threatened the sociocultural hegemony of the European American group. But we also need to keep in mind that the encounter occasioned signifi-

---

power relations maintained by a dominant cultural group over a subordinated cultural group, and *ethnicity* as the relative cultural homogeneity of a single people group. Neither "race" nor "ethnicity" is biological in the sense of genetic transmission. Race is a power relation, and eth-nicity is a cultural relation. For discussions on race and ethnicity, see Michael Omi and Howard Winant, *Racial Formation in the United States from the 1960s to the 1990s* (New York: Routledge, 1994), pp. 9-24; Montagu, *Man's Most Dangerous Myth,* pp. 41-98, 186-87, 521-29; Manning Marable, *Beyond Black and White: Transforming African-American Politics* (New York: Verso, 1995), pp. 185-200; Patterson, *Ordeal of Integration,* pp. x-xi, 72-77; Sow-ell, *Race and Culture,* pp. xiii, 1-35; Wilson, *Power, Racism and Privilege,* pp. 3-6; and Zack, *Thinking About Race,* pp. 29-38.

[78]Cited in Sniderman and Piazza, *Scar of Race,* p. 52. See also Pettigrew, introduction to *Preju-dice,* pp. 3, 31; and Doob, *Racism,* p. 39. William Graham Sumner was a professor of political science at Yale University and the leading advocate for social Darwinism in the United States. See Hofstadter, *Social Darwinism,* pp. 51-84; and Shipman, *Evolution of Racism,* pp. 107-21.

[79]Others who have articulated a similar view of "racism" as an ideology legitimating the patterns and practices constituting our sociocultural order are Kelsey, *Racism and the Christian,* pp. 22-23; Matsuoka, *Color of Faith,* p. 94; and Charles W. Mills, *The Racial Contract* (Ithaca, N.Y.: Cornell University Press, 1997), pp. 16-17.

cant critique and resistance that can be described only as solemn, sustained and remarkable. This response came mainly from within the oppressed communities as they drew on their own sociocultural resources and universe of meaning. But to varying degrees it can also be seen in countercultural movements emerging from within the dominant culture, as well as in movements that brought members of several people groups together in a common cause.

1. *Dominion.* The first strategy was dominion, and while it prevailed during the period of slavery (1619-1865), it was generally characteristic of the entire period of European exploration of the "New World." As the sociocultural order was initially developed, European emigrants and their descendants endeavored to establish sovereign control over indigenous peoples and their lands as well as the growing African slave population that provided labor in the Southern agrarian economy. The objective was to become *lord of the property,* both people and land. In order to accomplish this, the new European Americans had to reject the cultural life of their subject peoples and deny them their right to practice it. The African slaves and their descendants were regarded as aliens, having been brought to the American continent from a very different place with a way of life that could not be accommodated by the dominant group. This alienation, however, was not unqualified; the Africans were necessary to the developing economy and thus participants in the construction of the sociocultural order, but they were excluded from sharing the resources their labor produced and confined immovably to the status imposed on them by the dominant culture. Under duress, they contributed to the development of a "peculiar institution" that evoked in the dominant group both repugnance and attraction because it reminded them of both their growing economic dependence and their sociopolitical independence.

The ideology of racialized ethnocentrism, with its core notion of cultural superiority, emerged as a reflection of the needs, interests, values and beliefs of the Europeans and their descendants as they built their world. This ideology of supremacy legitimated the institutionalization of slavery with its practices of oppression and exploitation by imposing an inferior status on a subject people. And the extent to which the dominant group succeeded in rejecting and denying African cultural expressiveness only served to confirm the ideology; achieving dominion confirmed superiority. The ideology also justified the use of institutionalized power to confine a needed but despised people group in their assigned place. The threat had to be dispelled or minimized with the resources at hand: social attitudes and values, economic opportunity, legal and political structures, and where necessary physical violence in the form of slave beatings, murder and the forcible suppression of slave revolts.

As a religious heritage and faith institutionalized in the sociocultural order,

Christianity was made to serve the needs and interests of the dominant group. The ideology conferred superiority on the religion of the dominant group; thus the African religions were rejected because they were not Christian and their adherents were regarded as "heathen." The Bible was interpreted in ways that authorized both the institution of slavery and the assigned status and roles of the subordinate group.[80] Ivan Beals summarizes five reasons taken from the Christian Scriptures and tradition to legitimate sociocultural domination over the Africans and their descendants: "(1) Africans could be enslaved because they were under Noah's curse upon his son Ham. (2) Israel, God's chosen people, had slaves. (3) Jesus Christ did not forbid slavery. (4) Slavery was merely the lowest level in a divinely approved social order. (5) The enslavement of Africans actually improved their lives, by giving them access to the gospel."[81]

The "logic" of the ideology behind the strategy of dominion can be summarized as follows.

Why are black people slaves and excluded from the sociocultural order?

Because they are different and inferior.

Why are they different and inferior?

Because God made them that way, and they are unfit for anything but bondage.

2. *Segregation.* The second strategy was segregation, prevailing from the end of the Civil War until the passage of Civil Rights Act in 1964 and the Voting Rights Act in 1965. The Civil War can be regarded as a struggle for dominion

---

[80]The role played by Christianity and the contribution of its interpreters in the development of race and racism almost never goes unnoticed in the literature. But there are several studies that either in whole or in part address just this issue in ways that deserve attention: Beals, *Our Racist Legacy;* Alan Davies, *Infected Christianity: A Study of Modern Racism* (Kingston, Quebec: McGill-Queens University Press, 1988); Michael O. Emerson and Christian Smith, *Divided by Faith: Evangelical Religion and the Problem of Race in America* (New York: Oxford University Press, 2000); Tony Evans, *Let's Get to Know Each Other* (Nashville: Thomas Nelson, 1995), pp. 1-20; Fredrickson, *Black Image,* pp. 28-35; Gould, *Mismeasure of Man,* p. 103; Griffin, *Seeds of Racism;* Kyle Haselden, *The Racial Problem in Christian Perspective* (New York: Harper & Brothers, 1959); Hood, *Begrimed and Black,* pp. 2-22, 115-32, 155-80; Jordan, *White Man's Burden,* pp. 1-26, 87-98; Joseph H. Oldham, *Christianity and the Race Problem* (London: Student Christian Movement, 1924); Petigrew, *Prejudice,* 41-44; H. Shelton Smith, *In His Image, But . . . : Racism in Southern Religion, 1780-1910* (Durham, N.C.: Duke University Press, 1972); Willard M. Swartley, *Slavery, Sabbath, War and Women: Case Issues in Biblical Interpretation* (Scottdale, Penn.: Herald, 1983); and Forrest G. Wood, *The Arrogance of Faith: Christianity and Race in America from the Colonial Era to the Twentieth Century* (New York: Alfred A. Knopf, 1990).

[81]Beals, *Our Racist Legacy,* p. 7. To this should be added the fact that Paul's directives to slaves and their masters (e.g., Eph 6:5-9; Col 3:22—4:1) were construed as both tacit legitimation of the institution of slavery and a source of moral authority for controlling the demeanor of slaves.

within the European American community along the fault lines of the developing social, political, economic and religious order. On one level the war was
fought over different economic structures and the tensions between the North
and the South. At another level it was fought over political questions regarding
the autonomy of the states in relation to the federal government. And at yet
another level, the question was whether and how the union of states could be
preserved. Intersecting all of these levels was the question of the status and role
of African Americans, slave or free, in the sociocultural order. Some social,
political and abolitionist leaders advocated their full inclusion, while others
supported their repatriation to Africa. President Lincoln's belief in the inferiority
of the African descendants was exceeded only by his interest in salvaging the
Union at any cost.[82]

But the reestablishment of the Union with the victory of the North, the abolition of slavery with the Thirteenth Amendment, the granting of full citizenship
with the Fourteenth Amendment and the guarantee of voting rights with the Fif-
teenth Amendment did not bring alteration in the ideology of racialized ethnocentrism. These structural changes in the sociocultural order merely
precipitated a shift in strategy. Through segregation, the dominant order would
absorb the cultural life of the formerly subject people by taking it in and *isolate*
its expressions by separating it from the rest of society. Having achieved a measure of social, economic and political freedom, African Americans remained
subject to the European American effort to exclude and restrict by monopoliz-
ing as far as possible the sociocultural order.

The segregation imposed was physical as well as social and economic, but it
was also an imposition of limits on what roles, status and activities African
Americans could engage in as self-expression. They were free to develop their
sociocultural order within the limits of physical and social segregation, but
whenever and wherever they intersected with the dominant culture, their roles,
status and interactions were either dictated or forbidden—according to custom
or law—by the dominant group. The spheres and schemes, roles and rules in
which members of the two groups interacted remained under the monopoly of
the dominant group. The European Americans may have lost the control they

---

[82]On Abraham Lincoln's views on the inferiority of "Negroes," see C. Vann Woodward, *The
Strange Career of Jim Crow,* 3rd rev. ed. (New York: Oxford University Press, 1974), pp. 20-
21; and Fredrickson, *Black Image,* p. 91. In a letter to Horace Greeley, Lincoln declared: "My
paramount object in this struggle is to save the Union, and is not either to save or destroy Slavery. If I could save the Union without freeing any slave, I would do it; and if I could save it
by freeing all the slaves, I would do it; and if I could do it by freeing some and leaving others
alone, I would also do that. What I do about Slavery and the colored race, I do because it
helps to save this Union" (quoted in Paul Kivel, *Uprooting Racism: How White People Can
Work for Racial Justice* [Gabriola Island, B.C.: New Society, 1996], p. 121).

had exercised in the strategy of dominion, but they retained a measure of control in segregation.

Again, the ideology of racialized ethnocentrism emerged in the continuing development of the dominant sociocultural world. African Americans and their developing sociocultural order were still regarded as inferior; popular beliefs, attitudes, values and practices remained largely unchanged, embedded in the institutionalized world of European America. Within the African American community, the debate over whether to continue to seek full and free inclusion as equals in the sociocultural world or separate entirely to develop their own authentic institutions came to full flower.[83] For the dominant group, the ideology legitimated the separation, exclusion and restriction of African American citizens by the imposition of a status of inferiority, buttressed in the common sense by the institutionalization of inequality, the continuing development of the so-called science of race, influenced by Darwin's theory of biological evolution, and the culture of race, influenced by the application of Darwin's evolution theory to cultural development (i.e., social Darwinism). The extent to which the dominant group succeeded in absorbing and isolating African American cultural expressiveness only confirmed the ideology: establishing segregation confirmed superiority.

From the Social Gospel movement in the North to the participation of Southern ministers in the revival of the Ku Klux Klan, Christianity continued to be pressed to serve the dominant sociocultural interests framed by the presumption of African American inferiority.[84] Writing in 1929, H. Richard Niebuhr observed that "whether the dogma of white superiority and Negro inferiority has been openly avowed or unconsciously accepted, the white churches have nevertheless taken it for granted and have come to regard it as not incompatible with the remainder of their beliefs. . . . The assumption of superiority by one group—an assumption which became unquestioned social tradition—has been given the dignity of an impartial natural law and regarded

---

[83]The terms of this debate are known as *integration/assimilation* and *nationalism/separatism*, and within each position there is a range of opinions on strategies for achieving them. See Gates and West, *Future of the Race*, pp. 3-55; Wilson, *Power, Racism and Privilege*, pp. 50-61; West, *Prophesy Deliverance*, pp. 27-68; Marable, *Beyond Black and White*, pp. 185-200; and Stuckey, *Slave Culture*. Throughout his book *Race Orthodoxy in the South and Other Aspects of the Negro Question* (New York: Neale, 1914), Thomas Pearce Bailey argued for a scientific (i.e., social, psychological, anthropological) study of the "race problem," and thus in effect invited "science" to answer the question of whether African Americans should be permanently segregated or colonized elsewhere.

[84]In addition to the works cited in note 80, see Gossett, *Race*, pp. 176-97; Lincoln, *Race, Religion*, pp. 31-60; Myrdal, *American Dilemma*, pp. 83-111, 558-72; and H. Richard Niebuhr, *The Social Sources of Denominationalism* (1929; reprint, Gloucester, Mass.: Peter Smith, 1987), pp. 236-63.

as a self-evident truth."[85]

The "logic" of the ideology underlying the strategy of segregation can be summarized in the following way.

Why are black citizens segregated and restricted?

Because they are different and inferior.

Why are they different and inferior?

Because they are biologically and culturally incapable of achievement as a result of their place on the evolutionary scale.

3. *Integration.* The third strategy used to maintain the universe of meaning, one that has prevailed since the dismantling of legal segregation, the outlawing of discrimination in the wake of the civil rights movement of the 1950s and 1960s, and the advent of affirmative action in education and employment, is integration. The struggle against segregation and discrimination was a struggle for equality and inclusion in the sociocultural order; the struggle against exclusion and restriction was a struggle for the freedom and rights declared by the Constitution.

Through Supreme Court decisions, federal legislation and presidential executive orders, the government attempted to secure access to the sociocultural order and its opportunity for those who had previously been denied and isolated. But all these initiatives—and the systems of enforcement they spawned—did not originate from or alter the ideology of racialized ethnocentrism. Neither did they come without social, economic and political cost. These changes in the dominant sociocultural order only prohibited certain practices (e.g., discrimination) in many of the spheres and schemes of everyday life.

With the strategy of integration, the dominant sociocultural systems incorporated communities of color by admitting their members into systems already in existence, in effect constituting them parts of a larger whole. Furthermore, the dominant group contrived this solution with ingenuity and improvisation, continuing to control institutionalized power structures to advance its own interests and privileges. Integration made equality and access possible, but only on a limited basis; members of excluded and restricted communities could become part of the dominant culture and participate in its institutionalized systems to the extent that they played the roles and played by the rules it laid down. Achieving social, political and economic rights did not guarantee that these rights would be honored and respected, even with the creation of legal mechanisms of adjudication and enforcement (e.g., Equal Employment Opportunity Commission, state and federal courts). The European American response to the demand for equal rights in an accessible sociocultural order was, in effect, consent to *assimilation:* by suppressing their own sociocultural identities, interests,

---

[85]Niebuhr, *Social Sources,* pp. 236-37.

values and traditions, people of color could be made to accept—and perhaps even embrace—a sociocultural world previously closed to them.

Once again the dominant sociocultural order effectively employed the ideology of racialized ethnocentrism to manage itself. The force of law made it accessible, but practices of exclusion, restriction, discrimination and violence have continued to express beliefs, attitudes and values that take their point of departure in the presumed sociocultural inferiority of other people groups. Greater access to education and employment has made possible the growth of an African American middle class that nevertheless continues to encounter both subtle and blatant discrimination in spheres of everyday life. At the same time, the so-called underclass communities of color have grown as people confined to poverty, segregated housing and underfunded public education struggle to survive in an institutionalized system that regards them as incapable of achievement.[86] The ideology legitimates social, economic and political stratification in communities of color by contending that people of color produce a so-called culture of poverty[87] or can succeed only if they are given "special preferences" through the lowering of accepted standards, but that they will otherwise be expected to meet the same norms and expectations, express the same beliefs and values, and conduct themselves in the same manner as members of the dominant group. The extent to which the dominant group succeeds in incorporating and assimilating—and co-

---

[86]For general discussions of the social, economic and political situation in African America, see especially Roy L. Brooks, *Rethinking the American Race Problem* (Berkeley: University of California Press, 1990); Joe R. Feagin, *Racist America: Roots, Current Realities and Future Reparations* (New York: Routledge, 2000); Hacker, *Two Nations;* Gerald David Jaynes and Robin M. Williams Jr., eds., *A Common Destiny: Blacks and American Society* (Washington, D.C.: National Academy Press, 1989); Marable, *Black Liberation;* National Urban League, *The State of Black America 1999* (New York: National Urban League, 1999); Oliver and Shapiro, *Black Wealth/White Wealth;* Omi and Winant, *Racial Formation;* Patterson, *Ordeal of Integration;* Billy J. Tidwell, *The Black Report: Charting the Changing Status of African Americans* (Lanham, Md.: University Press of America, 1997); and Tom Wicker, *Tragic Failure: Racial Integration in America* (New York: William Morrow, 1996). For discussions of the African American middle class, see Stephen L. Carter, *Reflections of an Affirmative Action Baby* (New York: BasicBooks, 1991); Ellis Cose, *Rage of a Privileged Class* (New York: HarperCollins, 1993); Curry, *Affirmative Action Debate;* Early, *Lure and Loathing;* and Feagin and Sikes, *Living with Racism.* Analyses of the "underclass" in African America can be found in these publications by William Julius Wilson: *The Declining Significance of Race,* 2nd ed. (Chicago: University of Chicago Press, 1980); *The Truly Disadvantaged: The Inner City, the Underclass, and Public Policy* (Chicago: University of Chicago Press, 1987); *When Work Disappears: The World of the New Urban Poor* (New York: Random House, 1996); and *The Bridge Over the Racial Divide: Rising Inequality and Coalition Politics* (Berkeley: University of California Press, 1999).

[87]See Brooks, *Rethinking,* pp. 109-16; Feagin/Sikes, *Living with Racism,* pp. 2-14; Kivel, *Uprooting Racism,* pp. 95-98; Marable, *Black Liberation,* pp. 94-111; William Ryan, *Blaming the Victim,* rev. ed. (New York: Vintage, 1976), pp. 3-31; and Wilson, *The Truly Disadvantaged,* pp. 1-62.

opting—the cultural expressiveness of communities of color only confirms the ideology: establishing integration confirms superiority.

The religious communities and traditions of people of color are regarded as diverging from established norms and traditions; they are perceived as "different" in ways that make it possible for members of the dominant group to dismiss them. Religious communities in the United States remain largely segregated, constituted as culturally homogeneous assemblies committed to preserving the heritage of their faith tradition and its expressions. Each ethnic group, taking advantage of the freedom of religion guaranteed by the First Amendment, has developed—and institutionalized—its houses of worship and religious traditions in separation because of the legacy of dominion and segregation. Now in integration, these institutions remain mostly unchallenged in their peculiar exclusions; they stand as bastions to sociocultural autonomy, spheres and schemes where preferred norms, practices and experiences can be affirmed and validated virtually without interference.

The now-circular "logic" of the ideology implementing the strategy of integration can be summarized as follows.

Why are black people still excluded and unequal?

Because they are different.

Why are they different?

Because they are excluded and unequal.

Such is the rationale for our culture of dominance and the strategies employed to maintain its symbolic universe of meaning. At no time has the United States recognized or accorded in practice the equality of all, and at every time there have been communities of critique and resistance to the institutionalized inequality and privilege developed by European Americans. Some have always been more equal, more advantaged and more opportunistic than others; others have aspired to be so but been prevented, while still others have resigned themselves to the situation.

At no time have any of these strategies been absent. The reason? They emerge from and contribute to a symbolic universe of meaning that explains and legitimates the sociocultural order institutionalized at the hands of one group through racial oppression and exploitation of others.

●   ●   ●   ●

Indeed, the body does not consist of one member but of many. If the foot would say, "Because I am not a hand, I do not belong to the body," that would not make it any less a part of the body. . . . If one member suffers, all suffer together with it; if one member is honored, all rejoice together with it. 1 Corinthians 12:14-15, 26

Does the ear have the right to say the little finger is unimportant? If the arm is injured, is the rest of the body unaffected? If the exaltation of the hand comes at the humiliation of the foot, is there any glory in the body? With racism we have thoroughly distorted human interdependence; racism allows some to credit themselves by discrediting others, to justify themselves by alienating others, to defend themselves by attacking others. Racism deceives us by leading us to believe that some can be honored at the same time that others are suffering, and that the privilege of some is validated by the disadvantage of others.

4

THE CONSCIOUSNESS OF RACE

Not everyone who says to me, "Lord, Lord," will enter the kingdom of heaven, but only the one who does the will of my Father in heaven. On that day many will say to me, "Lord, Lord, did we not prophesy in your name, and cast out demons in your name, and do many deeds of power in your name?" Then I will declare to them, "I never knew you; go away from me, you evildoers." Matthew 7:21-23

Look, Lord, at all the things we have done in your name! And look at how strong and deep is our belief in you! Look at how we have served you and proclaimed you to others! No, Lord, we don't think we have used you to further our own interests, or co-opted your name to bless our preferred way of life. And we certainly don't think there is anyone or anything more deserving of our adoration than you. Is it our fault if the world in which we live doesn't know you like we do? Are we to blame if your name is disparaged by the unbelievers? Isn't that a mark of their sin? We're trying, Lord, we really are, but it's just so difficult at times . . .

• • • •

Each human being comes into the world as an entirely new and unrepeatable act of God's handiwork. Human agents are, of course, involved in these events, but the circumstances surrounding a child's conception and birth do not adequately explain the mystery of new life. Nor can the extraordinary advances made in medical science, including what we are learning about the human genome as the building blocks and road map of life, explain all that is at work as particular life begins and develops.

Yet while each human being comes into the world as a unique creation of God, the world into which she or he comes is already here; it exists before she or he is born, and it will undoubtedly exist after his or her life has reached its end. The world into which each new life enters is a "natural" world, a *created* world of mountains, plains, oceans, grass and other living creatures; and it is a "social" world, a *constructed* world of family, friends, organizations and places to interact with other human beings. In this twofold world we human beings are formed into the peculiar natural-social creatures we are, and grow in awareness of ourselves, others and our environment.

Our task in the present chapter is to continue exploring the social construction of race and racism by focusing attention on the ways they have influenced the formation of human subjectivity in our context. In a sense this is a turn inward, a look at consciousness as the awareness of ourselves—our identities, attitudes, beliefs and sensations. This look into the internal world does not put aside the external world; as I hope to show, the two are not so easily separated. Just as human beings build their social worlds as the expression of themselves, so these social worlds work on human beings to influence and form subjectivity and consciousness. Self-externalization and social internalization consist together in a relationship of reciprocity.

I do not aim to catalog the structures and contents of consciousness as such, but rather to inquire about the ways our awareness, perception and interpretation of race—or lack thereof—are formed subjectively in interaction with the objective sociocultural world around us. We will look not merely at the origins of racial consciousness but at the modes of consciousness and sense of personal identity that are influenced by the objective world of race and racism into which we entered at birth.

Exploring the subjectivity of race and racism require us to consider what is involved in the internalization of the sociocultural world, the formation of consciousness, and the development of a worldview that manufactures sense by holding internal and external together in a reciprocal relationship. Thus we will take up the mythology that has engendered the false consciousness of race that contributes to the formation of racial identity and the attitudes and beliefs that express it.

Race as a Mythical Construct: The Subjective Reality of Race
For most of us, life from day to day is taken up with activities and interactions in a variety of places. Many of these activities are familiar, as are many of the people we encounter, and most of the places where the encounters occur are places we have been to before. So familiar are we with the persons, activities and places in our daily lives that we tend to assume their stability, and we do not think much about them except when our experience of them falls outside what is usual or expected. We are generally aware of what we are doing, with whom we are doing it and where, but when something out of the ordinary occurs—someone acts differently from what we expected, a new kind of activity is under way, or a place is unfamiliar—we become particularly aware of the

situation as we attempt to find our way into or out of it, and we are conscious of ourselves and what we are experiencing.

So we pass through our days with a rather ordinary awareness of ourselves and the little corner of the world we occupy, and on occasion a little extra-ordinary awareness of ourselves and our world. There is a reciprocity between our consciousness and the outer world around us; the externality of the world evokes awareness and influences response, and the internality of our self affects the ways we perceive, interpret and engage that world. When we encounter someone from another people group, our awareness of this may be ordinary or extra-ordinary, but we are nonetheless aware of the other, and in all likelihood our engagement with him or her will draw deep from the resources of our inner wells—experiences, understandings, attitudes, values—to orient ourselves and our conduct as we read and make sense of the other.

How do those resources come to fill the inner wells of the self, and how does it happen that they are influenced by the external world? What is involved in taking the external world into the self and in making it possible to express the self into the external world? How does a relationship of reciprocity develop between the subjective and objective worlds? And how is it that as individuals we are enabled to *make* sense of ourselves and the world and the relationship between them? More important, how have race and racism shaped our subjective reality?

To aid us in taking up these questions, we will turn once again to Peter Berger and Thomas Luckmann, whose work will show that the answers have to do with the fact that we have been socialized into the myth of race. After examining their theory of socialization, we will explore the nature of myth and the mythology of race.

Socialization, subjectivity and identity. In their discussion of the social order, Berger and Luckmann argue that a society has both an objective and a subjective reality, and as such it is constituted by three interrelated dimensions: the expressions of the self into a world outside the self (*externalization* of self), the products that result from self-expressive activity and that are available to others in a world (*objectivity* of self and world), and the absorption of the objective world into the self's inner world (*internalization* of world).[1] The process by which an individual experiences and interprets objective events as the self-expressing activities of others, absorbs the meaning of such events into her or his own subjectivity, and adapts to and

---

[1]For the paragraphs that follow, see Peter L. Berger and Thomas Luckmann, *The Social Construction of Reality: A Treatise in the Sociology of Knowledge* (New York: Doubleday, 1966), pp. 129-77.

interacts with the objective world is known as *socialization.*

This process begins when one is born into an already-existing sociocultural order. Berger and Luckmann distinguish between two types of socialization. First and most important, *primary* socialization takes place in infancy and child-hood, when the persons responsible for the child mediate and interpret the objective world in accordance with their own location within it and their own stories and understandings of it. In the course of primary socialization the child begins to take on an identity that is both objectively assigned by "significant others" and subjectively appropriated by the child, resulting in a kind of "dia-lectic between identification by others and self-identification."[2] In other words, the child is *identified* by the self-expressive activity of others and internalizes this *identity* as the self *identifies* with the others. As the child is located in a rela-tional and objective world and internalizes the roles and attitudes of others, he or she also internalizes their world: "To be given an identity involves being assigned a specific place in the world. . . . Subjective appropriation of identity and subjective appropriation of the social world are merely different aspects of the *same* process of internalization, mediated by the *same* significant others."[3] Moreover, just as the child does not select his or her significant others from among several possible candidates, so the child does not select his or her "world" from among several possible worlds; the world internalized by the child is accepted "as *the* world, the only existent and only conceivable world" as objectively mediated and interpreted by the significant others.[4]

As socialization proceeds, the child develops the capacity to abstract pro-gressively from the attitudes and behaviors of specific others to attitudes and behaviors in general, and thereby to internalize the norms and expectations of others; the child moves from "I should not do this because the response from Mom is negative" to "*one* should not do this because the response from *others* is negative." For Berger and Luckmann, the consciousness of this "generalized other" is formed by abstracting from the attitudes and behaviors of significant others, and is indicative of the internalization of society as such. The individual discerns the intersections between self and others, recognizing the objective reality of others and their world and establishing the subjective reality of a self-with-others in a shared world. The child is in the world, and the world is in the child.

The second type of socialization begins when the "generalized other" has been established in the individual's consciousness and he or she is capacitated

---

[2]Ibid., p. 132.
[3]Ibid.
[4]Ibid., p. 134.

as a member of society (objective) with an internalized self and sense of the world (subjective). *Secondary* socialization takes place as the individual moves out into the objective world and begins to learn and internalize the roles, rules and language of the spheres and schemes that characterize its order. Thus it is "the internalization of institutional or institution-based 'subworlds.'"[5] This stage of socialization assumes an already-formed self and internalized world, so the socialization that then occurs does not *build* a subjective reality so much as it builds *on* a subjective reality. Because the already-internalized self and world have a tendency to persist, new internalizations must be added on to and integrated with the existing subjective reality, and this imposition runs the possible risk of inconsistency and contradiction.

A child who was socialized to take initiative and tell the truth may be disoriented in a sphere where passivity and equivocation are expected; a child who was told or led to believe that she is better than others who are different, or is entitled to something because she has earned it, or can accomplish whatever she desires, may not learn to respect and celebrate others and may begrudge their accomplishments or constrain their own self-expression. Responses such as these not only indicate a disrupted secondary socialization but manifest an inability to distinguish between the subjective self and the objective world one inhabits with others.

Knowledge, attitudes, values and behaviors internalized in the home may render an individual well- or ill-suited for functioning in institutional spheres. Nevertheless, our socialization is never completed, for we must continually learn and internalize roles and rules of the many new and familiar spheres and schemes that constitute the objective sociocultural order and correspond to the subjective reality of the self.

Validating subjectivity and identity. A society needs mechanisms to facilitate the internalization of the sociocultural order and the development and maintenance of an individual's subjective reality. Like the objective reality delineated by the institutionalized order, reality as perceived in the individual's consciousness needs protection and legitimation. For Berger and Luckmann, this is lent by the "plausibility structures" on which subjective reality depends. These are the social bases and processes that recognize and confirm one's identity. For example, the need to maintain one's identity as a professional basketball player requires the game of basketball, a context in which the game is played and an institutional structure that recognizes and confirms the individual's identity. Or one's identity as president of an organization requires an environment whose spheres and schemes, roles and rules recognize and confirm this identity.

---

[5]Ibid., p. 138.

Absent this recognition and confirmation, one's subjective reality is called into question and perhaps even invalidated. One's subjective reality corresponds to an objective reality in a relationship of reciprocity, and the maintenance of one's subjective reality is facilitated by the plausibility structures that make this reciprocity both possible and meaningful. As long as one is oriented by a plausibility structure that recognizes and confirms identity, one need not doubt one's subjective reality.

However, one's subjective reality is subject to change. Indeed, as an individual journeys through life and migrates from one sphere to another in the objective world, there are many opportunities to modify one's identity, even to have an identity transformed. If one's identity is virtually completely changed, one can be said to have undergone what our authors describe as an "alternation" that requires "re-socialization"; one "must replicate to a considerable degree the strongly affective identification with the socializing personnel that was characteristic of childhood" and "must cope with a problem of dismantling, disintegrating the preceding [affective and cognitive] structure of subjective reality."[6] For an alternation in subjective reality to be effective, the individual is required to identify with new significant others who mediate a new plausibility structure that recognizes and confirms the new identity.

For Berger and Luckmann, the premier model of alternation is religious conversion, a radical transformation of subjective reality that brings not simply a different identity but different loyalties, allegiances, beliefs, attitudes, values, behaviors and relationships, along with participation in different spheres and schemes, all of which are required to sustain—recognize and confirm—the new identity. "To have a conversion experience is nothing much. The real thing is to be able to keep on taking it seriously; to retain a sense of its plausibility. *This* is where the religious community comes in. It provides the indispensable plausibility structure for the new reality."[7]

Alternation is achieved when one's subjective reality correlates to a new objective world and its plausibility structure is mediated in new spheres by new people, and thus when one has effectively abandoned the former world and its plausibility structure. One cannot live in two different and contradictory worlds and still maintain an integral subjective reality; "No one can serve two masters" (Mt 6:24). The most important ingredient in alternation is a plausibility structure that legitimates not only the new subjective reality, but also the process by which it is formed.

Because the formation, maintenance and expression of one's identity never

---

[6]Ibid., p. 157.
[7]Ibid., p. 158.

occur outside a particular social sphere, Berger and Luckmann contend that there is a reciprocal, or "dialectical," relationship between subjective reality (identity) and objective reality (society). "Identity is formed by social processes. Once crystallized, it is maintained, modified, or even reshaped by social relations. The social processes involved in both the formation and the maintenance of identity are determined by the social structure. Conversely, the identities produced by the interplay of organism, individual consciousness and social structure react upon the given social structure, maintaining it, modifying it, or even reshaping it."[8] Berger and Luckmann make a distinction between *identity as such,* the phenomenon of an individual's subjective reality, and *identity types,* the socially constructed roles that have objective reality in the social world. Thus we might say that a particular person's sense of "I am . . ." is identity as such and ". . . a farmer" is an identity type, a socially constructed role objectified in the social world when the person self-expresses or acts as a farmer. Unless it is situated and expressed in a social sphere, identity is vague.

Furthermore, the ways we interpret both identity types and the self-expressive behavior of an individual as a particular type are specific to a particular context or social sphere and suggested by the worldview—symbolic universe—that ties the sociocultural order together as a whole. For example, in a sociocultural order whose universe of meaning includes belief in demon possession, certain behaviors will be regarded as objectifying such possession. Where an order's universe includes a theory of personality disorders, the same behaviors will be explained as objectifying mental illness. In a universe of meaning that includes belief in the superiority of some and the inferiority of others, the particular behaviors of an individual will be construed as objectifying one rank or the other. In this way, understandings and expressions of identity are rooted in construals of objective reality.

Socialization and race. At this point Berger and Luckmann offer us a way of understanding how *racial* identity and consciousness are formed through the processes of primary and secondary socialization. As the internalization of the sociocultural order (objective reality), socialization is the construction of personal identity and consciousness (subjective reality); and one's conduct in the spheres of everyday life is the externalization of the self into an objective world. The relationship of reciprocity suggests that who one perceives oneself to be correlates with the world one inhabits, and that this world is constituted as the expression of selves in ways that form, recognize and confirm identity.

Now when the sociocultural order objectifies *race* and is structured along the lines of an ideology of racism, internalizing the sociocultural world and

---

[8]Ibid., p. 173.

forming subjective reality amount to internalizing the objective reality of race and the ideology of racism. Racial selves are externalized, a racial social order is objectified, and socialization entails the internalization of this social order in ways that form identity and consciousness.

For a child, the process begins with internalizing racial identity and its social world as conferred by significant others, a reference group that consists largely of a child's family. It continues with self-differentiation from these others and the development of an awareness of a generalized other, an abstraction from the concrete others with whom the child interacts. And it continues with internalization of the roles and rules that structure the institutionalized spheres and schemes of everyday life in racialized social worlds, roles and rules mediated by plausibility structures that accept and confirm—or reject—racial identity.

In short, Berger and Luckmann offer a way to construe the internalization of a social world fabricated by and expressive of race, a world whose spheres render racial identity plausible. This is as far as Berger and Luckmann can take us.

We need, however, to take another look at the worldview or symbolic universe in relation to which the world of race and the practices that manifest racism can be thought to make sense. The concern here is the way a universe of racial meaning situates and explains not only the objective world of race outside ourselves but also the subjective world of racial identity and consciousness. We are interested now not so much in the spheres and schemes that objectify social reality as in the worldviews behind this objective reality. If, as Berger and Luckmann contend, socialization amounts to internalizing *both* an identity *and* the social world that makes the identity plausible, then socialization amounts to internalizing the worldviews that explain and legitimate the social world, apart from which both identity and social world are disconnected and meaningless.

As one progresses from one's particular subjectivity and physical location through the spheres and schemes that engender an objective sociocultural order to the universe of meaning that provides coherence and integration for this order, one is basically moving through the layers of the world one has internalized. This is the world that one expresses and contributes to in the course of everyday life. More important, this is the world that situates and makes sense of our lives. To the extent that this world with its identities, institutions, plausibility structures and worldviews is meaningfully shared with others, the knowledge of this world is a *common* knowledge, and the sense of this world is a *common* sense.

A view of the world. How shall we access and describe a worldview of race? One way to proceed is to regard a "worldview" simply as the overall perspective from which we see and interpret the world as a unified whole. As

Clifford Geertz defines it, a worldview is "the picture [a people has] of the way things in sheer actuality are, their most comprehensive ideas of order," or "an image of an actual state of affairs peculiarly well-arranged to accommodate . . . a way of life."[9] In other words, a worldview confirms a people's way of life, emotionally, morally, intellectually and socially.

Another way to proceed is to consider a "worldview" as an ideology, a set of ideas and beliefs about life and the world that serve to preserve an existing social order. In this regard, as Audrey Smedley has noted, a worldview is constituted by ideas that "meet some cultural need or advance the interests of those who hold them," coalescing to form "a culturally structured, systematic way of looking at, perceiving, and interpreting various world realities," so that "once established and conventionalized, worldviews become enthroned in individuals as mind-sets. They may even achieve the state of involuntary cognitive processes, actively if not consciously molding the behavior of their bearers."[10]

Yet a third way of proceeding is to regard a "worldview" as a myth, or a set of perspectives, beliefs, traditions, rituals and stories that situate a people's way of life in an ongoing narrative that explains the intersections of this and other worlds. In this sense a people's myth is "a conception of reality that posits the ongoing penetration of the world of everyday experiences by sacred forces. Such a conception naturally entails a high degree of continuity between the social and cosmic order, and between all their respective legitimations; all reality appears as made of one cloth."[11] Thus while we can say that *worldview* and *ideology*—and possibly even *paradigm*[12]—are somewhat synonymous in that they are consti-

---

[9]Clifford Geertz, *The Interpretation of Cultures* (New York: Basic Books, 1973), pp. 89-90.

[10]Audrey Smedley, *Race in North America: Origin and Evolution of a Worldview* (Boulder, Colo.: Westview, 1993), pp. 17-18.

[11]Berger and Luckmann, *Social Construction*, p. 110. This construal of myth appears in the context of their discussion of the various mechanisms for universe maintenance. There they argue that of all the mechanisms available, mythology is "the most archaic form of universe-maintenance." I shall argue, on the other hand, that the mythology of race, far from being the most archaic, is an all-inclusive form of universe maintenance, embracing in no small measure the other forms—theology, philosophy and science. For general discussions of myth, and the myth of race in particular, see Mark Nathan Cohen, *Culture of Intolerance: Chauvinism, Class and Racism in the United States* (New Haven, Conn.: Yale University Press, 1998), pp. 97-99; Tony Evans, *Let's Get to Know Each Other* (Nashville: Thomas Nelson, 1995), pp. 2-8; Ashley Montagu, *Man's Most Dangerous Myth: The Fallacy of Race*, 6th ed. (Walnut Creek, Calif.: AltaMira, 1997), pp. 41-42; and Richard J. Payne, *Getting Beyond Race: The Changing American Culture* (Boulder, Colo.: Westview, 1998), pp. 51-52.

[12]The use of this term to describe a way of perceiving and explaining a complex reality owes its origin to Thomas S. Kuhn, who used it in the sense of "model" in his *The Structure of Scientific Revolutions*, 2nd enl. ed. (Chicago: University of Chicago Press, 1970), to refer to the way scientists regard their areas of investigation and the changes that have taken place in their disciplines.

tuted by perspectives, pictures and beliefs that work in the social order, I will use the term *myth* because it not only includes these aspects but draws attention to the stories, traditions and rituals by which they are transmitted from generation to generation in a grand narrative that connects local and cosmic reality.

The functions of myth. Few have studied the mythology of various cultures in different historical periods more thoroughly than Joseph Campbell. In the final volume of his major work in cultural mythology, Campbell explores four interrelated functions that myths exercise in relation to a context. Each of these functions addresses a particular dimension of human existence in the here and now. An account of these functions will suggest how a myth of race deeply embedded in our sociocultural order works to shape personal identity and consciousness and unite subjective reality with objective reality.[13]

The first function described by Campbell is, for all practical purposes, distinctively religious. He labels it the *metaphysical-mystical* function of myth: it serves to harmonize consciousness with the ineffable mystery of the universe. A myth does not merely tell about this mystery in its narrative description. Rather it mediates the reality of this mystery to human consciousness. In this sense the myth functions "to waken and maintain in the individual an experience of awe, humility, and respect, in recognition of that ultimate mystery, transcending names and forms," a mystery that cannot be captured in language.[14] Thus the work of myth is to establish connection and continuity between one's life and that unfathomable mystery that renders all of reality a whole; it integrates subjectivity with "that which is both beyond and within [oneself] and all things."[15]

The second function of myth is to provide a picture or representation of the universe that can be grasped by the imagination and elevated on demand to consciousness. This is what Campbell calls the *cosmological* function, and it addresses the question of the nature of a knowable universe. In broad strokes, Campbell outlines the stages of the revolutions in cosmology that have occurred historically in the West, from Dante's *Divine Comedy* (1492) through Copernicus and Newton to Charles Darwin and Albert Einstein, all of whom in their time and place contributed admirably to the second function of myth by their "rendition of a cosmology, an image of this universe of wonder, whether

---

[13]For the paragraphs that follow, see Joseph Campbell, *The Masks of God: Creative Mythology* (New York: Penguin, 1968), pp. 4-8, 608-24, 677-78.

[14]Ibid., p. 609. The important thing to keep in mind here is that Campbell is not concerned with the "who" or "what" of the mystery but with human experience and recognition—the subjective reality—of the mystery. Furthermore, in describing the religious function of myth he does not have in mind any particular religion or religious faith, least of all Christianity. Rather his stress is on humanity's cultural capacity to express religiosity as a sense of ultimacy that embraces and yet transcends the here and now.

[15]Ibid., p. 6.

regarded in its spatial or its temporal, physical, or biological aspect."[16]

What is significant about this function of myth, as Campbell rightly observes, is that in the West we have turned not to religion but to science to broker our knowledge of the empirical universe, the seemingly knowable macrocosm beyond which there is only unfathomable mystery. In this sense all the ancient, medieval and modern theories of the origin and nature of the physical universe are, as cosmologies, human attempts to internalize, interpret and make sense of a physical ("natural") universe that in its complexity and totality is infinitely beyond the capacity of any human being actually to know. The cosmological function of myth, therefore, is to mediate the internalization of our physical universe, or, to use Campbell's language, to render "the fact-world that now has to be recognized, appropriated, and assimilated by the [myth-making] imagination."[17] We occupy a seemingly boundless place, but we experience this place locally as demarcated by boundaries. The purpose of myth, then, is to make this disjunction between boundlessness and boundaries meaningful in human experience. It answers the subjective need to know where we came from, and it explains the origins and development of the physical world we inhabit.

The third function of myth, the one that renders a sociocultural order intelligible and meaningful as a constellation of spheres and schemes, is the *moral-social* function of validating and enforcing the established order. Myth does this principally by "shaping . . . the individual to the requirements of [his or her] geographically and historically conditioned social group,"[18] thus providing the means for the individual to embrace the expectations and authorities at work in the sociocultural environment. Myth locates a place and a purpose for the individual in order that she or he may be part of a larger sociocultural order but—hopefully—not lost in or overwhelmed by it.

Another way to look at this function is that it explains why one's hopes and plans frequently collide with the boundaries of authority; what one chooses to provide meaning and direction for oneself must be confirmed in some way by others, or else one runs the risk of being cut off from the "herd." In a sense it makes little difference to the moral-social function of myth whether the source of this authority is external (God, government, guidelines) or internal (conscience, reason, instinct), for the fact remains that the individual must internalize and live by a code in order to be part of the larger established order. As a "mesocosm," the sociocultural world makes possible the decisions and choices an individual can make freely or by coercion, and the myth serves not only to connect the individual

---

[16]Ibid., p. 620.
[17]Ibid., p. 611.
[18]Ibid., p. 5.

to this order but to manage the individual's participation in it by grounding a system of rules and laws that define and reinforce acceptable behavior, restraints that when followed are thought to assure the realization of life's meaning and purpose.

Finally, and most important for Campbell, myth has a *psychological* function in that it provides an inward focus, a sense of balance and harmony with the whole of reality. This function of myth is "to foster the centering and unfolding of the individual in integrity, in accord with *d)* himself (the microcosm), *c)* his culture (the mesocosm), *b)* the universe (the macrocosm), and *a)* that awesome ultimate mystery which is both beyond and within himself and all things."[19] All the functions of myth achieve their integration at this most vital point: human subjectivity. The individual experiences connectivity with self, the moral-social order, the universe and the awesome mystery that infuses all. In a real sense, the individual experiences harmony with the universe, but in a metaphorical sense, the individual is the center of this universe because she or he has internalized its portrayal through the agency of myth.

As cultures undergo change, so does their mythology. In any given culture at any given time, its myth will work more or less effectively to stabilize the social order and provide places for its members to live out their lives. It also happens from time to time that the myth engenders in some an experience of dissonance and alienation; others may reject the myth entirely as dysfunctional or untrue to reality. In either case, however, these remain *subjective responses* to the myth and its work in the individual and the social order. An individual may reject a cultural myth, but an individual cannot change it; as long as one remains in a sociocultural order, its mythology will continue to work, more or less effectively, engendering subjectivity—experience and consciousness. Mythology is a *social* phenomenon, and human lives are lived in a society. As Campbell observes:

> For those in whom a local mythology still works, there is an experience both of accord with the social order, and of harmony with the universe. For those, however, in whom the authorized signs no longer work—or, if working, produce deviant effects—there follows inevitably a sense both of dissociation from the local social nexus and of quest, within and without, for life, which the brain will take to be for "meaning." Coerced to the social pattern, the individual can only harden to some figure of living death; and if any considerable number of the members of a civilization are in this predicament, a point of no return will have been passed.[20]

The myth of race. We can access and describe the myth of race by asking about its fourfold function. We must note at the outset that to regard it as a myth is to observe that race is a story, a narrative that recollects the past and antici-

---

[19]Ibid., p. 6.
[20]Ibid., pp. 5-6.

pates a future for the present; it speaks to where we came from and where we are going, and thus it is a story of origins and beginnings on the one hand and goals and completions on the other. The myth of race, then, can be seen as a story of lives lived in a sequence of events as occasions for human experience, a story not only of what happened "objectively" out there in the world but also what happened "subjectively" as people internalized, experienced and responded to their world in their thoughts, feelings and actions.

Race is not only "a way of knowing and looking at the world,"[21] or "an unstable and 'decentered' complex of social meanings,"[22] or "an unequal relationship between social groups."[23] Race is also an *experience* of self and world, engendered in and by a sociocultural order situated in a particular place and time and interconnected within a whole. Race is embedded in the common sense as a belief that there are distinct and different biological types of human beings, that all people can be categorized by type and that each type's way of life can be ranked on a sociocultural scale. The *myth* of race is the metanarrative that frames and interprets the experience of race in a sociocultural order, and as a story it chronicles—and explains—the origins and destinies of peoples, their migrations and removals, social development and stratification, domination and exploitation, war and peace, exclusion and discrimination, struggle and resistance.

1. *Dualism.* The myth of race performs its *metaphysical–mystical* (or *religious*) function by narrating the struggle between eternal forces of good and evil that are symbolized in this world by images of lightness and darkness, *white* and *black*. The awesome mystery in the mythology of race is the mystery of pure being opposing the threat of nonbeing, pure goodness unsullied by the corruption of evil, pure light that dispels encroaching darkness. The immateriality of ultimate being and its struggle with nonbeing is also symbolized in the ancient Greek and Gnostic dualism of eternal and temporal, mind and matter, spirit and body, in which each of the former is aligned with being and goodness while each of the latter is aligned with nonbeing and evil. The myth narrates the separation of light and darkness and ultimately the victory of light over darkness. While this dualist struggle is played out in the eternal realm, the spatiotemporal realm is not unaffected. The mystery of the dualism, symbolized here in white and black, has also been played out as "white" people have sought to exclude and control darker peoples. Those who identify as "white" align themselves with the being and goodness of ultimate reality, and whiteness

---

[21]Smedley, *Race in North America,* p. 15.

[22]Michael Omi and Howard Winant, *Racial Formation in the United States from the 1960s to the 1990s,* 2nd ed. (New York: Routledge, 1994), p. 55.

[23]Manning Marable, *Beyond Black and White: Transforming African-American Politics* (New York: Verso, 1995), p. 118.

becomes a sacred symbol that evokes a sense of awe; these claim to be the "children of God." The color or otherness of those whom "whites" identify as "nonwhite," "black," "brown," "yellow," "red" or "other" symbolizes the opposite side of the dualism, darkness, nonbeing, evil; these are labeled "creatures of nature." The myth of race embraces an ontological dualism of being and nonbeing, good and evil, light and darkness, symbolized as struggle between contending forces.[24] Its metaphysical-mystical function is to make sense of an oppositional experience, one's experience of being "over against" an other, an experience that sacralizes good and evil, lightness and darkness, by attributing them immutably to people on the basis of skin color.

2. *Science and evolution.* The *cosmological* function of the myth of race is executed when its narratives speak to the origins and nature of the universe and explain how and why it is as it is in all its complexity and interrelatedness. More important, the myth of race is at work when it addresses the origin and nature of living species in the universe. In the modern Western world this function has been discharged by science. We ought not to put science and myth over against each other, for as some have observed, science is a way of looking at and understanding the world, a way of interpreting and making sense of the world; as such, it is no less "mythical" than mythology is less "scientific." Mythology and science are both models of cognitive systems that seek to manage the complex phenomena of human physical and social existence. Indeed it is part of our mythology that science is more objective and less biased than myth; we have come to *believe* that science alone is the sure and certain path to true knowledge of empirical things. However, as Stephen Jay Gould has remarked, "science is rooted in creative interpretation. . . . By what right, other than our own biases, can we . . . hold that science now operates independently of culture and class?"[25] Ian Haney López expresses the same sentiment, but more forcefully: "Science was not and is not independent of culture and society; science *is* culture and society. The world out there beyond human knowledge is knowable only through social beliefs and practices, and among these number the beliefs and practices denominated science. . . . Race is purely a social construction, and the science of race is purely the science of social myth."[26] Science thus participates in the myth of

---

[24]See, e.g., Forrest G. Wood, *The Arrogance of Faith: Christianity and Race in America from the Colonial Era to the Twentieth Century* (New York: Alfred A. Knopf, 1990), pp. 49-53.

[25]Stephen Jay Gould, *The Mismeasure of Man*, rev. ed. (New York: W. W. Norton, 1996), p. 106.

[26]Ian F. Haney López, *White by Law: The Legal Construction of Race* (New York: New York University Press, 1996), p. 96. See also Cohen, *Culture of Intolerance*, pp. 90-99; Edward T. Hall, *Beyond Culture* (New York: Anchor, 1976), pp. 9-26; and Kuhn, *Structure of Scientific Revolutions*.

race; it is itself mythological as a way of seeing and interpreting "reality."

Placing science at a higher level of "truth" and "reality" than mythology is nothing more than an expression of Western cultural arrogance. The legs of our cosmology are shortened considerably, if not cut off from beneath us, when we recognize that much of what has passed for the "science of nature" in our common sense is really nothing more than a mask of theory that covers our lack of knowledge. Ashley Montagu presses this point: "In fact Nature is the name we give to the projection of the totality of our ignorance concerning the forces which are conceived to be involved in, or responsible for, the generation of life and its maintenance. Nature is not a 'thing-in-itself' that operates upon other things. The term denotes . . . an artificial construct whose function is to serve as a general stereotype for our ignorance. . . . For most people to say that a thing is 'natural' explains it. But does it? What do we mean by 'natural'?"[27]

These observations about science grow largely out of an assessment of the way science has contributed to the myth of race. Initially European American language of race developed in the seventeenth and eighteenth centuries to describe the differences noted by Europeans between themselves and other peoples. Physical differences were regarded by the Europeans as "natural" (that is, grounded in the natural created order), and this implied that divisions between human groups were distinct and permanent. The Europeans also noted social and religious differences and thought these were "natural" as well; these peoples were God's creatures, but they were not Christian and their way of life was altogether different. The language of "race" was used by natural scientists to name these physical and social-religious differences perceived by the Europeans and to compare them on a scale of physical-social similarity (i.e., equality and inequality). Race language entered the common vocabulary as the views of these natural scientists were read or heard by their public; the nonscientist now had a way to label perceived physical and social differences. Science took an inchoate idea of "natural" differences between people groups and "elevated [it] to the ranks of scholarly discourse when scientists began developing rationalizations and justifications for existing social realities."[28]

In the nineteenth century, theories of biological evolution began to emerge and soon became a major scientific model for studying living species, superseding religious-oriented interpretations of the origins and development of humankind. As Richard Hofstadter notes, "religion had been forced to share its traditional authority with science"; as a result, "evolution had been translated

---

[27]Montagu, *Man's Most Dangerous Myth*, p. 330.
[28]Smedley, *Race in North America*, p. 303.

into divine purpose, and in the hands of skillful preachers religion was livened and refreshed by the infusion of an authoritative idea from the field of science."[29] In 1854 Count Arthur de Gobineau published his *Essai sur l'inégalité des races humaines* (The Inequality of Human Races), in which he argued that history shows there has been only one truly great civilization, the European, and that its superiority results from the purity of its bloodlines (its "race"). Gobineau warned that European civilization would die out if European blood was intermixed with blood from inferior peoples.[30]

From Charles Darwin's *On the Origin of Species* (1859) and *The Descent of Man* (1871) advocates of "white" racial hegemony took the evolutionary ideas of "struggle for existence," "natural selection," "survival of the fittest" and "racial degeneracy" as scientific legitimacy for the belief that the races are unequal and that some are superior to others.[31] For evolutionists, nature was not a realm of equality; "struggle" and "survival" implied inequality and there were no "natural rights." Moreover, survival of the fit and demise of the unfit made sense to those who believed that some "races" are destined for both advanced biological development and greater cultural achievement.

In the United States, the growing abolitionist movement provoked defenders of slavery and "white" race superiority to appeal ever more to the ideas of science to justify slavery and their belief in the inherent inferiority—biological and cultural—of African and other peoples. Among evolutionists and religionists alike the debate raged on how best to explain human variation; some argued that humankind originated in a single place from a single pair from whom all have descended with biological variation (monogenesis), while others argued that humankind originated in several

---

[29]Richard Hofstadter, *Social Darwinism in American Thought*, rev. ed. (Boston: Beacon, 1955), p. 30.

[30]Gobineau's book was not translated and published in English until 1915, but his influence on thinking regarding the biological (or "racial") basis and determination of culture (or "civilization) is clearly evident between 1854 and 1915 in both Europe and America. A republication of this book has recently appeared: see Arthur de Gobineau, *The Inequality of the Human Races* (New York: Howard Fertig, 1999). In the preface to his book, Gobineau declared its purpose: "Recognizing that both strong and weak races exists [sic], I preferred to examine the former, to analyze their qualities, and especially to follow them back to their origins. By this method I convinced myself at last that everything great, noble and fruitful in the works of man on this earth, in science, art, and civilization, derives from a single starting-point, is the development of a single germ and the results of a single thought; it belongs to one family alone, the different branches of which have reigned in all the civilized countries of the universe" (p. xii-xiii).

[31]Editions of both publications continue to be printed in both complete and abridged editions. See, e.g., Charles Darwin, *The Origin of Species* (New York: Random House, 1993), and *The Descent of Man*, 2nd ed. (Amherst, Mass.: Prometheus, 1998).

places at different times, with each human type having separate progenitors (polygenesis).[32] In any case racial mixture, or miscegenation, was perceived by the descendants of Europeans in America to be contrary to humankind's "natural" instincts and damaging to the purity of their race.

It is a sign of the continuing cosmological function of the myth of race that the "naturalistic" or "biological" explanation of "races" continues in the common sense, in spite of the fact that, for the most part, science has abandoned nineteenth- and early-twentieth-century race theories. Biological differences are still thought by many European Americans to be the reason for social inequality. Others for whom biology is not *the* explanation nevertheless continue to struggle with separating out social inequality from "natural" variations. As Thomas Gossett has commented, "The great shift of emphasis from biology to social process as an explanation for cultural differences was a gradual one, and the increasing emphasis on the latter did not necessarily imply a rejection of the former."[33] One can say both that the myth precipitated science and that science accommodated the myth. But though science has moved away from its former empirical "findings" on race, they remain embedded in the consciousness of many as their cosmological view of origins and development of humankind, as their natural sense and their common knowledge. The myth remains and the myth works, as Richard Payne has noted: "Technological and scientific advancements do not necessarily destroy the myths upon which many contemporary perceptions are based. The persistent centrality of race in American society is evidence of how magic and science can coexist."[34]

3. *Dichotomy.* Whenever social aggregates are formed along the lines of an

---

[32]For the most part the monogenists prevailed in these debates, but not because of empirical evidence or even the Genesis narratives. The question was after all—and still is—one "shrouded in mystery" (Cohen, *Culture of Intolerance*, p. 41). For discussions of the terms, issues and personalities in these "scholarly" and "theological" debates, see George M. Fredrickson, *The Black Image in the White Mind: The Debate on Afro-American Character and Destiny, 1817-1914* (Hanover, N.H.: Wesleyan University Press, 1971), pp. 71-75; Gould, *Mismeasure of Man,* pp. 63-104; Robert E. Hood, *Begrimed and Black: Christian Traditions on Blacks and Blackness* (Minneapolis: Fortress, 1994), pp. 139-41; Pat Shipman, *The Evolution of Racism: Human Differences and the Use and Abuse of Science* (New York: Simon & Schuster, 1994), pp. 73-91; and Smedley, *Race in North America,* pp. 232-44.

[33]Thomas F. Gossett, *Race: The History of an Idea in America,* new ed. (New York: Oxford University Press, 1997 [first published 1963]), p. 416. Commenting on the debate over the arguments of Richard Herrnstein and Charles Murray regarding the correlation between biology and intelligence in their book *The Bell Curve: Intelligence and Class Structure in American Life* (New York: Free Press, 1994), Orlando Patterson asks, "Why is it that, in a land founded on the secular belief that 'all are created equal,' we are so obsessed with the need to find a scientific basis for human inequality?" (*The Ordeal of Integration: Progress and Resentment in America's "Racial" Crisis* [Washington: D.C.: Civitas/Counterpoint, 1997], pp. 135-36).

[34]Payne, *Getting Beyond Race,* pp. 49-50.

in-group/out-group dichotomy and these groups are characterized primarily by their "race," the myth of race is executing its *moral–social* function. The issue here is not merely the characterization of "differences" between groups but the formation of an in-group that self-defines and acts in ways that can be taught to its members. The characterization of the out-group(s) is important, then, as a counter-identity, inasmuch as the race myth upholds positive regard for the in-group and negative regard for the out-group(s); the identity, character and actions of the in-group are judged to be morally good and superior, while those of the out-group(s) are judged to be morally bad and inferior. Moreover, each group is regulated by a set of rules and expectations, customs and traditions, that are formed and preserved precisely to characterize and identify its members.

The myth's narratives include the stories of intergroup perceptions and relations, and how one group—European American—has dominated the other group(s) with an unwillingness to embrace them in fullness and equality. Certain ideas about the out-group(s) are taken for granted as common knowledge by the in-group: Once upon a time there were pure races, unmixed and distinct; differences between the races are biological and heritable; one race is physically and mentally superior to the others; race determines one's personality and intelligence; race and culture are interdependent; race mixing blurs the distinctions, dilutes the homogeneity, and ultimately degrades racial superiority. The narratives favor the historic formation of the in-group with the language of European discovery, exploration and claim to the "New World," the Puritans' "errand into the wilderness," the establishment of a national government to preside over the "land of liberty," and in the nineteenth century the doctrine of "manifest destiny"—a secularized version of "the chosen people"—which claimed that the United States had the right and responsibility to expand throughout the North American continent *because* the European Americans were a superior race,[35] all of which came together to substantiate the peculiarly Western myth of "progress."

More recently, in the wake of waves of immigrants and the civil rights movement, the consciousness of in-group versus out-group(s) has been only slightly modified with the assumption that the United States is now a land of "equal opportunity" for all. European Americans especially believe that the American creed of freedom, equality, civil and human rights, justice, and opportunity applies to all and that even those defined as out-groups do not have it so bad;

---

[35]See, e.g., Cohen, *Culture of Intolerance,* pp. 182-83; Christopher Bates Doob, *Racism: An American Cauldron,* 2nd ed. (New York: Harper Collins, 1996), pp. 40-42; John Hope Franklin and Alfred A. Moss Jr., *From Slavery to Freedom: A History of African Americans,* 7th ed. (New York: Alfred A. Knopf, 1994), chap. 7; Gossett, *Race,* pp. 310-38; Hofstadter, *Social Darwinism,* pp. 170-77; and Wood, *Arrogance of Faith,* pp. 206-42.

discrimination is no longer rampant or legal, and racism is on the decline. These perceptions are hardly shared by significant numbers of those regarded as members of the out-groups. Lack of individual and group achievement and indications of social inequality are explained not by lack of freedom or opportunity but by out-group biology or culture. Thus the myth's moral-social function serves both to differentiate and to disguise the boundaries between the preferred in-group and the undeserving out-group(s).

4. *Identity.* Finally, the race myth's *psychological* function is operative whenever identity and consciousness are formed by internalizing a racial in-group through primary and/or secondary socialization. Whenever an individual identifies with a racial "reference group" whose beliefs, values, attitudes and behaviors are instrumental in identity formation and the sense of social reality, the myth is at work. Whenever the moral judgments and aesthetic sensibilities of a racial group are preferred because of race, the myth is at work. Again, the issue here is not the characterization of "differences" between groups but rather the extent to which one *identifies with* an in-group that self-defines as a *racial* group.

An individual's socialization involves learning how to process sensory data, and as Gordon Allport has described it, this process includes selecting certain cues, accentuating them in our minds and interpreting them in accordance with prior knowledge, experiences and biases.[36] Identification with a racial reference group will moderate this process to one degree or another. One's own sense and assessment of the in-group in distinction from the out-group(s) results from internalizing the sense of significant others, whether family, other caregivers or peers. One can learn who is in-group and who is out-group in a variety of ways, including being told explicitly, or inferring from comments and judgments made by others about them, or from any situation in which one's innocent or positive behavior toward a member of the out-group is judged by one's in-group as unacceptable, thereby putting one at risk of losing the approval of significant others or being punished by one's own reference group.[37] In this latter

---

[36]Gordon Allport, *The Nature of Prejudice* (Reading, Mass.: Addison-Wesley, 1954), p. 166.

[37]Allport's analysis of in-group socialization and out-group prejudice remains an important resource in the psychology of racism. However, European Americans should also consult the work of Thandeka, who argues in her book *Learning to Be White: Money, Race and God in America* (New York: Continuum, 1999), that "the Euro-American child . . . is a racial victim of its own white community of parents, caretakers, and peers, who attack it because it does not yet have a white racial identity. Rather than continue to suffer such attacks, the Euro-American child defends itself by creating a white racial identity for itself. It begins to think and act like its community's ideal of a white self" (p. 13). See also Beverly Daniel Tatum, *"Why Are All the Black Kids Sitting Together in the Cafeteria?" and Other Conversations About Race,* rev. ed. (New York: BasicBooks, 1999), pp. 31-128.

case, one forms a racial identity as a defense mechanism to avoid rejection by one's own group.

It is an indication of the myth's psychological work when belief in the inferiority of other races is immune to rational arguments intended to disprove it. Reason does not form aggregates into in-group and out-group categories. Rather it is "the emotional appeal of an idea that holds together the members of each group and exalts their feeling of solidarity and greatness to such an extent that compromises with other groups become impossible."[38] The myth is assigned a kind of epistemological privilege when it is allowed to form the basis of our interpretation of experience, and especially when it determines what we do and do not see and hear. Members of a racial in-group filter—select, accentuate, interpret—their sensory data in accordance with the myth. An in-group and an out-group may share a common geography, social order and history, but "each group hears different echoes, tells a different story, creates a complete universe of perception that separates and disconnects."[39] Because the myth specifies the meaning of race, because the internalization involves the portrayal of both self and others, and because everyday life is experienced along the lines of dissonance between racial in- and out-groups, it should come as no surprise that race is thought of as *real.*

Is the myth of race *true*? This is the wrong question to ask. The correct question is, does the myth of race *work*? Here the answer is clearly yes. Myths do not admit to the canons of "true" or "false" with use of principles of verifiability, because by definition they are stories that narrate and interpret human experience in a world, and thus they are beyond the pale of the kind of truth or falsehood we associate with propositional statements.[40] The purpose of myths is to make sense of human experience in a world and to connect individual human lives with larger, more complex social and physical universes and ultimately with the transcendent mystery. The reciprocity between one's subjectivity and the "objective" world suggests that no human experience or construal of the world is unequivocal (unreflective or uninterpreted) but always framed and

---

[38]Franz Boas, *Anthropology and Modern Life* (1928; reprint, New York: Dover, 1986), p. 102.

[39]David K. Shipler, *A Country of Strangers: Blacks and Whites in America* (New York: Alfred A. Knopf, 1997), p. 151. See also Thomas Kochman, *Black and White Styles in Conflict* (Chicago: University of Chicago Press, 1981).

[40]For discussions of the canons of "true" in narratives, see Michael Goldberg, *Theology and Narrative: A Critical Introduction,* 2nd ed. (Philadelphia: Trinity Press International, 1991); James W. McClendon, *Biography as Theology,* new ed. (Philadelphia: Trinity Press International, 1990); and Terrence Tilley, *Story Theology,* Theology and Life 12 (Wilmington, Del.: Michael Glazier, 1985). For an insightful discussion of the canons of "true" regarding social reality and the correspondence theory of "truth," see John R. Searle, *The Construction of Social Reality* (New York: Free Press, 1995).

mediated by the world in which it is located. This world is a sociocultural world, portrayed by myths that work.

Embracing Ideology: The False Consciousness of Race

In everyday language we take *consciousness* to mean an awareness of ourselves and our environment, a sense of both our identity and the attitudes, beliefs and sensations that orient us to what is going on within and without. It is difficult to define "consciousness as such," because it is always filled with something other than itself; it is always an awareness of someone or something. When we talk about "consciousness," we are abstracting from the phenomenon of awareness of objects and reifying this awareness by supposing that it exists apart from the objects it holds or to which it is directed. As Berger and Luckmann observe: "Consciousness is always intentional; it always intends or is directed toward objects. We can never apprehend some putative substratum of consciousness as such, only consciousness of something or other."[41] The objects that are presented to consciousness are drawn from the spheres of our everyday life *(this person beside this car in this parking lot)*, our subjective states in relation to a sphere *(my anger at seeing that my car has been hit by this other car)*, or our memory, anticipation or imagination *(this happened before, and I wonder how this scenario will unfold as we do the hitter-hittee scheme)*. Consciousness holds together and integrates in some meaningful fashion the discrete aspects of inner and outer worlds so that we can interpret and make sense of them.

It is not altogether misleading to suggest that because our awareness is shaped and influenced by the social spheres of our daily lives, the patterns and structures of the social world are the patterns and structures of consciousness. A sociocultural world does not exist apart from the relationships and activities of its members; we live in a world that our predecessors built, and our living in this world contributes to its continuity. Because much of our activity and behavior is routinized and perfunctory, we are not likely to be conscious of the extent to which we are conditioned by our social world or how deeply we have internalized its patterns and structures until we find ourselves having to function in a social world that is fundamentally different in its patterns and structures, relationships and activities. We understand ourselves only as functioning members of the sociocultural order to which we belong, and our little corner of the world can be understood only on the basis of the peculiar spheres and schemes that make it objective to us. Our mental and emotional processes are never "pure," unconnected with spheres that stimulate them and to which they respond. The

---

[41]Berger and Luckmann, *Social Construction,* p. 20.

sociocultural world is thus not extraneous to awareness, thinking and feeling but rather is their presupposition and prerequisite.[42] Without a world to experience, there is no experience; without a structured world, there is no structure to experience.

It is possible, however, that our consciousness of ourselves and the world outside us may be a *false* consciousness: it may misapprehend or misinterpret something or someone, arise from mistaken ideas or assumptions, represent a distorted sense of social patterns and structures, exclude details or information that may be ominous, or be disconnected from our circumstances. Because of the reciprocal relation between subjectivity and objectivity, our consciousness can be said to be false when our subjective states appear to ourselves or others to be isolated from, or disproportionate to, the external situation. This is generally what we mean when we say, for example, that someone is "out of touch with reality": their consciousness as manifest in speech and action does not fit the situation.

Our inclination is to suppose not only that our experiences of the world are direct but that they are the arbiters of what is "real" and "true" in the world; if I experienced it, then it really happened and I know it to be true. We will also acknowledge that others may experience the same event differently and offer different interpretations of its significance, but we will nonetheless tend to prefer our reading. Be that as it may, there is no direct experience, no experience that is unmediated and uninterpreted, and thus no experience that is unfiltered and unrelated to prior and present subjective states and a reciprocal sense of the world. In any given situation there are far more data and stimuli than we can possibly acknowledge, far greater subjective and objective dynamics at work, and indeed far more background and history to the situation and the participants than can be discerned in the moment. So in spite of our inclination, we cannot really have confidence in the meaning of our experience and the subjective states that process it until these receive corroboration from others; I can trust my experience and the world in which it is located if and when I come to learn—or assume—that the experience and outlook of others are similar to mine. Only then can it be said that there is a *common* experience of a *common* world that makes a *common* sense. In other words, one's consciousness is intimately related to and confirmed by the expressions and products of the consciousness of others.

---

[42]For discussions of this interrelation between mental dispositions and culture, see Peter Berger, *Invitation to Sociology: A Humanist Perspective* (New York: Doubleday, 1963), pp. 93-124; Franz Boas, *Race, Language and Culture* (Chicago: University of Chicago Press, 1940), pp. 260-74; Geertz, *Interpretation*, pp. 82-88; and Hall, *Beyond Culture*, pp. 191-207.

Now suppose that this group or common consciousness is itself false in any—or all—of the ways described above. We regard outward expressions of an individual's false consciousness to be signs of irrationality, delusion or abnormal imbalance. When a false consciousness is *socially* shared and confirmed by the sociocultural order, the individual's irrationality becomes rational, delusion becomes reality, and the abnormal becomes normal. In a word, false consciousness becomes *ideology.*

Such is the effect of internalizing the sociality of race and racism. We are so convinced of the reality of race, so socialized into a sociocultural order that has been structured by racism, and so habituated to functioning in relation to its universe of meaning that it is very difficult to imagine that this reality has been humanly constructed as the externalization of a socially shared and false consciousness. The fact of this common knowledge and sense of race itself suggests that race has an objectivity in our world; we see it, and our peculiar experience of it is corroborated, because we have been socialized into it.

European Americans especially are socialized to function in the social world: it was designed to accommodate their experience. As a result, the experience of European Americans in the social order is regarded as the norm, and the social world as presented to the consciousness of European Americans is regarded as normal. Because the social world was not designed to accommodate and validate the experience of other people groups, their consciousness is regarded as abnormal and their socialization is far more conflictive. European Americans are socialized into a world suited to European American interests, and the presence and interests of other people groups is regarded as an anomaly, so that European Americans become, in effect, *mono*cultural persons. For others, socialization entails learning how to function in the spheres of the dominant group where they are disregarded, as well as in the spheres where their own group predominates, so that they become in effect *bi-* or *multi*cultural persons. Moreover, everyone internalizes some rendering of the system of racial classification, since everyone participates in a social order characterized by race, if only because each individual identifies with a group that either self-identifies or is identified as a racial group.

Consciousness that reifies something that does not exist is a false consciousness. Consciousness formed in relation to a social order arranged to accommodate the experience of some and minimize the experience of others is a false consciousness. When consciousness discounts the effect of a social world on the consciousness of others or imposes its own interpretation on the experience of others, a false consciousness is present. Consciousness that ignores patterns of exclusion and practices of discrimination in a social order is a false consciousness. Consciousness structured by a social hierarchy that assigns value, privilege and status according to station is a false consciousness. Consciousness that conforms to a set of standards that validate and normalize an oppressive social order is a false consciousness. Consciousness that interprets another in terms of a stereotype is a false consciousness. And perhaps most important, the *lack* of awareness is itself a form of false consciousness; ignorance may be bliss, but what one does not know may harm oneself and others.

The modes of false consciousness are many, and while it may not always be possible to characterize it at any given moment, there are several distinctive modes that demand our attention. Five of the most commonly expressed forms of false consciousness will be discussed. Keep in mind that one is not necessarily exclusive of the others, but one or more may be constitutive of the peculiar consciousness of race and racism.

The modes of false consciousness.

1. *Dualism.* With the earlier discussion of the myth of race as a background, it is appropriate to designate the first mode as consciousness of a dualism that posits two oppositional and irreconcilable entities, or two mutually exclusive realms to which are attributed different value and significance. A dualist consciousness not only distinguishes between two things but polarizes them, placing them antagonistically over against one another. As noted earlier, the fundamental duality that has shaped the dualism of race is good and evil, a duality that by definition cannot admit of concord. This is the unquestionable warrant for dual*ism:* structuring consciousness by grasping two inherently oppositional forces, and imposing this interpretive grid on the perception of cues that signal race. A dualist consciousness imposes an oppositional relationship between mind and body, reason and emotion, order and chaos, male and female, white and black; it uses this duality to vindicate an identification with, and preference for, the side of the polarity that it associates with "good" and attributes to others the side associated with "evil" or "bad." The dualism not only explains others but justifies the social order and its patterns of oppression.

Both primary and secondary socialization have enabled us to internalize the duality of good and bad and its companions, right and wrong, true and false. Our sense of these has been shaped by reward and punishment, acceptance and rejection, recognition and disregard, as these have patterned the spheres and schemes of our everyday lives with others. Our attitudes, values, beliefs and behaviors have evoked from others responses that have influenced us and nudged us toward identifying with one side as over against the other.

The point is that we have internalized duality in certain relationships and spheres, and on that basis a mode of consciousness has been formed that enables us to engage and make sense of ourselves and our world. But a duality is not the same as a dual*ism* that posits an oppositional structure in the external world. Noting similarities and variations is not dualist; categorizing differences and attributing value to them is. The dualist mode of consciousness distinguishes, for example, between people groups whose sociocultural way of life is regarded as "primitive," and the categorizers, who regard their own group as "civilized." It is expressed in the distinction between a people group that is "fit" and other groups that are "unfit" for existence and progress, such as in the nineteenth-century eugenics movement whose proponents believed that the selective breeding of the former and the restriction of breeding among the latter would eventuate in the triumph of a "superior" race and the extinction of those regarded as "inferior."[43]

The dualism of superiority and inferiority as a mode of consciousness, however, is not the result of disinterested empirical observation. Rather it is a false consciousness that imposes value judgments on phenomena. When coupled with identification with an in-group whose qualities and characteristics are assessed positively, as opposed to an out-group assessed negatively, a dualist consciousness manufactures a sense that superiority and authenticity are *inherent* in one's own group, while inferiority and defect are *inherent* in the out-group.

Perhaps the prototype of a dualist consciousness is to be found in what Berger and Luckmann called the "generalized other." For them, as we have seen, this notion referred to the child's ability to abstract progressively from particular attitudes and roles played by significant others to a more generalized or even impersonal sense of "others." One's identity and consciousness are formed as one moves from the undifferentiated "I/you" to their differentiation as

---

[43]The term *eugenics* was coined in 1883 by Charles Darwin's cousin Francis Galton (1822-1911). Eugenicists believed that the non-European "races" were inherently unfit for survival and would eventually die out. Their primary interest therefore was not so much in managing the breeding practices of these groups as in controlling breeding among the undesirables or "unfit" within their own "race" and fostering selective breeding among those judged to be "fit." These were largely the upper-class elite, whose biological and intellectual qualities and social status were eminently desirable as characteristic of a superior race. See especially Boas, *Anthropology and Modern Life,* pp. 107-17, and *Race, Language and Culture,* pp. 44-80; Gossett, *Race,* pp. 155-97; Hofstadter, *Social Darwinism,* pp. 163-69; Kenan Malik, *The Meaning of Race: Race, History and Culture in Western Society* (New York: New York University Press, 1996), pp. 9-91, 101-14; Montagu, *Man's Most Dangerous Myth,* pp. 297-310; Shipman, *Evolution of Racism,* pp. 107-45; and Smedley, *Race in North America,* pp. 255-72. One American popularizer of eugenic views was Madison Grant (1865-1937), who warned in his 1916 book *The Passing of the Great Race; or, The Racial Basis of European History* (New York: Charles Scribner's Sons, 1916) that the "Nordic" races in the United States were being diluted by the influx of foreign immigrants of "inferior" stock and that if this was not checked, the collapse of our "superior" civilization would be imminent.

"I" and "you," until one has apprehended oneself in relation to a "collective you." Throughout this process of formation, the individual's identity and consciousness require differentiation in the duality of self and other. Socialization into an in-group entails the internalization of the group's attitudes, values, beliefs, practices—in short, its social structures. Members of an in-group discern the duality of self-and-other, but it is a self-*with*-other, or self-*similar-to*-other.

However, socialization into an in-group also entails the portrayal and assessment of the out-group whose existence must be posited in order for the *in-group* to be the *in-*group. Thus a differentiated or dualist sense of the "other" is internalized; the self-*with*-other as characteristic of the in-group, and the self-*against*-other as characteristic of the in-group's awareness of the out-group. In effect, in-group members identifying with their group are also counter-identifying the out-group members, and consciousness of self requires consciousness of the other: civilized is not-primitive, fit is not-unfit, free is not-slave, white is not-black, etc. *and vice versa.* As Kenan Malik has expressed this dualism: "The Other . . . is that which lies outside a particular culture or society's epistemological boundaries. Not only is everything beyond the boundary treated as the Other, but society requires an Other without which there can be no sense of Self."[44] In short, a dualist consciousness is structured by a humanly constructed typology of generalizations about human beings, based largely on subjective impressions whose meaning is internalized as oppositional.

2. *Deception.* The second mode of false consciousness that requires attention is deception, both of oneself and of others. At its core, deception involves a deliberate or inadvertent act of misleading and disguising the truth in ways that prevent its recognition (for example, a cover-up that gives the appearance of reality but is known by the deceivers to be untrue). As a mode of consciousness, deception works in our selection of what we see and hear and then interpret as meaningful, in the spheres of our everyday life. These spheres are so complex that it is not possible to take in every detail, let alone interpret the whole with attention to all the detail.

In debriefing a group experience, a process observer will note not only what was said and how people responded to what was heard, but also the ways a person's response evinced understanding of what was said as well as the body language of those participating. Automobile salespeople will look for cues from a customer that suggest a strategy for a successful sale. A teacher will draw conclusions about a student who sits in the same seat every session while others always sit in different places.

---

[44]Malik, *Meaning of Race,* p. 221.

Defensive linemen rush the quarterback who is dropping back from the line of scrimmage; concluding that the quarterback is about to pass, they redouble their effort to tackle him before the pass is thrown. In the meantime the defensive backs, observing the quarterback's movements, back up in order to cover a potential receiver in their territory and position themselves either to make a tackle or to intercept the pass. But just when the quarterback would execute the pass, the ball is handed off to a running back who has stayed behind the line and who now runs through territory vacated by both defensive linemen and backs for (hopefully) a significant yardage gain. That is deception, and if the play worked for a positive gain, the defensive players can be said to have functioned under false consciousness.

In matters of race, European Americans especially practice deception, noticing in any given situation only those bits and pieces of information that have been predetermined as important cues to understanding the situation, regarding all other details as insignificant and ignoring them altogether, or misreading and misinterpreting them because they are thought to be irrelevant to the situation. This practice is what sociologists and psychologists call "selective perception," the tendency to see and hear what we have been socialized to see and hear, to anticipate and notice data that consciousness can construct into meaningful sense. A European American may encounter a group of Hispanic Americans in the hallway and conclude they are complaining or plotting revolt; or walk into a lunchroom and observe that the Asian Americans are sitting together as a group and wonder why they have segregated themselves from others; or choose to be served by the European American salesclerk because she is presumed to know her job and how to serve attentively.

Moreover, in its mode as deception, consciousness re-collects and reassembles the past, both one's own and that of others, in order to make it useful to a present situation or be of service to current notions and practices. We select, interpret and correlate "facts" to explain persons, places and events, all the while practicing deception by molding the past to conform to present sensibility. So Columbus "discovered" America, Lincoln "freed" the slaves, segregation was a "paternalism" that "protected" African Americans,[45] and America "won" the Cold War against the "evil" communist aggressor. This naive but nonetheless deceptive manner of retrieving a usable history is known by professional historians as "presentism" (privileging a contemporary sociocultural perspective that selectively re-forms the past in order to exclude or reframe the perspective of others), and among connoisseurs of literary fiction it is known as Orwellian

---

[45]So argues Dinesh D'Souza in *The End of Racism: Principles for a Multiracial Society* (New York: Free Press, 1995), pp. 170-79.

(the practice of rewriting history to exclude unfavorable events that would cast suspicion on the official rendering of current reality, a practice that figured prominently in George Orwell's novel *1984*). As a mode of false consciousness, deception disguises the fact that, as Berger has noted, "common sense is quite wrong in thinking that the past is fixed, immutable, invariable, as against the every-changing flux of the present. On the contrary, at least within our own consciousness, the past is malleable and flexible, constantly changing as our recollection reinterprets and re-explains what has happened."[46] Thus a society's view of itself is largely a fiction, and its system of explanation a delusion; by internalizing this social order, the individual comes to see and believe that its story is right and true.

European Americans believe, furthermore, that this rendering is normal, that failures can be explained away, that actions can be justified, and that anything that challenges this construal, especially if it is offered by members of another people group, can be ignored as a distortion of what "really" happened. In racial terms, European Americans may not perceive themselves as "white" or be aware of their environment as "white," but information from the sociocultural world is nevertheless arranged by the structures of a false consciousness that for the most part renders others as invisible. An African American executive in the board room is "unusual" only because the board room has been normally "white"; living in a homogeneous neighborhood is unremarkable until a Hispanic family moves in and is noticeable for "their" presence in "our" neighborhood; to say "some of my best friends are black" is another way of saying "most of my best friends are white"; and as Andrew Hacker observes, poverty among European Americans is "atypical," while among African Americans it is thought to be "a natural outgrowth of their history and culture."[47] And as noted in chapter two's discussion of Charles W. Mills, deception as a mode of false consciousness is a consensual "understanding about what counts as a correct, objective interpretation of the world," and thus, in effect, an "epistemology of ignorance."[48]

3. *Detachment.* A false consciousness is manifest as cognitive and emotional detachment. Over the course of their lives, people discover ways to remove themselves from situations. Sometimes this means physical removal, as when

---

[46]Berger, *Invitation to Sociology,* p. 57.

[47]Andrew Hacker, *Two Nations: Black and White, Separate, Hostile, Unequal,* rev. and exp. ed. (New York: Ballantine, 1992), p. 106. See also Nibs Stroupe and Inez Fleming, *While We Run This Race: Confronting the Power of Racism in a Southern Church* (Maryknoll, N.Y.: Orbis, 1995), pp. 46-52.

[48]See the section "The Racial Contract" on page 73, and Charles W. Mills, *The Racial Contract* (Ithaca, N.Y.: Cornell University Press, 1997), pp. 17-18, 92-97.

we walk out of a room. Other times it means cognitive or emotional removal, as when we cease to be involved in a discussion and begin to think of something else, or we choose not to feel or become emotionally engaged in what is happening. More often than not, these kinds of removal are an expression of our lack of interest in or inability to connect with someone or the situation. Attention wanders, emotions shut down, and our indifference turns into remoteness; for whatever reason, we just cannot or will not relate to what is going on. This is not necessarily false consciousness in its mode of detachment, but if the participants and situation involve race and racism at any level, it quite likely is.

False consciousness as detachment is indicated when European Americans are unable or unwilling to relate cognitively and emotionally to the experiences of members of other people groups, and regard these experiences as atypical or misinterpreted. Often when European Americans enter a situation where members of other people groups are present, they suppose themselves and the situation to be racially unbiased. In situations where only European Americans are present, the similarity of their experiences will be assumed, and therefore when they share their experiences, they will likely not be discounted but rather validated and confirmed by the common sense. European Americans see members of other people groups shop in the same stores, sit in the same restaurants, travel on the same airplanes, live in the same neighborhoods, see the same movies and work in the same occupations as they do, and conclude that discrimination in these spheres is no longer practiced. As Derrick Bell has observed, "The very absence of visible signs of discrimination creates an atmosphere of racial neutrality and encourages whites to believe that racism is a thing of the past."[49] When members of other people groups articulate their experiences of discrimination and humiliation, patronization and condescension, dismissal and invisibility, and when they declare that they have not been and are not now taken seriously, European Americans are detached because they lack the capacity or are reluctant to relate cognitively and emotionally to these experiences. Because no sense can be made of them, they go unacknowledged and are disbelieved.

This is not to say that European Americans have no *awareness* of racism. However, European Americans have no *experience* or *consciousness* of racism

---

[49]Derrick Bell, *Faces at the Bottom of the Well: The Permanence of Racism* (New York: BasicBooks, 1992), p. 5. The idea that casual contact and even friendship between members of different people groups can produce a false sense of sameness that ignores or denies sociocultural expressions of racism is explored at some length by Benjamin DeMott in *The Trouble with Friendship: Why Americans Can't Think Straight About Race* (New Haven, Conn.: Yale University Press, 1998).

that members of other people groups have; the consciousness of European Americans is detachment. Most European Americans regard racism as the attitudes, beliefs, prejudices and actions of a relatively few bigoted people; egregious acts of racism in our sociocultural world are regarded as hardly representative of the European American community as a whole. Rampant "racism" is thought to be a thing of the past, or at least in significant decline; the social situation is different now and racism is no longer ubiquitous. When racism is considered by European Americans, it is generally in personal rather than social terms, and thus its expressions are attributed to an individual's racial prejudices, stereotypes or ignorance. False consciousness allows European Americans to regard narratives of contemporary racism and discrimination with detachment and to remove themselves from sociocultural racism. It is a perk that comes with white privilege.

One reason European Americans have difficulty making sense of the experiences of racism shared by others is that they distinguish between an idea, principle or norm on the one hand and its implications or applications in concrete circumstances on the other. One can hold the principles of equality and fairness, for example, and at the same time be disinterested in or detached from a situation where they are absent; the lack of equality and fairness in a *particular* circumstance does not necessarily discredit the *principles* of equality and fairness. European Americans are good at believing in the principles but not at expressing them in situations where they could—or should—be incarnated. (Consider the public debates on "liberty" and "justice" during the colonial period of this nation's history.) This tendency allows them to affirm the principles of equality and fairness, and at the same time oppose a means to achieve them as advocated by others, or dissent from the view that a situation is unequal and unfair. (Witness the debates on, and demise of, affirmative action.) The truth and value of an idea inhere in the idea itself and are unaffected by whether it applies in a given situation. This tendency is a manifestation of false consciousness in the mode of detachment; it reifies an idea as a thing whose existence is separable from the concreteness of the spheres and schemes of everyday life. For members of other people groups in the United States, principles, ideas and norms do not exist as "things"; they do not exist at all apart from their concrete expressions in the patterns and structures of a shared sociocultural world.

Furthermore, detachment is a mode of consciousness that not infrequently involves projection—attributing one's own attitudes or feelings to another in order to protect oneself from the discomfort of uncertainty, fear or guilt. Saying to another who has shared a racial experience, "You shouldn't feel that way or think that way," often masks the speaker's uneasiness about the situation and the implications if the other's experience and reading were to be acknowledged. It may also project an accusation of responsibility for the situation ("Well, it was your fault, and you probably deserved it!") or the innocence of others ("She didn't mean it like that. She was just doing her job!").

European Americans may even acknowledge their inability or unwillingness to relate to the experience of racial discrimination and insult—to say nothing of oppression—but what remains is a fractured sense of what they would do or think or feel in a similar situation, and they interpret the experience of others by projecting these sentiments onto them, virtually oblivious to the dynamics of a racial situation ("If it had been me, I would have given her a piece of my mind and stomped out, even if she had threatened to fire me!"). European Americans find it remarkable sometimes that members of other people groups do not think or feel or respond like them in a situation. But most often this merely expresses a projection of hostility, fear, anxiety or guilt; European Americans want to be "objective" and "level-headed" in their assessment of the situation described by others, so they impose their cognitive and emotional sense onto others as the norm.

4. *Denial.* Common sense tells us that we should accept something if it is true and reject something if it is untrue. While it is not always possible to establish that something is one or the other, we nevertheless have to function from day to day by making judgments regarding the truth or falsehood of information, descriptions, assertions and so on. The fourth mode of false consciousness, denial, is the apprehension of a legitimate assertion as unwarranted, the thoughts and feelings of others as inappropriate, and the events that form a person's or people's narratives as untrue, misleading or biased in their favor. In short, denial is the refusal to believe, recognize or acknowledge that another's rendering may be correct, and so it is regarded as contradictory.

Like detachment, denial is a way of coping with conflicting impulses and claims. But unlike detachment, denial seeks to suppress the assertions of legitimacy that engender the conflict. As noted in chapter three's discussion of "white privilege," European Americans tend not to think of themselves as "white" because the world they live in and have internalized adapts readily and attends to their interests and objectives. This "transparency" is a detachment from the experience of others in a "white"-dominated world, but it is also a denial of the experience of these others because it is judged as contradictory. European Americans reject the assertions of other people groups because to acknowledge them not only would mean validating the assertions but might very well lead to a loss of tangible and psychological benefits. Thus denying the assertions of others is at the same time a denial of racism.

In no small part, this mode of consciousness is shaped by significant social distance between European Americans and other people groups. Perhaps it might be more accurate to say that it is a subjective byproduct of social isolation. Some European Americans have casual acquaintance with, and even work or study with, members of other people groups, but population demographics and public opinion polls suggest that the overwhelming majority of European Americans live in virtual or complete social isolation from other people groups. This social isolation tends to produce what Edward Hall has referred to as "fragmented, compartmentalized lives in which contradictions are carefully sealed off from each other."[50]

Contending that racism is expressive of racial prejudice and discrimination is a form of acknowledgment, but arguing that racism is only this is denial, and the defense of this denial requires the effective suppression of the contradictory assertion. If I believe I am not racist because I am not racially prejudiced, do not practice discrimination and hold strongly to principles of equality, justice and fairness, I may still retain denial as a mode of consciousness to the extent that the experience of another is disbelieved and rejected because it is viewed as contrary to my internalized norms. Additionally, all that is required to confirm a European American's sense that another's assertion of racism is groundless is that it be shared by another European American ("Did you think that was racist?" "No, it's not racism, just a difference of opinion!"). This legitimates one's socialization into the in-group and fortifies denial.

The inability to countenance a view that asserts the presence or experience of racism, and the interest in suppressing its expression and silencing its voice, is indigenous to the sociocultural order constructed and maintained by the dominant group. European Americans regard their experiences and sociocultural expressions as the norm, and the experience and expressions of other people groups contradict this. In race relations, European Americans are known to practice two variations of the tree-in-the-forest question (if a tree falls in the forest, and there is no one there, does it make a sound?): (1) If there are no members of another "race" present, is racism nonetheless a problem here? The answer usually given is no because if members of another people group are not present, racism *does not exist.* (2) If members of another "race" are present but no assertions of racism are made, is racism a problem here? Again, the answer is usually no" because if no assertion is put forth, there is no claim to reject, no position to argue, no experience to contradict. In either case, the question presupposes that racism is absent because racism is not the norm—and thus we see a preeminent illustration of false consciousness in its mode of denial. Likewise, if racism is denied or its assertions are suppressed, this is tantamount to

---

[50]Hall, *Beyond Culture,* p. 11.

declaring that racist attitudes, values, feelings and beliefs no longer exist or are not important—at least for European Americans. Thus consciousness in the mode of denial shields one not only from actual conflict but from the possibility of conflict.

5. *Dissociation.* Finally, consciousness is false when its mode is dissociation. When mental health professionals use this term to describe an individual, they generally mean that his behavior gives evidence that some psychological activities have been disconnected from others in such a way that more than one autonomous psychic core is operative. It is a kind of psychological segregation of painful or even hostile ideas and feelings; an individual can function from one segregated core or the other because they are psychologically independent of each other. James Newton Poling describes dissociation as "an unconscious defense mechanism where threatening attitudes, ideas, and feelings become distinctly separated from the rest of the psyche. This 'splitting' of mental processes may result in the display of wandering behavior, multiple personalities, and memory loss."[51] Thus in the behavioral sciences dissociation is indicative of cognitive and emotional dysfunction.

This is not how the term is being used in our present discussion, though there are some parallels. *Dissociation* here refers to the tendency to separate one's beliefs, understandings and conduct regarding "race" from the rest of one's convictions and behaviors. As a mode of consciousness, dissociation entails the belief that different races exist and that one's behavior in the presence of members of other races needs to be different from one's behavior in general or in unmixed settings. One's consciousness is different because of the perception of race: behavior is more guarded, language is more closely examined for fear of saying something that could be regarded as racially offensive, the situation and the member(s) of the other race(s) are assessed to determine whether the environment is safe or hostile, topics of conversation are pursued both to keep the conversation away from race and racism and to allow one to feel racially innocent, and questions, thoughts and feelings arise that one thinks might be inappropriate to express or would open the door to discussing race and racism.

In dissociation I experience myself in the moment as alien to a truer, more enduring self. It is as if I am playing a game, and when it is over I can take off the uniform and put back on the street clothes I usually wear. But dissociation may not end when the encounter ends. If the encounter has been unpleasant or confrontational, if I have been challenged or accused of racism, if mechanisms

---

[51]James Newton Poling, *Deliver Us from Evil: Resisting Racial and Gender Oppression* (Minneapolis: Fortress, 1996), 123.

of defense and resistance have overtaken my consciousness or behavior, or if I simply feel the absence of the respect and cordiality I deserve, in the wake of the encounter I must still find a place for this experience of a strange self, this identity that has been assailed. This troubled and uneasy self is not the usual self, and perhaps behaviors may be recalled as awkward and unnatural or even aberrant. But the self externalized in the situation is thought not to be my true self, so it is dissociated. *(That's not who or what I really am. I don't like acting that way and I don't like feeling this way now, so that wasn't the real me!)*

When dissociation is the mode of consciousness, it frequently disguises itself in a cause-effect manner. The physical, cognitive and/or emotional discomfort was the "effect" that was "caused" by the attitudes, statements or behavior of others. In this sense dissociation shows a kind of rationality, or better: rationalization. The presumption here is that a complex phenomenon can be reduced to its causes and effects, rather like the so-called modern scientific method. We also discern processes and interactions as the ebb and flow of effects generated by specific causes (the *effect* of my damaged fender has another moving vehicle as its *cause*). Reciprocity between subjectivity and the external world is construed as the ebb and flow of initiative and response, but in situations where race factors into the equation, initiative-response is converted into cause-effect. To the extent that I experience myself as having been "abused" in a racial situation, I turn and blame the "victimizer" and thereby preserve a sense of innocence. The strange self will be segregated from the true self, and because of the discomfort (anxiety, embarrassment, fear, shame, guilt, etc.) in previous situations where race was at work, I will seek to avoid such situations in the future if at all possible.

For European Americans who live their lives mostly in social distance or isolation from other people groups, this is indeed possible. For members of other people groups, this is virtually—or actually—impossible. Most European Americans consider themselves entitled to self-comfort and ease with others, a social disposition to be enjoyed and taken for granted as the default position. But this is in fact a "white privilege" in situations where race matters.

At its root, the "cause" of discomfort is thought to be not merely the presence and conduct of the others but the fact that they are acting as members of a different race. As noted earlier, for most people race is a biological fact beyond dispute; it is thought to be empirically evident in the different physical characteristics—or "types"—of people groups as well as their distinctive sociocultural expressions. The strange self and discomfited experience are thus thought to be the "effect" of others' race, or the externalization of racial selves. Moreover, this belief in the empirical existence and manifestation of "race" may be entirely unaltered by scientific data to the contrary; science may have discredited the notion of biological races, but the self needs an explanation for its discomfort, and so the "cause" of my discomfort will be identified as the others' *race* and the fact that they act as *racial others.* Thus as a mode of consciousness, dissociation is not merely a defense mechanism but, in a dysfunctional way, a survival mechanism, a way of preserving a sense of one's true identity in continuity. And in a bizarre sort of way, it makes it possible to preserve one's own *racial identity.*

Self-esteem and colorblindness. One common denominator in all modes of false consciousness regarding race and racism is the need to maintain one's self-esteem, and by extension the esteem of one's in-group. In a history like ours in the United States, where the self-aggrandizement of a dominant group has come through the ridicule, humiliation, disparagement and dehumanization of others because of their skin color and way of life, it is something of an oxymoron to talk of European American self-esteem. Nonetheless, perhaps because of the Cartesian "turn to the Subject" and the Western cult of individualism, we as a society have found it important to value and cultivate self-esteem. Like feeling comfortable with others, feeling good about ourselves is desirable because it makes life easier.

The modes of false consciousness have this as their foundational objective: We want to feel good about ourselves and we want to feel good about our group. It's just that this "right" to self-esteem has not been acknowledged historically by European Americans as "inalienable" to members of other people groups. The recognition, regard and respect that European Americans claim for themselves is withheld from others because of their putative race.

Another common denominator is the implied or expressed belief that one does not see color—one is "colorblind." On the surface, this is an unbelievable declaration. By this, European Americans *want* to say, "I don't see you as black [or brown, yellow, red, etc.]," but what is *meant* is "I see you on my terms, with my analogies and norms." What is usually heard is "You want to see me as white, but *you don't see me at all!"*

For me to say that I do not notice color or treat people differently because of color is a strategy of consciousness that has both negative and positive objectives: (1) to prevent myself from being perceived as a racist, and (2) to assert and establish myself as unbiased and fair-minded. In both cases, the modes of consciousness protect my self-esteem.

The problem is that the confession does not further the discussion of racism or introduce a dimension of trust into the dialogue, because it implies that the real culprits are those who see color. It is as though I were saying, "I'm not the problem, and the ones who are don't happen to be here." But colorblindness, as both Ellis Cose and James Waller have declared, "is not a racial equalizer but a silencer."[52] True colorblindness is the partial or complete inability to distinguish colors (primarily red and green) because of a physiological abnormality in the photo-sensitive receptors of the retina. The common sense construes the phenomenon that we designate as "color" as itself an element or property intrinsic to an object. This is contradicted, however, by physics, which tells us that it is a differential capacity to absorb and refract wavelengths of light that is inherent in an object. Thus in the spheres of race and racism, "colorblindness" is an aberration, a failure to see the obvious *and what it has come to symbolize,* and a fiction that serves to preserve self-esteem. It is, in a subtle way, not only a linguistic expression of racism but a contribution to the social construction of race. The net effect, to borrow from C. Wright Mills, is that the "common sense is more common than sense."[53]

Colorizing People: The Disposition and Conservation of Racial Identity

Earlier I noted Berger and Luckmann's observation that identity is a basic component of subjective reality, situated in a relationship of reciprocity with the environment outside ourselves and the persons with whom we interact. In the course of our everyday lives we are conscious of our environment and what we are doing and experiencing, but we tend not to focus a lot of attention on our "identity." We generally do not talk about ourselves in terms of identity, even though we are occasionally asked questions about ourselves (where do you live? where are you from? what do you do for a living?) that are camouflaged versions of the core identity question: *who are you?*

The assumption in these questions is that the inquirer can learn something about who the person is from the answers. Unfortunately, the assumption is false. Announcing where you were born, where you have lived and now live, and what you do for a paycheck reveals nothing about your identity. When someone asks the core identity question directly, we generally answer by saying our name and indicating our affiliation with a person, place or organization that we think will best help establish rapport with the inquirer. But we have not actually disclosed our identity. In fact, we have

---

[52]Ellis Cose, *Color-Blind: Seeing Beyond Race in a Race-Obsessed World* (New York: Harper-Collins, 1997), p. 209; and James Waller, *Face to Face: The Changing State of Racism Across America* (New York: Insight, 1998), p. 173. See also David B. Wilkins's introduction to *Color Conscious: The Political Morality of Race,* ed. K. Anthony Appiah and Amy Gutmann (Princeton, N.J.: Princeton University Press, 1996), who notes that "'color blindness' in our political and moral discourse has been little more than a smoke screen for the pervasive 'color consciousness' (and, more specifically, white supremacy) that has been a dominant feature of the American saga since the pilgrims first landed on Plymouth Rock" (p. 4).

[53]C. Wright Mills, *The Power Elite* (1956; new ed., New York: Oxford University Press, 1999), p. 313.

not really disclosed much of anything about ourselves.

What is identity? The notion of identity is rather obscure and ambiguous in popular discourse, perhaps because it is often confused with other aspects of subjectivity that are more evident to ourselves and expressed to others. But identity is not the same as *behaviors,* or even the *roles* we execute in social interaction, including the one we do to earn a living. Behaviors and roles are situational and occasional; they are momentarily expressed in some place, and then they are discontinued. *Personality* takes us a little closer to identity, inasmuch as personality can be understood as the combination of temperamental, emotional and mental traits that together make up one's disposition and come to be expressed in behaviors and roles. We get even closer to identity when we designate *character* as the peculiar constellation of beliefs, attitudes, values and commitments that distinguishes one person from another and that comes to expression in behaviors and roles through the agency of one's personality.

Underlying character, personality, behavior and roles is *identity,* the particular being of a self that subsists and endures through time and space, the existent sameness of a person that persists from time to time and place to place, and that is expressed in varying ways to oneself and to others. It is, as the etymology of the word suggests, the self as an entity being the same repeatedly. Identity is thus to be distinguished but not separated from its particular spatiotemporal expressions and the objective world with which it is correlated in reciprocity. Like roles and behaviors, personalities and characters, one's identity is subject to change, but unlike these others, identity is one's basic mode of subsistence and endurance, one's continuity through places and times.

Identity is formed and maintained in social interaction in everyday spheres in relation to those with whom we are more or less intimate. Our sense of identity is influenced by how we are seen by others and how they respond to us. It is not unusual to discern that another person is not recognizing us for who we are, or is recognizing us in ways that are not coherent with our self-identity. We have also had times when we experience another in ways that confirm our identity, so we discern that we are truly *known.*

This network of relationships is both our local social world and our means for connecting to the larger sociocultural environment. These social groups, coming as they do in varying sizes and degrees of intimacy, form the innermost core of our social world and represent the boundaries between our self and others. Our association with others in a social world assumes an awareness of our own identity and that of others, and we are more or less comfortable in the particular spheres that make up this core. We *identify* with these spheres and these others through shared memories and experiences of the ways our interaction has reciprocated influence. We seek and receive recognition, and we give it in turn. When there is recognition and acknowledgment of our selves from others and our identities are confirmed in social spheres, we are happy.

Group identity. It is possible to speak metaphorically of collective or group identity, as a set of characteristics (beliefs, attitudes, values, commitments and the behaviors that express them) that are generally shared by individuals who constitute a group. But it is only metaphorical in that the group has no existence apart from the constituent members who identify with it. Typically what makes an aggregate of persons into a group is shared interests, purposes or experiences. In this sense there is no difference between Alcoholics Anonymous and the Republican Party, though each could be said to have its distinctive "identity." What is characteristic of both groups is that there are criteria to be met before one can identify with the group, and there are certain behaviors or actions that are required in order to be identified with the group; this is how a group defines itself or construes its identity as a group.

A group may be self-selective or open, voluntary or involuntary. But any particular group, no matter how formal or informal, intimate or distant, small or large, will have to balance that which is common to or shared by the group with the uniqueness and idiosyncrasies of its individual members. Other than that which is common or shared by all, there remain the peculiar and stylized identities, characters and personalities of the individual members. This means that no group is or can be fully homogeneous. An individual's identity involves a degree of autonomy in that one thinks and feels, chooses courses of action and makes decisions in many different spheres, not just the ones that form the basis of a group's identity. Given the reciprocity between the subjective and the objective, the self and others, the extent to which an individual identifies with a group is measured by the extent to which the individual appropriates and shares in the identity of the group.

Racial identity. This brings us to *racial* identity. An individual's racial identity and concept of a racial self are shaped by identifying with a racial group, in much the same way that an individual's gender or occupational identities and concepts are shaped by identifying with those groups: through socialization and internalization. As one identifies with a racial group, its plausibility structures accept and confirm—make sense of—one's identity, and reciprocally, the individual contributes to the formation and maintenance of the group's identity. The group's narratives and memories, shared experiences and persistence through time and space become meaningful as frames of reference for locating oneself with others.

But as noted earlier, socialization entails positive identification with an in-group and negative characterization of an out-group, and in this country, one of the most prominent boundaries between groups has been race. This is an indication of a racially oriented oppositional identity and counter-identity. The patterns and structures of the dominant culture have enabled European Americans to arrogate to themselves the freedom to self-define and form individual and group identities in ways that imposed a negative identity on members of other people groups. As the dominant sociocultural "in-group," European Americans stigmatized and dehumanized those perceived as racial "out-groups" and forced them to bear these identities as they were marginalized. Any individual could be immediately assigned to a racial group on the basis of physical appearance, regarded as embodying most if not all the features thought to characterize the group's identity, and treated accordingly. As a member of the dominant racial in-group, one identified with and internalized the beliefs, attitudes, values and commitments that characterized group identity, and the member gave expression to these in her own behaviors both within and outside the group. Whether one's race was central or auxiliary to one's identity, one nevertheless identified passively or actively with a group whose identity was forged as oppositional to others.

In some otherwise unexpected ways this manner of forming "white" racial identity has contributed to the formation of group solidarity among members of other "races." The lengthy and violent history of racial exploitation, exclusion and restriction has engendered a group consciousness marked by common experience. This is what Manning Marable has in mind when he writes: "In the United States, 'race' for the oppressed has also come to mean an identity of survival, victimization and oppression to the racial groups or elites which exercise power and privilege. What we are looking at here is not an ethnic identification or culture, but an awareness of shared experience, suffering and struggle against the barriers of racial division."[54] When racial out-groups are subjected to domination and have negative identities imposed on them by their oppressors, one vital aspect in their resistance is self- and group-identification in other terms, so "the struggle for racial equality takes the form of a struggle for group identity."[55] The profound dissonance of this struggle to form an integral identity led W. E. B. Du Bois to describe it as a "peculiar sensation, this double-consciousness, this sense of always looking at one's self through the eyes of others,

---

[54]Marable, *Beyond Black and White,* p. 187.

[55]Malik, *Meaning of Race,* p. 217. See also Omi and Winant, *Racial Formation,* p. 99; Fumitaka Matsuoka, *The Color of Faith: Building Community in a Multiracial Society* (Cleveland, Ohio: United Church Press, 1998), p. 13; Gerald David Jaynes and Robin M. Williams Jr., eds., *A Common Destiny: Blacks and American Society,* (Washington, D.C.: National Academy Press, 1989), p. 13; and James Baldwin, "White Man's Guilt," in *Black on White: Black Writers on What It Means to Be White,* ed. David R. Roediger (New York: Schocken, 1998), p. 321.

of measuring one's soul by the tape of a world that looks on in amused contempt and pity. One ever feels [one's] two-ness,—an American, a Negro; two souls, two thoughts, two unreconciled strivings; two warring ideals in one dark body, whose dogged strength alone keeps it from being torn asunder."[56] In no small part the individual and group identities formed and maintained by members of oppressed groups can indeed be seen as counter-identities—identities that counter those imposed or attributed by the dominant group.[57]

But on closer inspection, there are three fundamental problems with racial identity, each of which contributes to the social construction of race and racism, both subjectively and objectively. First, because race is commonly supposed to be a matter of biology, a *racial* identity implies that one's identity is determined and immutable. It stipulates that one's race is the epicenter of one's existence, the primary if not exclusive mode of self-definition around which all other modes of self-definition revolve. If race is biology, one cannot change one's racial identity regardless of how individually stylized its expression may be. One simply *is* one's race. When race is construed as biological, it is possible to speak of an *ontological* "blackness," "redness," "brownness," "yellowness" or "whiteness," regardless of one's

---

[56]W. E. B. Du Bois, *The Souls of Black Folk* (1903; reprint, New York: Vintage, 1990), pp. 8-9. See also Victor Anderson, *Beyond Ontological Blackness: An Essay on African American Religious and Cultural Criticism* (New York: Continuum, 1995), p. 82; Manning Marable, "Staying on the Path to Racial Equality," in *The Affirmative Action Debate,* ed. George E. Curry (Reading, Mass.: Addison-Wesley, 1996), p. 5; Henry Louis Gates Jr. and Cornel West, *The Future of the Race* (New York: Vintage, 1996), p. 86; Marable, *Beyond Black and White,* p. 82; Sterling Stuckey, *Slave Culture: Nationalist Theory and the Foundations of Black America* (New York: Oxford University Press, 1987), pp. 265-98; and the essays in Gerald Early, ed., *Lure and Loathing: Essays on Race, Identity and the Ambivalence of Assimilation* (New York: Penguin, 1993).

[57]In addition to the works cited in the previous three notes, important discussions of racial identity, with a range of viewpoints and differences of opinion, can be found either as part or the whole of the following: Appiah and Gutmann, eds., *Color Conscious;* Stephen L. Carter, *Reflections of an Affirmative Action Baby* (New York: BasicBooks, 1991); F. James Davis, *Who Is Black? One Nation's Definition* (University Park: Pennsylvania State University Press, 1991); Michael Eric Dyson, *Reflecting Black: African-American Cultural Criticism* (Minneapolis: University of Minnesota Press, 1993); Joe R. Feagin and Hernán Vera, *White Racism: The Basics* (New York: Routledge, 1995); bell hooks, *Killing Rage: Ending Racism* (New York: Henry Holt, 1995); Noel Ignatiev and John Garvey, eds., *Race Traitor* (New York: Routledge, 1996); Bruce A. Jacobs, *Race Manners: Navigating the Minefield Between Black and White Americans* (New York: Arcade, 1999); Kathy Russell, Midge Wilson and Ronald Hall, *The Color Complex: The Politics of Skin Color Among African Americans* (New York: Anchor, 1992); Shelby Steele, *A Dream Deferred: The Second Betrayal of Black Freedom in America* (New York: HarperCollins, 1998), and *The Content of Our Character: A New Vision of Race in America* (New York: Harper Collins, 1991); Robert W. Terry, *For Whites Only,* rev. ed. (Grand Rapids, Mich.: Eerdmans, 1975); Thandeka, *Learning to Be White;* and Payne, *Getting Beyond Race.*

sociocultural environment or the actual hue of one's skin color. Amy Gutmann is correct to say, "Whether I like it or not, regardless of what I think or do or who I am in some more meaningful sense, I will be identified as white in this society."[58] But this does not mean that she *is* white, not even if she chooses to identify with those who so identify her. What Gutmann is saying is that a "white" racial identity is imposed on her by others, but her "regardless" implies her freedom to reject this identity, her capacity to self-identify in nonwhite ways. There is no question but that racism means this freedom has accrued to her in ways it has not accrued to others, but she remains a self able to form and maintain an identity by *identifying with* the reference group(s) of her own choosing. Ian F. Haney López argues that no one is "born White. Rather, one becomes White by virtue of the social context in which one finds oneself, to be sure, but also by virtue of the choices one makes."[59]

If *race* is biological, if one is born "white" or "brown" or "yellow," then there really is no basis to dismantle racism, because the expressiveness of racial identities is immutable (or we utilize advances in genetic science to revive the pseudoscience of eugenics). But race is not a matter of biology. Rather it is an institutionalized system of differential and stratified relations among people groups that serve the positions and interests of a dominant group—that is, it is socially constructed.

The second problem with racial identity stems from the fact that identity requires reference groups and plausibility structures for its maintenance and validation. In-groups define and maintain their own identities, and as we have seen, one ingredient in this is a characterization of out-groups. Democrats define themselves and maintain group identity in part through a characterization of Republicans. The group identity of workers is defined and maintained in part by a characterization of managers. Physicians are not-lawyers, Christians are not-Muslims, and women are not-men. The characterization of an out-group by an in-group is generally unfavorable and intended to buttress an adversarial relation. The negative identity is imposed on the out-group, who rejects or resists it because it is not consistent with its own sense of group identity; its members contend that this alien identity is false because it misconstrues or distorts something about themselves as individuals or a group.

Any group's self-definition will involve, then, three aspects: promotion of its own positive identity ("This is who we are"), advocacy of its identity in the

---

[58]Amy Gutmann, "Responding to Racial Injustice," in *Color Conscious,* ed. Appiah and Gutmann, p. 168.
[59]Haney López, *White by Law,* p. 190.

face of the negative portrayal by the oppositional group ("This is where you're wrong about us") and disparagement of the oppositional group's identity ("This is who you really are"). Thus a group identity is established and maintained by plausibility structures that make it possible for the member to identify with the group These are the bases and processes a group uses to articulate its purposes, beliefs and opinions, impose its entrance requirements, affirm benchmarks for good standing, and prescribe tactics and courses of action.

But just as a group imposes an identity on members of an oppositional group, so it also imposes an identity on its own members. The extent to which an individual identifies with the group is indicative of the extent of the group's ability to enforce its preferred identity and discern its expression in the conduct of its members. Members are expected to be loyal to the group as they share in and contribute to it, but they risk disapproval, criticism and possibly ostracism if their identification with the group is mitigated by sentiments, beliefs or demeanor the group perceives as disloyal or heretical.

Identity maintenance entails identity enforcement in the interests of solidarity, and herein lies a problem with racial identity. Identifying with a reference group means allowing the group to have a role in individual identity formation through socialization and internalization. Having a racial identity means allowing a *racial* group to have a role in this manner. In this regard Naomi Zack observes: "Racial identity . . . is connected with membership in groups and loyalties to the decisions made by other group members and leaders. Therefore, racial autonomy has traditionally meant the self-rule of groups rather than individuals."[60] Because race is thought to be permanent and biologically real with unambiguous indicators, and thus one's membership in a racial group is determined, this is tantamount to surrendering agency in one's identity formation and maintenance to the group, consciously or unconsciously, by consent or under duress. In this circumstance, one must either capitulate to the imposition and enforcement, in effect denying one's own freedom, or abandon the group altogether. However, the latter option is of course impossible because the indices of race, and therefore racial membership, are permanent. The individual, regardless of skin color, is encompassed again, but in a somewhat different way, by Du Bois's "two unreconciled strivings," being placed in a reference group he did not choose and cannot leave, and being unable or unwilling to gain access to and identify with another. Stanley Crouch notes that "the problem of a race consciousness of whatever stripe negates the question of the individual and imposes some sort of 'authenticity' that can trap

---

[60]Naomi Zack, *Thinking About Race* (Belmont, Calif.: Wadsworth, 1998), p. 107.

the single human life inside a set of limited expectations."[61]

Any group can tolerate and even encourage diversity within its ranks up to a limit, and that limit is generally marked by the boundary between stylized ways to affirm and express group identity and conduct the group (or its leaders) judges as clearly outside the scope of group identity. When individuals cross that boundary, they are regarded as, and become in effect, "race traitors." Thus an underlying dimension to this problem with racial identity is: Who in the "white" group gets to define—*identify*—what "whiteness" is? Who in the "brown" group gets to define what "brownness" is? What criteria are used, and who is empowered to apply them? So like any group, reference or otherwise, a racial group internally promotes its own identity, advocates for it in the presence of stylized variations to enforce conformity and solidarity, and disparages those who stray from the fold.

This problem in the phenomena of racial identity and racial group is only compounded all the more when we consider the long history of so-called miscegenation, or the "mixture" of races through "interbreeding," and the fact that "mixed-race" children are being born in increasing numbers to parents of different racial groups. Such persons who identify themselves with more than one racial group (for example, Tiger Woods, as a "cablanasian") are pressed or claimed to some degree by one or all groups to hold primarily or exclusively one identity or the other. Likewise, the creation of the category of "other" for the 2000 census generated considerable opposition from people groups who believed this would diminish the numbers in their group, thereby reducing the group's social and political power and the ability to hold federal and state governments accountable for enforcement of civil rights and continuation of governmental assistance programs. But as Zack has noted, echoing anthropologists and others who disbelieve in race, "if races were real, most people would be mixed, because there have been no lasting situations in history during which entire distinctive groups of people were isolated and bred exclusively within themselves. But races are not real, so racial mixture is not real either."[62] Again, individual and group racial identity is rendered problematic because of *intra*-group promotion, advocacy and disparagement.

The third problem with racial identity is that it is thought to determine or at least influence the way one performs various roles in the spheres of everyday life. One acts this way and does these things *because* one is a member of

---

[61]Stanley Crouch, "Who Are We? Where Did We Come From? Where Are We Going?" in *Lure and Loathing,* ed. Early, p. 84.

[62]Zack, *Thinking About Race,* p. 20. See also Cose, *Color-Blind,* pp. 228-30; Montagu, *Man's Most Dangerous Myth,* pp. 112-40, 253-96; and Smedley, *Race in North America,* pp. 232-72.

a particular race. Or one is predisposed to function in certain ways as a result of genetic inheritance. At best, a racial group is a sphere with its own stylized schemes and sets of roles, rules, perceptions, interpretations and power relations. These are the ways in which a racial group patterns its interactions at micro- and macro-levels. The fact is that individuals are members of many social groups, such as family, political, community, commercial, occupational, educational, recreational, benevolence and religious groups, each of which is patterned by spheres that eventuate one's interaction with others. One's identity is expressed—occasionally and contextually—in a multitude of social settings and roles, and to one degree or another one's identity will be formed and maintained as one *identifies with* more than one of these groups.

The problem emerges when an individual identifies with one group as paramount, or conceives of her identity as modeled after the identity of a particular group to the exclusion of others. This centralizing confuses individual identity with group identity, and individual identity with its spatiotemporal expressions in spheres. It also indicates the reification of a role by making it coextensive with one's identity ("I am a doctor!"). If I centralize race in my self-conception and acknowledge it as constitutive of my identity, then certainly I can be said to have a *racial* identity. But it also implies that my race determines or influences the ways I express myself in the execution of roles in the spheres of everyday life, so that I *am* and *can only be* a "white" married man who sells insurance, collects stamps, plays rugby on Saturdays and attends a Roman Catholic parish, or a "brown" single woman who designs software, reads poetry, convenes a political group and attends a Methodist church, and each does all of these things in individually stylized ways construed as characteristic of one's race because one *is* one's race in all spheres and in all other social groups. But as Michael Eric Dyson has observed, "biology is not identity,"[63] and if "race" is not a matter of genes, then it can hardly determine or influence one's identity or sociocultural expressiveness except as a matter of individual choice, by consent or under duress.

This is not intended to suggest that an individual's perspective on historical, social, economic and political matters should be unaffected by one's reference group(s). Rather it is to suggest that one's perspectives are not determined or influenced for all times and places by a reference group solely because it is a *racial* reference group. On this subject, K. Anthony Appiah believes that "there is danger in making racial identities too central to our conceptions of ourselves; . . . if we are to move beyond racism we shall have, in the end, to move beyond current racial

---

[63]Dyson, *Reflecting Black,* p. 26.

identities."[64] This conviction is echoed and extended by Richard Payne, who contends that an obstacle to dismantling race and racism is the notion that "race represents a fixed and inflexible identity" and that "the politics of racial identity demands an uncompromising and unambiguous loyalty to the myth of a racial group."[65] If one regards oneself only or centrally as *racial,* one has effectively made one's race essential to one's character, personality, behavior and roles.

Human identity is molded by many different elements and forces in a sociocultural world, including the social, economic and political opinions and concerns of those with whom we most closely identify, and the groups that cluster people by common interests and experiences. Many people define themselves by strong moral or religious convictions, the "tenacious beliefs which when held give definiteness to the character of a person or a community, so that if they were surrendered, the person or community would be significantly changed."[66] Such convictions guide persons in the course of their decision-making. But at its core, as reciprocity suggests, identity is the sameness of a person that endures, and thus identity has to do with the experiences of the self in relation with others. Identity is not rigid and inflexible but malleable and changeable in a network of places and times, activities and relations, memories and anticipations.

Elevating race to the status of ultimacy as an identity-forming determination, in George Kelsey's view, makes one a racist: "The racist relies on the race as the source of [one's] personal value. [One's] life has meaning and worth because it is a part of the racial context. It fits into and merges with a valuable whole, the race. As the value-center, the race is the source of value, and it is at the same time the object of value. No questions can be raised about the rightness or wrongness of the race; it is the value-center which throws light on all other value."[67] Thus it is unfortunate that, as Gerhard Lenski asserts, "when one surveys the human scene, one is forced to conclude that *when [persons] are confronted with important decisions where they are obliged to choose between their own, or their group's, interests and the interests of others, they nearly always choose the former*—though often seeking to hide this fact from themselves and others."[68] It is exceedingly tragic—and sinful—that in a racialized

---

[64]K. Anthony Appiah, "Race, Culture, Identity: Misunderstood Connections," in *Color Conscious,* ed. Appiah and Gutmann, p. 32.

[65]Payne, *Getting Beyond Race,* p. 5.

[66]McClendon, *Biography as Theology,* p. 19.

[67]George D. Kelsey, *Racism and the Christian Understanding of Man* (New York: Charles Scribner's Sons, 1965), p. 27.

[68]Gerhard E. Lenski, *Power and Privilege: A Theory of Social Stratification* (New York: McGraw-Hill, 1966; University of North Carolina Press, 1984), p. 30.

society such as ours, where race shapes and is thought by some to determine human identity and destiny, it is so easy to align oneself with one while maligning others.

Racial Attitudes: Americans' Opinions on Race

Suppose you answer a knock at your front door, and there stands a survey interviewer, asking if you would be willing to answer some questions about yourself and your views on various social, economic, political and race-relations matters. You agree, and the interviewer asks the first question: "We are faced with many problems in this country, none of which can be solved easily or inexpensively. I'm going to name some of these problems, and for each one I'd like you to tell me whether you think we're spending too much money on it, too little money, or about the right amount. First [interviewer reads first item] . . . are we spending too much, too little, or about the right amount on [this]?"[69] The items you are asked to respond to are as follows:

a. Space exploration
b. The environment
c. Health
d. Assistance to big cities
e. Law enforcement
f. Drug rehabilitation
g. Education
h. Assistance to Blacks
i. National defense
j. Assistance to other countries
k. Assistance to the poor
l. Highways and bridges
m. Social security
n. Mass transportation
o. Parks and recreation

How would you respond to these items in the survey? Pause to think about it for a moment. As you ponder each of these "problems," what goes through

---

[69]This is the first question on the General Social Survey (GSS), conducted each spring from 1972 to the present. This question, and the ones that follow, appeared on the 1998 GSS and were taken from James Allan Davis, Tom W. Smith and Peter V. Marsden, *General Social Surveys, 1972-1998: Cumulative Codebook* (principal investigator, James A. Davis; director and coprincipal investigator, Tom W. Smith; coprincipal investigator, Peter V. Marsden, NORC ed.; Chicago: National Opinion Research Center, producer, 1998; Storrs, Conn.: The Roper Center for Public Opinion Research, University of Connecticut, distributor), pp. 93-98. The response items listed as "a" through "o" are part of the survey question.

your mind? What pictures or scenarios appear in your memory or imagination? How do you sort through them to determine whether "we" are "spending" too much, too little or the right amount of money to "solve" them? Do you respond to each item with the same ease, or do some take more time than others? Think about it.

Now suppose the items are given to you with somewhat different wording. The question remains the same, but the items are phrased differently, as follows (with their other version alongside):

a. Space exploration program   (Space exploration)
b. Improving and protecting the environment   (The environment)
c. Improving and protecting the nation's health   (Health)
d. Solving the problems of the big cities   (Assistance to big cities)
e. Halting the rising crime rate   (Law enforcement)
f. Dealing with drug addiction   (Drug rehabilitation)
g. Improving the nation's education system   (Education)
h. Improving the conditions of Blacks   (Assistance to Blacks)
i. The military, armaments and defense   (National defense)
j. Foreign aid   (Assistance to other countries)
k. Welfare   (Assistance to the poor)
l. Highways and bridges   (*Same*)
m. Social security   (*Same*)
n. Mass transportation   (*Same*)
o. Parks and recreation   (*Same*)[70]

How would you respond to these items *now*? Pause and think again. As you ponder each of these "problems," what goes through your mind? What pictures or scenarios are conjured up in your memory or imagination? Again, how do you sort through them to determine whether "we" are "spending" too much, too little or the right amount of money to "solve" them? Do you respond differently now to each item, taking more or less time to decide? Think about it.

Notice several things about the question. First of all, you are not being asked to prioritize these problems, only to indicate what you think about the amount of money being spent on them. Second, you are not being asked if you know how much money is actually being spent in any area (though you are given a response option of "Don't Know"). Third, you are not being asked whether you think money should be redirected from one "problem" to another (though this

---

[70]This particular survey question was asked in both ways, each version being given to approximately half the respondents. The items in each version are coded differently so researchers can assess the relationship between how a question and its items are worded, and the distribution of responses across the range of response options.

might be implicit in your thinking when you respond by saying "Too Much" or "Too Little" to a given item). Fourth, you are not told who is actually referred to by the "we" in the question. There is no mention of any level of government or private enterprise, though with the very first item (space exploration), you probably associated "we"—consciously or unconsciously—with the federal government. But note: you have processed your thinking along the lines of the question's implicit assumptions: that (1) all these areas are "problems," (2) the *way* to "solve problems" is to "spend money," and (3) one *function of government* is to "solve problems" by "spending money." Fifth, the question does not ask what you know or even whether you care about these areas, but your association of "we" with government and your response to the question of spending levels probably raise the matter of taxes (where does the money come from?), and since you probably pay them in some form, you suddenly have a vested financial interest in the question and its items. Sixth, all of these areas are *social* areas, impinging to one degree or another on both personal and communal life. Describing each social area as a "problem" in need of a "solution" creates or confirms an impression that there is something *wrong* or incorrect or contrary about the area, but you are not told what the "problem" is or in what particular sense it is "problematic." The language of the question simply tells you that it is a problem, and that is how you think about it as you respond. And seventh, note what does not appear on the list at all. There is nothing listed that has to do directly with our economy itself or with government itself. There is no mention of such things as farm subsidies, oil and natural gas exploration, national political campaign funding, manufacture and sale of military hardware, or other such things.

Look again at the way these items are described in the two columns above, and consider the differences. The language of "problem" varies between the two lists. Notice that the list on the right lacks detail and specificity; the items appear to be rather generic, almost neutral. Only four of the items are given a particular slant by the use of the phrase "assistance to," implying the giving of help, support or aid, presumably in the form of money. The implication of "assistance to" is that the entity receiving assistance is *in need,* and the common understanding of this term is that the one receiving aid is in some way subordinate to the one giving aid. Thus the impression created by the items using this phrase is that "big cities," "Blacks," "other countries" and "the poor" are in need of financial aid that, if given, will mitigate whatever their "problem" is. Similarly, the list on the right identifies the "problem" with drugs as focused on "rehabilitation," generally regarded as a good thing. The "drugs" in question are unspecified and could presumably be over-the-counter, prescribed or illegal drugs, and they may or may not include tobacco and alcohol; the respondent supplies the specificity, if needed. In any case, the slant of "rehabilitation" evokes a sense of *recovery* or *restoration*, and probably focuses on rehab programs of one sort or another. Whether and to what extent the remaining items in the list are regarded as problematic is left up to the memory, imagination, knowledge, cognition and affect of the respondent.

Notice that the list on the left appears to be more specific by using a lot of verbs in the present progressive tense. These verb tenses impose a particular slant on the "problem" by presenting the item in a way that conforms to a particular bias or appeals to a certain audience. The language of "improving" and "protecting," for example, does not evoke the same sense of need or even "problem." Rather they imply making better and keeping from harm, or *amelioration* and *preservation,* so the "problem" appears to be strengthening and safeguarding "the environment" and "the nation's health." The slanting also focuses attention not on a vague "education" but on strengthening the nation's "educational system," however that might be construed. Likewise, the concern is not "assistance to" but rather making better the "conditions" of Blacks, whatever that may mean. Help for "big cities" is now more specifically "solving the problems" of big cities, prompting the respondent to look at cities from a different perspective. The question and the list on the right attribute a "problem" generically to "law enforcement," but the list on the left makes quite explicit a "problem" that may or may not be construed as directly related to law enforcement alone, "halting the rising crime rate." The implication of the way the question is posed is that this is a problem that "we" can—and *should*—address by spending money, though for what is unexpressed (more police officers, prosecutors and judges in the criminal court system, gun control, prisons, anticrime education programs or what?). The concern with "drugs" is now slanted not to rehabilitation but to "addiction," generally *not* regarded as a good thing. Even with drugs still unspecified, the item is directed toward "dealing" with "addiction," and this probably evokes thoughts of doing something about substance abuse, physical dependence, compulsive behaviors, and perhaps a host of other human conditions and activities associated with notions of addiction, most or all of which are probably assessed negatively as undesirable as over against a more positive assessment of "rehabilitation."

Suppose that after you have given your judgment of the spending levels on each of the items, you are then asked to explain *why* you think too much, too little or the right amount is being spent. What do you say now? Think about it. What reasons do you give for thinking that too much money is being spent in a particular area and too little in another? What judgments are you making and what criteria do you use? If you think that spending in a particular area is just about right, does this mean that you are satisfied with the spending results? If spending is too much in a particular area, does that mean you think money is being wasted or spent foolishly, or that the ways the money is spent are just not producing the desired results? What do your judgments mean, and why do you make them?

As it happens—perhaps fortunately—the interviewer does not ask this *why* question, so whatever your reasons may be for a particular response, and whatever you think or feel or imagine as a basis for your response, remain hidden to the interviewer and maybe even to yourself. Your "too little" responses to the "big cities," "Blacks" and "poor" items will be folded into all the other "too little" responses to these items, resulting in aggregate numbers that render your judgments and your reasons even more invisible and fractionalize your responses into a percentage.[71]

However, you may not be as unnoticeable as you might think. Through the wonder of computerization and what statisticians call cross-tabulation, a survey processor can "control" the data by segregating out all respondents who meet a set of criteria related to the responses given to other questions. Thus, for example, the survey processor can determine the distribution of responses to the "big cities" question given by unemployed single women who are over thirty-five years of age living in a suburb, or the distribution of responses to the "Blacks" question given by urban European Americans as compared to urban African Americans, or what respondents who think "too much" money is spent on space exploration also think about the amount of the spending levels on law enforcement. In short, responses to questions can be aggregated according to a range of criteria limited only by the answers given to other questions on the survey, including an aggregate that represents any demographic profile. Analyzing the distribution of responses among those who meet the profile's criteria leads to the observation that any given person who fits the profile is more likely or less likely to hold a particular opinion on a certain matter. Thus for example, if 58 percent of European American male respondents who are middle-class, have college degrees, live in the suburbs, work in the city and are registered Republicans think too much money is being spent on solving the problems of big cities, social scientists will observe that any individual in the general population who meets the profile is statistically more likely to hold the same opinion.

---

[71]Some of the questions in social science surveys do ask the *why* question, as we shall see momentarily. For the interested reader, of the total number of responses to the three items (including those who chose "No answer"), the percentages of those who responded with "too little" are as follows (ibid.):

Assistance to big cities: 18.9%	Solving the problems of the big cities: 45.5%
Assistance to Blacks: 26.2%	Improving the condition of Blacks: 33.9%
Assistance to the poor: 59.6%	Welfare: 16%

But by no means is any particular profile group uniform in its opinion on a particular matter. Quite the contrary, there are significant differences of opinion within each group, making it easy to generalize but difficult to be accurate with regard to the "characteristic" views held by a single group. It is possible to state unequivocally that *this* number of respondents chose *this* response option to *this* survey question. From this point on, everything is interpretation of these data, and while survey researchers can cross-tabulate responses and control for a variety of profiles, the only empirical data are *this* number of respondents matching *this* profile chose *this* response option to *this/these* question(s). Comparative numbers, profiles and percentages may be described statistically with the language of "tends" and "more/less likely to," but what this *means* is a matter of the researcher's interpretive judgment, and no reader of survey research is disinterested in or entirely objective about the data.

Opinion: Beliefs and attitudes . . . and principle. In general, the opinions that social scientists attempt to measure are the beliefs held by members of the population at large. Beliefs may or may not be substantiated or shown to be true, and they may be grounded in emotion or disciplined study and reflection, or based on something as thin as general impressions and naiveté. They are, nonetheless, what people think about various matters, and thus they are of interest not only to social scientists but also to pollsters who work for business, political and media decision-makers. From a social science perspective, opinions also reflect the attitudes people have or the judgments they make about certain matters, and thus opinions have an evaluative component. Opinions can be regarded, then, as a combination of what one believes about something and what one's attitude is toward it. For example, one can believe that a preschool child will be disadvantaged if the child's mother works, and this belief may entail a positive or negative judgment on working mothers. Social and behavioral scientists are not agreed on where the line should be drawn between beliefs and attitudes in public opinion surveys, but they are agreed that survey responses should not be confused with behavior; one's beliefs and attitudes as expressed in response to survey questions do not indicate or predict what one's behavior is likely to be.

Analysis of opinion on race relations in the United States has indicated that beliefs and attitudes have changed over the years since World War II. In some areas these shifts are substantial, while in other areas they are less so. One area where survey research has shown a change in opinion is racial equality, as measured by beliefs and attitudes regarding whether all persons regardless of race are entitled to equal treatment in such spheres as employment, education, housing, public accommodations and transportation. However, at the same point an anomaly begins to appear. As public opinion in general has moved over more than five decades toward affirmation of racial equality, equal treatment and equal opportunity, it has also shown increasing signs of resistance and opposition to initiatives designed to effect this equality in particular social arenas. Moreover, as opinion on equality has shifted, so has opinion on the reasons for inequality. As the sociocultural order has increasingly affirmed the value of racial equality, it has found itself divided over ways to understand and explain the causes of existing socioeconomic inequality, and thus over ways to remedy these and achieve equality.

This anomaly is described by social scientists as the gap between the *principle* of equality and equal treatment and the *implementation* of the principle in social spheres. American opinion in general strongly affirms the principle and is deeply divided over public policy and programs designed to put it into effect.[72] In a sense the public debate is not about whether Americans support equal political, economic, social and civil rights for all (egalitarianism); this they clearly do, though the affirmation is far from universal. Rather it is about the causes for inequality and the particular means by which they can be overcome. And because it is a matter of public policy, it is a political debate about whether and to what extent the government ought to be engineering equality in the sociocultural order.

Social survey data suggest that the fault lines in this debate run along the boundaries of racial groups, with European Americans on one side and virtually all other people groups on the other. These data appear to indicate that there are significant differences of opinion and perception on a host of race-related matters, including whether and to what extent racism is a problem in the sociocultural order. For example, in 1995 68 percent of African American respondents indicated that racism is a "big problem" in our society, while only 38 percent of European American respondents chose the same response.[73] When asked if they thought African Americans had "more opportunity, less opportu-

---

[72]See especially the analyses and conclusions in Donald R. Kinder and Lynn M. Sanders, *Divided by Color: Racial Politics and Democratic Ideals* (Chicago: University of Chicago Press, 1996); Howard Schuman et al., *Racial Attitudes in America: Trends and Interpretations,* rev. ed. (Cambridge, Mass.: Harvard University Press, 1997); Paul M. Sniderman and Edward G. Carmines, *Reaching Beyond Race* (Cambridge, Mass.: Harvard University Press, 1997); and Paul M. Sniderman and Thomas Piazza, *The Scar of Race* (Cambridge, Mass.: Belknap/Harvard University Press, 1993).

[73]From a survey conducted by Chilton Research for the *Washington Post*/Kaiser Family Foundation/Harvard University Survey Project (1995). Cited in "People, Opinions and Polls: An American Dilemma (Part II)," in *The Public Perspective* 7 (February/March 1996): 20. See also Gallup Organization, *Social Audit: Black/White Relations in the U.S.* (June 1997), available on the Internet at <www.gallup.com/poll/socialaudits/sa970610.asp>.

nity, or about the same opportunity to live a middle class life as whites," a majority of African American respondents (71 percent) chose "less," while a majority of European American respondents (55 percent) chose the "same" option.[74] An overwhelming majority of African American respondents think not only that the federal government can do something to help African Americans with "severe problems" (70 percent) but that the government is spending too little in assistance (74 percent). Among European American respondents, on the other hand, only a minority think the government can do something (38 percent), and an even smaller minority think the government is spending too little (16 percent).[75] A survey conducted by the *New York Times* in June 2000 asked how important improving race relations is to the future of the United States, and a majority of European American respondents said it was not the most important thing (65 percent), but a majority of African American respondents said it was (66 percent).[76]

Biased surveys? Though the purpose here is not to analyze the quantitative data of social surveys, we might well ask: Is it possible that in addition to measuring public opinion on race-related matters, survey questions mirror and manifest racial beliefs and attitudes? Do they not only presuppose what and how people think but also contribute to and validate in some ways the mythology and consciousness of race? Do survey questions illustrate the terms and patterns of racial-oriented thinking in that the conventional—commonsense—ways of construing race and racism are embedded in the questions themselves? In short, what can we learn about racial beliefs and attitudes by studying the questions and the response options? The way a question and its response options are posed not only elicits a response but also forms and influences the belief and attitude that underlie the opinion. Here we will consider one other survey question before turning our attention to the constellation of factors that contribute to the formation of opinion.

Consider this question: "On the average, (Blacks/African-Americans) have worse jobs, income, and housing than white people. Do you think these differences are . . . a) Mainly due to discrimination? b) Because most (Blacks/African-Americans) have less in-born ability to learn? c) Because most (Blacks/African-Americans) don't have the chance for education that it takes to rise out of poverty? d) Because most (Blacks/African-Americans) just don't have the motivation or will power to pull themselves up out of pov-

---

[74]*Washington Post*/Kaiser/Harvard (1995), cited in "People, Opinions and Polls," p. 21.
[75]*Washington Post*/Kaiser/Harvard (1995) and NORC *General Social Survey* (1994), cited in "People, Opinions and Polls," p. 26.
[76]*New York Times Poll* (June 2000), available at <www.nytimes.com/library/national/071100poll-results.html>.

erty?"[77] The first problem with the question is that it invites the respondent to think about African Americans and European Americans as groups and to compare them with each other. The question does not state explicitly that African Americans as such are "worse" but rather that the indicators of their socioeconomic status are. Declaring that their jobs, income and housing are "worse" thereby implies that, "on the average," the jobs, income and housing of European Americans are *better*. The question tacitly attributes some measure of superiority to one racial group, if only in the implication that their jobs, income and housing are better. By consenting to the terms of the question, the respondent has effectively embraced its declaration: one racial group is superior to another as expressed in socioeconomic indicators. Furthermore, the question is focused on African Americans, so the non-African American respondent is *looking at* the group from the *outside* and not considering his or her own racial group directly, let alone his or her own job, income or housing as the point of reference (the question does *not* state, "On the average, European Americans have better jobs . . .").

The question is not about *whether* one group is better off than another; this is stated. Rather the question asks *why* one group is worse off than another. To ascertain the opinion of the respondent, four explanations or causes are given, and the response options for each are "Yes," "No" and "Don't Know." Not being asked to identify a single explanation or rank the explanations in some order of influence, the respondent is given license to indicate whether any of the given explanations might be contributing factors. Thus it is possible to say none of them are at work, or all of them are at work, or some are but others are not. One can say *whether* a particular explanation applies, but not *to what extent* it may apply, or how it may relate to other explanations.

The first option, "discrimination," attributes the cause of "worse" to practices of exclusion and restriction, and by implication to the ones who practice exclusion and discrimination (generalized racial "others"). If the respondent is a European American, saying "yes" here points the finger at "us"; if the respondent is an African American, saying "yes" points the finger at "them." On the other hand, the second option, "less in-born ability," attributes the cause to African Americans themselves and implies biological inferiority in general, or cognitive capacity in particular ("intelligence"). Here the finger pointing is reversed: European American respondents who say "yes" point to "them," while African American respondents who say "yes" point to "us." The third option, "chance for education," appears to be straightforward but in fact is

[77]Davis, Smith and Marsden, *General Social Surveys, 1972-1998,* pp. 264-65.

rather vague. Presumably "chance" refers to the *opportunity for* education, but it could also imply the *likelihood of* education. In either case, the quality or level of "education" is unspecified, though it is stated to be related to the capacity to "rise out of poverty." This option implies that African Americans have been *deprived* of education; it does not say that they do not take advantage of opportunities given but that they do not "have" the opportunity or likelihood, and this invites the question *why*. Depending on how one responds to this option, the fingers could point in either direction. The fourth option, "motivation/will power," returns the respondent to the "us" versus "them" dualism and attributes the cause to African Americans themselves. This option says nothing about ability, inborn or otherwise, something that could conceivably be measured or assessed. Rather it speaks of an absence of motivation or will-power, presumably the absence of some incentive that might induce one to act, or the strength of resolve necessary to act. The implication here is that living in poverty is acceptable to those who so live because the incentive or will to rise "up out of" poverty is absent—as though one might prefer to live in poverty. This option also invokes the notion that hard work brings reward and that those who want to can achieve, a notion that, as we have seen, is firmly embedded in the race-myth and culture of dominance.

The fact that a respondent can say "no" to a particular explanation does not necessarily mean the respondent believes the explanation is not a factor. One could say "no" to discrimination by demurring at the word *mainly* yet still believe that discrimination is at work. A "no" answer could also indicate a belief that discrimination no longer exists or is not as widespread as it was once thought to be. One might say "no" to "less in-born ability" because the ability in question is "to learn," and one still believes that others are innately inferior. A "no" to the chance for education might mask a belief that African Americans are not entitled to, or should not be given, the opportunity for education. A "no" to lack of motivation or willpower might be a veil for the conviction that many African Americans living in poverty have extraordinary incentive and resolve but it is redirected to what is judged to be a "path of least resistance." Moreover, the inclusion of the superlative adjective *most* in the second, third and fourth options might very well be a caveat making allowances for the fact that *some* African Americans do have an inborn ability to learn, chance for education, and motivation and willpower to escape impoverished circumstances, and thus the language of the options avoids the appearance of blatant stereotyping.

Nevertheless, the question and options for explanation as a whole presuppose racial stereotypes. Indeed not only are stereotypes presupposed, at least with regard to European American respondents, but the fact that they are embedded in the question and its response options gives unspoken approval to believe, localize and activate them.[78]

Forming opinion. What are the factors that go into forming our opinions, the beliefs and attitudes we hold on a given subject? So far as public opinion is concerned, social scientists have identified several factors, and their surveys are designed to measure and correlate them so as to determine which are predominant in influence. When the subject is race relations, survey researchers are particularly interested in this because opinions have shifted over the years and yet differences of opinion between people groups on some race-related matters remain noteworthy. Here the goal is not to explain why a particular individual or group holds the opinion they do, or even why there are such differences of opinion. Rather our interest is in the types of factors that contribute to the formation of beliefs and attitudes on matters of race. More specifically, we need to consider the influences that form our consciousness because, as we saw earlier, consciousness is never empty but always has something as its object. The work of social scientists, especially in the area of race relations, is useful in this regard because in their attempt to measure and interpret opinion on race matters they have identified several variables that are opinion-makers.

Donald Kinder and Lynn Sanders have organized the discussion in their book *Divided by Color* entirely around the question of the factors or "ingredients" that shape opinion on race matters in an effort to determine which, if any, are predominant.[79] They argue for three, contending that "American public opinion—in general and on matters of race—is an expression of a small number of *primary ingredients:* the material interests that citizens see at stake in the issue; the sympathies and resentments that citizens feel toward those social groups implicated in the dispute, especially those groups that the policy appears to benefit or victimize; and commitment to the political principles that

---

[78]Space does not allow for a comparable analysis of other survey questions, but the discerning reader may find it illuminating to subject the following questions to his or her own analysis (paying particular attention to *italicized* words/phrases): "*Some people* say that because of *past discrimination,* blacks should be given *preference* in hiring and promotion. Others say that such preference in hiring and promotion of blacks is *wrong* because it *discriminates against whites.* What about your opinion—are you for or against *preferential hiring and promotion of blacks?*" (ibid., p. 168). "Do you agree strongly, agree somewhat, neither agree nor disagree, disagree somewhat, or disagree strongly with the following statement: Irish, Italians, Jewish and many other minorities *overcame prejudice* and *worked their way up.* Blacks should *do the same without special favors*" (ibid.). "Some people think that (Blacks/Negroes/African-Americans) have been discriminated against for so long that the *government* has a *special obligation* to help *improve* their living standards. Others believe that the government *should not* be giving special treatment to (Blacks/Negroes/African-Americans). Where would you place yourself on this scale, *or haven't you made up your mind on this?*" (ibid., p. 303).
[79]See Kinder and Sanders, *Divided by Color.*

the policy seems to honor or repudiate. Interests, attitudes toward social groups, and political principles are the core ingredients of public opinion."[80] There is also a fourth factor, one they refer to as the "frame," or the way an issue of policy is situated and described. Frames are "interpretive structures that are a part of political discourse, invented and employed by political elites to advance their interests," but they are also "internal structures of the mind that help individuals order and give meaning to the parade of events they witness in public life."[81]

Kinder and Sanders define the factor of "material interest" as the concern one has for the material well-being of oneself and immediate family, and whether one perceives a policy that threatens one's ability to develop and maintain financial resources and power to protect or advance these self-interests. In their review of social survey data, they conclude that there is little evidence to support the notion that opinions on race-related matters are influenced appreciably if at all by *self*-interest. However, the same cannot be said for *group* interests. Kinder and Sanders find an influence in the concern that the material interests of one's racial group may be jeopardized. They note, however, that for European Americans this is more perception than reality. Because "personal and collective racial threats seem so intertwined in the minds of white Americans," they conclude that to the extent that material interests are an influence on European American opinion on race matters, "it is through the threats blacks appear to pose to whites' collective well-being, not their personal welfare."[82] At the same time, nonetheless, survey data suggest that both African Americans and European Americans have a sense of intergroup competition that underscores some sense of threat and advantage: "On matters of public opinion . . . both black and white seem to be asking themselves not what's in it for me, but what's in it for my group?"[83]

The factor of "sympathies and resentments" is found to be a significant influence in the formation of opinion on race-oriented issues in public policy. Indeed, intergroup antipathy and intragroup solidarity loom large in these areas. Resentment is especially strong when the policy under discussion is thought to benefit the other group or disadvantage one's own. The authors find not only that racial resentment and prejudice are quite strong among European Americans but that their expression in survey questions accurately reveals the presence of racial stereotypes. European American resentment is no longer

---

[80]Ibid., p. 36.
[81]Ibid., p. 39.
[82]Ibid., pp. 84-85.
[83]Ibid., p. 90.

expressed in explicit language of inherent biological inferiority but in the language of motivation, desire, volition, work, merit and so on—the language of *individualism.* Kinder and Sanders interpret survey data to suggest that "most" European Americans do "subscribe" to racial stereotypes, believing that African Americans are less hardworking, less intelligent and more violent than European Americans, so that "prejudice is preoccupied less with inborn ability and more with effort and initiative."[84] However, this individualism can be regarded as a disguise for the *implicit* assumption that African Americans are racially inferior: "Some whites see no difference between the races, but most of the variation [in opinion] among white Americans is in *how* inferior black Americans are, whether the racial superiority that whites enjoy in essential capacities and fundamental qualities is overwhelming or slight."[85] Asserting that racial resentment "plays an important and expansive role in white public opinion," Kinder and Sanders conclude by saying that it "is not the *only* thing that matters for race policy, but *by a fair margin racial resentment is the most important.*"[86]

Kinder and Sanders's discussion of the "commitment to principles" factor underscores the *principle versus implementation* anomaly I noted earlier. Examining data on specific principles of equality, economic individualism and limited government, they note that there is greater unanimity among Americans in affirming the former two than there is for the latter one. Nonetheless, equality in principle does not easily translate into equality in application in such varied areas as the social, political and economic spheres (equal *rights, opportunities* and/or *results*). In general Americans hold to the value of hard work, believing not only that people should take responsibility for themselves but that people who do not have only themselves to blame for their failure. The principle of limited government is the belief that government's role is primarily to guard and preserve the rights of individual citizens and ensure their freedom to pursue their own individual interests.

So far as opinion on race-related matters is concerned, Kinder and Sanders observe that the principles of economic individualism and limited government do not exercise a significant influence *until* they are brought to bear on policy proposals for achieving racial equality. While survey data suggest that Ameri-

---

[84]Ibid., pp. 114-15.

[85]Ibid., p. 114.

[86]Ibid., p. 124. Kinder and Sanders link racial resentment with racial prejudice and racial stereotypes, so they are effectively arguing that prejudice and stereotypes play a very significant role in the formation of European American opinion on public policy matters related to race. Here they part company with others who acknowledge that prejudice and stereotypes do influence European American public opinion but argue that they are not the most important factors. On this score see, e.g., Schuman et al., *Racial Attitudes in America,* pp. 154-69, 320; Sniderman and Carmines, *Reaching Beyond Race,* pp. 61-73; and Sniderman and Piazza, *Scar of Race,* pp. 5, 13, 28-36, 64, 88.

cans desire a more inclusive and egalitarian society and that the principle of equality is important to them, they also suggest that this principle drops from sight entirely when the issues and policies under discussion are related to race. "Differences of opinion on topical matters of race can often be traced to differences over equality," but this only raises the question of "what it is, exactly, that equality means."[87] Take affirmative action. Opponents argue from the principle of equality that affirmative action "violates equal treatment," while supporters, arguing from the same principle, contend that affirmative action "brings the formal idea of equal opportunity to life."[88] Thus equality in principle is one thing, but equality with respect to any particular socioeconomic sphere or public policy proposal is another. This leads Kinder and Sanders to state, "Equality seems to mean, then, equality for *us*, not for *them*."[89]

As indicated above, the term *frames* as a central component in public opinion has a double reference. On the one hand, it refers to the way an issue is defined and how its essential elements are identified and connected. Definition is generally the work of what Kinder and Sanders call the "political elites," the principal contenders in public policy debates. Because there are differing positions on a question, the definition of frames turns on conflict and competition for public opinion and political action. "How citizens understand an issue, which features of it are central and which are peripheral, is reflected in how the issue is framed. . . . Every issue is contested; advocates of one persuasion or another attempt to define the issue their way. . . . Alternative frames are never even-handed: they define what the essential problem is and how to think about it; often they suggest what, if anything, should be done to fix it."[90] So, for example, "affirmative action "can be framed as "preferential hiring to remedy past discrimination" or as "reverse discrimination against European Americans," depending on the interests of the one(s) engaging the issue.

On the other hand, *frames* also refers to the "cognitive structures that help individual citizens make sense of the issues that animate political life. They provide order and meaning; they make the world beyond direct experience seem natural."[91] In this way opinion is influenced and formed by both what and how

---

[87]Ibid., p. 152.

[88]Ibid., p. 160.

[89]Ibid., p. 152.

[90]Ibid., p. 164.

[91]Ibid. While individuals may on occasion construct their own "frame," Kinder and Sanders state that "for the most part, we believe frames are assembled and promoted by others. They are the creation of a handful of intellectuals and activists, then brought to public attention by issue entrepreneurs and journalists. No doubt elites create and promote frames with public reaction in mind. And citizens certainly may reject frames they dislike and rework those they adopt. But by and large, citizens consume frames rather than produce them" (ibid., p. 165).

others think and what and how one thinks for oneself. But if the Kinder/Sanders element of frames is anywhere close to being accurate, then two observations need to be made at this point. First, in terms of reciprocity and internalization, it would appear that our "opinions" on race-related matters are formed under an influence more unidirectional than interactive—that is, we take in the thinking and definitions of others and make them our own. Second, in terms of myth or ideology, as our "opinions" are shaped by the views of others, both the arguments we choose to accept and those we choose to reject have been determined to some extent by those who speak from vested sociopolitical *and research* interests. So to the factors analyzed must be added the way survey questions and their response options are worded as a means to measure public opinion.

Other factors in opinion formation. Moving now beyond Kinder and Sanders, let's consider several other factors that do not figure appreciably in either their analysis and interpretation or that of other social scientists, but that are nevertheless important as influences in opinion—beliefs and attitudes—on race-related matters. Some of these additional factors may appear to be rather self-evident, but they still need mention because they orient our consciousness and the views we internalize.

First of all, there is a set of factors that make even more "plausible" what I have previously called a "reference group." To this point, such a group has remained largely diffuse in the discussion, except for use of the adjective *racial.* But when we identify such factors as *age* and *gender,* the reference group becomes a bit more narrowly construed—or better, there appear to be reference "groups." Sociologists refer to such groupings as a "cohort," a group of people forming a demographic aggregate. Survey researchers have noted that opinions and the strength with which they are held vary from cohort to cohort. In some ways an interracial young adult male cohort will have more in common in their experiences and opinions than, say, young Asian American males and middle-aged Asian American males. Likewise, *occupation* and *economic status* demarcate reference groups. Research into socioeconomic stratification shows that persons in a particular occupational or economic group are more similar in their life's experiences, outlook and sociocultural world than persons in disparate groups. Controlling for age, gender, occupation or economic status in survey responses reveals a basis for an interpretive statement that such-and-such persons "tend" or are more or less "likely" to hold such-and-such an opinion.

Further, *marital status* is a kind of differential gateway to a variety of social relations and connections among people. It is not so much that single people think differently from married people (though survey research tries to make this case) but rather that status as single or married places an individual differently in certain sociocultural spheres, if not in different spheres altogether, as points of reference. Research appears to justify the perception that single people socialize more with other single people, and married people more with other married people. This too, however, is moderated by other cohort factors.

Another factor to be added is *education,* specifically the level of education completed. Whether the group includes high school dropouts or possessors of multiple graduate degrees, there are indications of greater similarity among persons in an educational-level grouping then there are across levels. But again, this is largely a matter of social networks and shared experiences and outlooks in a sociocultural world.

Finally, we must include *religion,* understood as a distinctive set of beliefs, values, relationships and practices. What people believe in relation to a religious tradition, why they believe it and the extent to which their belief affects their manner of living are indices of the influence of a tradition on their opinion regarding sociocultural issues.[92]

Obviously any given individual will have several reference groups through which secondary socialization occurs, and whether any particular group is more or less influential will depend in no small part on the choices and preferences of the individual. And none of this is to suggest that one is socially confined within any of these groups, but rather that one's reference groups, however characterized demographically, are varied and influential in internalizing the sociocultural order.

A second set of factors is geographical in nature. First, one's *location* exercises an influence on belief and attitude, especially on race. We could narrowly define location as one's neighborhood and not be entirely misled. We do "live with" our neighbors—whether we like them or not—in that we share a physical place with them. But perhaps a truer place to begin might be one's municipality or geographical community. Whether one lives in an urban, suburban or rural area has an influence on one's social network, lifestyle and activities and therefore, through socialization, on one's beliefs and attitudes (for example, the opinion of farmers on issues of water rights will be framed quite differently from the opinion of urbanites). Further, a municipality does not exist in isolation but is connected in several ways—economic, political, social, cultural, religious—with a larger district or county, as well as state and region. We tend to think of these as marked

---

[92]See George Gallup Jr., "Keeping the Faith: Looking at God through America's Eyes," *The Public Perspective* 11, (May/June 2000): 14-17; Michael Shermer, "Why People Believe in God," *The Public Perspective* 11, no. 3 (2000): 18-20; Roper Center for Public Opinion Research survey data review, "Believer Nation," *The Public Perspective* 11 (May/June 2000): 24-35; and Michael O. Emerson and Christian Smith, *Divided by Faith: Evangelical Religion and the Problem of Race in America* (New York: Oxford University Press, 2000), esp. pp. 51-133, 153-68.

off by jurisdictional boundaries reflecting levels of government, but this can obscure the deeper and more pervasive features characteristic of an area—its economic bases, cultural mixture, predominant social and religious views and so on. Related to this is the *social distance* factor, the extent to which members of various people groups know and interact with one another. Physical proximity does not assure that personal and social interaction will occur, but it does make it possible and in some places more likely. Personal relationships among members of people groups do influence beliefs and attitudes.

The last set of factors underscores in a different way the reciprocity between the subjective and the objective. On the one hand, beliefs and attitudes regarding race matters are formed, clarified, moderated and changed in relation to a *critical incident* that has drawn the attention of individuals, organizations, government agencies and the media because of, say, wanton racially oriented violence or an appeal to racial stereotype to deflect personal culpability in criminal action. The history of race relations—indeed of *racism*—in the United States is characterized by such incidents, such as the videotaped beating of Rodney King by Los Angeles police officers; the beating of Leonard Clark by white teenagers in Chicago; the murder of James Byrd in Jasper, Texas, at the hands of three European American men; the murder of Mulugeta Seraw in Portland, Oregon, at the hands of a white supremacist; the slaying of Amadou Diallo by New York City police officers; the fatal shooting of Timothy Thomas by a Cincinnati police officer. Charles Stuart in Boston reported to police that the person who murdered his wife was an African American male, after he had murdered her himself. Susan Smith in Union, South Carolina, reported that the person who stole her car and abducted her two children was an African American male, when in fact she killed the children herself by pushing the car that contained them into a lake where they drowned. In both cases these perpetrators presumed that police officers would find their statements credible because they fit the stereotypic profile. Such incidents, under media scrutiny, have galvanized public opinion and precipitated reconsideration of race-oriented beliefs and attitudes.

On the other hand there is also the factor of *sheer indifference.* One's opinion may be influenced by racial events occurring nearby or far away to the extent that they evoke a strong response (anger and anguish or revelry and relish, or something in between). Sheer indifference is not cognitive or emotional dissonance but existential disconnection. It is disinterest and dissociation to the extreme, a *"quiet* toxin" whose "tracks are hidden in the overall attitude of 'each man for himself' that is so prominent a part of our society's ethos."[93] With

---

[93]Paul L. Wachtel, *Race in the Mind of America: Breaking the Vicious Circle Between Blacks and Whites* (New York: Routledge, 1999), p. 36.

regard to race and racism, the nonresponse of sheer indifference indicates that one not only *will* not but *cannot* find a way to engage and make any sense of the critical incident and all it expresses and symbolizes. For indifferent persons, the survey response option "Don't *Know*" really means "Can't *Care.*" Sheer indifference says, *I will not acknowledge you or internalize you, so I may remain unaffected and apathetic.*

•   •   •   •

Whoever says, "I have come to know him," but does not obey his commandments, is a liar, and in such a person the truth does not exist.   1 J o h n 2 : 4

It may not seem disingenuous to claim to know and love Jesus Christ and at the same time fail to heed his voice in all the spheres of our lives, but it surely is. It may not appear to us that the claim is false if we gravitate toward some people and position ourselves at some distance from others, but it surely is.

Where did we ever get the notion that we can be loyal to Jesus Christ without having to obey his commandments? How does rejecting others for whom Christ died manifest loyalty to him? For what purpose do we cling to the lie of racism and at the same time assert the truth of the gospel? Do we really think that knowing the truth in Jesus Christ allows us to live in opposition to others?

5

FRAMING A
THEOLOGY OF RACIAL
RECONCILIATION

You abandon the commandment of God and hold to human tradition. M a r k 7 : 8

We have a tendency to suppose that we know more and we know better than those who preceded us. We like to think we have the prerogative to determine what is best for ourselves and what is needed for others. We don't think that we're managing the gospel, but if we're not comfortable with what the gospel is saying, we'll find a way to make it fit into our lives so it becomes useful. After all, that's what our predecessors did, and what they have handed on to us is ours to shape. Aren't we the ones who have to interpret it for our situation? And don't we build on the interpretations of those who went before us?

•   •   •   •

All along the way in our discussion to this point we have repeatedly encountered the artful ways race and racism have arisen and become entrenched in our context. By attending to their objectivity and subjectivity we have observed their expressiveness in the warp and woof of the fabric of our history as a nation, and we have noted their presence and operation in the spheres and schemes of our everyday lives and the institutional systems that situate us in a shared world. Hopefully the discussion to this point has produced a sense of dissonance, a deep unease not merely with the status quo of race and racism but, more important, with the subtle and strident manifestations that dehumanize all who are caught in their grip. Racism is bad news for everyone, and no one who lives in the United States is untainted by its insidious evil.

But it is not supposed to be this way, and the good news is it does not *have* to be this way; the good news is that it can be changed! Those among us who have accepted and practiced it, who have ignored it and yet benefited from it, and who have been oppressed, exploited and restricted by it *can all be changed.*

Racism is neither the first word nor the last word, but in our context it has been a powerful interim word that has effectively challenged the first and the last words. Some have assumed or concluded that racism is a permanent structural feature of our sociocultural order, mostly because race is thought to be real. For these the prospect of change is nil: individuals may be more or less racist, and some may have their *personal* racism reduced to the point where it no longer registers on the scale, yet there will remain the social, cultural, economic, political and religious *systems* that are racist by design and in effect. Others devise strategies intended to counter the personal and systemic expressions of racism, working toward *solutions* that are themselves shaped by how the problem is perceived. If racism is the product of ignorance, then education is in order. If racism is a matter of personal antipathy, then a good therapist will do. If the problem is discrimination, then antidiscrimination laws are called for. If racism is some kind of moral flaw, then perhaps we need more ethicists. If the problem is biology, well—there's really nothing we can do about that, is there?

At the risk of sounding simplistic, racism is all of these—and much more— because at its root racism is *sin,* and therefore it is radically a *spiritual* problem, one that is firmly and deeply embedded in personal lives and the sociocultural order these lives have produced.

It is tempting at this juncture to ask, What can we as Christians do about racism? How should we respond to the micro- and macro-expressions of racism?[1]

---

[1]Readers interested in perusing literature that asks and answers these questions should consult the following works, all written by Christians who are committed to dismantling racism through racial reconciliation as an expression of their witness: Joseph Barndt, *Dismantling Racism: The Continuing Challenge to White America* (Minneapolis: Augsburg Fortress, 1991); James Breckenridge and Lillian Breckenridge, *What Color Is Your God? Multicultural Education in the Church* (Wheaton, Ill.: Victor, 1995); Harlon L. Dalton, *Racial Healing: Confronting the Fear Between Blacks and Whites* (New York: Anchor, 1995); Susan E. Davies and Sister Paul Teresa Hennessee, eds., *Ending Racism in the Church* (Cleveland, Ohio: United Church Press, 1998); Jefferson D. Edwards Jr., *Purging Racism from Christianity: Freedom and Purpose Through Identity* (Grand Rapids, Mich.: Zondervan, 1996); Tony Evans, *Let's Get to Know Each Other* (Nashville: Thomas Nelson, 1995); Clyde W. Ford, *We Can All Get Along: 50 Steps You Can Take to Help End Racism* (New York: Dell, 1994); Vincent Harding, *Hope and History: Why We Must Share the Story of the Movement* (Maryknoll, N.Y.: Orbis, 1990); William Pannell, *The Coming Race Wars? A Cry for Reconciliation* (Grand Rapids, Mich.: Zondervan, 1993); Spencer Perkins and Chris Rice, *More Than Equals: Racial Healing for the Sake of the Gospel* (Downers Grove, Ill.: InterVarsity Press, 1993); James Newton Poling, *Deliver Us from Evil: Resisting Racial and Gender Oppression* (Minneapolis: Fortress, 1996); Stephen A. Rhodes, *Where the Nations Meet: The Church in a Multicultural World* (Downers Grove, Ill.: InterVarsity Press, 1998); Columbus Salley and Ronald Behm, *What Color Is Your God? Black Consciousness and the Christian Faith,* rev. ed. (Downers Grove, Ill.: InterVarsity Press, 1981); Jody Miller Shearer, *Enter the River: Healing Steps from White Privilege Toward Racial Reconciliation* (Scottdale, Penn.: Herald, 1994); Clarence Shuler, *Winning the Race to Unity: Is*

It is also tempting to assert that as Christians we are equipped with the gospel and empowered by the Holy Spirit to engage racism and work for the reconciliation that God has accomplished in the life, ministry, death and resurrection of Jesus Christ. While this is true and the questions are appropriate, we are nonetheless confronted with a caution: Christianity as a faith and an institutionalized system has played not an insignificant role in fostering and defending racism[2] and is still culpable in its practices as manifest in its segregated congregations, denominational agencies and related organizations.

This book has been working from the premise that Christian faith and theology can and should respond to and engage racism in any and all of its expressions, but that in order to do so it must subject race and racism to critical scrutiny, seeking to discern how it has shaped and still shapes the contours of personal and sociocultural worlds. The gospel of reconciliation is the good news that authorizes Christian initiative in engaging racism and effecting racial reconciliation, but given the fact that this very racism has challenged, co-opted and compromised the gospel, it behooves us to attempt to make sense of it objectively and subjectively as characteristic of ourselves and our place and time. The gospel is a resounding *no!* to our racism, and to envision what the gospel's equally resounding *yes!* can and should be for us, it is necessary to understand our situation. The Word of God, the good news of the gospel of Jesus Christ, is addressed to us, here and now in our circumstances, and we ignore at our own peril what God has to say to us. The world of race is a false world, and racism is a counterfeit gospel in an idolatrous religion. God neither intends nor accepts what we have made of them, because we use them to alienate, abuse, overpower and destroy our fellow human beings. They are thus the indications of our own sinful revolt. We are, after all, implicated in racism.

The analysis of race and racism in the previous chapters has suggested a way to construe the reality of race and racism in our sociocultural world. Thus the matters discussed so far could be considered overtures to the first movements in a theology of racial reconciliation. In this final chapter we turn to the resources and convictions of our Christian faith in order to discern what impulses in the Christian story might warrant a stand against racism. Is there a vision for

---

Racial Reconciliation Really Working? (Chicago: Moody Press, 1998); Glenn Usry and Craig S. Keener, *Black Man's Religion: Can Christianity Be Afrocentric?* (Downers Grove, Ill.: InterVarsity Press, 1996), and *Defending Black Faith: Answers to Tough Questions About African-American Christianity* (Downers Grove, Ill.: InterVarsity Press, 1997); Raleigh Washington and Glen Kehrein, *Breaking Down Walls: A Model for Reconciliation in an Age of Racial Strife* (Chicago: Moody Press, 1993); and George A. Yancey, *Beyond Black and White: Reflections on Racial Reconciliation* (Grand Rapids, Mich.: Baker, 1996).
[2]In addition to the works cited in the previous note, see chapter three, n. 80.

another way to live as peoples, another world in which goodness, righteousness, justice, equality and truth are objectively and subjectively expressed in a sociocultural order? If there is, what does it look like from here, where we now find ourselves, and what does it mean for us and ask of us in the micro- and macro-expressions of our shared life? More important, what role if any do we as Christians have in dismantling the old world and building this new one? *If we built it, can we tear it down? If we tear it down, can we build another differently?* The task at hand is to suggest answers to these questions, answers that draw on the Christian faith as their source, answers that may indicate a theological foundation for taking up a ministry of racial reconciliation and an engagement with the sociocultural order.

What are these resources, and what is involved in drawing on them? First and foremost, we have the sacred literature of the Judeo-Christian traditions, the ancient Hebrew and Christian writings that together constitute the narratives of God and God's relation with God's people and the world. The Scriptures are our primary resource for developing a theological understanding and practice of reconciliation, racial or otherwise. But in order for these writings to function as a resource, we must access the convictions, perspectives, experiences, judgments and practices embedded in their narratives and retrieve them into our own situation. The Scriptures contain indications of sociocultural and religious worlds and the ways these worlds shaped and were shaped by the people who occupied them. These writings are themselves a product of God's self-disclosure. Written by very human authors inspired by the Holy Spirit, they chronicle God's presence, speaking and actions in the histories of God's people. They give an account of ways of life and responses to God's divine self-disclosure. They are, in other words, the story of God's initiative and the people's responses in places and through times, and they reflect their contexts—the cultures, environments, epochs and experiences of the people. They attest to the revelation of God in particular times and places, and they attest to the ways God attended and guided the people as they participated in those events, perceiving them and reflecting on them, interpreting them in order to understand more fully God's purpose for them and how they ought then to live as God's people.

Thus the sacred literature of our faith contains the narratives of God's *initiatives* in the actions of self-disclosure, the *responses* of people to these initiatives and the *experiences* that led to and flowed from their encounters with God in quite specific sociocultural and religious *contexts*. Each generation sought to access and retrieve this history of initiative and response, make sense of it by perceiving, reflecting, interpreting and understanding in order to warrant the actions that then served as the traditioning—the means of passing on—their faith and its meaning in new circumstances. This chronicle is our Bible, handed on to us through generations of God's people, each of whom, in their particular context and in relation to their experiences, had to access and retrieve the revelatory events of divine initiative and human response in order to warrant faith and conduct.

When we claim that this sacred literature is normative for our faith and conduct, we are acknowledging not only that it is inspired but that God continues to speak to us and act among us through it. We are acknowledging that it has been mediated to us by the sense others have made of its constellation of divine initiative and human response in concrete sociocultural environments, and that we must endeavor under the guidance of the Spirit of God to do as our predecessors have done: we too must perceive, reflect on, interpret and understand its witness for our circumstances in order that it might authorize our actions as response to God's initiative. Scripture is contextualized and expressive of the experiences of God's people. For us, here and now, the attempt to access and retrieve this resource entails attending not only to the narratives of God's speaking and actions but to the contexts in which they are situated and the responses and experiences of the recipients of God's revelation. To claim this sacred literature as normative means that our context, responses and experiences stand under its judgment, but this judgment is rendered in the hard work of discerning ourselves and our situation in the light of the initiatives, responses, contexts and experiences embedded in scriptural narratives.

To move toward a theology of racial reconciliation, we want to seek out the points of convergence between the constellation of resources in the Scriptures (initiative-response, experiences of the participants, context and traditioning) and the constellation of resources in our present situation of racism (Scripture, response-experiences, context). It is necessary to make clear at the outset that a theology of racial reconciliation is an attempt to situate or frame our engagement with race and racism with explicitly *Christian* perspectives. Thus my approach will be oriented by a theological understanding of Christian faith convictions and the sense they make of race and racism.

We will look first at the worldview of Christian faith, grounded in the revelation of the triune God. This is followed by a discussion of the *sin* of racism that so deeply afflicts us. We will then inquire into a New Testament impulse toward a radically new vision of inclusiveness and the abrogation of racism as the warp and woof of a sociocultural order. This challenge moves us into a description of what I will call a *critical consciousness,* whose purpose is to contest the racist status quo. We will conclude with attention to the ministry of reconciliation and a warrant for deconstructing a sociocultural order whose design and development have objectively and subjectively expressed race and racism.

Destabilizing Our Universe: The Initiatives of God

When we put our minds and hearts to thinking about our faith—what we believe, why we believe it and what it implies for how we should live—we are doing the work of theology. This reflection may be impressionistic, intuitive and undisciplined, or it may be rigorous, reasoned and methodical, or it may be somewhere in between.[3] In any case, theological thinking is concerned with correlations between the central affirmations of Christian faith, their biblical-historical bases and their implications for how we regard and conduct ourselves in our world. The primary subject of theology is the identity, character and actions of God; from this comes a secondary subject—our identity, character and actions as those who confess faith in God. In attending to its primary subject, theology asks about whether and how it happens that we discern God and what we can then say about who God is, what God has done and is doing, and why. Theological reflection presupposes and works from faith and attempts to understand faith and its object more fully and truly. Thus theology is a work of faith; we cannot step outside our faith to pursue the questions of faith, any more than we can step outside our histories to interrogate them. However, we can make the convictions of our faith and the God to whom they point the subjects of inquiry because both our faith and God can be present to consciousness (the subjectivity of faith). The inquiry explores the correlations and determinations between our faith on the one hand and the reality of God in our world on the other (the objectivity of faith). Theology is, in this sense, thinking about God *and* thinking about ourselves.

God's self-disclosure. Christians assert that God is discerned in and through God's revelation, or the disclosure of the divine self to us. Just as human beings are disclosed in their conduct, so God is disclosed in God's conduct. God's identity and character are manifest in God's actions, and as those toward whom God acts, we are positioned to recognize and acknowledge the One who acts, and thus to reflect theologically on who this One is. The story of Christian faith is the story of these actions of divine self-disclosure, what they mean and how

---

[3]For discussions of "theological reflection," each from a different point of view, see C. David Grant, *Thinking Through Our Faith: Theology for 21st Century Christians* (Nashville: Abingdon, 1998); Stanley J. Grenz and Roger E. Olson, *Who Needs Theology? An Invitation to the Study of God* (Downers Grove, Ill.: InterVarsity Press, 1996); Trevor Hart, *Faith Thinking: The Dynamics of Christian Theology* (Downers Grove, Ill.: InterVarsity Press, 1995); Patricia O'Connell Killen and John de Beer, *The Art of Theological Reflection* (New York: Crossroad, 1996); and Howard W. Stone and James O. Duke, *How to Think Theologically* (Minneapolis: Fortress, 1996).

they are understood. Indeed Christian faith is centered in and oriented by the affirmation that God has acted in many ways in different times and places to disclose the divine self, and that what we have to say about God is based on a construal of these actions. Moreover, Christian faith is centered on God's self-disclosure in Jesus Christ. The primary witness to the self-disclosing actions of God—the events of revelation—are the narratives of the sacred literature of our faith, the biblical accounts of God's presence and action in the history of the peoples of the older and newer covenants. These accounts also narrate the ways in which those toward whom God acted discerned and responded to God, how they experienced God's presence and the sense they made of it as well as its significance for their lives as a community. As participants, either directly or through the testimony of others, people encountered and responded to the God who was disclosed to them in word and deed, the One who formed them and accompanied them, rebuked and chastised them, forgave and restored them. The biblical witness focuses our attention on the drama of the interactions between God and particular persons in specific places in concrete situations, because it is through these actions and relations that the identity and character of God is revealed—and, one might add, the identity and character of the human participants are manifest. These participants and those who heard their report responded in one way or another to this God and internalized to one degree or another the meaning and significance of God's disclosure.

Taken as a whole, the witness of the Scriptures suggests a theological understanding of revelation as an event, situated in the places and times of human community, in which God discloses the divine self to human beings. It is the act in which God encounters human beings in their place and time, and enters into and sustains relationship with them, thereby becoming discernible and enabling human beings to respond. The preeminent expression of this revelation is the Christ-event, the birth, ministry, death and resurrection of Jesus Christ, Emmanuel, God-with-us. The language of both the Scriptures ("the Word became flesh") and the tradition ("incarnation") expresses the affirmation that in the Christ-event God is revealed. Put differently, the confession of Jesus Christ as God's revelation is the discernment of God's presence and action in and through the human Jesus of Nazareth.

Christians have historically confessed that the biblical narratives are themselves an agency or medium in and through which God continues to be disclosed, and that this disclosure is the presence and action of God as Holy Spirit. Thus Christian faith affirms that God not only *has been* revealed in the events narrated in the Scriptures but *continues to be* revealed to human beings through their agency. God's continuing self-disclosures are rooted in the biblical witness to God's originative self-disclosures.

A closer look at the "event" of revelation opens an understanding of the identity and character of God. Three interrelated aspects together constitute the complex event of divine self-disclosure. First, there is the One who acts, the primary subject in revelation, or the actor. Revelation takes place at the initiative of God, and unless God takes this initiative, there is no genuine *self*-disclosure. Second, there is the spatiotemporal medium in and through which Godself is present. God is manifest to us because God both "veils" and "unveils" the divine self in and through someone or something from our sphere. Another way to think of this is to suggest that in revelation God enters into our realm and clothes the divine self with something from it in order that God may be discerned. So God "appeared" to Abraham and Moses, "filled" the temple, "spoke through" the prophets and "dwelled bodily" in Jesus of Nazareth. In these media God is both present-but-hidden and present-and-revealed. This we may regard as the action of God.

Third, there is God's work of enabling a human response and effecting a divine-human relation. Whether the human participants are capacitated to respond and relate is dependent not on themselves but on God. This is not to suggest that human participants are passive in the event of revelation, but rather that discernment of God, response to God and relation with God are enabled or made possible by God's acting. If the first two aspects signal the objectivity of the event of revelation, then this third addresses the aspect of subjectivity. The event of revelation positions human beings to encounter God as subject in a medium that both hides and reveals, and enables them to respond to God's initiative. Having been enabled, human beings choose how to respond and whether to participate in the relationship with God. The Scriptures narrate accounts of God's people who chose to respond in ways unacceptable to God, and generally characterizes these responses as sin. But such responses were nonetheless enabled by the ongoing presence and activity of God. Thus the event of God's self-disclosure can be seen to consist in the presence and activity of God in the mediated encounter with humanity and the enabling of humanity's response.

The work of the triune God. Distinguishing the three aspects of the event of divine self-disclosure suggests a way to make theological sense of the Christian faith's affirmation of the *triune* God. When the early Christian communities confronted the question of the seeming contradiction that the one eternal God of Israel was present and active in the human Jesus of Nazareth and, following his resurrection, continually present and acting in the lives of believers, their answer—theologically—was the assertion that God is eternally one and yet three, both within the divine self and toward humanity. With the biblical language of "Father, Son and Holy Spirit," the early theologians distinguished the intradivine relations and contended that this one God is disclosed to humanity as the "Father who sends" (actor), the "Son who is sent" (action) and the "Spirit who indwells" (acting), with each "member" being truly and fully God yet distinguishable within the divine self and in their activities and expressions toward humanity. Moreover, to each is attributed a peculiar and distinctive work, a work primarily characteristic of one, but not excluding the involvement of the others. In all the divine works God is the subject, but each distinctive work portrays the activity of God in a threefold way: actor, action and acting. So, for example, God the Father is Creator in the action of creation and the ongoing activity of creating; God the Son is Reconciler in the action of reconciliation and the ongoing activity of reconciling; and God the Spirit is Transformer in the action of transformation and the ongoing activity of transforming.

In our faith-ful and theological imagination, we tend to attribute one aspect to each of the three, so we confess that God the Father is the Creator, God the Son incarnate in Jesus of Nazareth reconciled us to God, and God the Spirit transforms us. But the affirmation that God is *triune* stipulates that the God who created us is at the same time the Reconciler, and the God who created and reconciled us is at the same time the God who is transforming us. Thus there is a sense in which our discernment of God as Creator, Reconciler and Transformer is grounded in the biblical narratives that portray revelation as the action of a divine subject in which human beings are encountered and a divine-human relationship established with the enablement of human response-ability.

For Christians, the event of divine self-disclosure is centered in the incarnation of the Son or "Word of God" in Jesus of Nazareth (revelation), who manifests the one divine subject (revealer) and whose work as such made possible the indwelling presence and activity of God (revealing). This suggests, then, that God's initiative in self-disclosure indicates its origin, the incarnation of God in Jesus of Nazareth indicates its medium (humanity) together with its content (the divine self), and the response and effect it engenders indicates its purpose. In short, revelation is *God, with and in us.*

The Christian story. We have traveled—all too briefly—through the obscurity of revelation and the conundrum of the Trinity for one basic reason: to establish a theological foundation for a consideration of the overarching Christian Story as the constellation of stories that narrate and interpret our experience in our world and help us make sense of our connection with our human world and God. The Christian Story consists in the accounts of God's initiative and the human response in particular circumstances, and the ways these have shaped the perspectives, beliefs, traditions and rituals that have traditioned the faith to others. These stories are the narratives of the events of the self-disclosure of the triune God—the narratives of God and the narratives of our faith.

As this modest discussion of revelation and Trinity suggests, these narratives have served as the center and the agency of God's continuing self-disclosure. So for Christians faith means that those stories are *our* stories: we are implicated and situated in the originative and ongoing narratives of divine initiative and human response. One thing that is meant in claiming Christian faith is that we identify with these stories and that they have been internalized because in and through them God encounters us and enables us to respond in ways that acknowledge who we are in relation to God, and who God is in relation to us. Faith is that enabled response and relation. So when we speak about the Christian Story, we are speaking about how these narratives function not only as the media of God's self-disclosure but as a worldview that situates us and helps us interpret and make sense of our experience with God in the world. The central core of the Christian Story is the gospel of Jesus Christ, the good news of what God has done in and through him for us and even now is doing in and through us as Holy Spirit. What humanity has done with this gospel, and how it has been objectified and institutionalized in sociocultural environments, is the unsavory side of the narratives of human response and relation; they continue the unsavory narratives of human rebellion begun in the Garden of Eden. Thus the notion of the Christian Story in the present discussion is intended to underscore some of the ways Christian faith works to situate and identify ourselves in relation to God.

It would be misleading to imply that the Christian Story is the antidote to the poison of racism. As we have seen, race and racism were engendered in so-called Christian contexts by participants in sociocultural orders that claimed Christian faith and drew on the resources of that faith to legitimate themselves. Thus the myth of race and expressions of racism are a perversion of the Christian Story. Instead of a corrective to race and racism, the Christianity that preceded their rise contributed to their development. The first movements in a theology of racial reconciliation, then, must undertake a recovery of the Christian Story by reconsidering the function of its narratives as media of God's self-disclosure and means for locating ourselves in our world. How can the Christian Story function in the encounter with the myth of race, and in what sense can it challenge the worldview expressed in the myth? We can answer these questions by considering the Christian Story as an alternative rendering of a worldview.

The Functions of the Christian Story
1. *Metaphysical-mystical: God as subject.* Christian faith asserts God. More important, Christian faith asserts a consciousness of Yahweh, the God of Israel and Jesus Christ, who is and remains an ineffable mystery, even as this God is

manifest in human places and times. The narratives of the Judeo-Christian traditions portray the actions of the one God who transcends and cannot be identical with these places and times, but who nonetheless acts freely to enter and become immanent within human sociocultural worlds. In the main Christian faith has rejected pantheism and panentheism, refusing to divinize the world or identify the world as God. This faith acknowledges God as above or outside the world, but precisely through the events of divine self-disclosure this God is present and active in the world. The *metaphysical-mystical* or *religious* function of the Christian Story is to mediate the reality of the transcendent God to our times and places, and to the extent that these narratives function as media of God's revelation, an individual experiences and discerns the presence and action of God, who remains both hidden and revealed. Through this agency, consciousness grasps the objective and subjective presence of One who cannot be contained but can be disclosed in "names and forms," because this One is awesome *Subject,* preeminent *Person.* A human cannot look upon this Face and still live.

The imagery of the narratives envisions this One as enthroned on high in the heavenly court, from where all that transpires on the earth below is surveyed in a single glance; and in a lowly manger as a newborn child, whom no one would otherwise confuse with the One enthroned on high. It portrays the glory of this One as filling the temple with divine presence and the anguish of this One who is repeatedly rejected by the people. The Story works not only to identify the ineffable mystery but to disclose that this mystery is a *who,* a subject who is incomprehensible apart from self-disclosure but who in revelation is discerned truly if not fully. Thus the Story works to connect a human self with the divine self.

Moreover, this God is not one of several, or even one of two. This God is disclosed as *One.* God contends neither against the divine self nor against an equal. This one God does contend against the forces of evil that challenge, but the Christian Story does not posit another deity that threatens God's freedom and sovereignty, so there is *no dualism* in the narratives. The Scriptures contain the story of God's conquest of evil objectified in the human realm, the evil that originates in the human mind and heart and disqualifies itself as an acceptable response to God's initiative. Indeed the core of the narratives is God's initiative in overcoming evil; the Story accounts for the primal origin of evil, its contention against the rule of God, its vanquishing in the Christ-event and its assured destruction in the future. Thus the Story works to situate a Self in relation to the mystery who is named in self-disclosure, and through the recollection of a past and the anticipation of a future, this Self is located in the narratives that continue to unfold the Story.

2. *Cosmological: God as Creator.* The Christian Story also has a *cosmological* function: it portrays the physical universe in ways that make it possible to internalize and interpret it even in all its expansiveness. In the West we have looked more to the empirical sciences (biology, geology, physics, astronomy) to give us sure and certain knowledge of the physical world and less to the faith assertions of our religion(s). We have looked in the direction of science because we are curious about origins and causes and we want explanations. Science has served us well for the most part by making it possible for us to live longer lives in greater comfort. Science has also made quite a few people very rich, shortened the life span of countless others, and brought us to the point where we can destroy the whole planet in the twinkling of an eye. Science can answer, from its perspectives and assumptions, the questions of origins and causes, and if these conflict with the answers of religion—so be it. Science has its own myth or paradigm, with its own canons of definition and interpretation.[4]

But what science cannot do the Christian Story does do. Seeking out origins and causes, science does not address the more fundamental aspect of *purposes,* and this is constitutive of the Christian Story. Christian faith and the narratives in which it is embedded are *teleological,* concerned not only with the designs, origins and causes of the physical universe but more fundamentally with its ultimate purpose. Science answers the *what* questions; Christian faith addresses the *why* questions not merely for the human species but for the whole of the physical world. The Christian Story seeks to make sense of this world by narrating how its *telos* or goal comes to be recognized, appropriated and assimilated by the faithful imagination. The Story does not assert that this purpose is self-evident in the places and times of the physical world we inhabit. Rather it contends that this purpose is given in the events of God's self-disclosure. The disjunction between the seeming boundlessness of the universe and the boundedness of human spatiotemporal life is addressed by the Story that answers our need to know where we came from and where we are going, and why.

Grounded in the narratives that mediate the events of the self-disclosure of the triune God, Christian faith discerns and responds to God as Creator, whose work is creation in and through which the Revealer is disclosed, and who remains present and active in the ongoing work of creating. God creates life and a realm where it can be expressed, and God sustains them both within their boundaries. To God as Creator, all else is creature. To the creatures who are capacitated by the work of creation to respond to their Creator, there is nothing

---

[4]Ian G. Barbour has analyzed the similarities, differences and points of convergence in the work of interpretation and construction that goes on in both science and religion. See his book *Issues in Science and Religion* (New York: Harper & Row, 1966).

else but their response. Herein lies the purpose of creation: that God may reveal the divine self to an "other" who is not God, but to whom God chooses to give life in order that this other may respond to, enter into relationship with and thereby share in the divine life. Such creaturely life requires a realm suitable to it, different from the realm suitable to God's own life. So the creature is not made for its habitat, but the habitat is made for the creature; God placed the creature in its own suitable realm. The boundaries of space and time that measure and limit the life of the creature do not alienate and isolate the creature from the Creator. Rather they make response-ability and relationship possible. Thus the limitless life of the Creator is extended to and shared with the creature, but only under the conditions of creaturely life. The creature experiences and shares in the life of the triune God, but only in and through the bounded structures of space and time.

The narratives use the language of "covenants" to indicate the nature of the relationship between God the Creator and the human creatures who encounter God. God takes initiative to enter into relation with human beings and enables them to respond, and the covenants provide the conditions and obligations that shape the relationship. From the Garden of Eden through Noah, Abraham and Moses, to the people of Israel and Jesus Christ, God establishes relations with humanity that take a particular form: God promises and commits the divine self to do certain things for the human creatures, and in turn the creatures recognize their obligation to the Life-Giver and consent to the conditions laid on them in order that the promises may be fulfilled. Thus the relationship is patterned by promise and fulfillment, obligation and obedience, initiative and response. But in this way the communal life shared within the triune God is also opened to the participation of the creatures, whose life together is intended by the Creator to be communal. The creatures are obligated to live as a community that reflects, expresses and shares in the inner-trinitarian life of God. Human beings are created not to be *over against* one another but rather, as a reflection of the divine self, to be *with and for* one another, *open to* one another. As creatures, humanity is the "other" with whom God chooses to be in a particular kind of relationship, the patterns and structures as well as the conditions of which are stipulated by God, not by human beings. And as creatures, human beings are placed in relation to one another as fellow creatures who share life in community with God and one another. Thus the purpose of human beings is to share life in community with God and with fellow-creatures, and thus to respond and relate to an Other and to others.

This is obviously *not* a relation of equality. The biblical covenants established between God and God's people make it clear that the relationship and response-ability between Creator and creature is one of superordination and subordination, Life-Giver and life-receiver. But the status of human beings among themselves is grounded in their position as creatures and covenant partners in relation to God the Creator and Covenant-Maker. It is an inviolate and inalienable status because it is conferred by God. From the point of view expressed in the Christian Story, the only regard between human beings that is acceptable to God is *mutual* regard—one discerns not only a fellow creature but one who is a necessary complement, a person without whom one cannot be human, since the purpose of being human is to have and share life in response-able relation with an other. Differences between creatures therefore are merely what distinguishes *one* from an *other* with whom life is shared in community.

3. *Moral-social: God as Reconciler.* The narratives of Christian faith also exercise a *moral-social* function by grounding the life of the community in the shared life with God with structures and patterns of relationship that make response-ability possible. More specifically, the community is established by God as a community of love and harmony, whose structures are intended to realize the love God has for the creatures and the love they are to have for each other.

In freedom God chose to create an other out of God's love, and thus to share life in loving union with an other. It is love that characterizes God's initiative, and it is an answering love that is to characterize the creature's response. Thus the conditions and the obligations of the covenant of relation are intended to express objectively the love of God and the love of the creature. Likewise, the freedom of the creature entails the choice of whether to relate and respond in love toward God and others. But God is the one who determines the conditions and obligations in a relationship of love, and thus the patterns and practices of human life in community are demarcated according to whether they manifest the love that God intends. God's life and love are social, shared within Godself and with others, and with the terms of the covenant God stipulates what is and is not love, what is and is not an acceptable response, what is and is not a relation of love. The creature is free and enabled by God to experience love and express love toward God and others.

The narratives of the Christian Story recount how human beings were created to express love in obedience to their Creator and in mutuality toward one another. They tell how from the beginning the creature disrupted and altered the relation by disobedience to the divine command. But the narratives also recite the intervention of God, and thus Christian faith discerns and responds to God as Reconciler, whose work is reconciliation in and through which the Revealer is disclosed, and who remains present and active in the ongoing work of reconciling. From the Garden through Noah, Abraham and Moses, to the people of Israel and Jesus Christ, the narratives portray the pattern of God's ini-

tiative being met with a human response that breaks relation and puts the creature in jeopardy. For no other reason than divine love and grace, God takes the
initiative to reconcile the creatures and to declare how they shall live in relation
to God and one another, and what responses and patterns of communal life are
deserving of judgment and condemnation. We can thus regard the commands
of God as the disclosure of God's love and grace, expressions of how human
beings are to regard and relate to God and how they are to order their life
together as the people of God. It is because of their sin that God intervenes to
reconcile and specify a realm where justice and peace prevail. Thus God is disclosed as the Reconciler who intends that the patterns and structures of communal life enhance human life and express love and justice. Moreover, the
narratives express God's expectation that God's creatures will internalize and
live by the code of love and justice and express these in the patterns and structures of their external world.

In the self-disclosure of God the Reconciler, Christian faith discerns that
human beings are responsible for and accountable to one another and that all
share the same status under God: fellow creatures in need of reconciliation.
Quite unlike the myth of race, the Christian Story affirms explicitly that humanness is purposefully *co*humanity, that one can have life with and for others only
in a relationship of mutuality characterized by love, respect, honor, peace and
justice. Reconciliation presupposes a relationship that we have broken, and it is
we who have broken it by failing to respond and relate in the ways God's love
intends. The statuses that human beings impose on others or adopt for themselves do pervert, but cannot negate, the divinely conferred status of cohumanity. For the intention of the Reconciler is that who we are and how we live as
coparticipants in the life and love of God are to be revealed—*externalized*—in
our common life together.

4. Psychological: God the Transformer. Finally, the Christian Story has a *psychological* function in that the appropriation and internalization of the narratives situate an individual in the concrete circumstances of her life and orient
her in a quite particular way toward others, the world and God. This is not to
suggest that one's sense of self in relation to others and God is fully integrated
with no dissonance. Rather one's interior life or subjectivity is shaped in the
consciousness of relation to the presence and activity of God in the world. In a
significant sense, the scriptural narratives work to accentuate one's connection
with others and God in a shared world. They mediate the presence of God in
one's subjectivity, thereby enabling one to make a different sense of oneself,
others, the world and God. One thus identifies with others and with God, in a
world created by God, a world in which the Transformer is at work. One discerns God within oneself, altering one's identity so that one no longer endures

through places and times in opposition to God and others but as one who loves because one is beloved by God.

The narratives of the events of God's self-disclosure render God's identity and character as the One who loves the other and desires that this love be reciprocated. They tell how God's inward presence brings life out of death, changes minds and hearts, and restores identity so that one experiences God and others as a new self. God's presence enables and empowers one so that the former identity is regarded as alien, the old self, the broken identity, of which one can only make *non*sense. The initiative of God in reconciliation, so the narratives tell us, is accompanied by renewal. Thus Christian faith discerns God as Transformer, whose work is transformation in and through which the Revealer is disclosed, and who remains present and active in the ongoing work of transforming. Sin is the great disruption that moves the Creator God to respond in the work of reconciliation, but this work is not complete without the great alteration that transforms one into a new creature. The narratives express this in the language of new covenant and new creation, redemption and restoration, healing and wholeness, and of course resurrection, all of which are the work of God and all of which are experienced within as the presence and power of God. From the narratives set in the Garden through the stories of Noah, Abraham and Moses, to the histories of the people of Israel and the community whose center is Jesus Christ, the Story portrays human experiences in encounter with God, outwardly and inwardly, as God works to remake creation and creature and restore them to a shared life of love. The covenant partners cannot restore themselves; they are too broken. They cannot abandon their sin; they are too caught in its grip. They cannot live with God unless God renews them inwardly and enables them to respond in love toward God and others.

This, then, is the Christian Story, the narratives of God's initiatives in creation, reconciliation and transformation, and the response of humanity as God's creatures in estrangement, reunion and renewal. God created us as living and loving creatures and placed us in a realm conducive to shared life. But our response has been to deny our Creator and ourselves as creatures, and so we have fouled and shattered our true selves and the nest wherein we dwell. Rejecting the identity that God has bestowed, we have derived and formed our identities with reference to patterns of social relation that are contaminated by our rebellion. But the universe we have made for ourselves has been and continues to be destabilized by God's initiatives, and the functions of the Christian Story continue to work by God's love and grace as a medium for an encounter with God that unsettles and remakes us. God's initiatives in self-disclosure are also the means whereby God reveals us to ourselves and exposes the true nature of our responses and relations. If these initiatives of the triune God disclose who God is, what do they reveal about us and our response-ability? To this matter we now turn.

The Difference Sin Makes: The Response of Humanity

One need not be a Christian to take offense at racism. Persons who do not claim Christian faith have judged and categorically condemned racism, and many of these through the years have struggled to overcome it personally and dislodge its presence in the sociocultural order through a variety of strategies. Such persons view racism as a personal and sociocultural scourge that must be cleansed from the body politic. But from the point of view of Christian faith, racism can only be described as sin. Believers who have struggled to overcome racism—their own and that of others—and endeavored to eradicate it from our shared world have appealed to the resources of Christian faith to warrant and guide their efforts.

But there are also Christians who have not been and even now are not concerned with the devastation of racism. Persons who claim Christian faith and at the same time condone or ignore the expressivity of racism bring insult and injury to God and desecrate the humanity of others and themselves. This is a strong statement, to be sure. But the self-disclosure of God in our time and place brings this judgment upon us. Sensibility influenced by the Christian narratives regards racism as a moral wrong, and as such it is an offense to God the Creator, Reconciler and Transformer. The covenant is broken when the human partners misplace themselves in relation to God and one another. When the creatures place themselves over against God or other creatures, the divine purpose in creation has been thwarted and the relationship breached.

Recognition of the differences between ourselves and God is at the center of Christian faith; we are created and God is the Creator. As stated above, the differences between creatures are but indices that distinguish creatures who share the gift of life in community. Noting such differences between and among human beings in itself means nothing. But the sense we make of those differences means everything. To the extent that these differences are made by human beings, they nullify the relation or diminish the ability to share life with and respond to God and others. The narratives of the Christian Story recount over and over again how patterns of relation between human beings set aside God's purpose of interdependence and mutual regard. They also tell how the union of shared life and love has been shattered by our sin of withdrawing and redirecting love and placing ourselves over against God and one another in acts of defiance.

The texture of sin. Through the centuries, Christians have described their theological understandings of sin in a variety of ways, some very specific in their description and others more general. Some of these views have endured in the tradition, while others have long been abandoned. And some remain quite controversial. Nevertheless, there are several aspects that are common to all the views of sin, aspects that have been expressed in one form or another in any particular theology of sin. First and foremost, sin is against God. It may also be against others, but even then it remains fundamentally sin against God. Second, sin is related to evil, however this may be defined. Sin may presuppose evil that gives rise to it (sin follows from evil), or evil may presuppose sin (evil follows from sin), or both may hold. Third, sin is expressed in certain behaviors or practices, including the beliefs and attitudes that are manifest in them. Fourth, sin is thought to be a moral disability of some sort, an incapacity or unwillingness to choose and do the good or "right" thing. Fifth, sin is thoroughly personal in that it is centered in and expressed by a human being, but it can also be social or corporate, with its mode of expression involving the participation and consent of others. Sixth, sin is inescapable and therefore universal. Everybody does it, without exception. Whether and how it is transmissible from generation to generation remains an unresolved question, except for those few who believe it is transmitted biologically. Seventh, the sense and understanding of sin is contextual, related to the particular circumstances that characterize a time and a place.

This last aspect is important to mention because the particular forms or expressions of sin have changed over times and places. The particularity of sin is thus correlative to a people's way of life in a concrete sociocultural environment. The sense and understanding of sin are shaped in part by the patterns and practices of actual communities of people. For example, perhaps few now would regard the failure to wash one's hands before eating as a "sin," but the Pharisees in Jesus' day regarded hand washing as a ritual symbol of religious purity. Not many in the United States today consider overeating a "sin," but in earlier centuries when only the wealthy few could afford an extraordinary variety and quantity of food while the masses lived on the verge of starvation, gluttony was indeed a sin. Few would regard it as "sin" when a Christian attends a soccer tournament on Sunday morning or goes to a movie matinee on Sunday afternoon, but in Puritan colonial America a person was disciplined by the congregation if he engaged in any activity other than worship on Sunday. In short, sin is contextual. But let us hasten to add that it is not *only* contextual; it is not *solely* relative, but it is related to concrete times and places.

The sin of racism. For our time and place we need a theological understanding of the sin of racism, and such a theology needs first to be grounded in the self-disclosure of the triune God and the narratives that mediate that revelation to us. It needs, second, to focus on our responsibility and accountability (response-ability) and the manner of our relationship to God and to those with whom we share a common world (relation). It also needs, third, to address our sociocultural environment, because, as we have seen, the "world" in which we live is one that we have constructed, and it is structured as an expression of race and racism.

There is no intention in this theological reflection to impose Christianity on those who do not confess Christian faith. But racism is a very public (social, economic, political and religious) problem, a cancer that afflicts everyone in the sociocultural order, and for this reason we must raise our voices in the public square and speak from the convictions of our faith. In the tradition of the prophets of ancient Israel and with deep regard for the word spoken and enacted by Jesus Christ, we must speak and act against racism in all the spheres where it is manifest. To do this here, from a Christian perspective and drawing on the resources of our faith, we address racism as the sin of human response and relation to God and others.

One fairly unambiguous way to represent the sin of race and racism is to describe it as idolatry.[5] We have seen how "race" emerged as an abstraction and category that has become reified in the common sense. From the point of view of Christian faith, however, race has become much more than reified. It has been *deified* as the ultimate and immutable defining characteristic of humanness. Not only is it thought to exist, to be *real,* such that one has only to see it to believe in it, but it is unalterable, for one cannot change one's race. Just as the liberated Hebrew slaves bowed before the golden calf at Sinai, having demanded of Aaron that he "make gods for us, who shall go before us" (Ex 32:1), we have manufactured for ourselves a god of race that we have allowed to determine who we are, how we shall live and where we shall go, an idol to whom we ascribe our freedom or our bondage. Following Aaron, Jeroboam made golden calves and altars to establish the social and religious consolidation of the northern kingdom of Israel (1 Kings 12:25-33), and following Jeroboam, we have manufactured the idol of race in order to establish and preserve social and economic hegemony.

At its root, the idolatry of race results from idolizing the human, and the wor-

---

[5]In my opinion, the theological analysis of race and racism as idolatry found throughout George D. Kelsey's *Racism and the Christian Understanding of Man* (New York: Charles Scribner's Sons, 1965) remains unsurpassed. But see also Raymond Blanks, "Conversion, Covenant, Commitment and Change," in *Ending Racism in the Church,* ed. Davies and Hennessee, pp. 103-8; Gary W. Deddo, "Persons in Racial Reconciliation: The Contributions of a Trinitarian Theological Anthropology," in *The Gospel in Black and White: Theological Resources for Racial Reconciliation,* ed. Dennis L. Okholm (Downers Grove, Ill.: InterVarsity Press, 1997), pp. 58-67; and Fumitaka Matsuoka, *The Color of Faith: Building Community in a Multiracial Society* (Cleveland, Ohio: United Church Press, 1998), pp. 30-55.

ship of the idol of race consists in the beliefs, rituals and practices that acknowledge the claim of race to be the source of the meaning and value of human life
and the basis for loyalty and concern for others. The piety associated with the
idolatry of race is framed by the myth of race and is expressed not only in the
belief that race is real but also in the sense and sentiment—the devotion and
reverence—that fabricate racism.

The deification of race and the piety of racism are extraordinary examples of
the kind of idolatry that Paul described when he spoke of those who
"exchanged the truth about God for a lie and worshiped and served the creature rather than the Creator" (Rom 1:25). But as the first chapter of Romans as a
whole suggests, the idolatry of race and the cultic system of beliefs, rituals and
practices of racism are a *response* to God and others, one that shapes and in no
small way determines a *relation* to God and others. Race and racism have been
and still are the characteristically idolatrous, sinful responses and relations of
our time and place.

One theologian who has mapped the contours of an understanding of sin
along the lines of idolatry and relatedness is Daniel L. Migliore. While his theology of sin is not addressed specifically or as a whole to racism, his basic outline
lends itself to our purposes here, so I will draw in part from his construction and
develop a view of sin that speaks more directly to the patterns and structures of
racism explored in previous chapters.[6]

1. *Denying relation to God.* Migliore contends that the basic component
underlying the expressivity of sin is the denial of our dependent relation to God
and our interdependent relation to others. As such, sin is inherently oppositional and disruptive. With regard to our relation to God, Migliore maintains
that sin can take one of two forms of expression. On the one hand, there is an

---

[6]See Daniel L. Migliore, *Faith Seeking Understanding: An Introduction to Christian Theology*
(Grand Rapids, Mich.: Eerdmans, 1991), pp. 130-35. For other theological views of sin that address particular patterns and practices in our context, see James H. Cone, *God of the Oppressed*, rev. ed. (Maryknoll, N.Y.: Orbis, 1997), pp. 150-78; Curtiss Paul DeYoung,
Reconciliation: Our Greatest Challenge—Our Only Hope (Valley Forge, Penn.: Judson, 1997),
pp. 1-29; James H. Evans Jr., *We Have Been Believers* (Minneapolis: Fortress, 1992), pp. 99-
117; Justo L. González, *Mañana: Christian Theology from a Hispanic Perspective* (Nashville:
Abingdon, 1990), pp. 134-38; Stanley J. Grenz, *Theology for the Community of God* (Nashville: Broadman & Holman, 1994), pp. 234-314; Shirley C. Guthrie, *Christian Doctrine*, rev.
ed. (Louisville, Ky.: Westminster John Knox, 1994), pp. 192-227; Jung Young Lee, *Marginality:
The Key to Multicultural Theology* (Minneapolis: Fortress, 1995), pp. 101-9; Sallie McFague,
The Body of God: An Ecological Theology (Minneapolis: Fortress, 1993), pp. 99-129; Andrew
Sung Park, *Racial Conflict and Healing: An Asian-American Theological Perspective* (Maryknoll, N.Y.: Orbis, 1996), pp. 26-47; Ted Peters, *God–the World's Future* (Minneapolis: For-
tress, 1992), pp. 140-70; and Dorothee Sölle, *Thinking About God: An Introduction to
Theology*, trans. John Bowden (Philadelphia: Trinity Press International, 1990), pp. 54-67.

opposition to God's grace that comes with seeking to overcome the limits of our humanity and view ourselves as our own God. Migliore draws on the Christian tradition by describing this as the sin of *pride* and underscores it as the expression of an egocentric self. This is a form of idolatry that is active and self-centered, seeking to suppress all challenges or threats to one's freedom to be and do whatever is desired. One rejects God's grace because one acknowledges no need for it. On the other hand, there is a form of sin that moves in an altogether different direction but no less thoroughly opposes and rejects God's grace. Again drawing on the tradition, Migliore describes this as *sloth,* an expression of sin in which one places oneself beyond the reach of grace. It is not that one *cannot* be reached by God, but rather one chooses *not to be* reached or not to respond to God's grace, in effect opposing and rejecting God. Migliore emphasizes this paradox of sloth by pointing out that it typically is expressed as self-rejection or self-hatred that comes with idolization of an other. It is tantamount to a surrender and loss of self, an idolatry that is passive and other-centered, characterized by unwillingness to respond to God's summons to freedom.

The deification of race and the practices of racism amount to the displacement of God and the installation of our racial selves, our racial group or our race itself as the ruling power that shapes our lives. Both pride and sloth, activity and passivity, are indicative of our oppositional response to God the Creator, Reconciler and Transformer. We have opposed and rejected the Creator by usurping, either for ourselves or for others, the prerogative to define and limit the manner and quality of life. We take life as ours to shape or give our lives to others to determine. We believe our freedom can be expressed however we choose, or we deliver our freedom to another whose judgments we believe are truer because they are thought to know better how and why we should live. And we do this because of what we believe about race. We have opposed the Reconciler either by refusing to recognize the breach in our relation or by preferring the familiarity of our estrangement from God. We suppose our lives are without sin and have greater value because we are members of a greater race, or we imagine that there is only sin and that our lives have lesser value because we are members of a lesser race. We have opposed the Transformer by believing only in our racial selves and regarding our individual experience as the norm, or by believing only in racial others and regarding the experiences of the racial group as norm.

The sin of racism is manifest in our failure to acknowledge that our status as beloved creatures, our manner of loving and our identity as lovers are not ours to determine or to surrender to others because of either our race or the race of others. Loving oneself or one's group because of race and hating oneself or one's group because of race are equally reprehensible to God. Likewise, taking pleasure that one is not a member of some other group thought to be lesser is indicative of racial pride, and grieving because one is not a member of some other group thought to be greater is indicative of racial sloth.

The sin of racism is also manifest in the fact that human status, ways of life and personal and group identities have been established in a symbolic universe that has enthroned race as the ultimate arbiter of meaning. Racial self- and group-interest has become the motivation for human conduct, and the spurious strategies of dominion, segregation and integration have perverted God's intention for a community of love. We have rejected the promise and the Promiser, we disbelieve that God has a different purpose for us, and we submit only to assertions that make sense to us on our terms. And we have the audacity to claim that God intends it to be this way, that what we see as race and the differences we make of race are consistent with God's purposes. The notion that our identity, morality and sociality are grounded in and determined by racial interest is nothing more than the active or passive expression of egoism. Prideful people have no need for God, and slothful people have only an indifferent God.

2. *Denying relation to others.* When Migliore turns his attention to our relations with others, he contends that sin again takes two forms of expression, both of which oppose and disrupt human interdependence and mutuality, and both of which derive from a failure to acknowledge the triune God. On the one hand, *domination* rules over and uses others for one's own purposes, seeking to control or eliminate whatever or whoever stands in the way. This is *self-exaltation,* the need to exercise power over others, power to limit life and to impose and determine identity. On the other hand, *servility* gives in to the rule of others; it is an abject submission to the power and purposes of others, the abdication of oneself to others or the renunciation of oneself for others. This *self-destruction* comes when one no longer wills to live but rather is willed to live— or die—by others, a condition in which passivity and acceptance seem to be the only way to endure. Thus one's self becomes, in a way, what others say it is, and in the process one's self is destroyed. In the case of both domination and servility, aggressiveness and quietism, God's call to live in the freedom of relation with and for others is refused.

Race and racism place individuals and groups not only over against one another, but also *above* and *under* one another with the presumed dualism of racial superiority and inferiority. Sin is manifest in the mutual disregard we see, for example, in the racial stereotypes that orient our perceptions of one another. We view others on the basis of prejudgments we make regarding racial categories and their supposed meaning. We exalt ourselves by claiming the right to judge and interpret others because of their race, and we debase ourselves by acquiescing to others for the same reason. We look at each other and judge ourselves to be better or worse by comparison, when the standard by which we make these judgments is the tone of our racial regard for either ourselves or the other. But in effect we exalt ourselves only by diminishing others, and we debase ourselves only by exalting others. We oppose God's creation either by exploiting others and depriving them of their freedom because they are racially different or by succumbing to the determination of others and waiving our freedom because we are racially different. We oppose God's reconciliation either by requiring that our interracial relations take place on our group's terms or by consenting to the terms of others out of a desire to maintain the racial status quo. We oppose God's transformation either by regarding our own racial experience as the norm and rejecting the experience of others or by regarding as normal the experience of others while doubting ourselves.

The sin of racism is apparent when one grants that members of other races are human but then treats them in ways that express disrespect, dishonor and disinterest. It is manifest whenever racial beliefs and attitudes influence conduct that limits the response-ability of another. When one's self- and group-interests are given priority over human interests, when one's compassion is restricted to members of one's racial group, and when one's opposition and hostility toward members of other races are disguised by a veil of neutrality, the sin of racism is evident because it denies our interdependence. And whenever human interests are identified with the interests of some to the exclusion of others, when there is an inability to be compassionate toward any, and when all are regarded with neutrality, sin is evident because it denies our own response-ability. The belief in race and the misconduct of racism deny that the inalienable right to self-determination is only granted *under* God, *alongside* others; not above or below others, apart from God. In any form, racist expressivity either qualifies or diminishes the humanity of others and ourselves. Racial interests and racial rivalry, just like racial privilege and racial disadvantage, are inherently divisive when race is a category of division.

3. *Denying God's future.* The third pair of expressions that Migliore develops are oriented by visions for the future, the future of both God and humanity. Both of these forms of sin are characterized by denial and opposition to God's intended future and the destiny of humanity as God's covenant partner. On the one hand, the sin of *presumption* reflects confidence in our abilities and strategies to realize the fulfillment of our destiny by our own initiative. It is the belief that the future is ours to determine and that force and violence are more likely to achieve our objectives than the influence of God's love and grace. It holds that our own goodness will guide us in overcoming injustice, exploitation and

oppression. Even where our destiny is envisioned as the consummation of God's kingdom and reign over all, the sin of presumption claims the prerogative to bring that consummation in ways that serve our quest for our own fulfillment. On the other hand, the sin of *resignation* reflects doubt that anything can or ever will be any different than it now is and that nothing we do will make any difference. It is an attitude of indifference that in a bizarre way permits the scourge of injustice to go unchallenged. It is, in effect, a capitulation to inhumanity and a foreclosure on our future.

Race and racism offer a future of our own making, one way or the other. From the perspective of race and the history of racism, both of which are essentially oppositional, we can see only one of two possible visions: either we exclude and destroy or we are excluded and destroyed; either there will be only us or there will be only them. The sense that race and racism make for the future in our place and time is either the overthrow or the undertow of our humanity; cohumanity, coexistence and cooperation seem not be an option. In the sin of racism, we close ourselves off to God's creating work either by choosing for ourselves how we shall live and fulfill our self- and group-interests or by conceding to others the direction of our future. We reject God's reconciling work either by assuming that we know best how to manage our relations or by supposing that relations are simply unmanageable. We reveal our distaste for God's transforming work either by imagining the triumph of our cause over others and pressing God to authorize our initiatives on God's behalf or by discrediting the future of humanity with cynicism and sheer indifference. But arrogance can be both "we can do it" and "no one can do it," just as capitulation can be both "we give up" and "we know better."

Presumption exaggerates our sense of racial self and projects our own interests into a future; our objective is not racial reconciliation but racial establishment. Resignation, on the other hand, exaggerates our racist situation and projects it unaltered into a future; our objective is survival. Presumption disallows or minimizes the presence and activity of God, and resignation disqualifies the smaller and larger expressions of justice and peace that come with God's initiative and human response-ability.

False consciousness revisited. Running throughout this discussion are many of the more conventional ways of understanding sin. I have spoken of our sin as opposing and rejecting God and one another, and I have used the language of idolatry to describe the piety of race and our tendency to make God in our own racial image, suitable to our racial liking. We could also speak more directly of *disobedience* as our unwillingness to heed the new commandment that we love one another, or of *unfaithfulness* as our distrust of God and our wavering on our commitment or seeking after an other whose claim on us is illegitimate. We could describe our sin as our *rebellion* against God's rule and sovereignty, our *revolt* in which we set up rule in our own spheres. But no matter how it is described, the sin of racism is expressed in the characteristic features encountered earlier in the discussion of false consciousness.

Enveloped in objective and subjective expressions of racism, we are devoted primarily to ourselves and those others who are like us. We magnify our differences and venerate our opposition to one another, and we attribute goodness to ourselves and our group by maligning others. This is the sin of *dualism,* a relationship of opposition. Holding to race as a vital aspect of our humanity, we become in effect unbelievers, for we believe a lie and we disbelieve the truth. We are guilty of *deception* in seeing ourselves and others in terms of race instead of discerning God's gift of life and love for all. Our participation in racism misleads us to believe that our worth is related to our race in one way or another and that the history of our group tells it "like it is." The truth about ourselves as God's creatures and our status as fellow creatures is disbelieved and contradicted when in *denial* we dismiss others' appeals for justice and equality and regard their experience as meaningless. We impugn the integrity and response-ability of others by simply assuming they cannot be right in the account of their experience, or that God is not present to them in ways that would call our disbelief into question.

Traveling through the spheres of our everyday lives, it seems almost unthinkable to us that those with whom we come in contact have any but the most superficial relation to us. If they are racial "others," we are certain they have no relation to us. We think nothing of them, or we think they are useful only for our purposes, to assist us in obtaining what we want. They simply do not matter to us except as means to an end, and we care little about their welfare. We neither think about nor feel for them because we do not have the time to take an interest. With *detachment,* we remove ourselves because we think our responsibility is to ourselves while their responsibility is to us. A relation of interdependence takes on a twisted form: I am dependent on you only for this moment, only so far as you can serve my interests, and because you are different I am not interested in relating to what you think or how you feel. You are not only other to me, you are alien to me. Thus we draw not on the presence and activity of God but on our racial beliefs and commitments, orienting ourselves by what is familiar and comfortable, identifying ourselves with those whom we consider significant and discerning ourselves as unrelated to those who are racially different. We thus *dissociate* ourselves from these others by preferring some over against others and conducting ourselves differently with some over against others. Out of the desire to be true to ourselves, we prove to be false to God and to others. Out of the comfort of race, our sin discounts God and disparages God's way of life.

But must it be this way? Must we live with disinterest and disdain for one another? Must we continue in idolatry and false faith? Supposing for a moment that the way might be different than it is: what might it look like, and how then shall we live?

Vacating Habits: A New Vision

In the midst of their contentious relations over spiritual matters and their arrogant judgments about one another, the believers in Corinth were told by Paul that he would show them a way that was beyond comparison with any of their frames of reference, the way of faith, hope and love (1 Cor 12:31). Can we access and retrieve this way in our racist situation, as those who claim the biblical narratives as our own? Can our response-ability and relations with one another be changed? Is it possible that God's word through Paul to the Corinthians may implicate us, here and now, whose situation is different? Indeed we can draw on the Christian narratives that witness to the divine self-disclosure in particular situations by listening for God's address to us through them in our situation. The Scriptures contain instructions and exhortations that redirected the early Christians away from their habits and patterns of response and relation to God and one another, and for us these can not only raise questions but also point us in new directions.

There are far too many exhortations to faith, hope and love in the sacred literature for us to overlook their centrality in the way of life of the people of God. One thing that becomes clear in any careful reading of the Scriptures is that the people of God were expected not merely to *have* these virtues but, more important, to *express* them in their manner of life. The followers of God were expected to internalize and externalize—or objectify—faith, hope and love in their response and relation to God and one another in their sociocultural order. These virtues were expected to be their subjective and objective way of life; they were God's way, a way quite beyond comparison.

When we ponder these virtues, it is immediately evident that they are responses that presuppose an other, and thus they are inherently *relational*. Moreover, they are expected to characterize the human response to God's initiatives and to our fellow human beings, to structure the relationship with God and others in the particular situation of our lives. Faith, hope and love, then, were and are the corrective to our sin. They must be expressed in our lives and, through our conduct, in the world we share. The transforming work of God's self-disclosure is to enable and empower us to do so. Now let us consider some of the impulses in the Christian narratives that may address our situation of race and racism and serve as a biblical platform for developing the first movements in a theology of racial reconciliation.

A look at Ephesus. The Epistle to the Ephesians, like all the sacred literature, was directed to particular people living in a particular situation, and the author used the epistle to address both people and situation.[7] More specifically, Paul addressed the Ephesian hearers (the epistle would have been read to the assembled believers at their public worship) as *Christians* and instructed them regarding the nature of their Christian faith and its implications for their relationships with one another and their manner of life in their situation. Our first task is to access this situation as it is reflected in the epistle itself. We need to pay close attention to the epistle's themes and the way they are developed, using a bit of faithful theological imagination and listening for the voice(s). To then retrieve the epistle into our own situation, we will need to ask whether there are any points of convergence between theirs and ours, and whether the voice(s) may be addressing us as well.

Even a casual reading of the epistle suggests that there were problems in the church in Ephesus—problems of beliefs, attitudes, values, behavior, problems of a moral and theological nature. This should come as no surprise, given that each of the New Testament writings deals with situational problems confronted by the early churches. In the case of the epistles, however, the problems tend to be much more specific and more easily recognized. These writings were intended to serve as guides and correctives to the community in order that the problems in their situation might be dealt with effectively. The problems in Ephesus emerge for us when we note the instructions and exhortations laid down by the author. In other words, we not only listen to *what* the author is saying, but we ask *why* it is being said.[8]

---

[7]New Testament scholars disagree on whether this epistle was written by the apostle Paul; a majority reject Paul's authorship on the grounds that there are significant differences in grammar, syntax and vocabulary between this epistle and others recognized as genuinely Pauline. Because of space limitations, it is not possible to pursue the authorship question here. For our present purposes it is immaterial whether Paul actually wrote this epistle. It has been and continues to be regarded as part of the sacred literature of Christian faith, so out of deference to the debate on authorship, but with attention to stylistic matters, I will refer to the writer(s) of Ephesians as both "Paul" and "the author." When I engage other epistles that are uniformly recognized as genuinely Pauline, we will speak of him as their author. Furthermore, the earliest manuscripts of the epistle lack the phrase "in Ephesus" in 1:1, and it is largely the early Christian tradition that has this letter going to Ephesus. I will assume this tradition in this discussion.

[8]For example, why does the author makes the following observations: "I have heard of your faith in the Lord Jesus and your love toward all the saints" (Eph 1:15), "for surely you have already heard of the commission of God's grace that was given me for you" (3:2), and "surely you have heard about [Jesus] and were taught in him" (4:21)? Together, these observations seem to suggest that the author and the Ephesian believers did not personally know one another, as one would expect if the author had ministered among them as a preacher and teacher. This question is one other reason some doubt that Paul was the author of this epistle.

In general, the problems were of two kinds: their discernment and their manner of life as Christian believers. They apparently had either a lack of understanding or a misunderstanding of God, Jesus Christ, the church and themselves as Christians, and they had difficulty and discord as a result of the way they lived with one another as Christians in their environment. We could say, then, that their problems had to do with (1) their flawed discernment and (2) their response-ability and relatedness. We will begin with the discernment problem because it is central to the epistle as a whole and because the second problem stems from the first.

Problem 1: Discernment. In the opening blessing, Paul asserts that God has profusely bestowed wisdom and understanding on Christians by disclosing the "mystery" of the divine will, the knowledge that God's plan is to "gather up all things" in Christ, and that this has been God's purpose all along (Eph 1:7-11). The Ephesian hearers are then assured that because they have heard this gospel and believed in Jesus Christ, they too are to be included in this plan (1:12-14). Thus the author is aware of and grateful for their faith and love for one another (1:15-16). Now comes the first indication of the discernment problem. Paul does not merely want the Ephesians to know something he could tell them himself (that is, he does not simply want to pass on information). Rather, in his prayer he indicates his desire that God disclose something to them, or more accurately, that God give them wisdom and revelation in order that they might have a fuller understanding or discernment of God and God's purposes. The author indicates that there are three things that he wants them to discern: (1) the "hope" to which God has called them, (2) the "riches" of God's "inheritance" and (3) the "immeasurable greatness" of God's power for the believers (1:18-19). As a way of specifying "greatness," Paul asserts that this power for the believers is the very same power that was put to effect in the resurrection of Jesus and his exaltation to the position of supreme authority. What does this "power" look like and what can it accomplish? It raised Jesus from the dead and installed him as "head over all things" (1:22). Furthermore, later in the epistle the author again indicates the desire that the hearers will be able to understand, "with all the saints, what is the breadth and length and height and depth" of God's love and to know even that "love of Christ" that is unknowable, or that "surpasses knowledge" (3:18-19).

Presumably if the Ephesian Christians had the discernment the author describes, there would be no need to pray that it be given by God in revelation. It was the flaws or weaknesses of their current discernment that occasioned the epistle, and we can suppose that the author believed the rest of the letter could eventuate in this fuller discernment; insight could be shared with them because the author had received God-given discernment that could be expressed. This expression could become a medium of divine self-disclosure; God's voice could be heard in and through the written expression. Why else would Paul write? He apparently was concerned that the Ephesians had misunderstood or failed to understand altogether the correlation between God's purposes and plan, Jesus Christ, the church and themselves as members of the church. These are the principal themes taken up in the epistle.

As we move through the epistle, we will see how the author's powerful metaphors and vivid imagery address the Ephesians' status as believers, the meaning of what God has done in Jesus Christ, and the significance of the church as the community of faith, hope and love grounded in Jesus Christ. Interpreting God's purpose in Jesus Christ for them, the author exhorts them to perceive, reflect, interpret, understand and act *differently* than they have. The author places before the hearers a radically new vision of God and themselves, and therefore a radically new way to live.

Discerning themselves before the gospel. In relation to God, how is the status of the Ephesian believers described before they heard and believed the gospel, before their encounter with God? Paul says they were dead, separate from Christ, hopeless and atheists (Eph 2:1, 12-13). Before God's self-disclosure in the gospel, they probably would not have self-identified in quite this way. But that is precisely the point Paul is making. In their pre-Christian life they did not discern that they were God-less; on the contrary, they undoubtedly perceived themselves as "religious," having a plethora of deities and ritual practices through which to express their "piety." They simply were related to the wrong gods but did not discern this, and therefore they really had *no* relation to God. Their manner of life before the gospel is described as walking along a way that conformed to the temper of their times. In following this path they were being falsely led away from God; like everyone else, they were simply following the way of their own interests and ideas into disobedience to God (2:1-2). Again, they probably would not have regarded themselves as being misled and disobedient but rather as living ordinarily like everyone else within the socioeconomic ranks and religious practices that constituted their milieu. But from the perspective of Christian faith, their former manner of life and their world externalized sin and disobedience, and they did not discern this, about either themselves or others.

We need to pause here to ask, who were the people in the church in Ephesus to whom this epistle was addressed? The author refers twice to "you Gentiles" (2:11; 3:1), so we can suppose that the majority of the congregation were Gentiles who had converted to Christianity. Even though the author never addresses any of the Ephesian believers as "Jews," it is reasonable to suppose that there were also Jews in the congregation who had converted to Christianity. Indeed, as we will soon see, it is *necessary* to suppose the presence of Jewish Christians among the believers in Ephesus.[9] But who were the Gentiles? They were *not*-Jews. In other words, "Gentiles" was an out-group identity, imposed by in-group Jews on all other people groups. Gentiles were simply the "peoples" who inhabited other regions, developed different cultures, spoke Greek or languages other than Hebrew and practiced a variety of religions.[10] So far as the Jews were concerned, all other peoples were "Gentiles," practitioners of impure ways of life and followers of idolatrous religions. *Gentiles* was a term of derision and condemnation when used by Jews. The Jews had their own distinctive sociocultural order, rooted in the practice of their distinctive religion. "Jew" was a particular identity expressed concretely in beliefs, attitudes, values and practices institutionalized in a distinctive sociocultural and religious order. The Jews regarded themselves and their religion as superior to others. All other people groups with their sociocultural and religious life were just that: *other* than—and inferior to—Jews.

In the first century of the common era in Judea and Galilee, Jews were the predominant social and religious group, even though they lived with limited autonomy under the political rule of Rome. Outside Judea and Galilee, Jews lived as cultural and religious minorities among the "Gentiles." Whether living in the homeland or in the dispersion among the Gentiles, Jews managed to establish and maintain their social and religious ways of life by using universe-maintenance strategies of dominion (rejecting and excluding Gentiles altogether), segregation (separating and isolating themselves from Gentiles) or integration (assimilating Gentiles who converted to Judaism) to one degree or another, depending on the extent of their social and religious power. So in places like Ephesus there would have been two groups, Jews and Gentiles, who for the most part, as the New Testament writings suggest, scorned one another and kept themselves separate from one another, with each having their distinctive group identity, worldview and characteristic ways of living. The emergence of Christian churches in places like Ephesus meant in effect

---

[9]If this epistle was not in fact sent to the church "in Ephesus," this does not exclude the possibility that Jewish Christians were part of the congregation to which the epistle was first sent. The presence of Jewish Christians in the churches of Asia Minor is well established in both Acts and Paul's letters. The author's argument in Ephesians makes no sense unless the congregation consists of both Jewish and Gentile Christians.

[10]The English word *Gentile* is used to translate the Greek word *ethnos*, meaning "nation" or "people." *Ethnos* is used most often in the plural to refer pejoratively to the non-Jewish "nations" or "peoples." The word *Gentile* comes into English from early Latin *gentiles,* which referred to persons of the same clan. In later Latin it was used to refer to "pagans," and thus to peoples who were non-Latin (that is, non-Christian).

that two groups became four: Jews, Gentiles, Jewish Christians and Gentile Christians. In no small part the *religious* conflicts between and among these four groups as narrated in Acts and the epistles was related to *sociocultural* conflict.

In terms of relation to the Jews, and by implication relation to the God of the Jews, how is the status of the Ephesian Gentile believers described before they heard and believed the gospel? Paul describes them first with a term used by the Jewish in-group to refer to the out-group: they are "called 'the uncircumcision' by those who are called 'the circumcision'"(Eph 2:11). He goes on to make it clear that as Gentiles they were the out-group, a people separate and excluded from all that made the Jews the people of God. They were *separated* from Christ, *alienated* from the citizenship of Israel, *estranged* from the covenants of the promise, *dispossessed* of hope and thus *had no* God (2:12). In relation to the history of Israel as the people of God and Israel's heritage in Yahweh the God of the covenant, the Gentiles were far distant strangers and aliens (2:13, 19).

Note, however, that the perspective represented in these pronouncements was the perspective of *Judaism*. The Gentiles were being identified as the out-group in relation to the Jews of Israel, the in-group. It strains imagination to think that Gentiles would have identified themselves in these ways before their conversion to Christianity. Certainly their manner of identifying themselves is not expressed in the Ephesian text. Their *way of life* before their conversion is described, but it is described as a problem for them as *Christians*—an issue that will be addressed more directly in a moment.

Discerning the mystery. The center of the Ephesians' discernment problem is that they have not recognized God's purpose for them, and as a result they continue to live in ways that contradict this purpose. In the early portion of the epistle the author contends that God's plan had been hidden, kept secret as a "mystery" (Eph 1:9) that only now has been disclosed in and through Jesus Christ. The intent of this plan is to bring or gather together everything in the heavens and on the earth into Christ, and thereby to establish a household for all in the completion of time (1:10). Thus the destiny that God has determined for both the Jews and the Gentiles is that they are to be *together* in Christ. This eternal purpose of God has now been discerned by Paul and God's "holy apostles and prophets" (3:5) because God has disclosed it to them. Specifically, what has now been disclosed as the "mystery of Christ" is that the Gentiles are included in the household of God; it is not "for Jews only"!

The relation between the Jews and other people groups had been characterized by arrogant claims to superiority and assertions of inferiority, practices of exclusivism and isolationism, domination and oppression, and in-group and out-group antipathy. In short, between Jews and all others there was a "hostility" that functioned as a "dividing wall" (2:14).[11] The beliefs, attitudes and conduct of each group with regard to the other effectively expressed a contentious relation of *over-against.* But the revelation of God's mysterious plan in and through Jesus Christ is discerned by the author as the abrogation of this hostility, this over-against. Separation and exclusion are not God's purpose; cohumanity together with and under God is. The old ways of life expressed by the Jews have been nullified in Christ, who "has abolished the law with its commandments and ordinances" (2:15). The ways of life expressed by the Gentiles have also been nullified, as we shall soon see.

The mystery of Christ is that in his humanity ("flesh," 2:14) he has made the two groups into one, gathering them into himself. In his humanity he has created the two as *one new humanity* (2:15); he has broken the hostility and made peace between them. Moreover, the two groups have both been reconciled to God *in one body,* Christ's body that suffered death on the cross and his body the church.

The author wants them not only to hear this but to *discern* it, and as a result to live differently with one another in their shared world. Whatever "one new humanity" may have meant to the author, it is clear that its significance for the Ephesian believers is a matter of God's self-disclosure, and that its appearance in the humanity of Jesus Christ has eventuated in the complete rejection of their beliefs, attitudes and practices—former ways of life—as inconsistent with God's purpose for humanity. They have been reconciled to one another and to God, and therefore those who claim to be followers of Christ, whether "Jew" or "Gentile," are intended to express this reconciliation in their beliefs, attitudes and practices—their new way of life together and with God. Jesus Christ as the new and true human is the One to whom all must look to discern God's intention for humanity.

Discerning themselves* after *the gospel. In relation to God, how is the status of the Ephesian believers described *after* the life, ministry, death and resurrection of Jesus, and after they heard and believed the gospel? Paul describes them as having been destined to be adopted as God's children (Eph 1:5), and so they have an inheritance that has been committed to them (1:11, 14, 18). They are now close to God (2:13) so they may approach God (2:18). Moreover, they are fellow citizens with all other believers, and members of God's household (2:19).

---

[11]The Greek term translated into English as "dividing wall" is literally "middle wall of the partition," evoking the physical wall in the temple area that separated the court where Gentiles could go from those areas where only Jews could go.

All this imagery underscores a manner of relation and response-ability to God and to others. Any person adopted by the head of a household in Greco-Roman culture had the same legal privileges and right of inheritance as the biological children of the householder. Adopted persons were full members of the household, entitled to the householder's protection and benefits, but obligated thereby to live by the stewardship of the household as laid down and presided over by the householder. The imagery of being adopted into membership with equal rights and privileges in God's household would have made sense to Gentiles. Where once they were excluded as inferior aliens, they were now to be included as equal brothers and sisters. Where once there had been estrangement and hostility, there was now to be a manner of life that expressed reconciliation and unity.

The imagery of household is centered in the humanity of Jesus Christ, who is described as its "cornerstone" (2:20), and this leads the author to assert that around Christ the members of the household are being structured as building blocks that "grow" into a "holy temple" suitable to be God's dwelling (2:21-22). The Jewish and Gentile believers are joined together as a habitation of God. The "mystery," therefore, is that "the Gentiles have become fellow heirs, members of the same body, and sharers in the promise in Christ Jesus through the gospel" (3:6). Paul seeks to enlighten them concerning this mystery so that through their common life in the church as the "body" of Christ, God might disclose the eternal plan that has been executed in Jesus Christ (3:9-11). The church as the "household," "temple," and "dwelling place" of God, then, has a role to play as a medium of divine self-disclosure, an expression of God's purposes for humanity.

The transition from their old way of life to their new way of life is signified by Paul with the assertion that though they were dead, they have now been made alive (2:5) and raised with Christ (2:6) in the place of his exaltation and rule. In this way Paul links their transition directly to Jesus' own death and resurrection. In ways extraordinary and mysterious, the believers participated in the life, death and resurrection of Jesus; Paul now presses them to claim Jesus' new humanity as their own. He reminds the Ephesian believers that they had previously been instructed to abandon their former way of life and rid themselves of their old humanity, to be renewed in their thinking and to put on the new humanity that has been created according to God's purpose (4:22-24). Jesus' humanity is now to be their humanity. Their old humanness and its expressivity have been abolished in the divine plan executed in Jesus Christ, so it is no longer necessary that they live as they had; they have a choice because God has revealed this new humanity in Jesus Christ and called them to it in the gospel. Where once they were unable to respond, they now have response-ability.

Where once their relation with the Jews as the people of God was hostile and estranged, there is now reconciliation.

Problem 2: Response-ability and relatedness. Now here is the other problem writ large. The Ephesians' new status authorizes them to live differently, but in effect they have not done so, though they claim to be followers of Jesus Christ. The epistle contains one other prayer that is important here. Having interpreted the significance of Jesus Christ for the reconciliation between Jews and Gentiles—and thus between Jewish Christians and Gentile Christians—and between all and God, Paul prays that his hearers may be empowered inwardly through the Spirit and that through their faith Christ might be at home in their hearts (Eph 3:16-17). He desires that the Spirit of God strengthen their inner selves so that they might express Christ through their faith, for this power of God "is able to accomplish abundantly far more than all we can ask or imagine" (3:20). The fact that they have not been so empowered and have been unable to manifest their "new humanity" is indicated by this prayer, but not only by this prayer.

The remainder of the epistle is given largely to instructions and exhortations that make sense to the hearers—and to us—only because they were needed in the situation. We can hear *what* Paul said to them, but we can also ask *why* he wrote as he did. The answer is: they continued to walk in a manner of life that was inconsistent with God's purposes for them as disclosed in the new humanity in Jesus Christ. They had neither discerned nor expressed this new humanity and the reconciliation it entailed. Why else would the author encourage them to walk—live—in a manner "worthy of the calling to which you have been called" (4:1)? Why would Paul exhort them to live together "with all humility and gentleness, with patience, bearing with one another in love, making every effort to maintain the unity of the Spirit in the bond of peace" (4:2-3) unless this manner did *not* characterize their life together? Why would he assure them that "there is one body and one Spirit, just as you were called to the one hope of your calling, one Lord, one faith, one baptism, one God and Father of all, who is above all and through all and in all" (4:4-6) unless they were fragmented, continuing to be over against one another, haggling over the meaning of faith and baptism, disposing of the oneness of God? Moreover, why would Paul tell them that they "must no longer live as the Gentiles live" (4:17) unless that was precisely what they were doing? Rather than humility, gentleness, patience, forbearance and unity, their life together reflected misunderstanding, alienation from the life of God, ignorance, hard hearts, lack of remorse, lewdness, unwholesome practices and greed (4:18-19). Rather than speaking the truth to one another, they spoke falsehood, and instead of speaking in ways that would encourage and edify one another, they spoke corrupt words (4:25-29).

As incredible as it may appear, the believers in Ephesus remained over against one another even as they claimed to be Christians. Their beliefs about each other in the church remained consistent with the beliefs each group held about the other. Their attitudes toward one another in the church were no different from those expressed in their in-group and out-group hostility. They were Jews and Gentiles who were bringing their Jewishness and Gentileness into the church, and this was tantamount to disrupting and opposing one another and God. Why else would the author exhort them to "put away from you all bitterness and wrath and anger and wrangling and slander, together with all malice, and be kind to one another, tenderhearted, forgiving one another, as God in Christ has forgiven you" (4:31-32)? The corrective to this old humanity is recognized not only in the new humanity of Jesus Christ but in the author's exhortation that they "be imitators of God, as beloved children, and live in love, as Christ loved us and gave himself up for us" (5:1-2).

The corrective to their problem was this: they were to live in relation as God intended, express God's life in their divinely empowered response-ability to one another, and imitate God, now that they were coming to discern God's purpose in a new way. As God's children, they were to walk in goodness, righteousness and truth, and thereby demonstrate what was well-pleasing to the Lord (5:9-10). So Paul exhorts them to watch how they live, to live as those who are wise and to comprehend what God's will is for them (5:15-17). Even the thieves among them were told to quit stealing and to work honestly (4:28). Why? The reason given was not that stealing was an immoral practice. Stealing in the ancient world was a way of life, a way to make a living economically: one stole in order to survive. But stealing was still taking something that belonged to someone else, and if one stole for survival—or any other reason—rather than "work honestly," one had nothing to "share with the needy" (that is, one had nothing to give to others).

Materializing new humanity. How then is the church to be regarded? We have seen the rich imagery of church as "body," "household," "temple" and "dwelling place." All these metaphors work linguistically because they serve to *materialize* that to which they point. The church is like and unlike a "body," "household" and so on. The metaphors work because they are the images by which the church as such is *conceived.* They make it possible for the Christian to perceive and internalize the church, to make sense of it. More important, they externalize a sense of the church and locate the member within it in a particular relational way. The same is true with all the metaphors Paul uses to describe the status of the Jewish and Gentile believers in Ephesians 3—4. These metaphors are used to express their status in relation to God and the history of God with the people of God. Likewise, "one new humanity" is a metaphor that the author begs the hearers to externalize; they are to think of (identify) themselves and externalize (conduct) themselves in ways that express (reveal) their participation in Jesus Christ.

In the epistle, however, the controlling image is the unity and reconciliation that are to characterize the response-ability and relation of members of the church, to each other and to God. The goal of God's purpose is a people of God whose maturity is measured not by the standards of Judaism or Gentileism but by Jesus Christ and the "new humanity" realized and disclosed in and through him (4:13).

In the Epistle to the Romans, Paul contends that believers have participated in Jesus' death and resurrection in their baptism; those who have been baptized into Christ have been baptized into his death, and as Christ was raised from the dead, so believers may live a new life (Rom 6:3-4). For Paul, this baptism of believers is the crucifixion of their old humanity, their death to the sin of their former way of life (6:6). The Roman Christians are to regard themselves as "dead to sin and alive to God in Christ Jesus" (6:11).

In his Galatian epistle Paul had declared the same conviction regarding the significance of baptism, only with a more explicit qualification. The believers who have been baptized into Christ have *put on* Christ, meaning the humanity of Jesus Christ (Gal 3:27) that supersedes the old humanity of the believers. But he presses on to clarify the significance of this putting on Christ. For Paul it means that the fractious and oppositional ways of regarding and relating to one another that had heretofore characterized intergroup relations have been effectively abolished in Jesus Christ. In-group and out-group identities and patterns of relation are abolished in Christ, and therefore among those who have been baptized into Christ. Ways of living that express estrangement, opposition and discord are rejected by God in Christ, so "there is no longer Jew or Greek, there is no longer slave or free, there is no longer male and female," for believers are one humanity in Christ Jesus (3:28). Jews and Greeks, slaves and free, male and female: these are all essentially oppositional relations, characterizations of in-groups and out-groups, powerful and powerless, dominant and subordinate, and in all cases the patterns of relation and regard are nullified in the new humanity of Jesus Christ.

In the Epistle to the Colossians,[12] a letter that contains a more concise presentation of the same themes encountered in Ephesians, the author grounds Christian faith and life not only in the Christ-event but more specifically in believers' participation in the death and resurrection of Jesus Christ. The believers are

---

[12]Paul's authorship of Colossians is also disputed. For the same reasons indicated in note 7 above, I refer to the author(s) of this epistle as either "Paul" or "the author."

exhorted to "put to death" their former way of life and all its expressions (Col 3:5-8), and having removed their old humanity and its expressions, they are to put on the new humanity that is being restored through their discernment of its portrayal in Jesus Christ (3:9-10), who is himself the "image" of God the Creator (1:15; 3:10). As a parallel to the audacious assertion in Galatians, the author now proclaims that there is no place in this restoration for "Greek and Jew, circumcised and uncircumcised, barbarian, Scythian, slave and free" person, but Christ is all things and in all things (Col 3:11). To the Greeks, barbarians were simply those who did not speak Greek; *barbarian* was not necessarily a pejorative term, though it did refer to those who could not communicate in the common language of Greco-Roman culture. Eventually, however, it became a term of derision, referring to those whose cultural ways of life were judged by the Greeks to be ignorant, crass and unrefined; barbarians were not Greek (they were "savage"). Scythians, on the other hand, were nomadic warriors and slave traffickers from the northern regions of the Crimean Sea (Black Sea), so the moniker *Scythian* referred to either the slaver or the slave. Again, these were all essentially oppositional relations, characteristic of in-groups and out-groups, patterned by power relations of domination and subordination—modes of relation and mutual disregard that are abolished in the new humanity of Jesus Christ.

Retrieval. How, now, can we retrieve this construal into our racist situation? To begin, we must acknowledge that the voice of God may be speaking; we cannot afford to foreclose on that possibility. The author of these epistles intended that the voice heard be discerned as God's speaking in human language, drawing on human relations, patterns of interaction, beliefs, attitudes and behaviors expressed in very particular sociocultural worlds. Second, we must regard the portrayal of ways of life as dichotomized between acceptable ("new humanity") and unacceptable ("old humanity") according to the disclosure of God's purposes in Jesus Christ. Third, we must consider the significance of status and mutual regard as ways of internalizing and expressing group identity. And fourth, we must attend to the ways, socioculturally located as they were, in which the virtues of faith, hope and love were either discredited or expressed, and the response-ability and relations were externalized in life together under God.

The keynote of our retrieval is the notion of *a way of life in a shared world.* How we live with one another, how we perceive and relate to one another as individuals and groups, is not solely a matter of our own determination. As we have seen, through socialization we are taught to view ourselves, others and the world around us in particular ways; the world is presented to us as *there* to be lived in, but we interpret it in the ways we have been taught. The world around us does not make sense; rather we make sense of the world. Through internalization and the reciprocity of our subjectivity and the world's objectivity, we interact with others and the world in ways that are more or less expedient and meaningful. We learn how to function in the spheres of our daily lives where we play roles, follow rules and accomplish our objectives. We identify more with some of these spheres and less with others, and we identify more with some people and less with others. We have a lifestyle, a way of life, and we live it in a world that is shared with others.

But this world, our sociocultural order, is premised on *race* and the meaning that is ascribed to it as an element of our humanity. And this world is structured by *racism,* which expresses these judgments we make about our humanity. The category of race divides humanity into groups, and the expressions of racism alienate groups by placing them over against one another. With race, human beings distinguish themselves from one another by attributing differential value to human groups, and in racism, this differential value is expressed concretely in patterns of response and relation. Race engenders in-groups and out-groups, and racism engenders structures of inclusion and exclusion in the sociocultural order. Race contributes to group identity, and racism fosters identification with a group. Race assigns status, specifying location and standing in the sociocultural order, and racism maintains this status by institutionalizing inequality. Race influences roles and rules in the spheres of everyday life, and racism either enhances or restricts the capacity of human beings to express themselves in these spheres.

Race and racism are human creations, and with them the humanity of some is exalted over the humanity of others. The history of race and racism is the history of the ways we have formed and expressed our humanity over against one another as people groups and as individuals, and they are so embedded in the structures of our sociocultural order and our consciousness, so characteristic of our response-ability and relationships, that it is not an exaggeration to say they are the temper of our times.

Race and racism are inherently oppositional and disruptive of human community because they express differential status and power relations and require that human beings identify with one group over against another. When human beings identify with a racial group as a primary reference group, they are effectively internalizing an oppositional identity. In this sense there is very little difference between Jews over against Gentiles and "whites" over against "others" (black, brown, red or yellow).

It is true that the notions of "identity" and "consciousness" are largely a modern Western phenomenon, but as we have seen, they refer to one's sense of self and sense of one's group. In the ancient world a person's status was determined almost entirely by membership in a particular family, gender, place of origin, occupation and affiliation with political or religious groups; our notions of identity, individuality and personal autonomy would have been strange to them.[13] One's status in an ancient sociocultural and religious order was largely assigned and basically unalterable. In our own sociocultural order we are relatively unconcerned about these demographic indicators, and we do not necessarily regard them as constitutive of a person's identity, though as individuals we tend to identify ourselves in terms of these indicators. However, we do regard these as indicators of status and identity when we racialize them. Then they become the indicators of a person's racial status and identity, the markers of a person's humanity. They become, in effect, the indication of primary racial reference groups in relation to which identity is formed.

The new humanity disclosed to us in Jesus Christ calls into question our ways of forming and expressing our oppositional humanity. The abrogation of Jew over against Gentile, male over against female, free over against slave is the abrogation of sociocultural and religious expressions of response-ability and relations that are inherently oppositional and disruptive. To draw on the terms used in previous chapters, "Jew" was a socially constructed group identity and role, played out by individuals in the social, economic, political and religious spheres of everyday life. And so was "Gentile." But they were oppositional to one another, patterned by practices of exclusion and the presumption of superiority and inferiority. They were in-group over against out-group. The same is true of "male" and "female." A person's sex is a matter of biology, but a person's gender is a matter of sexual identity in relation to others, and therefore it is a social identity expressed in social spheres and schemes, patterned by roles, rules, perceptions, expectations and power relations. Moreover, the ways individuals internalize and externalize these roles in the schemes of gender relations contribute not only to the formation of gender identity but also to the institutionalization of gender in the sociocultural order. To the extent that male-female gender relations are oppositional—exploitive and oppressive—they are manifestations of the old humanity nullified in Jesus Christ. And the same is true of "slave" and "free." The difference between our history of slavery and the ancient institution of slavery—and it is a singular difference—is that American slavery was based on race, that is, the perception and valuation of differences thought to be biological. In the ancient world "slave" was primarily a social and economic status, and one became a slave either voluntarily or forcibly. But per-

---

[13]See Ivan Hannaford, *Race: The History of an Idea in the West* (Washington, D.C.: Woodrow Wilson Center Press, 1996), pp. 184-86; Gerhard E. Lenski, *Power and Privilege: A Theory of Social Stratification* (Chapel Hill: University of North Carolina Press, 1984); and David F. Wells, *Losing Our Virtue: Why the Church Must Recover Its Moral Vision* (Grand Rapids, Mich.: Eerdmans, 1998), pp. 164-66.

sons were not forced into slavery because of their "race," and it was possible for slaves to gain freedom from their servitude. In the ancient world persons were not slaves because of their biology; in America they were.

Jew or Gentile, male or female, slave or free, black or white, brown or yellow—all these are socially constructed ways of defining and expressing ourselves over against others, and as such they contradict God's purpose for humanity, the purpose of cohumanity with and for one another, as disclosed in the one new human, Jesus of Nazareth. *Christian* is also a group identity and therefore a personal identity. It is also a reference group. The question that Jesus' new humanity forces upon us is this: Has our ability to internalize and externalize Christian identity been constrained and even contradicted by our loyalty and allegiance to other reference groups, including our racial group? Has our old oppositional humanity compromised the response-ability and relations that God intends for God's human creatures? Have we failed to discern God's self-disclosure in the reconciliation in Jesus Christ because we prefer the blinders that come with self- and group-interest? Have we declined to express this reconciliation because we are more comfortable with our old ways of living and our default position is consistent with the temper of our times?

The Christian virtues of faith, hope and love need to be retrieved. These virtues are not primarily something we believe in but something we express. They are a way of life that surpasses all other ways, because they are essentially characteristic of abilities and relations. So far as the Christian narratives are concerned, they are the means by which we discern God, ourselves and others. The way of faith is the way of acknowledging our dependence on God as the One whom we can trust; it positions us in a quite specific way in relation to God and qualifies our response to God's gracious initiative, enabled by the Holy Spirit. Our belief, attitude and expression in relation to God is thus *humble* faith.

The way of love responds to God's initiative and draws us into unity with God. It is the way of acknowledging God and our interdependence with others whom we need; it positions us in a specific way in relation to God and others and distinguishes our response to them, enabled by the Holy Spirit. Belief, attitude and expression in relation to others is *obedient* love, a love that responds to God's command that we love one another, that we demonstrate loving regard for one another, that we be with and for one another.

The way of hope responds to God's purposes for us and points us toward a common future marked by the fulfillment of God's purposes. It is the way of acknowledging that this future is God's future with us; it positions us in a particular way in relation to this world as the habitat for our shared humanity. As a response enabled by the Holy Spirit, it distinguishes our commitment to a realm where justice and peace prevail and our cooperation with God in securing this realm from all that threatens and opposes God's purposes. Belief, attitude and expression in relation to this shared future is *witnessing* hope, a hope that envisions the consummate reign of God and proclaims that vision to all.

The way of faith, hope, and love is therefore the *way of reconciliation,* the way of living with God who has reconciled us to Godself and the way of living with others. The Christian way of living is intended to express this reconciliation. As Paul said, "So if anyone is in Christ, there is a new creation: everything old has passed away; see, everything has become new!" (2 Cor 5:17). If this is to be our way of living, we need to think—again.

Having Second Thoughts: The Art of Contestation
In his book on the state of race relations in the United States, David Shipler recounts a story about a training event held by the Defense Equal Opportunity Management Institute. The trainer began by telling the assembled participants that if they were going to be silent during the event, then he would operate with three assumptions about their silence. He told them that with their silence he would assume, first, that they *understood* everything he said; second, that they *agreed with* everything he said; and third, that they *supported* everything he said. After reiterating that he would make sense of their silence with these assumptions, and stating that the only way he would know any differently would be if they broke their silence, he paused. And there was . . . silence. After a few moments he said, "So you just sent me a message: you understood, you agreed, and you certainly supported me in your silence."[14]

In racism, the silence is deafening. Whenever racism is expressed in word or deed and the response to it is silence, the racism goes unchallenged and the racist takes the silence as confirmation of understanding, consent and acceptance. But the conspiracy of silence is deadly, destroying both perpetrator and victim. Silence can be a form of resistance,[15] but in the consciousness of those who express racism and to whom racism is invisible, silence is interpreted as license to continue. Even among those who are aware of racism in a particular situation, it is hard to know what to think and how to speak and act. And so— silence. What is needed is insight and discernment, that spirit of wisdom and revelation about which the author of the epistle to the Ephesians wrote. What is needed in the encounter with the expressers and expressions of racism is the ability to think and act differently, to externalize the new humanity.

Living in the ways of our old humanity is living a lie, not only because it fal-

---

[14]David K. Shipler, *A Country of Strangers: Blacks and Whites in America* (New York: Alfred A. Knopf, 1997), p. 547.
[15]See for example Poling, *Deliver Us from Evil,* pp. 106-7.

sifies God's intention for us but because it locks us into the sociocultural patterns and practices of oppositional relations. Our old humanity does not recognize or acknowledge that there is any other way to live, and so we are most accustomed to expressing old humanity, our over-against humanity. Expressing the virtues of faith, hope and love, however, entails not only growing discernment of God's purposes and empowerment to express them in relation to God and others, but also looking at what was previously overlooked. It involves recognizing that what was once thought to be the truth is really a lie, that what was customary and habitual is really counterfeit. Race and racism are old humanity and therefore lies. The new humanity in Jesus Christ is incomparably different from the old humanity, and its new ways of living in relation to others are radically different. And its expression involves unmasking the old for what it is: a lie. As the author of Ephesians exhorted the hearers, those who express the new humanity must not participate in the expressions ("works") of the old humanity but rather *expose* them (Eph 5:11-13). Exposing the old humanity entails recognizing it, and recognizing it involves thinking about it, and thinking about it requires the new perspective given in the self-disclosure of God. Exposing the old requires thinking with and from the truth of new humanity in Jesus Christ. But exposing the old also requires our speaking and acting, so with regard to the ways the old humanity is expressed in racism, it requires that we not maintain silence.

Critical consciousness: Why and why not. Why is *thinking* so important? Why is it necessary to perceive, reflect on, interpret and understand the old humanity? Is it not sufficient to discern and express the new humanity in our ways of living together?

It is necessary to *think* differently because the objective is to *live* differently. The reciprocity between our consciousness and the external world—our internalization of the patterns and structures of the world around us—means that we have internalized old humanity and that we express it in an external world suitable to it. From the perspective of the new humanity, we are sinners in a sinful world, and that is fundamentally our default position. Reciprocity between subjectivity and objectivity means that we take the structures of the world in and these shape our consciousness, *and* as we conduct ourselves in the world, this expresses our consciousness. Psychologists and philosophers regard thoughts, ideas, myths and fantasies as the symbolic portrayal of actions in consciousness, but reciprocity suggests that our actions may be regarded as the "symbolic representations of thoughts."[16] Reciprocity means that thinking in different ways

---

[16]James Gilligan, *Violence: Reflections on a National Epidemic* (New York: Vintage, 1997), p. 61.

leads to living in different ways, *and* living in different ways leads to thinking in different ways. Moreover, reciprocity means that our identity and character are not immutable, that they can be formed and reformed when we think and act differently. As James McClendon has observed, "By being the persons we are, we are able to do what we do, and conversely, by those very deeds we form and re-form our own characters. . . . Thus, character is paradoxically both the cause and consequence of what we do."[17] Internalizing new humanity as constitutive of Christian identity, then, involves externalizing this identity in a shared world and contesting the consciousness, patterns and practices of the old humanity as externalized in race and racism. New ways of living expose old ways of living, and this entails both thinking and living differently, with *critical consciousness.*

Among other things, this involves reassessing our histories. We cannot engage racism in our situation without rethinking our racist past. We remain locked in the deception of false consciousness if we do not access and retrieve our stories from the perspective of the new humanity in Jesus Christ. The history of racism is the history of our old humanity in its sociocultural development; it is the history of godlessness and disobedience, the history of our lie about ourselves and God. The only time we have is now, and we deceive ourselves if we believe that it is under our control. But our time in the present is shaped by a synthesis of our recollections of the past and our anticipations of the future. In our consciousness both the memory of no longer and the hope of not yet are together influencing us in the now.[18] Accessing and retrieving our histories as people groups, however, is not simply a matter of rewriting them. Rather it is interrogating them from the perspective of new humanity, asking about evidence of ways of living and relating characteristic of the old humanity, and denouncing these expressions as counterfeit humanity.

One of the many reasons racism prevails in both blatant and disguised forms is that we have not discerned our histories as groups in relation to one another.

---

[17]James W. McClendon, *Biography as Theology,* new ed. (Philadelphia: Trinity Press International, 1990), p. 16. McClendon's work on the sociality of character-in-community has been developed further in his three-volume systematic theology. See his *Ethics,* vol. 1 of *Systematic Theology* (Nashville: Abingdon, 1986); *Doctrine,* vol. 2 of *Systematic Theology* (Nashville: Abingdon, 1994); and *Witness,* vol. 3 of *Systematic Theology* (Nashville: Abingdon, 2000).

[18]Augustine's reflection on "memory" is superb. See books 10-11 in his *Confessions,* trans. Rex Warner (New York: Mentor/New American Library, 1963), pp. 210-84. Perhaps more than any other, Augustine has influenced the development of narrative theology with this book. For an excellent discussion of "past, present and future" as modes of consciousness, see Stephen Crites, "The Narrative Quality of Experience," in *Why Narrative? Readings in Narrative Theology,* ed. Stanley Hauerwas and L. Gregory Jones (Grand Rapids, Mich.: Eerdmans, 1989), pp. 65-88.

European Americans especially are uninformed regarding the history and contributions of the cultures represented among people groups whose ways of living have been constrained by the dominant group. The human response-ability to the divine initiative in reconciliation must involve a commitment to historical truth.

Thinking with and from the resources of Christian faith in light of the new humanity disclosed in Jesus Christ is not easy. If it were, perhaps it would not have been necessary to send epistles to the early churches. But critical consciousness, thinking through the discernment of God's self-disclosure, is necessary if we are to engage racism and express reconciliation in Christ.

Programmatically, such Christian thinking involves three things.[19] First, it requires recognizing and contesting the assumptions behind the beliefs, attitudes, values and practices that express racist humanity; it amounts to answering the *why* questions regarding the common sense and the patterns of sociocultural life that shape it. Take racial stereotypes: *why* is it believed that African Americans are lazy or less intelligent? Or the leadership of corporate America: *why* are the vast majority of corporate CEOs white men? Or the way an institution operates: *why* do we have these policies? The analysis involved in critical thinking does not stop at the first answer. Rather it continues contesting in order to work all the way back to the underlying assumption, the premise, the a priori or first principle.

Second, it requires recognizing and contesting the influence of the context of our thinking and living. Reciprocity involves internalizing an outer world, and so what we see and how we interpret it are influenced by the patterns and structures of this environment. Critical consciousness is an awareness of the fact that beliefs, attitudes, values and practices are never neutral or purely objective but always relative to contextuality. Take poverty: believing that "whites" are superior to all other people groups is correlative to the perception that members of other groups have less income and live in poorer-quality housing. Educational institutions: administrators and teachers think and conduct themselves in ways that mirror the beliefs, attitudes, and values of their constituencies. Business practices are shaped by an atmosphere of free enterprise and competition with attention to business law, actual competitors and the specific market. Thinking critically about context means asking about the ways it influences consciousness and conduct, because context validates them as "normal."

---

[19]See Stephen D. Brookfield, *Developing Critical Thinkers: Challenging Adults to Explore Alternative Ways of Thinking and Acting* (San Francisco: Jossey-Bass, 1987), esp. pp. 5-14. Brookfield does not write as a Christian, and thus his analysis is not a theology. Nonetheless I have found his discussion to be most relevant to theological thinking, especially in engaging racist expressivity.

Third, it involves imagining and exploring alternatives to customary ways of thinking and living. Beliefs and habits, who we are and how we express ourselves, are not immutable. Neither are sociocultural ways of identifying and expressing ourselves. Critical consciousness discerns that "That's just the way it is!" is a mask for "It can't and *won't* be any other way." Conventional thinking and living (old humanity) is self-protective and resistant to change; critical thinking (new humanity) contests this by exposing its falsehood and envisioning an alternative that is more consistent with God's self-disclosure in our place and time.

Take hierarchy. The rule of some over others is the norm in our personal and sociocultural worlds. It expresses over-against, dominant and subordinate, the rule of the few, and invalidates the essential equality God intended in creating us as cohumanity. All the arguments against the expressivity of equality in a shared world (e.g., it would lead to social and economic chaos and is basically utopian) are really arguments for preserving hierarchy and the privilege of the few. Arguing for hierarchy is nothing more than extraordinary resistance and opposition to equality, justice and reconciliation; it is old humanity. Imagining alternatives is a threat to this status quo, and therefore exploring alternatives is contestation.

As Christians, we take the license for such imagination and exploration to have been granted in the discernment of God and the new humanity in Jesus Christ. Those who confess Christian faith and loyalty to Jesus Christ, who seek to express the virtues of faith, hope and love, should not be surprised when their contestation brings ostracism, repression and suffering. It certainly happened to Jesus, and an indicator of our participation in his new humanity is the extent to which it happens to us. The believers in Philippi were encouraged thus: "Only, live your life in a manner worthy of the gospel of Christ, so that . . . I will know that you are standing firm in one spirit, striving side by side with one mind for the faith of the gospel, and are in no way intimidated by your opponents. For them this is evidence of their destruction, but of your salvation. And this is God's doing. For he has graciously granted you the privilege not only of believing in Christ, but of suffering for him as well" (Phil 1:27-29). More important, the authorization for imagining and exploring alternatives is the future of God, the consummation of humanity's destiny with God and one another as envisioned in the sacred literature of our faith. The warrant is the presence of God's future *now,* expressed in the new humanity.

Thinking with and from the resources of Christian faith and the discernment of God is a new consciousness that contests old beliefs, values and practices and their institutionalized expressions in the sociocultural order—including the intended and unintended expressions of racism, whether statements and actions that symbolize thoughts (objectivity) or ideas and beliefs that symbolize the world (subjectivity). Christians must not fear the truth or be reluctant to contest racism. As discerners of God and practitioners of the new humanity, Christians must join with all those who are committed to living with contestation, for if we blindly accept everything ("It's OK, and besides it's not my job") we are guilty of the sin of resignation, and if we naively accept anything ("It's better than nothing, and besides we can do it") we may very well be guilty of the sin of presumption. Thinking through faith, hope and love is an exercise of empowered response-ability that requires time, energy and most of all thinking with and for others; it is the opposite of "automatic cognitive processing" that absorbs and reflects racist sensibility and worldviews.[20]

Expressing reconciliation entails a different awareness of self and others and living in ways that manifest this new awareness. It requires asking ourselves and others just what we stand for in the times and places of our lives where the old humanity prevails. If we are not prepared and equipped to stand for new humanity in all the spheres and schemes of our lives, then we will have compromised not only ourselves and our claim to Christian faith but the gospel itself. Consciousness of ourselves and others in everyday spheres that objectify the sociocultural order must be essentially different, formed by the discernment of God. As we have seen, the racist sense we have made is abrogated in Jesus Christ. It is expected of us as Christians that our *non*sense be transformed by *God*sense.

Critical consciousness: Contestation. Critical thinking is manifest in the questions evoked when we discern the expressions of race and racism in our sociocultural order at its micro- and macro-levels and all levels in between. In addition to *why,* critical thinking asks about *who* and *what,* and it is characterized by suspicion because it recognizes that racism is deeply embedded in both the fabric of our sociocultural environment (institutional systems and practices) and our own identities and consciousness (dualism, deception, detachment, denial, dissociation).

The questions are directed to ourselves and our neighbors, coworkers, supervisors, retail merchants, bankers, service providers, teachers, boards of directors, media representatives, politicians—everyone who has a hand in shaping ways of living and the beliefs, attitudes, values and behaviors externalized in them. Critical thinking asks not only whether racism is expressed in a given situation but also how this expression disguises and perpetuates racism. It asks not only "Is this racial discrimination?" but also "Is there a pattern of discrimination that is likely to continue?" Critical thinking asks not only "Why do you disregard my [or that person's] view and experience?" but also "Do you believe your view and experience are normal?" It asks not only "Why are these policies

---

[20]See James Waller, *Face to Face: The Changing State of Racism Across America* (New York: Insight, 1998), pp. 171-89.

operational?" but also "What do these policies manage?" and "Who makes them?"

It is not sufficient simply to identify a problem and propose a solution, because the "problem" we see may be only a symptom of a more widespread disease. Discrimination, inequality, ill-treatment and disregard are not, in and of themselves, the problem. Rather they are concrete expressions of the underlying problem of race and racism. Critical thinking, then, directs attention not only to the problem but, more important, to the self- and group-interests of those in a power position to direct and solve the problem, asking, "To whose benefit is it that the problems not be solved?"[21] In institutional spheres, including the church, critical thinking asks whose voices are heard and whose are discounted, whose frames of reference predominate and whose are excluded, who has the power to name—label and define—the situation and who is named in the process, who is in control and who is not, indeed who is present and who is absent.

Old humanity hides itself in the appearance of fairness and equality, but to the extent that the expressions of fairness and equality are produced by "old humans," they can be regarded only as sin masquerading as righteousness. Old humanity contrives justice, goodness and truth; new humanity contests these contrivances. As Christians who discern the goodness, righteousness and truth of God embodied in the new humanity of Jesus Christ, we are not invited to manufacture justice, peace and equality on our own terms; that would be presumption all over again. Nor is it necessary that we acquiesce in the injustice, discord and inequality of our sociocultural order; that would be resignation all over again. It is expected of us, instead, that we incarnate in our thinking and ways of living—our response-ability and relations—practices of contestation and resistance in all spheres of life where the "Domination System" is expressed.[22]

This does not mean that Christians should seek to "christianize" the sociocultural order by taking up social-political causes or by imposing Christianity on others. That is what got us into the trouble of racism in the first place. Nor

---

[21]Jonathan Coleman, *Long Way to Go: Black and White in America* (New York: Atlantic Monthly Press, 1997), p. 14. See also Ronice Branding, *Fulfilling the Dream: Confronting the Challenge of Racism* (St. Louis: Chalice, 1998), pp. 50-55

[22]In his "power trilogy" Walter Wink has explored the New Testament language and world of the "powers" and shown these to be the characteristic spirit—or spirituality—of humanly constructed sociocultural worlds, the inner life expressed in and through the outer structures and patterns—institutions—of social, economic, political and religious life. See Walter Wink, *Naming the Powers: The Language of Power in the New Testament* (Philadelphia: Fortress, 1984); *Unmasking the Powers: The Invisible Forces That Determine Human Existence* (Philadelphia: Fortress, 1986); and *Engaging the Powers: Discernment and Resistance in a World of Domination* (Minneapolis: Fortress, 1992). A summation of these three volumes can be found in *The Powers That Be: Theology for a New Millennium* (New York: Doubleday, 1998).

does it authorize us to form political parties or commit our loyalty to existing political parties in order to politicize the new humanity. Politics, whether democratic or totalitarian, is the expression of our old, fallen humanity, and old wineskins will not hold new wine. Besides, the majority does *not* rule when it comes to truth and justice. Rather, discerning the new humanity in Jesus Christ authorizes us to raise our voices and live in contestation, exposing the old humanity and all its expressions as nullified in Christ, with a willingness to express faith, hope and love and a refusal to align ourselves with any kingdom of this world. It is the authorization to proclaim the gospel in word and deed in the particularity of our circumstances; it is not authorization to co-opt the gospel for social or political purposes (again, presumption and resignation).

Contestation, then, is the practice of subversion, characterized by humility, obedience and witness; it is countercultural in that it questions the expressions of old humanity endemic to our sociocultural order. Communities of Christians who practice critical thinking with and from the discernment of God are authorized to express response-ability and relations as "peculiar people" or "colonies of resident aliens" who are in but not of the world.[23] As the embodiment of the new humanity, communities of Christians are authorized to live in ways that contest racism; they are empowered by the Holy Spirit to manifest themselves in the sociocultural order as communities of inclusion, justice, truth—and reconciliation.

Counting the cost. Following the unsuccessful end to a Camp David summit between Palestinian Authority President Yasser Arafat and Israeli Prime Minister Ehud Barak, an editorial cartoon drawn by Jim Morin of *The Miami Herald* appeared in the July 29, 2000, issue of *The Denver Post*. The words of God come out of a cloud addressing these two as they stand side by side, gazing upward: "I have a solution to your Jerusalem problem. . . . You have both Israelis and Palestinians live and work next to one another in peace, harmony, and brotherhood. . . . Recognize one another's freedoms of worship and speech, and love your fellow man as a child of God." In response, the caricatured Arafat and Barak cry out in unison, "Are you crazy?!" and all that comes from the cloud is an exasperated sigh.

---

[23]See Rodney Clapp, *A Peculiar People: The Church as Culture in a Post-Christian Society* (Downers Grove, Ill.: InterVarsity Press, 1996); and Stanley Hauerwas and William H. Willimon, *Resident Aliens* (Nashville: Abingdon, 1989). For a constructive argument contending for a Christian community that is "in but not of the world," see Loren B. Mead, *The Once and Future Church: Reinventing the Congregation for a New Mission Frontier* (Bethesda, Md.: Alban Institute, 1991), and Robert Wuthnow, *Christianity in the 21st Century: Reflections on the Challenges Ahead* (New York: Oxford University Press, 1993). For a prognostication of the church that implies capitulation to the sociocultural order, see Lyle E. Schaller, *The New Reformation: Tomorrow Arrived Yesterday* (Nashville: Abingdon, 1995).

According to media reports, both leaders had been under considerable pressure from their constituents not to give in to the opposing side. Undoubtedly each leader knew that any agreement they might reach would inflame some of their constituents, perhaps to the point of escalating violence. Oppositional forces within and between people groups, political pressures at home and abroad, and the threat of violence prevented these leaders from achieving a peace agreement at that point. Perhaps they knew what needed to be done but were prevented from doing it because of the cost. Peace agreements that occasion violence are not peace agreements, because they are either broken or enforced by suppression and more violence.

Critical Christian thinking—thinking that works with and from the discernment of God in the new humanity disclosed in Jesus Christ, draws on the resources of Christian faith and scrutinizes the expressivity of our situation of racism—is *integral* thinking, essential for wholeness and conformity to the purposes of God. It is, to be sure, situated thinking: it does reflect the contours of our situation (it is influenced by our context). And of course it is human thinking and therefore subject to the sin that afflicts our humanity. It is committed to dialogue, not self-absorbed in monologue, for no one has a corner on the truth except *the* One. It is obligated only to the presence and activity of the God who judges all things and invites us to participate in the ongoing divine work of creating, reconciling and transforming humanity. It is thinking that makes a different sense, choosing not to assume that the subjectivity and objectivity of our common world are true. But most important, it is thinking that intends to be expressed concretely in our response-ability and relations—ways of life—in a shared world. But to think thus, and to live thus, is not without its cost. So far as race and racism are concerned, Christian thinking must also be *integrity* thinking.

In the first of a series of volumes on the "pre-political" virtues of human communal life, Stephen Carter argues that expressing the personal and civic virtue of integrity stands on three interrelated criteria: "(1) *discerning* what is right and what is wrong; (2) *acting* on what you have discerned, even at personal cost; and (3) *saying openly* that you are acting on your understanding of right from wrong."[24] The point of his threefold definition is that integrity is not manifest unless and until its expression moves through to the third aspect, witness or confession that one's conduct is grounded in discernment and that one is willing to pay the cost, suffer the consequences. "The first criterion captures the

---

[24]Stephen L. Carter, *Integrity* (New York: BasicBooks, 1996), p. 7 (see also p. 123). The second volume in the series has appeared as *Civility: Manners, Morals and the Etiquette of Democracy* (New York: BasicBooks, 1998).

idea of integrity as requiring a degree of moral reflectiveness. The second brings in the ideal of an integral person as steadfast, which includes the sense of keeping commitments. The third reminds us that a person of integrity is unashamed of doing the right."[25] *Unashamed of doing the right!*

Critical thinking endeavors to be *integral* or wholistic, attending to all persons and all the perceptions, beliefs, attitudes and values expressed in human conduct. It asks questions that seek to expose the dynamics and intersections of institutionalized patterns and practices, recognizing that how one reads and interprets any given situation is deeply influenced by the reciprocal relation between subjectivity and objectivity, and thus one's own assumptions and perceptions need to be probed. But critical thinking is also *integrity* thinking in that its intended objective is not merely to *discern* and expose right and wrong, truth and falsehood, but to *act* and thereby express one's discernment with willingness to pay the price, and to *confess* to others what one is doing and why.

That is the art of contesting the sin of racism, but as it happens, it is also the expression of humble faith, obedient love and witnessing hope, grounded in discernment of the new humanity in Jesus Christ. It expresses new humanity in word and deed, and for this reason it may be—by God's gracious initiative—a medium for others to discern the self-disclosure of God.

To Have and to Hold: *Embracing* All "Others"

In his second epistle to the church in Corinth, Paul asserts that he is compelled by the love of Jesus Christ to continue his ministry. He is certain that Christ died for all, and on the basis of that conviction he concludes that all have participated in his death. But he presses on to affirm that the reason Christ died for all is "so that those who live might live no longer for themselves, but for him who died and was raised for them" (2 Cor 5:15). Why did Paul say this? Apparently some in the Corinthian church were living for themselves and not for Christ. Perhaps quite a few of the Corinthian believers were continuing to live over against one another; there certainly is indication in both the Corinthian epistles that the congregation was split into factions and that relations among the believers were wild and unruly. The death and resurrection of Jesus Christ, however, was the realization of God's purpose for humanity, so for those who have died with Christ the old ways of living have come to their end. Those who live not for themselves but for Christ practice new ways of living, for those who participate in Christ's new humanity *become* new, having been newly created (5:17).

Paul then makes a bold assertion: This death of the old and this creation of

---

[25]Carter, *Integrity*, p. 7.

the new are God's work, God's initiative in reconciling humanity to the divine self through the agency of Jesus Christ. Moreover, they are God's initiative in reconciling the *world*—the realm or habitat where the human creature lives— to the divine self (5:18-19). The words *reconciled* and *reconciliation* in this pas- sage are intended to convey the meaning of "making different, changing toward or restoring." Alteration from death to life, old to new, is an extraordinary work of creating and transforming.

Paul's contention here is that reconciliation is a changed relationship because the participants have been changed. In the relation between God and humanity, it is humanity that has been changed in the death of the old and the creation of the new humanity. The transforming work of God, centered in the reconciling work of Jesus Christ and executed in the believer by the Holy Spirit, engenders new response-ability to and relation with God. Thus the humanity of the creature is *changed toward* and *restored* in relation to God. In the relations between human beings, *all things* have been changed for those who are in Christ, in whose life the human and divine are together in unity. The transform- ing work of God engenders new response-ability to and relation with fellow human beings. Thus human creatures are *made different* and *changed toward* others, and their ways of living together are the expressions of the new creation. In both relations, what was once *over against* has been transformed into *with and for* an other. Reconciliation is change in the partners, and it is expressed toward the partners in relation.

The reconciled as medium. Paul has yet another bold assertion to place before the Corinthians, as though his declaration of God's reconciliation were not enough to press upon them. Undaunted by the Corinthians' undisciplined faith and combative lives, he audaciously declares that God not only has placed them in the *service* of reconciliation but has placed within them the *message* of reconciliation (2 Cor 5:18-19). Serving on behalf of another and speaking a message for another make one an "ambassador" for another, a repre- sentative whose words and actions are construed as coming not from the one who is sent but from the one who sends. Paul is saying, in effect, that the Corin- thians speak for God: we are ambassadors on behalf of Christ as though God were imploring through us (5:20). He is contending that the Corinthians are not only agents in the service of reconciliation but an agency of God's self-disclo- sure.

Implicit in all of these bold declarations is recognition that their present manner of life has contradicted this divinely given service and announcement. Why would Paul say these things to the Corinthians? Would he beg them to be reconciled to God (5:20) if their personal and communal lives were not calling the gospel into question? Their reconciliation to God is negated by their disservice and by their remaining over against one another; they disagree with one another and their life together is wracked with conflict. Because their situation is so discordant, he must exhort them to "put things in order, listen to my appeal, agree with one another, live in peace," because it is only as they do so that "the God of love and peace will be with you" (13:11).

Like creating, reconciling occurs at the initiative of God the Reconciler, and reconciliation comes as the initiative of the transforming God whose presence and action enable a transformed response-ability and issue in new relations. The creating, reconciling and transforming initiatives on God's part change and position human beings to be representative agents on behalf of the new and true human, Jesus Christ. God is present and working in and through those who respond and relate out of their new humanity. But this reconciling work is not manifest in and through us until we respond and relate in reconciliation. This is important, because our expression of reconciliation is a medium through which God discloses both Godself and the new humanity to others. As practitioners of Christian faith, we are ambassadors on behalf of Christ, and God appeals to others through us.

Competing lords. Professing to be Christians but expressing old humanity in our conduct and relations is discrediting Jesus Christ and invalidating the gospel of reconciliation. One cannot express racism in any form and at the same time claim to be loyal to Jesus Christ. No person is able to serve two lords, Jesus tells us; either you will detest one and cherish the other, or you will cling to one and disregard the other (Mt 6:24). Well enough, but even in agreeing with this saying of Jesus, we overlook what is perhaps the most important element in it: lord*s* (plural). In the New Testament context, *lord* referred to a socioeconomic relation between individuals; it was an acknowledgment of the status of one over another. Specifically, it referred to the one whose status and position were dominant in a socioeconomic relationship stratified by superordination and subordination. More important, in the master-servant scheme it referred to the fact that the master had a legal claim on the servant, and the servant was obligated to serve the master. From this perspective, the weight of Jesus' saying falls on "lords," not on the "either-or." One cannot serve two lords, both of whom have a legal claim on the servant.

We live in a sociocultural world in which the God of Jesus Christ and the god of race/racism both lay claim to us, and we are obligated to serve because we participate in the realm claimed by both. As Jesus' saying suggests, when we find ourselves in a situation where two competing "lords" command our loyalty, we either hate one and love the other or we reject one and cling to the other, but either way we remain in relation to both. The issue then is not whether we are obliged to one or the other; we are obligated to both. Rather the issue is this: If we resist and contest the claim of one, *are we prepared to suffer the consequences?*

In the ancient world, if two lords both had valid legal claim to a servant, the servant would never have been given the opportunity to choose between the two. That would have been tantamount to giving power and control to the servant. Instead the competing claims of two lords would have been brokered and resolved by mediators in ways that entirely excluded the servant, and the result would be that the servant was declared as obligated to one and not the other. In Jesus' saying there is an implication that the "servant" remains in relation to two "lords." The question is, how is the servant related to these two lords? Jesus' answer: Love one and hate the other; cling to one and reject the other.

The ultimate question is, which one do you hate and reject, and which one do you love and cling to? You are obligated to both, since both have a claim on you. But you have to choose, because you cannot divide your loyalties. Moreover, in choosing one you must be prepared to suffer the wrath of the other. So which one do you hate and which one do you love? Choose—now, this day. Which one will you serve? Jesus Christ and racism have claims upon us, but we cannot serve them both.

The requirements of reconciliation. To live as those whom God is reconciling requires many things, but we will consider five aspects in particular.

1. *Repentance.* Reconciliation as a way of living requires that we repent of the sin that has estranged us from God and from one another. As we have seen, it is God who enables response in humble faith, obedient love and witnessing hope, with the ongoing presence and work of the transforming Spirit. It is also the working of God that enables us to discern our sin and confess our culpability. Racial reconciliation cannot be expressed without acknowledging that our racist ways of living have repudiated God and dehumanized others. Personal and institutional expressions of racism have deprived others of their inalienable dignity and worth as God's creatures. Dishonor, disrespect, disregard and distrust have characterized our relations. Repentance of the sin of racism entails not only acknowledging the forms and expressions of racism in our personal and sociocultural worlds but also denouncing them, turning away from them and refusing to express them or be drawn into their expression by others.

Repenting of racism is not something we do once, after which we are finished with it. It is a way of living in a sociocultural order that expresses racism in its everyday spheres and institutionalized systems. Whether conscious of it or not, we live with and participate in the patterns and practices of racism.

Repentance is both turning *from* sin and turning *to* God. Repenting of this sin, then, is both turning from racism and turning to the One whose life and love we have discredited. As a way of living, repentance is a response-able condition, a position in relation to God and others; it marks a transition from living over against an other to living with and for an other. It must be concretely manifest in and through our ways of living together. Repentance is not repentance unless it is *expressed* and *recognized* in a way of living. This means that repentance must be understood as both speaking and acting, and so it must take the form of confession *of sin to* the other and conduct that reflects a transformed life with God and others.

There is no other way to express the subjectivity of repentance than by objectifying it in our relations with those against whom we have sinned. Expressed in this way, repentance becomes an indication of our resistance to the old humanity of racism. The path to reconciliation is traveled by those who manifest humility rather than arrogance, obedience rather than rebellion. For these, the life of repentance can be an enduring witness to Christian hope.

Reconciliation requires repentance, and repentance must be followed with restitution. Inwardly and outwardly racism is our sin against other human beings as well as God. By practicing it, and by living in a sociocultural environment that expresses it, we have violated other human beings and deprived them of their rightful share in the gift and quality of life. The righteousness and justice of God and the appearance of the new humanity in Jesus Christ require that we restore what we have taken from others. If our sinful ways of racist living have privileged some and disadvantaged others, if our pursuit of self- and group-interests has come through the oppression of others, if our quality of life has come at the expense of others, then our new ways of living together under God must give back what has been taken. God's justice requires that what has been wrong in our practice of racism must be made right, and we cannot express repentance and reconciliation if the structures and circumstances of our relations are not changed. Repentance must be both a giving *up* and a giving *to.* Personal repentance is not sufficient, because racism is not only personal.

The sin of racism is embedded in this nation's history and the development of its sociocultural order. We participate in this sociocultural order and in its valuation of some and devaluation of others. As European Americans, members of the dominant group, we are naively foolish to believe we can repent of our individual racism yet continue to enjoy the benefits that have been handed down to us by the history of racism and our sociocultural order, set up and maintained to assure the benefit of some and the deprivation of others. We cannot turn from our personal sin and still live neutrally, passively and agreeably with the sin embedded in our shared world, the sin that advantages us by restricting others, the sin that continues to influence and shape patterns of human living. We cannot give up our sin and continue to give in to the sinfulness of our world. In order to express reconciliation, our repentance must lead to restoring what our history and way of life have taken from others. Repentance acknowledges and works to restore the dignity and worth of the one who has been aggrieved.

2. *Forgiveness.* Expressing reconciliation as a way of living requires that we practice forgiveness. Like repentance, forgiveness makes the expression of reconciliation possible. It can be misleading to ask whether repentance and forgiveness precede reconciliation or whether reconciliation gives rise to repentance and forgiveness. We should not concern ourselves with the sequence of steps, because such concern tends to freeze us in the circularity of the "chicken or egg" question. Besides, sequencing steps—stage one, stage two, stage three, *voilà!*—is influenced by cause-effect thinking. All of the steps have already been taken in God's creating, reconciling and transforming initiatives; what is required of us is that we express in our response-ability and relations the new humanity of Jesus Christ. My forgiveness of you is not contingent upon your repentance to me; that is over-against relation. Rather my forgiveness is expressed with and for your expression of repentance, and my obligation is to forgive whether you repent or not; your obligation is to repent whether I forgive or not. But we remain over-against in estrangement unless repentance and forgiveness are both expressed in our relation. Reconciliation is expressed when we each discern that repenting and forgiving are ways of living together, and that we each are enabled by the transforming Spirit to repent and to forgive.

As a way of living together, reconciliation is grounded in the belief that humanness entails interdependence as well as interrelation. We need one another, because humanity is essentially *co*humanity. We need others in order to be human. Forgiveness acknowledges the inherent dignity and value of one who has injured another, of those who have harmed others. No one is beyond the reach of forgiveness; there are only those who limit their forgiving reach. The question, then, is not "How *can* I forgive those who have rejected and injured me?" but "How *will* I extend the forgiveness I have received from God to others?" Robert Schreiter poses the latter question this way: "How can I discover the mercy of God welling up in my own life, and where does that lead me?"[26]

The limited reach of forgiveness preserves the hostility of an over-against relation. The forgiveness expressed in reconciliation is intended not only to characterize the with-and-for relation but to objectify the forgiving initiative of God in our relations. Anger, bitterness, hatred and rage are prisons we construct in response to injurious actions of others. They confine us within ourselves,

---

[26]Robert J. Schreiter, *Reconciliation: Mission and Ministry in a Changing Social Order,* Boston Theological Institute Series 3 (Maryknoll, N.Y.: Orbis, 1992), p. 43.

locked away from God and others, and in a grotesque way they hand us over again to the power of those who have injured us. Forgiveness frees us from this prison and extends the witness of God's forgiveness to others.

But forgiveness by itself, just like repentance by itself, is not yet the expression of reconciliation. Just as we cannot claim to repent and remain unchanged in our ways of living in a sinful environment, so we cannot claim to forgive and remain unchanged. Reconciliation with God and others is expressed in patterns and practices of repentance and forgiveness. Repentance is limited in its expression and does not achieve its ultimate purpose without acknowledgment and acceptance by the other. Likewise, forgiveness is limited in its expression and does not come to full flower without acknowledgment and acceptance by the other. Reconciliation is living in and practicing such *mutual* recognition and consent. The "dividing wall of hostility" remains in place if both repentance and forgiveness are unacknowledged and unexpressed in the ongoing life of onetime enemies.

Reconciliation is mutual regard exhibited tangibly in the practices of repentance and forgiveness, and therefore the boundary between "exclusion and embrace" is crossed by responding to the initiative of the other. Unacknowledged repentance or forgiveness leave what Miroslav Volf has called "a distance between people, an empty space of neutrality, that allows them either to go their separate ways . . . or to fall into each other's arms and restore broken communion."[27] Repentance is very important, and so is forgiveness. But either can be confessed generally and unilaterally. Reconciliation, on the other hand, is relational and therefore mutual. It requires turning toward and changing with one another in order for it to be a way of life.[28]

3. *Relationships.* Reconciliation as a way of living requires that we actually be in relationship with others. So far as racism is concerned, reconciliation requires that we have relationships with members of other people groups. For European Americans, it requires that we have relationships with those whom we and our sociocultural order have disregarded and marginalized. Racial estrangement, animosity and indifference have characterized the over-against relations between people groups, and racial reconciliation requires a transformation of these relations, not resistance to them. The divine initiatives in creation, reconciliation and transformation are grounded, as we have seen, in the

---

[27]Miroslav Volf, *Exclusion and Embrace: A Theological Exploration of Identity, Otherness and Reconciliation* (Nashville: Abingdon, 1996), pp. 125-26. See also Charles R. Foster, *Embracing Diversity: Leadership in Multicultural Congregations* (Bethesda, Md.: Alban Institute, 1997), esp. pp. 1-20.

[28]See Walter Wink, *When the Powers Fall: Reconciliation in the Healing of Nations* (Minneapolis: Fortress, 1998), pp. 13-16.

inner-relations of the triune God, and Christian faith discerns that relation is essential to Godself and therefore to humanity. We cannot be creature with the Creator or human with one another without relationships. The new humanity disclosed in Jesus Christ is humanity with and for others, and how much we express this new humanity in our ways of living is connected to whether we actually participate in concrete relationships.

Personal relationships between members of various people groups often remain locked in distrust and suspicion. The patterns and practices of these situated relationships tend to establish and maintain unequal power relations between groups. The history and practice of racism certainly have given no reason for trust. Indeed this history has revealed time and time again how trust was abused or destroyed by the conduct of some in relation to others. But trust is necessary for reconciliation, and for this reason initiative and response in personal and social relationships across racial lines must work toward establishing mutual trust. In order to establish ourselves and be perceived as trustworthy, we must practice integrity and express sincere regard toward others. In order for others to have confidence in and rely on us, we must be deliberate and disciplined in our commitment to others. As McClendon suggests, we form trustworthy character by engaging in actions that are worthy of the trust of others.

Trust is a quality of personal relationships and is grounded in experience with others. It involves learning about others and their stories and taking a vital interest in their world. It is opening oneself to the influence of another person, being willing to travel together down a common road. Trust comes as the result of interactions and shared activities that engender a consciousness of living with and for another. Trust does not come from superficial or infrequent contact, and it will not likely develop within the racialized schemes that occur in the everyday spheres where persons from various people groups interact. These are not relationships, and they do not in themselves express reconciliation. On the other hand, doing something together, talking with each other about ourselves and our experiences, actively listening and responding in ways that evidence our regard and respect for one another, working together for a common cause—all of these are ways to develop and express trust. More important, these are ways to *identify* with one another and have our beliefs, attitudes, values and conduct transformed. It is not necessary that we agree on all things, only that our disagreement not estrange us from one another and dissolve the relationship.

A relationship with *anyone* takes work, whether it is a relationship of spouses, parents and children, coworkers, fellow tenants or neighbors. Such phenomena as the national divorce rate, abuse of children and spouses, violence in the workplace, waiting rooms outside therapists' offices and general disregard for our fellow human beings suggest that we are not skilled in human relations. As a consequence, relations become destructive. Relationships with members of other people groups are especially difficult, because not only are we unskilled in interpersonal relations but we have all the destructiveness and dehumanization of racism to contend with—our own racism, the experience of the racism of others, racism embedded in our sociocultural environment.

Working to develop the trust necessary to express reconciliation, then, is *hard* work. Trustworthiness and trust in others expresses how we value one another. When self- and group-interest supersede or diminish our interest in others, we are unable to express or engender trust. Racial reconciliation means having to learn how to "receive the gifts, offerings, stories and talents that we may have not known we needed; by accepting these things, however, we may change the course of our life and ministry."[29] It also means acknowledging, valuing and expressing the essential equality of others, an equality established by divine initiative in creating us in "the image of God."

Working at relationships with members of other people groups entails giving up something. It means giving up our pride and sloth, our domination and servility, our presumption and resignation. It means giving up the sin of the old humanity. But as the narratives of Christian faith make plain, we do not give up something in order to *achieve* something else. Rather we give up something in order to *be freed for* something better. It is misleading to think of this giving up as a "sacrifice."[30] Giving up our sin is hardly a sacrifice. The language of sacrifice makes sense in the context of religious practices wherein an individual or a group surrenders to God something that they have lawfully acquired and that therefore belongs to them. When I lay the first fruits of my harvest or the first-born of my flock on the altar of God, I am ritually giving up something I hold to God. In our everyday discourse, the notion of sacrifice functions as a metaphor that depicts giving up something in order to achieve something else. But so far as racism is concerned, we European Americans have *nothing* to give up that is rightfully or legally ours; we have only our *sin* to surrender. Nothing that *is* ours is worthy of God's unmerited favor or positive regard toward us. Racial identity, both individual and group, is among these. Giving up racial identity is not a sacrifice, because racial identity is a sinful identity inasmuch as it expresses the precedence of race. Giving up our sin is not a limitation on our autonomy but the liberation of our true humanity. For all have sinned and are unable to reflect God (Rom 3:23).

---

[29]Rhodes, *Where the Nations Meet,* p. 101.
[30]This is one of the "principles" of racial reconciliation suggested by Washington and Kehrein in *Breaking Down Walls,* pp. 186-97.

Loyalty to Jesus Christ is our liberation. The obligation to express his humanity in and through our conduct is our freedom. Our committed relationships to those from whom we had been estranged because of racism is our own emancipation. The unalterable commitment to relationships with persons from other people groups is not the limitation of our humanity but the expression of our *new* humanity. Giving up white privilege is not surrendering advantage but gaining the freedom to secure the rights of others. Giving up our racial identity is not losing our "reference group" but being liberated to identify with others. As Paul observed in Ephesians, giving up stealing is not the loss of an economic way of life but rather the liberation from greed and the freedom to give to others. As the title of this section suggests, abdicating our sin of racism is not forsaking some but receiving freedom to embrace all "others."[31]

The way of reconciliation is not constriction but liberation, and liberation is always *in relation to* others. Those who express racial reconciliation will therefore be those who have committed relationships with those previously regarded as alien "others."

4. *The church.* Expressing reconciliation as a way of living requires the church as a community of the reconciled. This is particularly important for many reasons, but two should be stated at the outset: the church is the community of *sin,* and the church is the community of *salvation.* To state it differently, the church as a community of sinful human beings has fostered some of the most egregious expressions of racism, but the church also materializes our only hope of expressing, by the transforming presence and activity of God, the objective reality of the new humanity in its own spheres and schemes and in our sociocultural order. Granting these two fundamental reasons as the framework of the church's objectivity, we need to consider other reasons.

In order to live our lives as Christians, we need each other. We need a community in which we can express our faith, hope and love with and for others. We need a Christian "reference group" whose convictions, values, relationships and actions are instrumental in forming our own identities and ways of living as believers. It is through the church that we have access to the Christian Story and the resources of Christian faith, because a community of faith affirms, interprets

---

[31] I am indebted to far too many people for this construal of "surrendering of _____ is freedom for _____" to list their works here. Their names, however, include Augustine, John Calvin, Martin Luther, Karl Barth, Charlotte von Kirchbaum, James Cone, Leonardo Boff, Robert McAfee Brown, Benjamin Reist, William Herzog, Diane Hayes, James Evans, J. Deotis Roberts, Gustavo Gutiérrez, Cheryl Sanders, Carter Heyward, Jürgen Moltmann, Eugene Rivers, Letty Russell and Rosemary Radford Ruether. But I am especially indebted to Stephen Carter, whose discussion brought extraordinary focus to this "from _____ to _____" motif in the arena of public virtues. See his *Civility,* esp. pp. 97-121.

and identifies with this Story. Individual members of churches share in a kind of ecclesial group identity that is internalized as they participate in a congregation's ongoing life. As an ecclesial group with its own constellation of persons, patterns and structures, a congregation can be understood as an objectivity in reciprocal relation with members' subjectivity. Members internalize the congregation as an external reality, and so it forms and influences consciousness, and members externalize themselves with others in the patterned life of the congregation and so contribute to shaping the external reality of the congregation. In this way, a congregation is constituted as a sphere in which a variety of schemes are used to express interaction and objectify its life. Members share a common knowledge regarding the congregation's history, its way of life and what the typical roles and rules are. Over time there emerges a common sense about what it means to "do church," and participation in congregational life helps individuals orient themselves to the Christian Story.

Thus a community of believers is indispensable if one is to be nurtured and sustained in Christian faith in personal and sociocultural life. It is precisely as a community of believers that a church represents a "plausibility structure" in relation to which an individual identifies and is identified as a Christian and is capacitated both to make sense of the Christian Story and to express the life of faith, hope and love.

We might take a more theological approach to describing the "social reality" of the church by drawing attention to what the church does that internalizes and expresses the Christian Story. This modest attempt to develop an ecclesiology is grounded in Paul's metaphor of the church as the "body of Christ," an objective expression of the presence and activity of Jesus Christ in our spatiotemporal realm. As such, the church as a community has the purpose of participating in and extending the ministry of Christ the Incarnate One to the world. The church discharges this purpose in three interrelated ways, each of which contributes to the formation and expression of its ecclesial identity, because each responds to God's initiative in Jesus Christ.

First, God is *calling* persons to be *gathered to* the church, and persons respond by receiving Christ's saving work and entering into the community of believers, Spirit-enabled to express humble faith. By manifesting its life through *koinōnia* or fellowship, the community *lives* the Christian story. The central act exemplifying response to God's calling is *baptism,* the enactment that confirms one's new status and relation to God and ordains one to service as a Christian; in an ecclesial sense, this is the *beginning* of a Christian way of living. The effect of God's initiative and human response is the creation of communion in the body as a community *in* the world.

Second, God is *empowering* persons to be *built up within* the church, and persons respond by participating in Christ's saving work and serving the community of believers, Spirit-enabled to express obedient love. By manifesting its life through *leitourgia* or worship, the community *celebrates* the Christian story. The central act exemplifying response to God's empowering is the *Lord's Supper,* the enactment of the recollection of Christ's work and the expectation of his coming and presence; in an ecclesial sense, this is the *sustaining and growing* of a Christian way of living. The effect of God's initiative and human response is the qualitative growth of the body as a community *for* the world.

Third, God is *sending* persons to *entreat outside* the church, and persons respond by extending Christ's saving work and service out of the community of believers, Spirit-enabled to express witnessing hope. By manifesting its life through *kerygma* and *diakōnia,* proclamation and service, the community *tells and does* the Christian story. The central act exemplifying response to God's sending is *demonstration,* the enactment of God's own testimony to the divine purposes for humanity in human speech and action; in an ecclesial sense, this is the *authenticating* of a Christian way of living. The effect of God's initiative and human response is the quantitative growth of the body as a community *with* the world.

As has been stated, human beings do not participate in the new humanity of Jesus Christ unless they express humble faith, obedient love and witnessing hope. For this the church as the community that practices faith, love and hope is necessary. It is the sphere in which persons can be formed, nurtured and sustained as Christians— and we might add: as Christians in a sociocultural order whose prevailing values and practices are indifferent, hostile and frequently opposed to Christian faith.

The question that is posed to us as believers gathered into, upbuilt within and sent from the church, the question evoked by the fact that the church is a community of sin and salvation, is this: How can Christian faith be received in, expressed in and made relevant for a diverse sociocultural environment patterned and structured by racism? What is the church's witness, how is it expressed, and does it make any sense? New Testament epistles revisited!

Discerning the self-disclosure of God—God's ongoing presence and activity in creating, reconciling and transforming—entails acknowledging that the church is intended to embrace rather than exclude. The church is intended by God to be grounded in the loving fellowship of the triune God ("one"), to participate subjectively and objectively in this love and its justice, righteousness and peace ("holy"), to express itself as the preeminently inclusive and partisan community ("catholic") and to extend Christ's word and work to all "others" ("apostolic"). To be this kind of community, the church must categorically reject all humanly constructed barriers that separate persons from one another. It is not given to Christians to determine whether and how to "do church"; it is rather expected that Christian community will manifest the new humanity of Jesus Christ and contend against the rules and ways of the old humanity nullified in him. The experience of Christian community among believers is expected to be the experience of the new humanity, human beings with and for others in interdependence and equality.

Gathering ourselves as Christians into racially homogeneous communities contradicts our new humanity and resists God's calling; building up ourselves as Christians by appealing consciously or unconsciously to a racial group identity rejects our new humanity and resists God's empowering; entreating ourselves as Christians by appealing only to those who belong to our racial group subverts our new humanity and resists God's sending. Response-ability and relation expressed only with and toward those who are in the same people group diminishes God's Spirit-enablement. "You have heard that it was said, 'You shall love your neighbor and hate your enemy.' But I say to you, Love your enemies and pray for those who persecute you, so that you may be children of your Father in heaven. . . . For if you love those who love you, what reward do you have? Do not even the tax collectors [a despised out-group] do the same? And if you greet only your brothers and sisters, what more are you doing than others? Do not even the Gentiles [another despised out-group] do the same?" (Mt 5:43-47). Especially in a racist sociocultural order, homogeneous groups do not demonstrate the gospel as the way of living for new humanity. Instead they compromise the discernment and expression of new humanity in Jesus Christ, contribute to the expressivity of racism and thereby help others—whether Christian or not—to make nonsense of Christianity.

5. *Sociocultural transformation.* Finally, expressing reconciliation as a way of living requires the transformation of the sociocultural order. As we have seen, the construction of social reality engendered race and racism, and the maintenance of social reality preserves them both. This social reality, then, must be deconstructed if it is to be an expression of racial reconciliation. There can be little doubt that the racism in our sociocultural order needs to be dismantled, but to the extent that this racism is characteristic of the sociocultural order, the order itself needs to be changed. The history and institutionalization of our politics, economics and social ways of living have generated and expressed the racial domination and subordination characteristic of racism. The question then is not really *whether* to change this order. Because of the reciprocal relationship between subjectivity and objectivity, change is necessary if racial reconciliation is be expressed—objectified—in human social environments. The question is *how* to change this order, and thus it is a matter of strategy, or better: strategic thinking and acting.

Ensuring the freedom of all to be whoever they want and to express themselves however they want is not reconciliation. Liberation in itself is not living with and for another. But human freedom is a prerequisite for reconciliation, freedom from the over-against relations of oppression and dehumanization that constitute our objective reality. There can be no genuine reconciliation between people groups if there is not freedom for all, and there is no freedom for all if a sociocultural order is structured to prefer, value and advantage some over against others. Thus reconciliation requires the deconstruction, or transformation, of our shared world.

The Christian narratives express the conviction that people are changed through the presence and activity of God in the ongoing work of creating, reconciling and transforming. The theology—and even the sociological theory—of this book has contended that social change is possible in and through individuals as Spirit-enabled agents of God—ambassadors—in the world. We deceive ourselves as Christians if we think we can turn toward God and at the same time relinquish our response-ability to serve God's purposes in the human realm. Expressing reconciliation entails expressing the new humanity in the practices of humble faith, obedient love and witnessing hope. Christians hold the singularly compelling vision of the consummation of God's purposes for humanity, the integral fulfillment of human beings with and for God and others in a community of peace, truth and justice. Expressing this humanity here and now, under the sinful conditions of human life, is the presence of God's future in our shared world, the already and the not-yet of the consummation of the unbounded reign of God. God's purposes are for this world and for all humankind, and expressing these purposes means a shared sociocultural environment suitable to this expression. The task then is to participate with God in the ongoing work of transforming our sociocultural order.

Our personal and ecclesial transformation is integrally connected not only with Christian witness but also with social practice. As Christians, we are engaged in works of reconciliation and the practices of peace, truth and justice because we have been called, upbuilt and sent for this purpose. The Christ who is our life is also our authorization. We give food to the hungry and drink to the thirsty, welcome the stranger, clothe the naked, and visit the sick and imprisoned ones because Jesus Christ has licensed us to do so in his name (Mt 25:31-46). But the Christ-event and the justice of God demand of us that we ask: Why are people hungry and thirsty (without the means to sustain life)? Why are there strangers and aliens (foreign out-groups)? Why are people naked (publicly shamed)? Why are people ill (outcast without healthcare)? Why are people imprisoned (unable to repay usurious debt) in any sociocultural order, but especially in one like ours that trumpets freedom, equality and economic opportunity? Why? The answer is: Because that is the way our order was built, and that is how it is maintained!

To dismantle racism, feeding the hungry in itself is not sufficient. We must feed the hungry *and* we must contest the structures that produce hunger, *and* we must work cooperatively to dismantle these structures, *and* we must foster development of sociocultural expressions of integral freedom and equality with and for others.

Robert Schreiter observes that reconciliation has two faces. One he calls the "social" and the other he calls the "spiritual" (the *personal* and *interpersonal*). He clarifies this distinction by noting that the social "has to do with providing structures and processes whereby a fractured society can be reconstructed as truthful and just," while the personal "has to do with rebuilding shattered lives so that social reconciliation becomes a reality."[32] Later he contends that "for social reconciliation to be successful, there must be reconciled individuals present to help give leadership to the process, as well as a cadre of people who understand the meaning of individual reconciliation. Individual reconciliation helps nurture and strengthen social reconciliation, but social reconciliation cannot be reduced to individual reconciliation."[33]

Clearly Schreiter is pointing to the priority of individual reconciliation as a means of achieving social reconciliation. However, one aspect is missing from his construal, and I have drawn attention to it at several points. It might be imagined as a kind of "chicken or egg" matter, a loop that we think has to begin somewhere. But this is cause-effect thinking. Individual response-ability and relationships are necessary in reconciliation, but I am suggesting an integral loop: In order to transform the sociocultural order, we need transformed and reconciled persons—*agents* of the new humanity—to express themselves in the spheres and schemes that constitute the sociocultural order. But in order to transform and reconcile persons who can express the new humanity, we need a transformed sociocultural order—*agencies* of the new humanity—that is suitable for nurturing and sustaining reconciliation. In terms of socialization (internalization and externalization) and plausibility structures, this has been rendered by the church as the community of faith, hope and love, but not all that well. The church's mission is to express new humanity in the world as an agency of God's transforming work, and therefore the church's sociocultural environment, wherever and whatever it might be, is intended to be not only the church's mission field but, more important, a sociocultural habitat that fosters the expression of the new humanity. Reciprocity suggests that reconciled persons externalize themselves as communities of reconciliation and that communities of reconcilia-

---

[32]Robert J. Schreiter, *The Ministry of Reconciliation: Spirituality and Strategies* (Maryknoll, N.Y.: Orbis, 1998), p. 4.
[33]Ibid., p. 111.

tion socialize reconciled persons who internalize their world.

In the meantime, short of the consummation of God's reign, we have work to do. We are ambassadors, and our churches are our embassies. We are where we are in order to serve the interests—talk the talk and walk the walk—of the Sovereign who commissions and sends us. We dare not capitulate to racism by segregating ourselves from either other believers or those who do not—or no longer—live with the Christian Story. In the meantime, as the church, we commit ourselves to the practices of humble faith, obedient love and witnessing hope, and through this expression of our new humanity we resolve to resist, contest and dismantle racism in our shared world. In this meantime, as Willie James Jennings has asserted, "we need a church made up of people who refuse to live out racial politics, who refuse to participate in the racial realities of this nation, who refuse the power and privileges of whiteness, who reject the stereotypes of [other people groups], who claim a new way of life born at the cross and the resurrection, who will not be known even by family, tribe, friends or nation after the flesh, but who would know themselves only through the power of resurrection and the call of the cross of Christ."[34]

Who knows? Perhaps by externalizing ourselves in habitualized activities involving multiple actors, each playing their role effectively, through time we might *institutionalize* the new humanity! Isn't it worth a thought?

●   ●   ●   ●

Do nothing from selfish ambition or conceit, but in humility regard others as better than yourselves. Let each of you look not to your own interests, but to the interests of others. Let the same mind be in you that was in Christ Jesus. . . .

Do all things without murmuring and arguing, so that you may be blameless and innocent, children of God without blemish in the midst of a crooked and perverse generation, in which you shine like stars in the world.   P h i l i p p i a n s   2 : 3 - 5 ,   1 4 - 1 5

Why does Paul exhort the Philippians in this way? They must have been long on ambition and conceit and short on humility. Apparently they looked out for themselves and disregarded one another. What a witness they were!

What would it look like if Christians in community thought as Christ did? What would it mean for believers to think the same things? What is required to make murmuring and arguing cease? What do we have to do to shine like stars? For openers, we need to consider others as surpassing ourselves, and we have to take an interest in them.

---

[34]Willie James Jennings, "Wandering in the Wilderness: Christian Identity and Theology Between Context and Race," in *The Gospel in Black and White,* ed. Okholm, p. 48.

Postscript

Dear Reader,

Race. Racial. Racism. Racist. These words elicit an awareness of ourselves and of others, as well as how we perceive one another. . . . That is how we began, and that is how we will end.

I do not expect—and I certainly do not assume—that you will agree with everything I have written here. There is much that has been left unsaid, much that I do not know how to say and much that countless others have said already. After all, racism infects everything that makes up our society, and throughout U.S. history it has drawn the critical scrutiny of far more persons than we can ever really know. Most of them have not written a single word on the subject, and among those who have written there remain significant differences of opinion on the origins and development of racism. We come to recognize racism not from reading books but from relating with people and looking at our shared world from the perspectives of others. Speaking with others and listening carefully as they recount their experiences is the most important way to begin the journey of recognizing racism.

But reading can help, just as writing can help. Reading and writing on the subject of race and racism constitute a kind of surrogate conversation in which the dialogue partners are unable to face one another and look into each other's eyes. In the conversation of reading and writing, one person—the author—gets to do all the talking for an extended period. But as in a face-to-face conversation, the other person—the reader—has the opportunity to take notes and jot down questions for clarification and follow-up, and maybe even begin the development of a counter-argument. When the first person is finished, the other partner in the dialogue has the opportunity to respond. In reading and writing, unlike a face-to-face conversation, the first person does not often get the opportunity to hear what the partner has to say.[1] The value of a surrogate conversation is the author's stimulation of the reader's thinking and the challenge it may pose to the reader's way of living.

So I do not expect that your thinking will correspond to my own or that you will consent to all of my arguments. Perhaps your social and anthropological analysis is different, so that you come to a different set of observations and conclusions about race and racism and about what it means to be human in a social world. But if there is any response to what I have said, I would expect it would include a willingness to look at your social and anthropological understandings of race and racism. I suspect that my theological method is somewhat different from yours, so I do not expect you will consent unquestioningly to my theological contentions. But I do expect that if you profess faith in Jesus Christ and earnestly seek to live as his disciple, you will consider the resources of your faith and ask how they address race and racism and just exactly what they say about such matters.

Let me, dear reader, be a little more specific. Whether you agree with me or not, I do expect that as a result of your reading you will reflect on your own experience with members of other people groups as well as with members of your own group, and ask where and how race and racism might be manifest. Reflect on what was said and what was left unsaid, and how you were affected by the interaction. Did the language used disclose or disguise matters of racism? Did you talk about it or talk around it?

Whether you agree with me or not, I expect you will take a closer look at and think about the places and times of your day-to-day life, your particular places of work, recreation, socializing, school, business and of course home. Where and how is race present, and is racism there as well? How is it manifest and how is it hidden? Don't look only at the obvious. Look at the people and the environment, but look also for values, assumptions, contentions and patterns of interaction. What are the formal and informal procedures and regulations, and how do people behave? What is there about the setting that you cannot see and do not really know?

Whether or not you agree with me, I expect you will take a turn inward and inventory the contents of your awareness of yourself and others. Ponder your identity and character, and maybe even ask someone, "Who do you think I am?" Reflect on your personality and behaviors, especially in situations where you are with others of your own people group, but also where you are in mixed company. What are you thinking about, what are you aware of about yourself

---

[1] My e-mail address is: drsharp@seminary.edu. You write; I'll respond.

and the others? What are you *not* thinking about, and what escapes your awareness? I'm sure you have friends and significant others. What difference do these people make in your life, and just how do you identify with them? Most of all, what exactly *do* you think about race and racism?

Whether you agree with me or not, I suspect you have a view of the world that helps you to make sense of it. You have some idea about how it works and how it doesn't. You probably have views on social, political, economic and religious matters, and hopefully these have some interconnections to form a sort of comprehensive worldview. I expect that after reading this book you will mull over this worldview and look for indications of what role race plays in it. Caution is in order here: The absence of any indication of race in a worldview does not necessarily mean that race doesn't play any role. It may be camouflaged. Furthermore, if you are a Christian, I expect you will consider what Jesus Christ, the Bible and the church have to do with racism, and not answer with: *Nothing!*

Above all else, whether you agree with me or not, all my efforts in writing and all your time in reading will be to no avail if what is said here does not stimulate—even *provoke*—your conversation with others, members of other people groups as well as your own. If you have stayed with me to this point, if I've written anything that has appealed to your response-ability, then please *do not be silent.* As you look back on your reading and ponder your own experience and worldview in relation to race and racism, *share your self with an other.*

Some of this book was written at a cabin in southern Colorado. During one summer a robin's nest with three eggs sat on a crossbeam that spanned the arched overhang of the cabin's front porch. For the first several days, whenever I left or came in through the front door, the mother robin would fly away out of fear, leaving her eggs unprotected. But eventually, seeing that I moved slowly and stayed as far away from the nest as possible, she apparently came to accept that I was not a threat, and so she would remain in the nest as I came and went. For a while she kept her eye on me, but then she just ignored me. Shortly thereafter the eggs hatched, and three chicks emerged into my little mountain world.

As I watched the mother and father robin feed them one afternoon, I caught myself thinking about the robin world these chicks would soon be entering, wondering what that world would be like for them and how it would greet them as they fell from the nest and learned to fly away. Was it conflicted and polarized like our human world?

I am well aware that there are dangers in the robin world, including some predators that threaten them. But I doubt that robins are their own "natural" enemy, or that mother and father robins teach their young to hate other robins, to oppress, exploit, disregard or derobinize other robins. Only we humans do that to one another.

I think the robin world is a parable for us. Do you suppose it might also be a way of living?

●   ●   ●   ●

If the world hates you, be aware that it hated me before it hated you. If you belonged to the world, the world would love you as its own. Because you do not belong to the world, but I have chosen you out of the world—therefore the world hates you. John 15:18-19

I give you a new commandment, that you love one another. Just as I have loved you, you also should love one another. By this everyone will know that you are my disciples, if you have love for one another. John 13:34-35

Beloved, let us love one another, because love is from God; everyone who loves is born of God and knows God. Whoever does not love does not know God, for God is love. God's love was revealed among us in this way: God sent his only Son into the world so that we might live through him. In this is love, not that we loved God but that he loved us and sent his Son to be the atoning sacrifice for our sins. Beloved, since God loved us so much, we also ought to love one another. No one has ever seen God; if we love one another, God lives in us, and his love is perfected in us. 1 John 4:7-12

Simon son of John, do you love me? John 21:16

May your way of living be your commentary.

Bibliography

Allport, Gordon W. *The Nature of Prejudice.* Reading, Mass.: Addison-Wesley, 1979.

Andersen, Margaret L., and Patricia Hill Collins, eds. *Race, Class and Gender: An Anthology.* 2nd ed. Belmont, Calif.: Wadsworth, 1995.

Anderson, Victor. *Beyond Ontological Blackness: An Essay on African American Religious and Cultural Criticism.* New York: Continuum, 1995.

Appiah, K. Anthony, and Amy Gutmann, eds. *Color Conscious: The Political Morality of Race.* Princeton, N.J.: Princeton University Press, 1996.

Asante, Molefi Kete. *Afrocentricity.* Rev. ed. Trenton, N.J.: Africa World Press, 1988.

Bailey, Thomas Pearce. *Race Orthodoxy in the South and Other Aspects of the Negro Question.* New York: Neale, 1914.

Barbour, Ian G. *Issues in Science and Religion.* New York: Harper & Row, 1966.

Barndt, Joseph. *Dismantling Racism: The Continuing Challenge to White America.* Minneapolis: Augsburg Fortress, 1991.

Beals, Ivan A. *Our Racist Legacy: Will the Church Resolve the Conflict?* The Church and the World 9. Notre Dame, Ind.: Cross Cultural, 1997.

Bell, Derrick. *Faces at the Bottom of the Well: The Permanence of Racism.* New York: BasicBooks, 1992.

Bennett, Lerone, Jr. *Before the Mayflower: A History of Black America.* 6th rev. ed. New York: Penguin, 1993.

———. *The Shaping of Black America.* Rev. ed. New York: Penguin, 1993.

Berger, Peter L. *Invitation to Sociology: A Humanistic Perspective.* New York: Doubleday, 1963.

Berger, Peter L., and Thomas Luckmann. *The Social Construction of Reality: A Treatise in the Sociology of Knowledge.* New York: Doubleday, 1966.

Blassingame, John W. *The Slave Community: Plantation Life in the Antebellum South.* Rev. and enl. ed. New York: Oxford University Press, 1979.

Blumenbach, Johann Friedrich. *On the Natural Varieties of Mankind.* 1775 and 1795 eds. New York: Bergman, 1969.

Boas, Franz. *Anthropology and Modern Life.* 1928. Reprint, New York: Dover, 1986.

———. *The Mind of Primitive Man.* Rev. ed. New York: Collier, 1963.

———. *Race, Language and Culture.* Chicago: University of Chicago Press, 1940.

Branding, Ronice. *Fulfilling the Dream: Confronting the Challenge of Racism.* St. Louis: Chalice, 1998.

Breckenridge, James, and Lillian Breckenridge. *What Color Is Your God? Multicultural Education in the Church.* Wheaton, Ill.: Victor, 1995.

Brookfield, Stephen D. *Developing Critical Thinkers: Challenging Adults to Explore Alternative Ways of Thinking and Acting.* San Francisco: Jossey-Bass, 1987.

Brooks, Roy L. *Rethinking the American Race Problem.* Berkeley: University of California Press, 1990.

Campbell, Joseph. *The Masks of God,* vol. 4 of *Creative Mythology.* New York: Penguin, 1976.

Carter, Stephen L. *Civility: Manners, Morals and the Etiquette of Democracy.* New York: BasicBooks, 1998.

———. *Integrity.* New York: BasicBooks, 1996.

———. *Reflections of an Affirmative Action Baby.* New York: BasicBooks, 1991.

Clapp, Rodney. *A Peculiar People: The Church as Culture in a Post-Christian Society.* Downers Grove, Ill.: InterVarsity Press, 1996.

Cohen, Mark Nathan. *Culture of Intolerance: Chauvinism, Class and Racism in the United States.* New Haven, Conn.: Yale University Press, 1998.

Coleman, Jonathan. *Long Way to Go: Black and White in America.* New York: Atlantic Monthly Press, 1997.

Collum, Danny Duncan. *Black and White Together: The Search for Common Ground.* Maryknoll, N.Y.: Orbis, 1996.

Cone, James H. *God of the Oppressed.* Rev. ed. Maryknoll, N.Y.: Orbis, 1997.

Cose, Ellis. *Color-Blind: Seeing Beyond Race in a Race-Obsessed World.* New York: HarperCollins, 1997.

———. *The Rage of a Privileged Class.* New York: HarperCollins, 1993.

Crenshaw, Kimberlé, et al., eds. *Critical Race Theory: The Key Writings That Formed the Movement.* New York: New Press, 1995.

Curry, George E., ed. *The Affirmative Action Debate.* Reading, Mass.: Addison-Wesley, 1996.

D'Souza, Dinesh. *The End of Racism: Principles for a Multiracial Society.* New York: Free Press, 1995.

Dalton, Harlon L. *Racial Healing: Confronting the Fear Between Blacks and Whites.* New York: Anchor, 1995.

Darwin, Charles. *The Descent of Man.* 2nd ed. Amherst, Mass.: Prometheus, 1998.

———. *The Origin of Species.* New York: Random House, 1993.

Davies, Alan. *Infected Christianity: A Study of Modern Racism.* Kingston, Quebec: McGill-Queen's University Press, 1988.

Davies, Susan E., and Sister Paul Teresa Hennessee, eds. *Ending Racism in the Church.* Cleveland, Ohio: United Church Press, 1998.

Davis, F. James. *Who Is Black? One Nation's Definition.* University Park: Pennsylvania State University Press, 1991.

de Gobineau, Arthur. *The Inequality of the Human Races.* New York: Howard Fertig, 1999.

Delgado, Richard, ed. *Critical Race Theory: The Cutting Edge.* Philadelphia: Temple University Press, 1995.

DeMott, Benjamin. *The Trouble With Friendship: Why Americans Can't Think Straight About Race.* New Haven, Conn.: Yale University Press, 1998.

Derman-Sparks, Louise, and Carol Brunson Phillips. *Teaching/Learning Anti-racism: A Developmental Approach.* New York: Teachers College Press, 1997.

DeYoung, Curtiss Paul. *Reconciliation: Our Greatest Challenge—Our Only Hope.* Valley Forge, Penn.: Judson, 1997.

Doob, Christopher Bates. *Racism: An American Cauldron.* 2nd ed. New York: HarperCollins, 1996.

Du Bois, W. E. B. *The Souls of Black Folk.* Introduction by John Edgar Wideman. 1903. Reprint, New York: Vintage, 1990.

Dyson, Michael Eric. *Race Rules: Navigating the Color Line.* New York: Vintage, 1997.

———. *Reflecting Black: African-American Cultural Criticism.* Minneapolis: University of Minnesota Press, 1993.

Early, Gerald, ed. *Lure and Loathing: Essays on Race, Identity and the Ambivalence of Assimilation.* New York: Penguin, 1993.

Edwards, Jefferson D., Jr. *Purging Racism from Christianity: Freedom and Purpose Through Identity.* Grand Rapids, Mich.: Zondervan, 1996.

Emerson, Michael O., and Christian Smith. *Divided by Faith: Evangelical Religion and the Problem of Race in America.* New York: Oxford University Press, 2000.

Evans, James H., Jr. *We Have Been Believers.* Minneapolis: Fortress, 1992.

Evans, Tony. *Let's Get to Know Each Other.* Nashville: Thomas Nelson, 1995.

Ezorsky, Gertrude. *Racism and Justice: The Case for Affirmative Action.* Ithaca, N.Y.: Cornell University Press, 1991.

Fanon, Frantz. *Black Skin, White Masks.* Translated by Charles Lam Markmann. New York: Grove, 1967.

Feagin, Joe R. *Racist America: Roots, Current Realities and Future Reparations.* New York: Routledge, 2000.

Feagin, Joe R., and Melvin P. Sikes. *Living with Racism: The Black Middle-Class Experience.* Boston: Beacon, 1994.

Feagin, Joe R., and Hernán Vera. *White Racism: The Basics.* New York: Routledge, 1995.

Flagg, Barbara. "'Was Blind, but Now I See': White Race Consciousness and the Requirement of Discriminatory Intent." *Michigan Law Review* 91 (1993): 953-1017.

Ford, Clyde W. *We Can All Get Along: 50 Steps You Can Take to Help End Racism.* New York: Dell, 1994.

Foster, Charles R. *Embracing Diversity: Leadership in Multicultural Congregations.* Bethesda, Md.: Alban Institute, 1997.

Franklin, John Hope, and Alfred A. Moss Jr. *From Slavery to Freedom: A History of African Americans.* 7th ed. New York: Alfred A. Knopf, 1994.

Fredrickson, George M. *The Arrogance of Race: Historical Perspectives on Slavery, Racism and Social Inequality.* Hanover, N.H.: Wesleyan University Press, 1988.

———. *The Black Image in the White Mind: The Debate on Afro-American Character and Destiny, 1817-1914.* Middletown, Conn.: Wesleyan University Press, 1988.

Fukuyama, Francis. *The Great Disruption: Human Nature and the Reconstitution of the Social Order.* New York: Free Press, 1999.

Gallup, George, Jr. "Keeping the Faith: Looking at God Through America's Eyes." *The Public Perspective* 11, no. 3 (2000): 14-17.

Gates, Henry Louis, Jr., and Cornel West. *The Future of the Race.* New York: Vintage, 1996.

Geertz, Clifford. *The Interpretation of Cultures.* New York: BasicBooks, 1973.

General Social Surveys, 1972-1998: Cumulative Codebook. Principal investigator, James A. Davis; director and coprincipal investigator, Tom W. Smith; coprincipal investigator, Peter V. Marsden. NORC ed. Chicago: National Opinion Research Center, producer, 1998; Storrs, Conn.: The Roper Center for Public Opinion Research, University of Connecticut, distributor.

Gilligan, James. *Violence: Reflections on a National Epidemic.* New York: Vintage, 1997.

Goldberg, David Theo, ed. *Anatomy of Racism.* Minneapolis: University of Minnesota Press, 1990.

———. *Racial Subjects: Writing on Race in America.* New York: Routledge, 1997.

Goldberg, Michael. *Theology and Narrative: A Critical Introduction.* Philadelphia: Trinity Press International, 1991.

González, Justo L. *Mañana: Christian Theology from a Hispanic Perspective.* Nashville: Abingdon, 1990.

Gossett, Thomas F. *Race: The History of an Idea in America.* 1963. Reprint, New York: Oxford University Press, 1997.

Gould, Stephen Jay. *The Mismeasure of Man.* Rev. ed. New York: W. W. Norton, 1996.

Grant, C. David. *Thinking Through Our Faith: Theology for 21st Century Christians.* Nashville: Abingdon, 1998.

Grant, Madison. *The Passing of the Great Race; Or, The Racial Basis of European History.* New York: Charles Scribner's Sons, 1916.

Gregory, Steven, and Roger Sanjek, eds. *Race.* New Brunswick, N.J.: Rutgers University Press, 1994.

Grenz, Stanley J. *Theology for the Community of God.* Nashville: Broadman & Holman, 1994.

Grenz, Stanley J., and Roger E. Olson. *Who Needs Theology? An Invitation to the Study of God.* Downers Grove, Ill.: InterVarsity Press, 1996.

Griffin, Paul R. *Seeds of Racism in the Soul of America.* Cleveland, Ohio: Pilgrim, 1999.

Guthrie, Shirley C. *Christian Doctrine.* Rev. ed. Louisville, Ky.: Westminster John Knox, 1994.

Hacker, Andrew. *Two Nations: Black and White, Separate, Hostile, Unequal.* Rev. and exp. ed. New York: Ballantine, 1995.

Hall, Edward T. *Beyond Culture.* New York: Anchor, 1976.

Haney López, Ian F. *White by Law: The Legal Construction of Race.* New York: New York University Press, 1996.

Hannaford, Ivan. *Race: The History of an Idea in the West.* Washington D.C.: Woodrow Wilson Center, 1996.

Harding, Vincent. *Hope and History: Why We Must Share the Story of the Movement.* Maryknoll, N.Y.: Orbis, 1990.

Hart, Trevor. *Faith Thinking: The Dynamics of Christian Theology.* Downers Grove, Ill.: InterVarsity Press, 1995.

Haselden, Kyle. *The Racial Problem in Christian Perspective.* New York: Harper & Brothers, 1959.

Hauerwas, Stanley, and L. Gregory Jones, eds. *Why Narrative? Readings in Narrative Theology.* Grand Rapids, Mich.: Eerdmans, 1989.

Hauerwas, Stanley, and William H. Willimon. *Resident Aliens.* Nashville: Abingdon, 1989.

Herrnstein, Richard J., and Charles Murray. *The Bell Curve: Intelligence and Class Structure in American Life.* New York: Free Press, 1996.

Hill, Norman. "Race in America—Through a Glass, Darkly." *The Public Perspective* 7, no. 2 (1996): 1-4.

Hochschild, Jennifer L. *The New American Dilemma: Liberal Democracy and School Desegregation.* New Haven, Conn.: Yale University Press, 1984.

Hofstadter, Richard. *Social Darwinism in American Thought.* Rev. ed. Boston: Beacon, 1955.

Hood, Robert E. *Begrimed and Black: Christian Traditions on Blacks and Blackness.* Minneapolis: Fortress, 1994.

hooks, bell. *Killing Rage: Ending Racism.* New York: Henry Holt, 1995.

Huxley, Julian, and Alfred C. Haddon. *We Europeans: A Survey of "Racial" Problems.* New York: Harper & Brothers, 1936.

Ignatiev, Noel, and John Garvey, eds. *Race Traitor.* New York: Routledge, 1996.

Jacobs, Bruce A. *Race Manners: Navigating the Minefield Between Black and White Americans.* New York: Arcade, 1999.

Jaynes, Gerald David, and Robin M. Williams Jr., eds. *A Common Destiny: Blacks and American Society.* Washington, D.C.: National Academy Press, 1989.

Jordan, Winthrop D. *The White Man's Burden: Historical Origins of Racism in the United States.* New York: Oxford University Press, 1974.

Katz, Judith H. *White Awareness: Handbook for Anti-racism Training.* Norman: University of Oklahoma Press, 1978.

Keener, Craig S., and Glenn Usry. *Defending Black Faith: Answers to Tough Ques-*

tions About African-American Christianity. Downers Grove, Ill.: InterVarsity Press, 1997.

Kelsey, George D. *Racism and the Christian Understanding of Man.* New York: Charles Scribner's Sons, 1965.

Killen, Patricia O'Connell, and John de Beer. *The Art of Theological Reflection.* New York: Crossroad, 1996.

Kinder, Donald R., and Lynn M. Sanders. *Divided by Color: Racial Politics and Democratic Ideals.* Chicago: University of Chicago Press, 1996.

Kivel, Paul. *Uprooting Racism: How White People Can Work for Racial Justice.* Gabriola Island, B.C.: New Society, 1996.

Kochman, Thomas. *Black and White Styles in Conflict.* Chicago: University of Chicago Press, 1981.

Kovel, Joel. *White Racism: A Psychohistory.* Reprint ed. New York: Columbia University Press, 1984. (First published 1970.)

Kuhn, Thomas S. *The Structure of Scientific Revolutions.* 2nd, enl. ed. Chicago: University of Chicago Press, 1970.

Lee, Jung Young. *Marginality: The Key to Multicultural Theology.* Minneapolis: Fortress, 1995.

Lenski, Gerhard E. *Power and Privilege: A Theory of Social Stratification.* Chapel Hill: University of North Carolina Press, 1984.

Levine, Lawrence W. *Black Culture and Black Consciousness.* New York: Oxford University Press, 1977.

Lincoln, C. Eric. *Race, Religion and the Continuing American Dilemma.* Rev. ed. New York: Hill and Wang, 1999.

Lubiano, Wahneema, ed. *The House That Race Built.* New York: Vintage, 1998.

Malcomson, Scott L. *One Drop of Blood: The American Misadventure of Race.* New York: Farrar Straus Giroux, 2000.

Malik, Kenan. *The Meaning of Race: Race, History and Culture in Western Society.* New York: New York University Press, 1996.

Marable, Manning. *Beyond Black and White: Transforming African-American Politics.* New York: Verso, 1995.

―――. *Black Liberation in Conservative America.* Boston: South End, 1997.

Matsuoka, Fumitaka. *The Color of Faith: Building Community in a Multiracial Society.* Cleveland, Ohio: United Church Press, 1998.

McClendon, James W. *Biography as Theology.* New ed. Philadelphia: Trinity Press International, 1990.

―――. *Doctrine.* Vol. 2 of *Systematic Theology.* Nashville: Abingdon, 1994.

―――. *Ethics.* Vol. 1 of *Systematic Theology.* Nashville: Abingdon, 1986.

―――. *Witness.* Vol. 3 of *Systematic Theology.* Nashville: Abingdon, 2000.

McFague, Sallie. *The Body of God: An Ecological Theology.* Minneapolis: Fortress, 1993.

McIntosh, Peggy. "White Privilege: Unpacking the Invisible Knapsack." *Peace and Freedom,* July/August 1989, pp. 10-12.

Mead, Loren B. *The Once and Future Church: Reinventing the Congregation for a New Mission Frontier.* Bethesda, Md.: Alban Institute, 1991.

Migliore, Daniel L. *Faith Seeking Understanding: An Introduction to Christian Theology.* Grand Rapids, Mich.: Eerdmans, 1991.

Mills, C. Wright. *The Power Elite.* 1956. New ed. New York: Oxford University Press, 1999.

Mills, Charles Wade. *The Racial Contract.* Ithaca, N.Y.: Cornell University Press, 1997.

Montagu, Ashley. *Man's Most Dangerous Myth: The Fallacy of Race.* 6th ed. Walnut Creek, Calif.: AltaMira, 1997.

Myrdal, Gunnar. *An American Dilemma: The Negro Problem and American Democracy.* 2 vols. New Brunswick, N.J.: Transaction, 1996.

National Urban League. *The State of Black America 1999.* New York: National Urban League, 1999.

Niebuhr, H. Richard. *The Social Sources of Denominationalism.* 1929. Reprint, Gloucester, Mass.: Peter Smith, 1987.

Okholm, Dennis L., ed. *The Gospel in Black and White: Theological Resources for Racial Reconciliation.* Downers Grove, Ill.: InterVarsity Press, 1997.

Oldham, Joseph H. *Christianity and the Race Problem.* London: Student Christian Movement, 1924.

Oliver, Melvin L., and Thomas M. Shapiro. *Black Wealth/White Wealth: A New Perspective on Racial Inequality.* New York: Routledge, 1995.

Omi, Michael, and Howard Winant. *Racial Formation in the United States from the 1960s to the 1990s.* 2nd ed. New York: Routledge, 1994.

Pannell, William. *The Coming Race Wars? A Cry for Reconciliation.* Grand Rapids, Mich.: Zondervan, 1993.

Park, Andrew Sung. *Racial Conflict and Healing: An Asian-American Theological Perspective.* Maryknoll, N.Y.: Orbis, 1996.

Patterson, Orlando. *The Ordeal of Integration: Progress and Resentment in America's "Racial" Crisis.* Washington, D.C.: Civitas/Counterpoint, 1997.

Payne, Richard J. *Getting Beyond Race: The Changing American Culture.* Boulder, Colo.: Westview, 1998.

Perkins, Spencer, and Chris Rice. *More Than Equals: Racial Healing for the Sake of the Gospel.* Downers Grove, Ill.: InterVarsity Press, 1993.

Peters, Ted. *God—the World's Future.* Minneapolis: Fortress, 1992.

Pettigrew, Thomas F., et al. *Prejudice.* Cambridge, Mass.: Belknap, 1980.

Polanyi, Michael. *Personal Knowledge: Towards a Post-critical Philosophy.* New York: Harper & Row/Harper Torchbooks, 1964.

Poling, James Newton. *Deliver Us from Evil: Resisting Racial and Gender Oppression.* Minneapolis: Fortress, 1996.

Raboteau, Albert J. *Slave Religion: The "Invisible Institution" in the Antebellum South.* New York: Oxford University Press, 1978.

Rhodes, Stephen A. *Where the Nations Meet: The Church in a Multicultural World.* Downers Grove, Ill.: InterVarsity Press, 1998.

Roediger, David R., ed. *Black on White: Black Writers on What It Means to Be White.* New York: Schocken, 1998.

——. *Towards the Abolition of Whiteness: Essays on Race, Politics and Working Class History.* London: Verso, 1994.

——. *The Wages of Whiteness: Race and the Making of the American Working Class.* London: Verso, 1991.

Roper Center for Public Opinion Research. "Believer Nation: A Roper Center Data Review." *The Public Perspective* 11, no. 3 (2000): 24-35.

——. "People, Opinions and Polls: An American Dilemma (Part II)." *The Public Perspective* 7, no. 2 (1996): 19-42.

Russell, Kathy, Midge Wilson and Ronald Hall. *The Color Complex: The Politics of Skin Color Among African Americans.* New York: Anchor, 1992.

Ryan, William. *Blaming the Victim.* Rev. ed. New York: Vintage, 1976.

Salley, Columbus, and Ronald Behm. *What Color Is Your God? Black Consciousness and the Christian Faith.* New York: Carol, 1993.

Schaller, Lyle E. *The New Reformation: Tomorrow Arrived Yesterday.* Nashville: Abingdon, 1995.

Schreiter, Robert J. *The Ministry of Reconciliation: Spirituality and Strategies.* Maryknoll, N.Y.: Orbis, 1998.

——. *Reconciliation: Mission and Ministry in a Changing Social Order.* Boston Theological Institute Series 3. Maryknoll, N.Y.: Orbis, 1992.

Schuman, Howard, et al. *Racial Attitudes in America: Trends and Interpretations.* Rev. ed. Cambridge: Harvard University Press, 1997.

Searle, John R. *The Construction of Social Reality.* New York: Free Press, 1995.

Shearer, Jody Miller. *Enter the River: Healing Steps from White Privilege Toward Racial Reconciliation.* Scottdale, Penn.: Herald, 1994.

Shermer, Michael. "Why People Believe in God." *The Public Perspective* 11, no. 3 (2000): 18-20.

Shipler, David K. *A Country of Strangers: Blacks and Whites in America.* New York: Alfred A. Knopf, 1997.

Shipman, Pat. *The Evolution of Racism: Human Differences and the Use and Abuse of Science.* New York: Simon & Schuster, 1994.

Shuler, Clarence. *Winning the Race to Unity: Is Racial Reconciliation Really Working?* Chicago: Moody Press, 1998.

Sleeper, Jim. *Liberal Racism.* New York: Viking, 1997.

Smedley, Audrey. *Race in North America: Origin and Evolution of a Worldview.* Boulder, Colo.: Westview, 1993.

Smith, H. Shelton. *In His Image, But . . . : Racism in Southern Religion, 1780-1910.* Durham, N.C.: Duke University Press, 1972.

Sniderman, Paul M., and Edward G. Carmines. *Reaching Beyond Race.* Cambridge: Harvard University Press, 1997.

Sniderman, Paul M., and Thomas Piazza. *The Scar of Race.* Cambridge, Mass.: Belknap/Harvard University Press, 1993.

Snowden, Frank M. *Before Color Prejudice: The Ancient View of Blacks.* Cambridge, Mass.: Harvard University Press, 1983.

―――. *Blacks in Antiquity: Ethiopians in the Greco-Roman Experience.* Cambridge, Mass.: Belknap/Harvard University Press, 1970.

Sölle, Dorothee. *Thinking About God: An Introduction to Theology.* Translated by John Bowden. Philadelphia: Trinity Press International, 1990.

Sowell, Thomas. *Race and Culture: A World View.* New York: BasicBooks, 1994.

Stampp, Kenneth M. *The Peculiar Institution: Slavery in the Ante-bellum South.* New York: Vintage, 1956.

Steele, Shelby. *The Content of Our Character: A New Vision of Race in America.* New York: HarperCollins, 1991.

―――. *A Dream Deferred: The Second Betrayal of Black Freedom in America.* New York: HarperCollins, 1998.

Stocking, George W. *Race, Culture and Evolution: Essays in the History of Anthropology.* New York: Free Press, 1968.

Stone, Howard W., and James O. Duke. *How To Think Theologically.* Minneapolis: Fortress, 1996.

Stroupe, Nibs, and Inez Fleming. *While We Run This Race: Confronting the Power of Racism in a Southern Church.* Maryknoll, N.Y.: Orbis, 1995.

Stuckey, Sterling. *Slave Culture: Nationalist Theory and the Foundations of Black America.* New York: Oxford University Press, 1987.

Swartley, Willard M. *Slavery, Sabbath, War and Women: Case Issues in Biblical Interpretation.* Scottdale, Penn.: Herald, 1983.

Tanner, Kathryn. *Theories of Culture: A New Agenda for Theology.* Minneapolis: Fortress, 1997.

Tatum, Beverly Daniel. *"Why Are All The Black Kids Sitting Together in the Cafeteria?" and Other Conversations About Race.* Rev. ed. New York: BasicBooks, 1999.

Taylor, Jared. *Paved with Good Intentions: The Failure of Race Relations in Contemporary America.* New York: Carroll & Graf, 1992.

Terry, Robert W. *For Whites Only.* Rev. ed. Grand Rapids, Mich.: Eerdmans, 1975.

Thandeka. *Learning to Be White: Money, Race and God in America.* New York: Continuum, 1999.

Tidwell, Billy J. *The Black Report: Charting the Changing Status of African Americans.* Lanham, Md.: University Press of America, 1997.

Tilley, Terrence. *Story Theology.* Theology and Life 11. Wilmington, Del.: Michael Glazier, 1985.

Ture, Kwame, and Charles V. Hamilton. *Black Power: The Politics of Liberation.* New York: Vintage, 1992.

Usry, Glenn, and Craig S. Keener. *Black Man's Religion: Can Christianity Be Afrocentric?* Downers Grove, Ill.: InterVarsity Press, 1996.

Vanhoozer, Kevin J. *Is There a Meaning in This Text? The Bible, the Reader and the Morality of Literary Knowledge.* Grand Rapids, Mich.: Zondervan, 1998.

Volf, Miroslav. *Exclusion and Embrace: A Theological Exploration of Identity, Otherness and Reconciliation.* Nashville: Abingdon, 1996.

Wachtel, Paul L. *Race in the Mind of America: Breaking the Vicious Circle Between Blacks and Whites.* New York: Routledge, 1999.

Waller, James. *Face to Face: The Changing State of Racism Across America.* New York: Insight, 1998.

Washington, Raleigh, and Glen Kehrein. *Breaking Down Walls: A Model for Reconciliation in an Age of Racial Strife.* Chicago: Moody Press, 1993.

Wells, David F. *Losing Our Virtue: Why the Church Must Recover Its Moral Vision.* Grand Rapids, Mich.: Eerdmans, 1998.

———. *No Place for Truth: Or, Whatever Happened to Evangelical Theology?* Grand Rapids, Mich.: Eerdmans, 1993.

West, Cornel. *Prophesy Deliverance! An Afro-American Revolutionary Christianity.* Philadelphia: Westminster Press, 1982.

———. *Race Matters.* New York: Vintage, 1994.

———. "Toward a Socialist Theory of Racism." 1996. <http://eserver.org/race/toward-a-theory-of-racism.html>.

Wicker, Tom. *Tragic Failure: Racial Integration in America.* New York: William Morrow, 1996.

Wilson, William Julius. *The Bridge over the Racial Divide: Rising Inequality and Coalition Politics.* Berkeley: University of California Press, 1999.

———. *The Declining Significance of Race: Blacks and Changing American Institutions.* 2nd ed. Chicago: University of Chicago Press, 1980.

———. *Power, Racism and Privilege.* New York: Free Press, 1973.

———. *The Truly Disadvantaged: The Inner City, the Underclass and Public Policy.* Chicago: University of Chicago Press, 1987.

———. *When Work Disappears: The World of the New Urban Poor.* New York: Random House, 1996.

Wink, Walter. *Engaging the Powers: Discernment and Resistance in a World of Domination.* Minneapolis: Fortress, 1992.

———. *Naming the Powers: The Language of Power in the New Testament.* Philadelphia: Fortress, 1984.

———. *The Powers That Be: Theology for a New Millennium.* New York: Doubleday, 1998.

———. *Unmasking the Powers: The Invisible Forces That Determine Human Existence.* Philadelphia: Fortress, 1986.

———. *When the Powers Fall: Reconciliation in the Healing of Nations.* Minneapolis: Fortress, 1998.

Wood, Forrest G. *The Arrogance of Faith: Christianity and Race in America from the Colonial Era to the Twentieth Century.* New York: Alfred A. Knopf, 1990.

Woodward, C. Vann. *The Strange Career of Jim Crow.* 3rd rev. ed. New York: Oxford University Press, 1974.

Wright, Lawrence. "One Drop of Blood." *New Yorker,* July 24, 1994, pp. 46-55.

Wuthnow, Robert. *Christianity in the 21st Century: Reflections on the Challenges Ahead.* New York: Oxford University Press, 1993.

Yancey, George A. *Beyond Black and White: Reflections on Racial Reconciliation.* Grand Rapids, Mich.: Baker, 1996.

Zack, Naomi. *Thinking About Race.* Belmont, Calif.: Wadsworth, 1998.

Index

alternation (conver-
sion), 177
apprehension, 135-36
assumptions, 23-27
biological determinism,
122-25
biology. *See* science
Christian Story, 240-41,
243
functions of, 244-50
Christianity
racism and, 167, 170,
237, 164-65
resources of, 237-39
church
community/sociality,
293-96
externalizing new
humanity, 269-70
colorblindness, 206-7
common knowledge,
24-25, 31-32, 36,
159-61
common sense and,
33, 179, 193-94
(*see also* common
sense)
institutions and, 107-8
intersubjectivity, 33
race and, 43-44, 46-
47, 50, 78-79
stereotypes, 127
common sense, 114
colorblindness, 206-7
language, 30

race and, 39, 48, 49,
81-82, 184, 188
See also common
knowledge
community, 248-49
consciousness, 173,
176, 192-93
critical thinking, 276-
84
false, 192-207, 258-
60
identity, 178-79
of race, 17
racial, 194, 178-79
contestation, 277-84
critical questions,
280-82
context, 238-39
definition of, 12
conversation
and assumptions/per-
ceptions, 23-27
factors in, 27-29
fear, 22-23
on race/racism, 20-30
creating, 243
Creator-creature, 243,
245-48
creature, 246-50, 251,
255
critical consciousness,
276-84
critical theory
definition of, 59
significance of, 95-98

culture, 66-67, 73, 144-
45
deception, 197-99
denial, 202-4
detachment, 199-202
dichotomy, 189-90
dissociation, 204-6
divine self-disclosure.
See revelation
dualism
in consciousness,
195-97
in myth, 184-85
ethnicity, 162-63
ethnocentrism, 162-63
experience, 238-39
definition of, 12
of race, 184
externalization, 106-7,
144-45, 174-75,
178, 194
Christian identity, 274
of Christian Story, 249
church as, 293-96
faith, hope, love, 260,
284
new humanity, 269,
277
faith
consciousness (sub-
jectivity), 249-50
as response, 244
faith/hope/love, 260,
263, 271
externalization, 274-76

false consciousness, 17,
  192-207, 258-60
forgiveness, 289-90
frames. *See* opinion
generalized other, 175,
  179, 196-97
genotype, 102-3
identity, 175-79, 190-
  91, 196-97, 206, 208-
  9, 272-73
  and biology, 211-12
  Christian, 249-50,
    274, 293-96
  racial, 209-17
  racial group, 209-17,
    255-56, 272
ideology. *See* racism
idolatry, 253-60
in-group/out-group, 189-
  91, 196-97, 209-14
  Jews and Gentiles,
    263-65, 268-71,
    273-74
initiative-response, 238-
  39, 241-44, 245-50,
  284-85, 286
  church, 294-95
  faith/hope/love, 260
institutional system,
  141-46
institutionalization, 141,
  145
  gender and status,
    273-74
  of race, 113-14
See also objective reality
institutions, structure of,
  141
integral thinking, 283-84
integrity, 283-84
internalization, 173-76,
  178-79, 195-97, 231
  Christian identity, 274

of Christian Story,
  241, 244, 246, 249
faith, hope, love, 260
interpretation, 136
Jesus Christ, 241-43
new humanity, 265-71,
  273-74
language, 19-20
  abstraction, 37
  categorization, 38-39
  objectifying, 34-35
  reification, 39-40
  world-construction,
    30-40
legitimation of institu-
  tions, 109-13
miscegenation, 119,
  188, 214
myth, 180-81
  Christian alternative,
    243-50
  functions of, 181-83
  of race, 182-92
objective reality, 32-33,
  141, 174-78
  institutionalization of,
    104-14
one-drop rule, 116-22,
  124
opinion, 217-34
  factors in formation,
    227-34
  frames, 230, 228-31
  racial group, 228-29
perceptions, 23-27
phenotype, 102-3
plausibility structures,
  176-77
power, 137-38, 150-51,
  153
  institutional, 143-44
  social and economic,
    89-94

prejudice, 73, 125-31
presentism, 198
privilege. *See* white
  privilege
projection, 201-2
protocol. *See* rules
psychology of racism,
  66-73
public opinion and race,
  17. *See also* opinion
race, 19, 272
  definition of, 43-48,
    102-3
  European American
    view of, 21, 122
  myth of, 173
  objectifying human
    variation, 115-16
race essentialism, 50,
  211-12
race science, 52-53
racial, 19
  definition of, 48-50
racial identity, giving up,
  292-93
racism, 19, 272
  bioscientific and envi-
    rorelational, 52-53
  definition of, 50-54
  dominative, aversive,
    metaracism, 68-73
  ideological, behav-
    ioral and sociocul-
    tural, 51
  ideology of, 17, 61,
    74, 92, 162-70
  as idolatry, 253-54
  models of, 17
  myth of race and, 17
  as sin, 18, 236, 251-
    60
racist, 19
  definition of, 55-57

rationality, 55-57
  of racism, 61-66
reciprocity
  and critical con-
    sciousness, 276-80
  in reconciliation, 296-
    99
  of subjectivity and
    objectivity, 174,
    177-78, 193, 209,
    231, 233, 271-72,
    284
Reconciler/reconcilia-
  tion, 243, 248-49
reconciliation, 237, 239
  agents of (medium),
    285-86
  change, 284-85
  church and, 293-96
  forgiveness, 289-90
  freedom, 297
  relationships, 290-93
  repentance, 287-89
  sociocultural, 296-99
reference group, 159-60
  Christian, 274
  church, 293-96
  racial, 190-91, 212-
    14, 272-73
  racial opinion, 231-32
reification
  of race, 50
  roles, 134
  social order, 111
relationships, 290-93
relevance structures, 36,
  54
repentance, 287-89
restitution, 288-89
revelation, 238-39, 240-
  43, 245
roles, 108-9, 133-34
rules, 134-35

sacrifice, 292-93
schemes, racial, 138-40.
  See also typificatory
  schemes
science, 246
  natural, 44-47 (see
    also race science)
  and race, 56, 65, 167,
    122-25, 185-89
Scripture, 238-39, 241
selective perception,
  198
self-esteem, 206-7
semantic fields, 36, 54
silence, 275-76
sin, 236, 242, 248-50
  sociocultural environ-
    ment, 252-53
  racism as, 251-60
slavery, 67, 86-88, 164-
  65, 187, 273-74
social Darwinism, 123-
  24, 167, 187
social distance, 22, 202-
  3, 205, 233
socialization, 174-76,
  197, 271
  primary, 175
  race, 194-95
  racial, 190-91, 209-17
  secondary, 175-76
sociocultural environ-
  ment, 104-5, 141, 144,
  176, 238-39, 271-72
  transformation of,
    296-99
sphere, 125, 131-32,
  140-41
  Christian community,
    293-96
Spirit, 242-43
stereotype, 125-31, 195
  racial, 138-40

subjective reality, 173-
  77
  and language, 34-36
  myth, 181-83
symbolic language, 36
symbolic universe. See
  worldview
system. See institutional
  system
theological method, 12,
  238-39
theology, 240
theories of race, 17
tradition(s), 238-39
  definition of, 12
transformation, socio-
  cultural, 296-99
Transformer/transforma-
  tion, 243, 249-50
triune God, 241-43
trust, 291-92
types, 132-33
typification, 106
typificatory schemes,
  34, 53-54, 125, 131-
  38, 140-41
universe maintenance,
  111-13, 118
  strategies for, 158-70,
    256, 264
white privilege, 149-58,
  201, 205, 293
worldview, 179-81
  and assumptions/per-
    ceptions, 24
  Christian, 244-50
  myth, 180-83
  racism and, 56, 92
  symbolic universe,
    110-13, 159-70,
    179-80